Refusing Death

REFUSING DEATH

Immigrant Women and the Fight for Environmental Justice in LA

Nadia Y. Kim

STANFORD UNIVERSITY PRESS
Stanford, California

STANFORD UNIVERSITY PRESS
Stanford, California

Printed in the United States of America on acid-free, archival-quality paper

Library of Congress Cataloging-in-Publication Data

Names: Kim, Nadia Y., author.

Title: Refusing death : immigrant women and the fight for environmental justice in LA / Nadia Y. Kim.

Description: Stanford, California : Stanford University Press, 2021. | Includes bibliographical references and index.

Identifiers: LCCN 2020051465 (print) | LCCN 2020051466 (ebook) | ISBN 9780804792660 (cloth) | ISBN 9781503628175 (paperback) | ISBN 9781503628182 (epub)

Subjects: LCSH: Environmental justice—California—Los Angeles Region. | Women immigrants—Political activity—California—Los Angeles Region. | Asian American women—Political activity—California—Los Angeles Region. | Hispanic American women—Political activity—California—Los Angeles Region. | Pollution—Social aspects—California—Los Angeles Region.

Classification: LCC GE235.C25 K56 2021 (print) | LCC GE235.C25 (ebook) | DDC 363.70086/9120979494—dc23

LC record available at https://lccn.loc.gov/2020051465

LC ebook record available at https://lccn.loc.gov/2020051466

Cover design: Angela Moody

Cover image: Adobe Stock

Typeset by Newgen North America in 10.5/15 Adobe Garamond Pro

For my dear daughters, Taybi Hanna and Kitani Yina, when I grow up I hope I can love just like you.

And for Mariee Juárez, Jakelin Caal, Felipe Gómez Alonzo, Rathanar Or, Ram Chun, Oeun Lim, Thuy Tran, Sokhim An, Ruya Kadir, Yusef Hawkins, and the countless other young souls taken by hate. May you, George, and Breonna come alive where love flows like a mighty stream and where air is as clear as crystal.

CONTENTS

ACKNOWLEDGMENTS

IT IS AMAZING HOW, until we sit down to write the acknowledgments of a book, most of us don't realize how many people it took to make it all happen. In recollecting every single student, reader, knowledge-sharer, networker, listener, and willing participant over the years who was gracious enough to share some of their precious time with me, I cannot help but feel infinitely humbled and slightly misty-eyed.

As the world wouldn't run without activists, there is no group in the world whom I respect more. If it had not been for the generosity, trust, and good nature of the following unsung mountain movers, this research project would never have taken off and no reader would have ever held this book in their hands. My warmest gratitude to Marta Cota, Elena Gutiérrez, Elina Green, Jesse Marquez, Kim Baglieri, Fe Koons, John Harrison (Manila Ryce), Marisol Barajas, Milton Nimatuj, Ashley Hernández, Bahram Fazeli, Darryl Molina, Yuki Kidokoro, Maura Dwyer, Sylvia Betancourt, and the many community organizers, too many to name, whom I consider not just my s/heroes but LA's s/heroes.

And, of course, the academy could not run without academics, administrators, and activist scholars. Worth noting is that every one of them whom

I name below is special to me: none of them are caught up in the (very seductive) seduction of status, intransigence, and envy. Instead, through their own work and engagement of mine, they make me a better scholar, public intellectual, and person. Not only did many of them support me through the writing of this book, but some of them also helped me through a particularly difficult time during it.

Special thanks to the City University of New York's Asian and Asian American Research Institute (AAARI) for generously awarding me the Thomas Tam Visiting Professorship (2018–2019) that gave me time off from teaching and service to complete this book. Led by the indomitable Joyce Moy, AAARI's Antony Wong, Claire Chun, and Diana Pan also offered support (Antony provided and oversaw research assistance). I thank as well the Sociology Department of the CUNY Graduate Center for serving as my home base for the year: Nancy Foner, Margaret Chin, and Rati Kashyap were especially helpful in organizing talks, getting me on-boarded, and integrating me into the local intellectual community. On the Los Angeles side, I must recognize Loyola Marymount University's Bellarmine grants programs for seeing promise in this project and providing funding accordingly.

In particular, I must thank those busy souls who performed the arduous task of reading a chapter or two and offering sharp feedback. The people who improved *Refusing Death* in this way are Miliann Kang (my frequent writing partner and wonderful human), Andrew Dilts, Daryl Maeda, Glenda Flores, Eileen Díaz McConnell, Rachel Washburn, Diane Fujino, Robyn Rodriguez, Liz Clark Rubio, Russell Leung, and David Brunsma. Those who sat through presentations of this book and gave thoughtful feedback that shaped its direction are Judy Park, David Marple, Monisha Das Gupta, the scintillating South Korean scholars of the American Studies Association of Korea (ASAK, with special thanks to Jim Lee), Angie Chung (a New Yorker who also helped me get settled, and wonderful human), Vivian Louie, Pyong Gap Min, Richard Alba, Tom Guglielmo, Kyeyoung Park, Roger Waldinger, Irene Bloemraad, and the energetic scholars of the Politics of Race, Immigration, and Ethnicity Consortium (PRIEC—thanks to Karthick Ramakrishnan for organizing). Finally, David Pellow, Phil Brown, Eddie Telles, Rene Zenteno, Alice Krozer, and Patricio Solis offered invaluable knowledge and resources for this project.

When I combed through my records to include everyone who had helped with library searches, annotation, transcription, co-interviewing, translating, coding, Endnote, archiving CBO records (requested by some CBOs), and attending meetings or events when I could not, I was astounded by the number of names. To these persevering research assistants, I owe a deep debt of gratitude: Armine Marukyan, Abigail Rawl, Stephanie Hernandez, Claire Ramirez, Lauro Cons, Snejana Apley, Caitlin Campbell, Angelica Jazmin Ceja, Crystal Reyna, Marianna Hernandez, Cindy Medina, Genevieve Franco, Elisabeth Moolenaar, Sherilyn Colleen, and Lara Ullrich (and advance forgiveness is asked of anyone whom I may have forgotten).

I could not have asked for a more brilliant and amicable editor than Marcela Maxfield of Stanford University Press. Despite having manuscripts piled high on her desk, she knew my book intimately and cared about shepherding it through. Most notably, Marcela, alongside editor-in-chief Kate Wahl, kept an embattled Stanford Press thriving and glowing. Special thanks to David Palumbo-Liu for all his work on behalf of the press.

Looking institutionally, I must mention here that while I have, over my life course, experienced physical assaults for being an Asian-descent woman (most recently being nearly run over in the street by a driver enraged by "Chinese virus"), the hostile climate of academia over the past twenty years has perhaps felt the most chilling. At Loyola Marymount I must thank my past and present department colleagues who (try to) understand what this is like by regularly checking in, being supportive, and just being a pleasure to work with: Eric Magnuson, Sylvia Zamora, Ravaris Moore, Rob Cancio, Rosalio Cedillo, Natasha Miric, and Philippe DuHart. Outside my department, the past and present LMU colleagues whom I'm grateful to for the same are Deena Gonzalez, Curtiss Takada Rooks, Ed Park, Stella Oh, Judy Park, Diane Meyer, Kirstin Noreen, Csilla Samay, Brad Stone, and John Zepeda-Millán.

Beyond LMU, my "colleagues" whom I have yet to name but deserve thanks are Wendy Roth, Catherine Lee, and Tommy Wu (who answered many a question about the most exciting but cryptic city in the world; Tommy helped in immeasurable ways); Tanya Golash Boza and Ayu Saraswati (who organized the Peru Creative Connections writing retreat that lit the fire under me to finish, and to do so with feeling); Sonya Rose, John Lie, Eduardo Bonilla-Silva, G. Reginald Daniel, Dick Flacks, and John Foran (all mentors of yore who believed in me first); Joe Feagin, Yen Espiritu, Tom Romero,

Laurie Blumberg-Romero, Prudence Carter, Karen DeGannes, Darrick Hamilton, Mina Yoo, Larry Hashima, Kelly Chong, Bandana Purkayastha, Joseph Jewell, Min Song, Grace Kim, James Wu (may he rest in peace and power), Kevin Escudero, Lila Sharif, Dennis Brown, Jinah Kim, Eric Tang, Ben Carrington, and Pawan Dhingra.

Last but not least, my soul tribe: Ayesha Robinson, Leo Vargas, Erika Schmidt, Hampton Cantrell, Dave Brady, Janice Sasaki, Nina Ha, my daughters (and my Shih Tzu mix Cookie), my siblings and family here, and my family in Korea, Brasil, and Canada. Without your hugs, hilarity, and helpful favors, I wouldn't have much of a career or, really, much inner peace. I hope you know that I love you to the moon and back—and back again.

Refusing Death

INTRODUCTION

FIGHTING FOR BREATH IN THE OTHER LA

ONE OF THE first actions I participated in with People's CORE, a Filipin@[1] American–led social justice organization, was to help its activists—a handful of staff and K–12 teachers—mobilize Carson and the surrounding community against BP Arco's renewal of their permit to refine oil. When the day of reckoning had come in September 2008, I walked into a packed room anchored by an all-male panel of four well-dressed officials from government agencies and BP. One appeared to be Latino, the rest, White American. Turning toward the audience I saw mostly middle-aged women and men of color: primarily Latin@s and Asian and Pacific Islander Americans (AAPIs), but also a smattering of Black Americans and White Americans. Per standard procedure, the meeting began with the panel's presentations on various dimensions of BP's operations and the renewal of their permit.

When it came time for the official public comment period, one soft-spoken elderly woman of Japanese American descent slowly approached the mic. In a calm but apprehensive tone, she shared that she did not come to attack them but to share her concerns as a Carson resident, adding, "My husband worked his whole life at your refinery, and, please, don't get me wrong because I'm *not* saying that BP caused his cancer, but after he retired he *did* get cancer, and he passed away." Subtle sighs came from the audience. Amidst the muttering and headshaking, the officials did not express sympathy for her loss but instead chose to quickly reassure her that BP met legal regulations and that cancer rates were down and still within their allowable limits—a poster child for Foucault's claim that the state uses race to justify the deaths of Others so that the racially superior can live; that is, industry is "allowed" to cause a certain number of deaths. The non-emotionality of the representatives of BP and of the Air Quality Management District (the state regulating body) ultimately served to delegitimate any possible link between a BP employee's death by cancer and the BP oil refinery itself. Indignant, the typically calm Cindy, a Samoan American K–12 teacher, raged into the mic, which I had never before seen her do. As I jumped in my seat and straightened my back, she, with palpable exasperation, inveighed against the BP officials for being less than truthful about the frequency and severity of the oil refinery's illegal flaring (a major release of toxic gases), all to the great detriment of the air. Making our ears ring slightly, she punctuated her remarks with, "I am *so angry*! I am so *tired* of being sick, of seeing sick children at my elementary school where I work: we've all got asthma, constant bloody noses! You know, it's very possible that her husband's cancer was caused by all of this pollution." [Turning to the elderly widow] "I'm really sorry for your loss."

What struck me most was not Cindy's rage piercing the air and our eardrums at an otherwise hushed and understated public gathering. Her rage was understandable, and over the years, I had seen many activists across myriad movements shape-shift emotionally. Thus when women like Cindy chose to tell officials of the regulatory agencies and industry about running in horror to ERs with blue-faced children seemingly choking to their deaths as they bobbed and flailed in their arms, of how their "baby" contracted asthma as early as two, of how the children cry because they cannot study in school nor exercise outside in brown air, the tears sometimes flowed or the spit sometimes flew. For me, the take-home point, rather, was how she strategically denormalized the officials' emotions (that is, apathy) as inappropriate (and broke "feminine" ideals in the process).[2] Long before the meeting, she, and all of us, knew that BP's permit would be perfunctorily renewed. Nevertheless, Cindy was sure to make a political splash by showcasing her unapologetic conviction that the emotion had to match the crime. She did so not by focusing on the fancy statistics and chemical names that she was intimately familiar with, but by delving into the politics of the body and of feelings. After she relayed the emotional and physical toll of being sick ("I'm so angry . . . tired!"), she followed up with an offer of emotional support to the widow ("I'm really sorry for your loss"). By being sad and enraged for the widow while the mostly White and all-male officials sat stonefaced, Cindy did not just legitimate the widow's conjecture that a lifetime of work at an oil refinery and a death by cancer were more than coincidence; she also worked hard to paint an image of callous jerks, the very image the male officials worked to undermine precisely (and ironically) by presenting "professionalism"—emotional apathy—as normal.

Another affective touchpoint for the immigrants' politics was their disquiet over officials and outsiders frequently quipping, "Why don't you just move, then?" when mostly mothers raised concerns about their dirty, unbreathable air and their asthmatic children. Notwithstanding the bias and privilege enmeshed in a "just move" retort, even a slight difference in air quality could mean the difference between an asthma attack or a preempted one, between, in the ultimate, life and death. When I asked the activists why they roundly rejected "moving to another part of LA" (although I could conjecture why), they echoed the sentiments of Tanya, a Mexican immigrant mother of high schoolers who lived in a vortex of diesel in West Long Beach. Thinking first of her neighbors, whom she cared for as fictive kin, she huffed, "Well, if I want to leave, I'll leave! If I don't, I won't! *I would be leaving them all alone* (shaking her head)!" Tanya was indignant not just because the question was infused with social privileges, but because it had no regard for the value that she and other immigrants placed on fighting for one's neighbor and community. If she stayed put, yes, she might be subjecting herself and her children to an early death, but if she "escaped," who would fight for her community? Certainly not the government and certainly not BP Arco. Yet activists like Tanya were far from unclear on the deadly consequences of her "choice." Arrayed against raced, classed, and gendered neoliberal power, Tanya was so dejected by the elites' empathy deficit that she proposed that her two grassroots organizations—Community Partners Council (CPC) and Long Beach Alliance for Children with Asthma (LBACA)—adopt the most embodied strategy, one of last but necessary resort:

TANYA: They need more like—for example, every person that's dying of asthma—take a picture of them and all the people who are dying of asthma to show them. *It's not enough*, but it might help a little bit; we have to give the government even more of these images, and the City of Long Beach.

NADIA: Because you don't think they'll do anything for you without pictures of death?

TANYA: Not if I don't fight, no.

Striking about Tanya's macabre strategy is that she herself was not even convinced that forcing photographs of dying or dead children would be "enough" to move the elites, so deep was their emotional apathy. Also striking is that Tanya, as Foucault theorized about state racism, was well aware that the state—rooted in neoliberal[3] racial capitalism[4]—was "letting die" immigrants of color like her, while it privileged whiter and richer "legals" with health and life. In fact, Ruth Wilson Gilmore (2007:28) conceptualized it more capaciously *and* precisely than Foucault when she wrote, "Racism, specifically, is the state-sanctioned or extralegal production and exploitation of group-differentiated vulnerability to premature death." Yet Tanya knew—as Cindy knew of the Japanese American widow—that the state's and industry's full knowledge that they were causing premature deaths, even of children, would likely still not be enough to move the system to care.

I devote most of the pages of this book to understanding moments like these. After all, Cindy and Tanya are among the growing number of Asian and Pacific Islander and Latina immigrant women who have assumed the helm of grassroots community organizing for environmental justice.[5] While we may not know these women, they are part of a broader collective mobilization that has finally gotten Americans to pay attention to environmental racism: the Flint water crisis, the Dakota Access Pipeline, the Mauna Kea telescope, and the disproportionately compromised lungs of Black, Brown, and Pacific Islander people under COVID-19. Immigrant women have not stopped at EJ movements, however; they have also led on immigration reform (Pallares 2014; Milkman and Terriquez 2012; Zepeda-Millán 2017—see also García Bedolla 2014), schools (Pardo 1998; Terriquez 2011), labor (Milkman 2006; Terriquez 2015a), domestic violence (Coll 2010), welfare (Fujiwara 2008;

Naples 1998b), and social service reform (Võ 2004; Carney 2014—see Fujino 2008).[6] For a population that has been racialized as America's foreigners and "illegals" and gendered as hyperfertile mothers, their marginalization by the electoral system has not tempered, but rather buoyed, community organizing (see Fujiwara 2008; Ishizuka 2016; Nicholls 2013; Truax 2015; Võ 2004; Zepeda-Millán 2017). Furthermore, this pattern, as *Refusing Death* explains, owes to immigrants no longer viewing formal citizenship as the only avenue to political legitimacy and efficacy. In this context, the women of my study, alongside immigrant men and their children, are changing the political landscape of global cities like Los Angeles and less glittery cities across the nation. They do so while being slowly choked by neoliberalism's physical and emotional violence, as we just witnessed in the lack of action and empathy for those who die from oil refineries, or in flip comments about moving.

To understand these change-makers whom we know little about, I spent close to four years with these fierce activist women (and men and youth) in the port-industrial belt of South Bay Los Angeles and Long Beach. Society would deem improbable their existence and political significance. Studies have shown that, despite improvements, Asian Americans broadly have been weaker politically than their non-White counterparts, in part because of barriers and cultural issues such as language (see Lien 2017; Wong, Ramakrishnan, Lee, and Junn 2011); similarly, studies have shown that immigrants of Mexican ethnicity who do not speak English, are low income, and are unauthorized (the vast majority of the Latin@s in this study) tend to be less civically active than their Central American[7] and other non-White peers (Feliciano 2005; Jones-Correa and Andalon 2008; Leal 2002; Turney and Kao 2009; Verba, Schlozman, and Brady 1995; Wong, Ramakrishnan, Lee, and Junn 2011). Yet the mostly Mexican as well as Filipin@-led Asian immigrants in LA have gone from being barely legible in the US polity—especially the women, who until the 1990s were missing in leadership—to relentlessly fighting polluting behemoths and their tentacle reach into schools. These organizers buck every trend line, and thus we should know who they are: a growing chorus of Asian and Latin@ immigrants who galvanize everyday people to bring truth to power despite power killing them quietly.[8] Save for intermittent coalition work, the Asian and Latin@ ethnics tended to work discretely from each other given mostly insular organizations and neighborhoods: Mexican (and Central

American) immigrants in Wilmington and West Long Beach and mostly Filipin@s and other Asian Americans in Carson. Yet I was able to draw conclusions from taking together their mostly independent movements, a rare but eye-opening comparative approach to environmental justice and other community mobilizations.

As noted, a potent similarity I learned was the attentiveness to inequalities of the body among the Latin@ and Asian immigrant organizers, which I detail throughout *Refusing Death*. Of course, one might expect activists who fight disproportionate environmental poisoning of their communities to center embodiment; what, then, was so interesting about that? Yet I was struck by how much the immigrants, in the fight for environmental justice, recast the ambit of nativist racism and classism by spotlighting not just their bodily injustices but their emotional ones. In other words, grassroots leaders like Cindy and Tanya saw an arc of physical and emotional neglect in the racism and classism endemic to environmental injustice. Such a perspective, affirmed by transnational experiences, prompted the immigrants to identify and draw boundaries as an *embodied community*, one that carried and felt the hazards, sickness, and beauty of their collective in their bodies. To fight "the (White) healthy wealthy," a neoliberal system built on privileging some bodies and emotional lives at the expense of others, the activists stepped into these gaps by practicing what I call *embodied citizenship*. More than the language of assimilation, voting, campaigning, and rights (see Boggs and Kurashige 2011), then, these immigrants used the emotive metric of care to define "good" and "moral" citizenship and to contest corporatist state violence. Therefore, they innovatively remapped environmental justice movements. Unfettered by political party and social movement conventions, their activism for clean air often seemed to integrate seamlessly issues of education (and immigration) justice, as explored in Chapter 3. Of course, political creativity is not without its surprising contradictions, as the immigrants' liberty and latitude to redefine often yielded inventive and confounding politics. Beyond informing theories and studies of environmental justice, movements, race, class, gender, citizenship, migration, transnationality, and embodiment, these grassroots actors challenge and stretch Foucaultian biopolitics (and biopower[9]), a running thread throughout this book that, at its end, I stitch together into a full theoretical tapestry (see Chavez 2007; Cisneros 2016; Halse 2009; Brendese 2014; Carney 2014).

THE IMPORTANCE OF THE INVISIBLE— KNOWING THE UNKNOWN

These immigrant activists with whom I spent nearly four years are not the glitterati of Los Angeles, nor do they typically have a bank of cameras trailing them. Just as they live in the shadows of massive commercial ports, sky-high freeway overpasses, and Goliath-like oil refineries, they—especially the Latin@s without papers—live in the shadows of Los Angeles. Yet these political innovators have transformed global metropoles like the City of Angels and countless others that light up the nation's sky.

Their transformation of the racial and ethnic face of cities like Los Angeles largely began with the landmark 1965 Immigration and Nationality Act, as Asian and Latin@ ethnics have since composed the vast majority of immigrants to the United States. To be sure, some have been Afro-Latinx, Afro-Asian, and African, but as the vast majority of the influx have been neither-White-nor-Black Asians and Latinxs, these migrants have profoundly complicated America's prevailing White-Black race hierarchy. This population revolution has also generated such questions as, Where do these newer immigrants fit in such a hierarchy? Are they seen and treated as, or do they see themselves as, Americans? What is the impact of Latinxs representing the largest "minority" group in the United States, surpassing the African American populace since the 2000 US Census? We have witnessed, for instance, the centrality given to "the immigrant and Latino vote" in electoral politics in the United States. Indeed, most mainstream political pundits argue that no one can win the US presidency, and many down-ticket offices, without some backing from Latinx and other immigrant groups. While much mainstream discourse and growing scholarly work have been devoted to the role of immigrants of color in the dramatic transformation of America's electoral landscape, another political watershed has received surprisingly less attention. Not only have sociologists of social movements, as noted earlier, long overlooked the activism of immigrants of color (Zepeda-Millán 2017)—most especially immigrant women—the role of racial politics in immigrant movements remains underappreciated (Menjívar 2010).

Yet in recent decades, as noted, what society might see as the improbable mountain movers—the of color, low-income, first-generation, undocumented immigrants, many of whom are women and mothers—have in fact been on the front lines of influential grassroots community movements of all kinds.[10] Despite their wave-making for environmental (health) justice[11]—asthma politics, antitoxics, and anti-goods-movement work—sociology and Asian American, ethnic, and American studies[12] have not paid sufficient attention to them, in part because the scholarship across the board has not been commensurate with the catastrophic reality of our environmental and climate crises. Excepting the incredible individual work that has already been done, perhaps these disciplines do not see environmental issues as people- and interaction-centered as, say, criminal justice or education. Yet not only is environmental (and climate) justice always about people and relationships, it is inextricably tied to race, class, and gender as well as the less appreciated axes of nation and citizenship, which I have previously argued must be integrated into our intersectionality frameworks (N. Kim 2013; see also Pellow 2007). As Pulido (1996a, 1996b) and Pellow (2007) have argued, race scholars, for instance, continue to underappreciate the primacy of environmental racism to *racism in toto* (as the current COVID-19 pandemic has thrown into relief [Bagley 2020]), yet "critical environmental justice studies" has never decentered race (Pellow and Brulle 2005). Indeed, Pulido (2017b:19) writes that in uniting two great movements of the twentieth century—environmentalism and civil rights—environmental justice was also, in part, a strategic move to contest the country's 1980s reactionary wave against antiracism; EJ was, in turn, attacked by this wave of intensifying neoliberalism.

As an example of the need for more research on Asian American environmental justice movements, the Filipin@ Americans I worked with are part of a longer legacy of Filipinx environmental justice activism and compose the majority and leadership of today's fight in LA's port-oil belt, yet remain largely unknown and unheralded.[13] If Los Angeles knows anyone, it might be the pioneering farmworkers and labor leaders Larry Itliong and Philip Vera Cruz, who mobilized for environmental justice on behalf of Filipinx and Mexican immigrant farmworkers who prematurely died, lost babies, or had disabled babies owing to being sprayed with the cancer of pesticides (Guillermo 2015; Vera Cruz 1992).[14] *Refusing Death*, therefore, seeks to be a window into Filipin@ ethnics' battles on the front lines of environmental racism and classism in communities where they concentrate, such as Carson, Los Angeles, where over 20 percent of the populace is Filipinx (80 percent of Carson's APIDAs[15] [see Ocampo 2016]). Carson is also ethnoracially mixed, mostly middle class (also mixed income), proximal to the Ports of LA and Long Beach and the nation's most cancerous freeway (Interstate 710)—freeways being among the most "racist monuments" in LA (Fleischer 2020)—and home to a diesel-spewing railyard, a Marathon oil refinery (formerly BP Arco, then Tesoro, then Andeavor), and a Phillips 66 refinery.

The mostly unauthorized Mexican immigrant organizers of West Long Beach and Wilmington have also become a major headache for the hazardous corporations and the state agencies tasked with regulating them. Although the vast majority of these activists were not socialized by formal or movement politics in Mexico and only joined and led social movements after settling in LA, we lack sufficient social scientific and ethnic studies research on Mexican immigrant environmental justice movements, especially in urban centers, despite the pioneering work and clarion calls since the 1990s of Pulido (1996a, 1996b), Pardo (1998), Peña (1998), Moses (1993), and Gallegos (1998).[16] Further, ethnoracial-specific disciplines such as Latinx and Asian American studies benefit greatly when they prioritize relational and comparative positionings vis-à-vis other racialized groups.[17] Indeed, it is often easier to grasp the specificities of each group's social locations, perspectives, and experiences—and to tap multiple types of social hierarchies—when we interrelate and compare groups with one another.[18]

Goods, Oil, and Asthma

Los Angeles is not just the City of Quartz (Davis 1990) but the City of Oil. Although most known for Hollywood and fashion, Los Angeles is actually the largest urban oil field in the country (Sadd and Shamasunder 2015:7). Today, oil wells that span the greater Los Angeles region, most of which run along the narrow belt from Long Beach to El Segundo, yield approximately twenty-eight million barrels per year from production both on- and offshore. As an extensive structural web exists to support the refining of millions of barrels (see ibid.:5), the Ports of Los Angeles and Long Beach must receive and store nearly all of the region's crude oil, tar sand, and asphalt. Per "goods movement," this means that the lungs of the activists and their children take in the diesel spewed by all the gargantuan cargo containers (from China, mostly) and then by the trucks and trains that transport refined oil or the myriad stuff that we Americans buy—from cars and furniture to TVs and smartphones to food and tchotchkes—to the dealerships, Walmarts, Targets, Best Buys, and grocery chains across the country. This vast network needed for goods movement also relies heavily on other polluters, from ancillary industries such as truck-washing companies to battery recyclers, and invites in still others, such as plastics manufacturers. The communities of West Long Beach, Wilmington, and Carson are among the hardest hit along this port-industrial belt (see Figure 1 for one example).

Predominantly Latinx West Long Beach, for instance, is not just a stone's throw from one of the largest shipping ports in the world, but also bounded by the Terminal Island Freeway (SR-103) to the west and the I-710 to the east. Owing to research pressure from Coalition for a Safe Environment (CFASE) and other groups with whom I worked, California environmental agencies found that the more disadvantaged parts of Wilmington ranked in the state's top 5th percentile in highest pollution exposure and highest levels of social vulnerability (Sadd and Shamasunder 2015). In addition, their estimated cancer risk exceeds *one thousand* additional cancer-stricken residents per one million, the highest recorded in Southern California and three orders of magnitude higher than the National Clean Air Act goal of *one* in one million cancer cases.[19] Also owing to intense community pressure from CFASE, Wilmington became one of the few cities in Los Angeles to be monitored for benzene, a cancer-causing toxin spewed mostly by oil refineries.

Not surprisingly, oil refinery contamination is connected to the asthma epidemic in the region insofar as refinery emissions are a trigger (see Koren 1995). Asthma matters not just because most of the children of the organizers (and some adults) in this book were afflicted by it, but because it is one of the country's fastest-growing diseases, poses a major health care and financial burden, and costs the nation a lot of lives.[20] Yet compared to most industrialized countries, the United States collects only sparse data on asthma (Brown, Mayer, Zavestoski, Luebke, Mandelbaum, and McCormick 2003). Moreover, the US government has never had a federally directed effort to monitor and address asthma—an oversight so curious that even the Pew Environmental Health Coalition raised it as an issue in their nationwide study of the epidemic (Corburn 2005:143).[21] In effect, the government regulatory world is engineering an asthma populationwide health crisis.

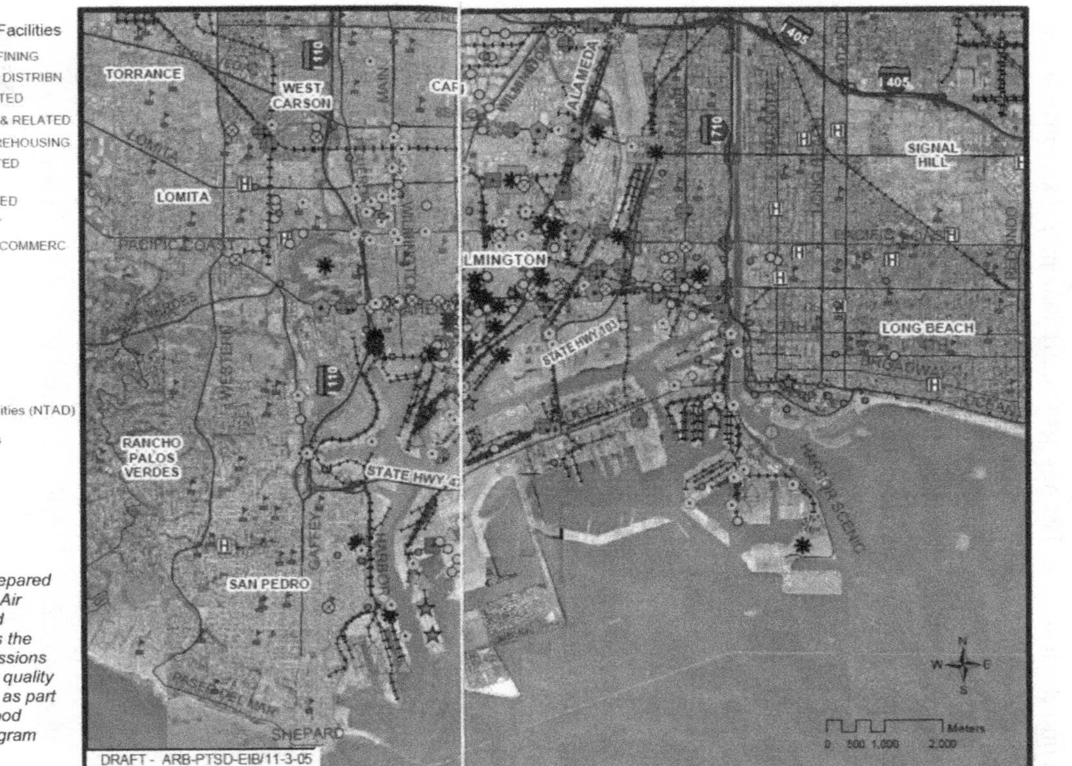

FIGURE 1. "Wilmington Pollution Sources." Source: Communities for a Better Environment.

Asthma became a nationwide problem in large part after asthma rates had increased noticeably in communities of color.[22] By 2000, Black American and Latino children across Los Angeles County were more likely than White Americans to report asthma-related limitations in physical activity and the need for urgent medical services, while Asian American children reported a higher asthma prevalence than Latino youth (Simon, Zeng, Wold, Haddock, and Fielding 2003). Another 2003 national study found that after controlling for other possible factors, Hispanic, African American, and Asian and Pacific Islander mothers were more than twice as likely as White mothers to live in the most air-polluted counties in the country (Woodruff et. al. 2003, cited in Sze 2006:103–107). Asthma is therefore not just a racialized and classed[23] disease but a gendered one.[24] Parents and other caretakers of children—especially mothers—must often shoulder the burden of managing chronic diseases such as childhood asthma.

While this book is attentive to the fact that we need to better address how patriarchy can partly account for environmental injustices (see Alaimo 2010), most researchers have found race and class (Pellow and Brulle 2007)—or race alone—to be at their root.[25] For instance, race and class have been found to explain why about half of all Asian ethnics, Pacific Islanders, and indigenous people live in communities with uncontrolled toxic waste sites and why more Latinxs in Los Angeles have these sites near their homes than in any other US city. Beyond the City of Angels, the United States and other advanced nations have exploited their position at the top of the (raced and gendered) global economic order by committing "toxic imperialism," specifically against nations in Africa, Asia (such as the Philippines), and Latin America; namely, by dumping all our cancerous e-waste there (Bullard 1993, Bullard et al. 2007; Hamilton 1993; Pellow 2007) but also by environmentally devastating developing nations through endless war and nuclear testing (Alston and Brown 1993).

As most of the immigrants in the book hailed from these global southern nations and maintain personal to political ties with them, *Refusing Death* shows that a transnational lens is paramount for a full grasp of their political vantage points and lives (see N. Kim 2006b, 2008b; Lacroix 2014; Levitt 2001).

THE ENVIRONMENT OF NEOLIBERAL NATIVIST RACISM

There is very little, arguably nothing, that does not relate to the discourse and politics of the "environment" in one way or another (Alaimo 2010; Peña

2005; Pulido 2017b). In immigration terms, for instance, the borders of our postmodern United States—a part of the "environment" that requires (sacred indigenous) land, kills ecosystems, and generates hazardous pollution—are crisscrossed by the world's migrants, capital, and ideas and serve as portals to global cities like Los Angeles. In another example, drastic privatization and militarization, the weakening of government, the sparse regulation of industry, and the valorization of the market—all staples of neoliberalism (Giroux 2006)—have meant that environmental pollution has become a commodity, "disingenuously promoted" by corporations and government allies as "race-neutral policies that benefit everyone equally" (Sze 2006:10–11; see also Christopherson 1994).

Yet environmental injustice, and neoliberalism writ large, are anything but race (or gender or class) neutral. Most dramatically marked by the retrenchment of the welfare state, neoliberalism was the product of shifts in global capital (no longer binding capital and industry to borders) and of an intense expansion of racisms to center nativist racism (Fujiwara 2008; Omi and Winant 2014). Federal welfare reform and anti-immigrant policies such as California's Proposition 187—all in the 1990s era—were traceable to this new nativism (Fujiwara 2008; Park 2011), ultimately serving as antecedent to the country hoisting a White supremacist into the White House in 2016, reifying white nationalism despite his 2020 election ouster and promulgating the global movement of strongman racism against migrants and Muslims. In 1996, President Clinton's watershed welfare "reform" ("welfare-to-work" program) discursively targeted women of color—Black, immigrant, and refugee—and dropped them from life-saving benefits (SSI), compelling some Asian refugee mothers to kill themselves (Fujiwara 2008). In 1994, Governor Pete Wilson's Proposition 187 emerged, targeting the Latinx population (and its "hyperfertile" mothers) by denying nonemergency health care and public education to "illegals." These biopolitical state actions—what I deem in this book physical and emotional assaults—have made (female) immigrant groups of color, especially Latin@s, more vulnerable to premature death or, in the words of Mbembé and Meintjes (2003), to the necropolitics of death. Ultimately, there is no neoliberalism without killing "those minorities" quietly or, in Berlant's (2007) words, killing them slowly.

As immigrants and refugees of color have been one of the central targets of the neoliberalism 2.0 that commenced in the 1990s (Fujiwara 2008), the hierarchy of citizenship is one of its pivots. The racial "foreigner" discourse of Asian Americans and of "Latin@s" as threats and competitors who are not-American—alongside "terrorists," or Mid-Eastern, Muslim, and Black immigrants—emblematizes nativist racism. As Telles and Ortiz (2008) found, the nativist racism against Mexican Americans largely accounts for the decades of exclusion, such as from the highest strata of the education system, of even the third and higher generations. And although certain Asian American groups—namely, East and South Asian ethnics—have been racialized as monolithic "model minorities" for select White supremacist purposes, data have revealed that nativist racism is responsible for the jade or bamboo ceiling that even these ethnics hit, for the high rates of anti-Asian hate crimes, and for their frequent reports of discrimination.[26] And more than any other group of color, Asian Americans suffer the widest economic disparity within (see Lai and Arguelles 2003; Pew Research Center 2018). Both for Latin@s and Asian Americans, nativist racism is what denies their belonging[27] in a country that they aspire to call home and that seemed to reach its apotheosis under Trump's cages and concentration camps and under coronavirus/Kung-flu racism.[28] Furthermore, because both racialized groups, especially the undocumented among them, do not have the electoral political history and power that White Americans—and secondarily, Black Americans—do, grassroots communities become an important site of immigrant-, refugee-, and citizenship-centered politics. In many ways, the immigrants of my study who saw environmental justice as a broader fight against nativist racism and nativist classism were anticipating the advent of the Trump Era of White supremacist nationalism and its shelf-life long after Trump.

IMMIGRANTS MOVING IN MOVEMENT—IMPLICATIONS FOR ENVIRONMENTAL JUSTICE SCHOLARSHIP

As environmental justice history is American (race) history, one could feasibly trace the environmental justice movement to the Great Plains tribes' pushback against White Americans' massive slaughter of buffalo as a form of (indirect) genocide (see Alaimo 2010) or to the Black American workers who, in 1930, protested their silica dust poisoning and their co-workers' deaths at the hands of a willfully negligent Union Carbide (Cherniack 1986). Or, one could turn to the Yellow Power struggle against the use of Agent Orange in Viet Nam

(Waugh 2010) or to the Filipino and Mexican farmworkers who refused to be poisoned by agribusinesses' DDT (Marquez 2012; Moses 1993; Pulido and Peña 1998; Schwartz et al. 2015; Vera Cruz 1992). The official origins, however, are usually identified by Robert Bullard (1993), the founding father of environmental justice studies, as being in 1982, when Black Americans rose up in Warren County, North Carolina. Hundreds of activists and residents came together to oppose the expansion of a chemical landfill, setting off a ripple effect of people in neighborhoods and small towns challenging other LULUs (locally unwanted land uses). Since these notable origins, the movement has pressured industry to demonstrate the safety of new processes and chemicals rather than have to bear the burden of proof themselves (the precautionary principle). In addition, marginalized people like the clean air warriors of this book have publicized the alarming incidence of asthma among children of color when the state neglected to do so and have drawn a clear, political line from racism and classism to asthma (Brown, Mayer, Zavestoski, Luebke, Mandelbaum, and McCormick 2003). Taken together, the US environmental justice movement has been impressive in its growth, gaining prominence in other nations (Bullard 1993) and across transnational networks (Pellow 2007). In the United States, it is now more racially diverse than both the Civil Rights and traditional environmental movements and skillfully combines insights from both (Pellow and Brulle 2007).

White American women have long been noted as tour de force leaders for environmental justice (see Seitz 1998). In her classic *Silent Spring*, Rachel Carson popularized the danger of pesticides for women and children and translated science for the masses, prompting not just the elimination of toxins such as DDT but, in part, the creation of the Environmental Protection Agency (Peña 2005). In the early 1980s, Lois Gibbs's leadership of the National Toxics Campaign after she discovered that her and her neighbors' homes sat on a deadly toxic soup led to the 1986 reauthorization of the Superfund Act (to clean up the worst toxic waste sites in the country). Yet Carson's history-making book failed to address Mexican and Filipinx immigrant laborers' deadly exposure to DDT, and Gibbs's movement was criticized for accepting the lion's share of federal Superfund resources at the expense of cleanup in communities of color (Peña 2005).

Although White women laid the groundwork, women of color have resoundingly taken up the mantle (Bullard et al. 2007). They are the Chicanas who have seen the worst dimensions of poverty's effect on nature (Kirk 1998), who rise up after their barrios and Lao communities are dumped on (Pardo 1998 and Shah 2011, respectively), and who connect military waste to decimation of reservation lands (LaDuke 1993), and the Asian and Latina immigrants who realize that their toiling in Silicon Valley factories halted their pregnancies and turned their breast milk orange (Pellow and Park 2002). Often connecting the vectors of environmental health and racial justice, non-White women make up nearly three-fourths of the leaders profiled in the 2000 *People of Color Environmental Groups Directory* (Bullard, Johnson, and Torres 2011).

The Latinas with whom I worked most resembled the Mothers of East Los Angeles (MELA)—the longest-standing and most famous Latin@ environmental justice movement in LA—who successfully fought off a prison, a toxic waste incinerator, and an oil pipeline in their segregated East LA neighborhood (Pardo 1998). Like MELA, most of the participants in my study did not begin their life of organizing until after the 1980s. And, like MELA, the Latinas of Long Beach and Wilmington were fiercely proud of their community and took great pains to subvert the poor image of it. Asian Americans in environmental justice have been resisting as immigrant chipmakers in antitoxics and prolabor movements in Silicon Valley (Pellow and Park 2002), as immigrant seamstresses in toxic garment factory "sweatshops" (Louie 2001), and as teenage girls fighting hazards in Richmond, California (Shah 2011). While my study similarly foregrounds the women who constitute the majority of the EJ organizers, I also treat the men—who, not surprisingly, were often the founders and leaders of the community organizations—and the male youth activists as the key players that they are. Gender—and its relationality with race, class, and citizenship—is therefore a key part of my analysis of political process, embodiment, and emotionality.

Robert Bullard's tour de force vision and unflinching commitment gave rise to environmental justice scholarship starting in the early 1980s. Since, the burst of work that has emerged from sociology as well as environmental, American, ethnic, and women's and gender studies, and other disciplines, has been nothing short of stunning. Indeed, it is on the shoulders of these giants that this book stands. Environmental justice mobilizations and scholarship have forcefully redefined "the environment" beyond unpeopled wilderness—as enjoined by mostly class-privileged White male leaders—to where people live, work, and play (and go to school), as exhorted by less affluent White women and people of color (Cole and Foster 2000; Seitz 1998; Novotny 2000). Analysts of such environmental justice movements have also been the most adept and trenchant in their vision for the field, pushing it to center: ecology (Peña 1998; Alaimo 2010), race-class community identity and culture (Brodkin 2009; Pardo 1998; Sze 2006), immigrant political citizenship (Shah 2011), privilege (Park and Pellow 2011), transnational movements (Pellow 2007), political economy and racial capitalism (Pellow 2007; Pulido 2017a), settler colonialism (Pulido 2018; Steinman 2012), spirituality (LaDuke 2005), indigenous experiences of land (Vickery and Hunter 2016), bodies (Alaimo 2010), and emotions (Norgaard and Reed 2017). Yet these thoroughgoing contributions have not been given the attention, especially theoretically, needed to redefine the broader disciplines of sociology, American studies, ethnic and race studies, Asian American studies, and Latinx and Chicanx studies.

Refusing Death seeks to address these critiques and developments. It starts from the premise that environmental injustices flow from racial capitalism (Robinson 1983; Pulido 2017a—see also Pellow 2007) and its relation to autonomous racial formations (Omi and Winant 2014). Arrayed thus, the book conceptually integrates the ecological, the intersectional, the (neo)imperialist, and the transnational to pursue how a particular Filipin@- and Mexican-women-led movement of immigrants creatively and comprehensively processes *the embodied nature* of racism and classism; in so doing I highlight the women's leadership in forging gendered resistance and community citizen-making.

As environmental justice research has been accused of not sufficiently dealing with nature, this book seeks to correct for that. Inspired by the ecological school of thought and world-renowned biodiversity activist Vandana Shiva (1988, 1998), Devon Peña (1998, 2005) explains its application to the Chicano community:

> The ecologist locates truth *in place*, within the contextual limits of both natural and cultural landscape mosaics that constitute a bioregion at a given point in time. . . . The Western scientific worldview privileges expert universal knowledge against the traditional, place-bound local knowledge of various unruly Others—women, workers, colonial subjects (Shiva 1988, Peña 1997a). . . .

> Ecology merely reminds us how to live in our "niche," in our place [and with non-humans]. (Peña 1998:3–5)

This situated knowledge is especially crucial for people of color who are often forced to live in places determined by race, ethnic, and class segregation, whether these are urban Chicanos "living across the tracks" or New Mexico farmers losing their land: "Perdimos la libertad. Nos encercaron" ("We lost our liberty. They fenced us out") (Peña 1998:11). In fact, Peña finds that, until the rise of environmental justice movements, Chicano/a scholars had reasonably associated environmentalism with middle-class Whites; yet Chicano communities had forged ecologically sustainable livelihoods long before the advent of "conservation," long before White men such as Thoreau and Muir had popularized environmental ethics (6).

Scholars contend that we could extend this ecological environmental justice approach to the entire swath of US history, using it to reconceptualize manifest destiny and the institution of plantation enslavement (Alaimo 2010:29; see also Norgaard and Reed 2017), as well as, I would add, the maladies and violent deaths of Chinese immigrant transcontinental railroad workers from dynamite explosions and subzero winters. In light of the richness of this revisionist history, Alaimo (2010) agrees with Peña that we cannot excise ecology, or "nature," from the theories, analyses, and empiricism of a very urban-centered environmental justice—that the pendulum has swung too much the other way from the natural environment.

As a revision, Stacy Alaimo (2010) contends that environmental justice should center the relationship between nature and the body. I agree that we must first start by moving beyond the conceptualization of the body as largely a discursive production, as proffered by feminist theory and cultural studies; even the cyborg in "The Cyborg Manifesto," she writes, is "rarely embraced as an amalgamation of human and nature" (7). Most embodiment theorists operate in the Foucaultian tradition of seeing the malleability of the body but not registering how individuals, partially in and through their bodies, can create and change discourse and culture (Turner 1984). Alaimo moves us to rethink:

> Bracketing the biological body, and thereby severing its evolutionary, historical, and ongoing interconnections with the material world, may not be ethically, politically, or theoretically desirable. Trans-corporeality offers an

> alternative. . . . [A]s a theoretical site, [it posits that] the movement across human corporeality and nonhuman nature necessitates rich, complex modes of analysis that travel through the entangled territories of material and discursive, natural and cultural, biological and textual (2010:3).

In this book I adopt this transcorporeal perspective, as environmental justice is primarily about how bodies are changed by their hazardous environments, thereby summoning material connections between the two (ibid.:61). By examining the Asian and Latin@ immigrants' mobilization for cleaner air, not only do we learn how they fundamentally work through transcorporeality, but we move beyond sociology's tendency to write theories of the body without commensurate empirical analyses.

Norgaard and Reed (2017) integrate the critical relationship between nature and emotions. On their insightful research on the Karuk people, they find that the natural environment is part of the stage where social interactions happen and is a central influence on emotional experiences, such as grief and shame; for instance, the degradation of the river and resultant loss of salmon species bear profoundly on Karuk individuals' internalization of identity, social roles, and power structures, and their resistance to racism and ongoing colonialism. To arrive at such analyses, Norgaard and Reed argue that we must move beyond a focus on the physical health impacts of environmental pollution or on the mental health impacts of environmental disasters; rather, we must take seriously the concept of environmental harm and other relationships in terms of emotions, environmental change, and systemic injustices.[29]

Taken together, I contend that there has been too much of a split in our understanding of "nature" and "city" such that we lose sight of the fact that urban communities are effectively both. Of course, we must broadly distinguish between agricultural land grants and inner-city neighborhoods, but the Asian and Latin@ immigrants with whom I worked never ceased to see their urban community as nature. Beyond wanting to clean up nature (air), these are communities right along the shoreline and next to one of the world's largest ports; nature is therefore also the sand, the ocean, the rocks, the jetties, and the salty sea breeze. A transcorporeal perspective, then, allows us to focus on how the immigrants forge, at once, an ecological and embodied—and, I would specify, an affective—approach per nature and the built environment.

David Pellow (2007) registers another major critique of the US environmental justice movement and our related scholarly precepts about what constitutes "victory": that local EJ communities ultimately kick the can down the road whenever they prevent the siting of a toxic incinerator, oil pipeline, or power plant in their neighborhood; they, in effect, kick it to another disadvantaged neighborhood or a poorer nation down the road. In this way, most resistance movements and even their "victories" can problematically reproduce inequalities within the movement or reinforce one hegemony by battling another (see Collins 2000; Espiritu 1997, 2003; Moraga and Anzaldua 1983; Pyke and Johnson 2003). During my time with LA's immigrants, their main fights did not concern the siting of a new facility, however. They sought instead to make state regulators drastically cut the amount of diesel or toxins that entered their lungs by way of the shipping ports, train yards, freeways, and oil refineries, and to actually *enforce* these regulations that neoliberalism had allowed them to flout. Figure 2, for instance, shows how close Long Beach is willing to put a diesel-pumping BNSF SCIG train yard to Hudson Elementary School, Cabrillo High School, and two homeless service centers, not to mention people's apartments and homes.

FIGURE 2. Proposed railyard project by Burlington, North Santa Fe. Source: Long Beach Alliance for Children with Asthma (LBACA).

The other key campaign was to stop the proposed expansion of the Interstate 710 freeway that would allow many more eighteen-wheelers enshrined in black haze to move product to stores, exacerbating rates of asthma (especially children's), cancer, and death. As "racist monuments" (Fleischer 2020), freeways require the razing of people of color's homes; unleash noise and light pollution; obstruct the sun and sky; and disproportionately sicken and kill nearby residents with diesel, oil slick, dust, and safety hazards. As for smaller mobilizations, the teachers of Carson tried to shut down the truck-washing business leaking toxic chemicals onto their elementary school campus next door, but this campaign died down after People's CORE's effective young female leader moved away and the teachers grew overwhelmed with other activist pursuits (such as union and workers' compensation fights). Communities for a Better Environment was also involved in a campaign called "Clean Up, Green Up" to reduce community contamination by asking small businesses to ecologically clean and green their operations.

As Pellow (2007) would appreciate, however, Carson's Filipin@ American organizers also peered beyond the local, seeing with clear eyes the transnational environmental justice struggles in the Philippines; as we shall see, they were conscious of fighting the battle on two fronts, even if most of their energy was devoted to LA. In this vein, Aimee Suzara (2003), a Filipina American activist, reflected on her participation in the Second National People of Color Environmental Leadership Summit in 2002, noting that she attended with a "heavy heart":

> Just a few months earlier, cuts were made in funding for Superfund site cleanups, representing a trend of post-9/11 attacks on environmental policy in the United States by the Bush administration. Meanwhile, in the Philippines, residents living near former U.S. military bases were continuing to suffer from toxic waste-related illnesses such as congenital defects, leukemia and other cancers—a tragedy for which the [US] military still refused to take responsibility. A renewed military presence in the Philippines as part of the "War against Terrorism" highlighted this toxic legacy. With those concerns in mind, I attended the summit as the representative of the Filipino/American Coalition for Environmental Solutions (FACES)—a young national organization that works toward the cleanup of U.S. military installations in the Philippines

> [and as a delegate of the Asian Pacific Environmental Network, a Northern California organization].

Suzara makes plain that she, FACES, and APEN conceived of "environmental justice" not just as the fight for Filipinos poisoned by oil refineries in Richmond, California, but as the transnational fight for Filipinos poisoned by US (neo)colonial military bases and American wars abroad. In parallel fashion, Latin@ immigrants approached environmental justice with a sense of solidarity with all poor and exploited people across the globe. This seemed to afford an understanding that they were fighting for more than just clean air, even as it remained their main focus; their inventive blending of school issues with environmental justice bore this out most forcefully. Both sets of activists show us that an ecological and transcorporeal perspective requires us to be attentive to the specificities of the community, while acknowledging that local politics can always in some way inform transnational politics, and vice versa (Aparicio 2006; see also Lipsitz 2001).

This broader theorization also addresses a major point about environmental justice scholarship that has been registered by Laura Pulido (2017b). She has argued convincingly that the environmental justice movement should give up on the state, that it needs to take stock of the government's commitment to its neglect and the fact that, on average, officials have done very little to change the environmental status quo. Without taking anything away from the blood, sweat, and tears of America's EJ movement actors who have long fought to close the race-class gap in environmental suffering, Pulido concludes that, on balance, fundamental change has been sparse and far between. After all, the neoliberal racial state—under racial capitalism—genuflects at the altar of the market, corporations, and more affluent White America. Writing in a similar vein, activist Grace Lee Boggs has eloquently enjoined marginalized communities to jettison the fight for state rights and inclusion and engage instead in various modes of self-determination (see Boggs and Kurashige 2011). While this book contends that, on balance, most social movements endure many more losses than "victories," if victory is ever realized at all, the Asian and Latin@ immigrants had a contradictory relationship to the state of engagement and disengagement; as we shall see, this owed to reasons that ranged from a greater focus on personal and communal development than on outcomes and to the invisibility (and hegemony) of capitalism. Importantly, the immigrants' "Come close, go away" relationship with the state was also partly traceable to their transnational distaste for sending states and colonial states.

THE BODY, EMOTIONS, GENDER, AND BIOPOWER

Body and Emotions

A transcorporeal perspective allows *Refusing Death* to posit the body as a site of political identity and struggle whereby the asthmatic or cancerous body is as corporeal as it is symbolic. Among the clean air activists I studied, for instance, they drew boundaries to deem all healthy bodies that did not care about them politically, emotionally, or physically as outside their "community" bounds. This study thereby empirically examines inequalities of the body and emotions, in relation not just to the margins (women, people of color) but to dominant bodies, institutions, and practices. It centers the mutual constitution between sociopolitical conditions, on the one side, and body and emotions, on the other (for example, Wolkowitz 2006; Lorber and Moore 2010).

When disciplines move beyond *theories* of the body and embodiment, the questions become more nuanced. For instance, given groundbreaking studies such as Shah's (2001) work on Chinese immigrant contagion, R. Lee's (2014) work on Asian bodies and resistance as fragmented, and Hayot's (2007) work connecting Asian immigrant biology to critiques of modernity, how might we conceptualize "environments" in our current epoch and see racism as bodies and feelings? To this end, I build on the incisive Foucaultian analyses of state power over migrant bodies within Latinx and Chicanx studies,[30] but also seek to move toward critiquing and reformulating Foucault from a perspective that centers women and men of color as well as migrants of color.

As I analyzed my interview and field notes, I found that the emotions literature, particularly in sociology but also in American and ethnic studies, could not fully account for the movement participants I studied, in part because the connection between bodies and emotions has not been clear or consistent (Calhoun 2001). Historically, the Enlightenment Period first separated the body from the mind,[31] a binary opposition to normalize injustices, such as that of men over women and Whites over non-Whites. Yet psychologists have long agreed that our thoughts largely determine our emotional state (Forward and Buck 1989; Levine and Heller 2010—see also Zembylas 2016), and sociologist Peggy Thoits (1989) writes that "reason" and emotion operate together and shape the other. Furthermore, scholars such as Deborah Gould (2009:18–22) have conceptualized unintentional, reactive bodily responses to stimuli as "affect." While this holds true at the individual and group levels, *Refusing Death* seeks to theorize the treatment (that is, abuse) of bodies and emotions as structurally embedded in systems and institutions, which also spawns—and becomes embedded in—bottom-up collective processes, such as social movement resistance. In this vein of defining emotions, feelings, and affect more broadly, more systemically, and more dialectically, I conceive of embodiment as also necessarily about emotional life; I thereby subsume affective states under a broader rendering of embodiment. At the same time, bodies and emotions certainly have their own characteristics and structurally manifest in distinct ways; subsequent chapters thereby highlight a different vector of each, and overlaps them where appropriate. To elaborate on the point about systems, sociological, American studies, and ethnic studies research have not sufficiently addressed the affective structures of institutions, nor the fact that they run on an "economy of emotions" (see Ahmed 2004) and, specifically, a racialized one (Bonilla-Silva 2019). On this racial lacuna, Mirchandani (2003:721) writes that social scientists have paid "little or no attention . . . to the racialized dimensions of emotion work." Yet beyond clarion calls and theoretical treatments, this book empirically examines a racial—and intersectional—emotional economy with respect to environmental justice and to political processes from the top down; this allows us to extend beyond the traditional focus on how racism harms the mental health and emotional life of those on the bottom, its importance notwithstanding.

Furthermore, while racialized emotions focus on the White-Black dynamic (Bonilla-Silva 2019), *Refusing Death* sees clearly that systemic White supremacy could not exist without relating racialized emotions to Latin@s, among others; Trump's Latinx-centered White racist nationalist movements and terrorism worldwide threw this into sharp relief. Furthermore, scholars contribute inadvertently to the White supremacist status quo when they neglect to study and integrate (nativist) racism against APIDAs, Muslims, and Mid-Eastern Americans (some of whom are Black), particularly in light of Trump's revival of post-9/11 racism, which also targets South Asian Americans, and revival of the antivirus racism against Asian ethnics traceable to Chinese arrival in the 1800s (Shah 2001). In other words, it is precisely White supremacy's *concealment* both of its racism against APIDAs and its pitting of Asian ethnics against Black Americans that affords its vitality and long shelf life over *all* groups of color. The more scholars, activists, and journalists believe such concealment to mean that racism does not (really) apply to APIDAs, which, in turn, cyclically fosters their lack of study of the population, the more potent and long-lasting White (nationalist) supremacy is, and will be, in toto. In other words, it wins at its own game.

Not only does *Refusing Death* center body and emotion politics in an environmental justice scholarship that has not widely done so, it addresses the racialized—and nationalized, gendered, classed—affective structures of systems (such as neoliberalism) and its institutions (for example, regulatory agencies); moreover, it examines these institutions' dialectical dynamic with resistance movements, as the traditional focus has been on the emotional economy of resistance movements alone. When we intersect race and gender, for instance, we understand better why institutional officials who battle environmental justice activists tend to ridicule the women and their expressed emotionality as a symptom of being "hysterical housewives" and to "trivializ[e]" their street science research as "emotional and unscholarly" (Kirk 1998). In this context, it is difficult to understand how the women push back if we do not analyze their view of how (White male) elites, and the system and institutions they represent, deploy emotions for power projects. With respect to the predominant Whiteness of the state and industry elites and the non-Whiteness of the Asian, Latin@, and other of color activists under a racial economy of emotions, Bonilla-Silva (2019:6) would see White "hegemonic emotional domination" (Matias 2016) being normalized over the "dubious" emotions of the margins. In my empirical examination of this process, with race I also intersect gender, class, and citizenship given the largely male, more affluent, and legal status of the dominant institutional actors.

In highlighting the relations between men and women and an attendant masculine-feminine hegemony, I also depart from previous gendered analyses that conclude that these immigrant mothers do not deem what they are doing as political but an extension of their mothering (Hardy-Fanta 1993; Pardo 1998). While the women in my study certainly differentiated between what they considered big-P Politics versus small-p politics (Chapter 6), they did not question whether or not their organizing was political. In analyzing the women and the men together, I find that both contest environmental racism and classism by waging resistance in the form of embodied citizenship. Yet it was the women who truly led on the issue of prioritizing the politics of care and who fleshed out its realization; although the men saw more purchase in the language of rights, it was the women who taught them how to "nourish . . . bodies and social ties" (Pérez and Abarca 2007:141). In their *embodied* citizenship practice, the women showed that citizenship was not just a top-down, individualized, legal,[32] and US-centric hierarchy; it was also a bottom-up, relational, transnational, and sociocultural process (Fujiwara 2008; Glenn 2002; Ong 1996, 1999, 2003; Rosaldo 1994). The capacity to redefine politics in this way was especially important for the Asian and Latina ethnic women who have been muted and rendered politically insignificant by nativist racism, classism, and sexism.

Although environmental injustices largely flow from White supremacist and capitalist systems, research attentive to gender has offered striking findings. For instance, the potency of the movements led by Mothers of East Los Angeles (Pardo 1998) and Lois Gibbs of the Love Canal disaster (Hay 2009) stemmed from their gendered and affective appeal to respecting the family, namely its mothers and children. The Latinas' and Gibbs's appeals to the common decency of the heteronormative family, to be sure, holds up alternative family formations as abnormal and not ideal, as Hay critiqued of Lois Gibbs's movement specifically. As we shall see, not only do the majority of the immigrant organizers in my study presume "the family" as heteronormative, their emphasis on the body fostered unconventional views on political issues related to embodiment, as I detail in Chapter 6.

Biopower and Bioneglect

Refusing Death is broadly about how Asian and Latin@ immigrant activists navigate their lucid awareness and experience of being slowly and quietly killed. More specifically, my time and interviews with them in the field taught me how they navigated the neoliberal biopower of environmental racism and classism. Yet Foucault's own theorizing could not fully account for both their suffering and their social justice work in this hypercontaminated corner of

Los Angeles. As critiques by Mbembé and Meintjes (2003) and Henry Giroux (2006) have made clear, Foucault did not give the "let die" (or "make die") dimension of biopower as much theoretical or empirical due as "make live." While he argued that the biopower of "making live" relied on the circulation of beneficial forms (money, fresh air) and the suppression of negative forms (circulated disease), he does not tell us about a state that circulates deadly air (Foucault 2007). Similarly, Mbembé and Meintjes argued that racism against Africans and those in the diaspora had long featured overt violence and the power of the sword to "make die," what they term necropolitics. And through its own drastic acceleration of neoliberal neglect, the George W. Bush administration had let African Americans of the Lower Ninth Ward die preventable deaths at the merciless hands of Hurricane Katrina, as Giroux (2006) writes.[33] Yet my orientation toward "let die" is not quite coterminous with necropolitics insofar as slow or quiet deaths often do not happen in overtly violent regimes or in formal states of emergency; in fact, the regimes, particularly those in the United States, pride themselves on being humanitarian, democratic, and more sophisticated than states of emergency.

Inspired by this literature and the pursuit of a better theoretical grip on the LA community organizers, I move beyond critique to reformulate a more expansive and inclusive process I call *bioneglect*. I argue for bioneglect's insertion into, not supplanting of, biopower, as a top-down, discursive-material process of "letting die" waged by neoliberal racial capitalism and the racial state. As "the set of mechanisms through which the basic biological features of the human species became the object of a political strategy, of a general strategy of power" (Foucault 2007:1), biopower needs to interrelate "let die" on an equal and balanced level with "make live." As the latter process should also do, I use bioneglect to give "let die" a neoliberal update (which Foucault would not live long enough to realize), make racial capitalism and its materiality as important as discourse (especially in terms of the neoliberal state), posit that the state originates populationwide health crises as much as it responds to them, and also center the following: racism (in a non-European context), an enlivened body that feels and is agentic (and is as material as it is textual), and Foucault's more disfavored form of power: top-down power (what he calls, "negative," "repressive"). In turn, I reconceive bottom-up movements to be central to, and by extension, to round out biopower writ large; as Foucault's canon did not include a systematic theory of resistance, I document what resistance looks like in the systemically polluted streets of Los Angeles and, in turn, how the state and industry respond (or, perhaps more appropriately, do not). In this way, biopower is relational and dialectical, and needs to be theorized and applied as such.

DATA AND METHODS

Regarding the intersectional nature of fieldwork, Espiritu (2003) writes that it is gendered insofar as women's efforts to conduct systematic ethnographic research can be constrained by motherhood or the extra burdens that women of color faculty face. As a mother and someone who advises, mentors, and counsels many (female) students of color, this certainly applied to my case, especially in the early stages of fieldwork. At the same time, being a mother was one of the key commonalities that allowed me to conduct this research project in the first place. For context, I inadvertently approached this study in an atypical and ineffectual manner. Normally, scholars have a preexisting relationship to the social movement prior to studying it, and thus relationships are already firmly established. Yet I had been living outside of California (where I am from) for much of the decade prior and had just moved back, really wanting to conduct ethnography on the local environmental justice movement. I was therefore a complete stranger when I asked to conduct research on, and with, the immigrants in LA's South Bay and Long Beach. After they expressed having been "burned" by professors and journalists before, I would have been utterly skeptical and wary of me as well, so I kept assuring them that I had been a movement activist for the previous sixteen years (on immigration, race, affirmative action, women's issues; secondarily, environmental justice), that they could read the completed manuscript before it was published, and that I would help out with whatever research and organizing needs they had. The latter certainly helped, but it was once they learned that I was a fellow mother and once they met my happy, chubby little baby girl, that the walls they were slowly lowering seemed to come down completely (much to my surprise). Other times, the organizational leaders would arrest me with their comments, like when Anya, LBACA's project manager, remarked out of the blue after I had already been working with them for a few months, "You know what, Nadia? I just want to say that I appreciate that when you asked to study us, that you mentioned that you could also help with the day-to-day, like putting chairs away and cleaning up; also, that you actually did it! I can't tell you how much that matters to us!" I remember smiling widely, my heart feeling warm, and thanking Anya. I really did not think that would matter as much as my "activist bona fides" or the research and organizing help I could offer LBACA. At the same time, Anya reminded me that putting chairs away and cleaning up *was* organizing, one of its many and boundless tasks.

After several months of my working to gain their trust and build relationships, I was able to employ a mixed-methodological and intersectional approach of three-and-a-half years of ethnographic participant-observation with the Asian American and Latin@ activists and allies in the port-industrial cities of LA. I also conducted in-depth interviews with a subset of the aggregate group. Finally, I conducted systematic analysis of political literature, public policy reports, and presentations. I collected the data between mid-2008 and late summer 2010, then again from mid-2011 to late 2013.

The ethnographic participant observation and interviews drew mostly from members and unaffiliated allies of community-based organizations (CBOs) serving the predominantly Asian American and Latin@ populations from Carson, Long Beach, Wilmington, and the surrounding area. The first, People's Community Organization for Reform and Empowerment (People's CORE or PCORE), was founded and predominantly staffed by Filipin@ Americans and mostly serves their co-ethnics, who compose over 20 percent of Carson's population, but also the smaller numbers of Samoan, Cambodian, hapa, and other Asian-descent groups who reside there. PCORE focuses its organizing on environmental justice—namely, the effects of port, railway, and freeway diesel pollution and oil refineries on local schools and on the broader community—and on issues of education and multilingual translation, military veterans' benefits, housing and tenant rights (including smoke-free rentals), and arts and cultural enhancement. Their theory and practice is that Filipin@ and other Americans of color should live in self-sustaining, locally controlled, just communities.

The second, Long Beach Alliance for Children with Asthma (LBACA), boasts a diverse staff that primarily serves the Latin@ but, at times, the Asian and Pacific Islander Americans (AAPIs) who call Long Beach home, namely the Cambodian immigrants who compose 4 percent of the city (roughly twenty thousand). LBACA focuses its organizing on curbing the same asthma-inducing hazards as PCORE but devotes more time and energy to providing asthma health services, a mix of organizing and services that many social justice groups provide today (Luft 2009; Shah 2011; Tang 2011) and that has roots in the Black Panther Party (Nelson 2011).

The third, Communities for a Better Environment (CBE),[34] largely serves Latin@ and AAPI residents but works with all people of color from the listed cities, as well as Huntington Park (headquarters) and surrounding cities, and has a San Francisco office where it originally started in California. CBE specializes in the above-noted environmental justice campaigns but also power plants and smaller polluting businesses. In its own brochure, they write, "Community organizing is the central component of CBE's strategy. The goal of our organizing is to help low-income communities of color build the power to influence environmental decisions that affect their lives." Although I partook in various CBE actions and events, I spent most of my time with its Youth for Environmental Justice (Youth for EJ) program, for which the organization is renowned. Both LBACA and CBE overlap in some capacity with the immigrant rights movement.

I also worked with three predominantly Mexican-Latinx-serving organizations. First, Coalition for a Safe Environment (CFASE) was founded and is run by Jesse Marquez, a multigeneration Mexican American leader. Overseeing a very small Latin@ staff (and assisted by a multiethnic coalition of organizers), CFASE largely serves the nearly 87 percent of Latinxs (largely Mexican) who make up the working-class Wilmington population. LBACA, mentioned above, was the second one. CFASE started out grassroots, became a nonprofit soon afterward, and has relied heavily on lawsuits and community pressure to effect change. I also worked with Community Partners Council (CPC), a mostly service-providing community organization that overlapped with LBACA on environmental justice work when CPC was not focused on immigrant rights, crime prevention, gang reduction, gaining green space and parks, and offering community health (diet, exercise, lifestyle) classes and workshops, and the like.

The three supplementary organizations with whom I worked informally and intermittently were East Yard Communities for Environmental Justice (EYCEJ), Semillas de Esperanza (SE), and Latinos in Action (LIA). I connected with EYCEJ by way of the regular presence in organizing circles of the charismatic leader and other members and by my close relationship with Laura, who left LBACA to work for EYCEJ. The organization mostly served the (unauthorized) Mexican immigrant population of working-class East Los Angeles. The interface between me and Latinos in Action was Marta Cota, who also left LBACA to work with LIA, which serves the Latinx population in Long Beach and the surrounding environs; their core issues are immigration rights and education.

Regarding the Asian American informants, I spent three-and-a-half years in the field with up to twenty-four professional and volunteer community organizers. Of those, I was able to secure in-depth interviews with ten women and five men, all self-identified as such. The gender imbalance is explained by the predominance of women in environmental (health) justice movements (see, for example, Brown and Ferguson 1995; Kirk 1998; Sze 1999). The average age of the Asian ethnic informants was thirty-nine, and the immigrants' average length of time in the United States was thirty years. Most of the women worked in the paid labor force as CBO staff, K–12 teachers, child daycare owners, and social workers, while the remainder were undergraduate or graduate students and stay-at-home mothers. All but one of the men were paid activist staff. Most of the women and men had grown up in lower- to mid-middle-class households, were presently earning middle-class incomes, and were citizens or legal residents.[35] Two Filipin@ American youth were unauthorized, one of whom left EJ partway to focus solely on the cause of Dreamers.

Regarding the Latin@ informants themselves, I conducted thirty in-depth, semistructured interviews mostly with the staff, leaders, members, and loose affiliates of the noted organizations; twenty-two identified as women and eight as men. About nine of the women were currently working at the time of the interview, nearly all had held odd jobs at some point or other (usually low-skilled service, such as in factories or as domesticas), and the remainder were stay-at-home mothers. The average age was thirty-nine, the average length of time in the States for the immigrants was eighteen-and-a-half years, and thirteen activists were either citizens or legal residents, six of whom were second-generation Latin@.

The final method was systematic analysis of CBO and affiliate literature, public policy reports, and presentations so as to ascertain how the groups and their members politically framed issues, inequalities, and injustices; to learn how they strategized per this framing; and to help me recall the purpose and details of events and meetings.

Although some of the Asian American and Latin@ activists and their environmental justice organizations periodically came together to work in a loose Southern California coalition (for example, Coalition for Environmental Health and Justice), most often they worked discretely from each other owing to a focus on different cities and neighborhoods (hence, populations) and on different political strategies (as noted, grassroots organizing, service provision, or, most typically, a mix).[36] And although I recruited from CBOs for my sample, I focused on the activists and allies rather than on the CBOs per se. What motivated my decision was my key research question, which was not how *organizations* are redefining politics from an immigrant-specific standpoint (which is more the province of organizational sociology), but how the *activists* who move in and out of these CBOs and the *social movements* they make and remake, are doing so. I often found the membership in these collectives to be fluid and seasonal, and therefore organizations were not the most reliable measure of what shaped the subjective dimensions of politicization; meaning-making; and race, class, and citizenship inequality, and in turn, how these subjective dimensions related to the larger CBOs.

Regarding process, I always communicated in English with all of the Asian American first generation and the youth, whether in the field or in formal interview settings. I spoke a combination of English and very basic Spanish with the majority of the Latin@ immigrant and youth activists; for formal interviewing, a fluent and bilingual Spanish speaker was always present to translate.

CHAPTER OUTLINE

Chapter 1 addresses the physical and emotional violence of the racial state and racial capitalism under neoliberalism and how it manifests in discourse, power-knowledge, and false choices that prop up environmental injustice. The chapter is rounded out by the Angeleno activists who fight everyday bioneglect in a specifically embodied way, often by way of their own "street science" power-knowledge. Chapter 2 conducts an in-depth analysis of the emotional politics unleashed by bioneglecting elites and their institutions in line with a raced, gendered, and classed economy of emotions. This chapter focuses equally on how the movement actors navigate dominant emotional power and how they turn it against the system. In Chapter 3 I chronicle the nuanced ways in which the Asian American and Latin@ activists, and some of the community-based organizations, conceived of the politics of embodiment, from illness to mobility to bodily adornment. It also examines how these notions of the body (and emotions) spurred the female change-makers to creatively blend their clean-air activism with organizing for school reform. In Chapter 4 I detail how the activists use embodied inequalities to broadly define racism and classism and to politically determine "us" versus "them." Specific attention is paid to how transnational and local factors shape the Latin@ immigrants' view of classism as the key enemy—and class inequality as the main moral boundary—while the Filipin@-led Asian immigrants pinpoint racism and race inequality as such. In Chapter 5 I continue the focus on the politics of emotion by detailing how emotional support of one's neighbors against the assault of bioneglect—the women-led act of embodied citizenship—constituted the key resistance strategy. Chapter 6 analyzes the immigrants' unconventional, unbounded, and seemingly contradictory politics that extend from being excluded from political institutions and/or being rendered bit players in the country, and from an embodied focus. Here we also address the immigrants' contradictory relationship to the state and the motivations behind it. The final analytical chapter, Chapter 7, spotlights the youth activists and how growing up most or all of their lives in neoliberal, nativist racist America, and with the very asthma that their parents sought to curb, textured their fully embodied and less-assimilationist politics. In the afterword, I detail how this female-led Asian and Latin@ immigrant movement for clean air problematizes Foucaultian biopower. As his conceptualization could not fully accommodate this LA case, I theorize a newer process—bioneglect—and emphasize how it can be interrelated with resistance, the focus of *Refusing Death*.

CHAPTER 1

NEOLIBERAL EMBODIED ASSAULT

ADDRESSING THE biopolitics of disposability, Giroux (2006:187) trenchantly writes,

> Underneath neoliberalism's corporate ethic and market-based fundamentalism, the idea of democracy is disappearing and with it the spaces in which democracy is produced and nurtured. Democratic values, identities, and social relations along with public spaces, the common good, and the obligations of civic responsibility are slowly being overtaken by a market-based notion of freedom and civic indifference in which it becomes more difficult to translate private woes into social issues and collective action or to insist on a language of the public good.

Giroux's is an apt description of the neoliberal context in which the Asian and Latin@ immigrants labored for clean air. As neoliberal racism and racial capitalism are the fulcrum of environmental injustice (Pulido 2017a; see Pellow 2007), this chapter examines how the state and industry spurn democracy by coopting the environmental justice movement. The discursive gymnastics is dizzying, to say the least. In reality, the state and industry cause the environmental degradation and visit it upon communities of color, but use the language that it is fixing the very problem it is causing. In so doing, they steal credit from the environmental justice movement for any "progress" in cleanups and improved health, a progress that they hail as significant but that is typically modest. Yet studies have not addressed enough how the state and industry feign an emotive ethics of care in their cooptation of the movement; that is, how they deploy emotional structures in the operation of power. As with "fixing" a problem that state agencies and big business pretend not to have created, their discursive gymnastics serve as cover for what is actually a physical assault on people of color's bodies and an emotional assault on their mental health.

Although I spent years with the Asian American and Latin@ organizers before the reality star and real estate mogul launched his long presidential campaign down a short gold escalator, these immigrants had always been organizing under the cloud of neoliberal discourse and material decline. Writing during George W. Bush's second term, Giroux seems to presciently anticipate the apotheosis of neoliberalism under Trump. In explaining today's biopolitics, Giroux (2006:181–182) sees it as inseparable from racism and classism but deems the current state of affairs to be much more deadly than the Jim Crow era:

> While the murder of Emmett Till suggests that a biopolitics structured around the intersection of race and class inequalities, on the one hand, and state violence, on the other, has long existed, the new version of biopolitics adds a distinctively different and more dangerous register.[1] The new biopolitics not only includes state-sanctioned violence but also relegates entire populations to spaces of invisibility and disposability. As William DiFazio points out, "the state has been so weakened over decades of privatization that it . . . increasingly fails to provide health care, housing, retirement benefits and education to a massive percentage of its population" (2006:87). While the social contract has been suspended in varying degrees since the 1970s, under the Bush Administration it has been virtually abandoned. . . . The state no longer protects its own disadvantaged citizens—they are already seen as dead within a transnational economic and political framework.[2]

Omi and Winant would add that, in this post–World War II context, ostensibly "color-blind" racism has been used to justify the shrinking of government and the abandonment of poor people and poor people of color (Omi and Winant 2014; see also Duggan 2003). As Nobel Prize–winning economist Paul Krugman says without equivocation, "race" is the "major reason America treats its poor more harshly than any other advanced country" (2005:A27 cited in Giroux 2006). For instance, one need only skim the health literature to know that race (more so than class and gender) is often the most powerful determinant of morbidity, mortality, and maltreatment by the medical industry (Sims 2010; Williams 2008). Race is also most responsible for why the White and Black wealth gap will likely never come to a close in our lifetimes (Oliver and Shapiro 1995; Shapiro 2004), and for why the American people in the battleground states chose to cast their vote for a nativist racist, or "White nationalist" (not to mention, sexual predator, class elitist, and ableist) (Major, Blodorn, and Blascovich 2016; Tesler 2016; Schaffner, MacWilliams, and Nteta 2017) and did so again in 2020 despite Trump's missteps with, among other crises, the COVID-19 pandemic.

Pulido (2017b:18) writes that neoliberalism is primarily responsible for the state's cozy partnership with industry when it comes to environmental racism and classism (Heynen et al. 2007; Liévanos 2012; London et al. 2013; Kohl 2014; Harrison 2015). This "pollution industrial complex" (Faber 2008) manifests in pro-industry and pro-market EPA appointments, priorities, "regulations," and the vacating of laws like the Toxic Substances and Control Act (Silbergeld and Mandrioli 2015). In fact, Bullard, Johnson, and Torres (2011:18–19) largely trace the existence of environmental racism to the predominantly White American developers that proliferate on zoning boards and planning commissions and whose own special interests guide decision-making, while people of color are systematically excluded from these powerful bodies (or given only token representation). Even President Bill Clinton's unprecedented Executive Order on Environmental Justice, born of movement pressure, was declared by the inspector general to have "no plans, benchmarks, or instruments to evaluate progress" by the early 2000s (Bullard et al. 2011:40). As E.O. 12898 has replaced substantive regulatory power with superficial and voluntary policies, Holifield (2007) has dubbed it "classic roll-out neoliberalism" (recall that a staple of neoliberalism is little to no regulation of big business and the market).

Accordingly, contaminating facilities and transportation projects continue to railroad through working-class neighborhoods and neighborhoods of color (Pellow and Brulle 2007). While environmental hazards are committed against low-income White Americans as well, even middle-class people and immigrants of color have at times been dumped on and "intoxicated" more severely than low-income White communities (Bullard et al. 2007; Bullard and Wright 2009). I saw this manifest in myriad ways during my fieldwork. With regard to environmental justice, one only needs eyes to see that communities of color, often lower income and often immigrant, are the sites for a disproportionate number of toxic industries relative to their absence when I drive through predominantly White communities, especially the infamous concentrations of the affluent in the likes of Beverly Hills, Palos Verdes, Bel Air, and Brentwood.

To be sure, detractors sometimes ask, "Didn't the poor and people of color move into these neighborhoods after the pollution sources were already there? Which came first, people or pollution?" In the case of our country's commercial hazardous waste facilities, since 1965 they have been found to be disproportionately sited in neighborhoods already dominated by people of color. More recent evidence on over four hundred such facilities corroborates these earlier findings (this time including poor White neighborhoods) (Bullard et al. 2007:29). At the same time, one might ask whether the chicken or the egg question even matters. If neighborhoods where pollution sources abound are generally more affordable, have more public housing, and/or are populated by more people of color (including immigrants of various statuses), then the fault lies with broader structural forces that have created and sustained inequalities in housing and neighborhoods; perhaps what got there first—people or pollution—arrives too late in this political chain of events, and is thus too myopic a political question. Following the data, however, not only is the unequal siting of toxic release facilities a product of racial capitalism and Giroux's claim of indifference to non-White life, it effectively creates population crises rather than responds to the disease epidemics or food or resource shortages that were Foucault's focus. I want to stress that upon originating these ecological and health crises, the state then withholds protection from them—tantamount to two forms of "letting die"—whilst declaring that it cares about helping the margins live (healthfully). All of these discursive gymnastics require emotional and affective structures. As I have not seen environmental justice studies focus empirically on the emotional and affective processes from the top down, we turn now to a brief overview of the related literature.

THEORETICAL BACKGROUND

Arlie Hochschild is widely received as the founder of the sociological study of emotions, an area that had long been around, though mostly applied to gender, work, and social movements; currently, it is enjoying more widespread attention, such as in studies of race (Bonilla-Silva 2019). Hochschild made clear that emotions are social processes shaped by societal norms, social locations, and cultural factors (1979, 1983; see also Wharton 2011:460). These dovetail with economic structures and, together, emotive processes teach people not only what to feel but "how they make sense of their feelings, how they manage their feelings, how their feelings affect their actions" (Garey and Hansen 2011:5). Similarly, Sara Ahmed (2004) conceives of emotions as our responses to objects and actors, those that animate our actions, boundaries, and worldviews. Emotions appear only as objects because the history of their production, exchange, and circulation are hidden from view. Per these building blocks, Ahmed (2004:13) theorizes about a "sociality of emotions," one that operates across the individual and collective levels in a form of sociality that connects or divides, that is, as an emotional or affective economy.

After Hochschild's (1983) analysis of emotional labor performed by workers in the service economy (for example, flight attendants), her most well-known concept is arguably "emotion work." Emotion work is a set of rules governing most life situations concerning the emotions that people involved in these situations should experience, and particularly the optimum pitch at which they should be expressed (Albas and Albas 1988:259). In other words, people do "emotion work" to align their public and private emotions with feeling rules to avoid societal sanctions and secure privilege (see M. Kim 2018). "Feeling rules," Hochschild specifies, "guide emotion work by establishing the sense of entitlement or obligation that governs emotional exchanges" (1979:56).

One of the signal contributions of emotion work and feeling rules is precisely its ability to tie emotionality to power. Much of the sociological literature on emotions in social movements has focused on the marginalized activists. Yet Hochschild notes that dominant groups act as the keepers of feeling rules who often dictate appropriate feelings to lower-status individuals.

For instance, on the basis of status positions, those with higher status often expect gratitude from those lower on the ladder ("As minorities, you should be grateful"), a move that secures their own privilege. Also writing about the power-laden nature of emotions, Ahmed (2004) writes that emotions such as hate, fear, disgust, shame, pain, sorrow, and pity can be enacted and politicized to "Other" a particular community. In a more explicit linkage to stratification, Davis (2011:177) writes that "all emotions are politicized and bound up with the securing of social hierarchies." Although coming from different approaches, these scholars demonstrate that emotions are tied up in sociocultural structures and processes and, importantly, that emotions are bound up in and with power. Perhaps one of the most common ways that dominant institutions deploy power is by way of nationalism, as Benedict Anderson (1983) detailed about the ways that states secure an imagined community of millions who know nothing of each other. With the rise of the nation, governments had to hegemonically use affective desires, pride, and fear to shore up the patriotic loyalty of their people and, by extension, shore up the power of the nation-state.[1]

Focusing on a misguided "culture of fear," sociologist Barry Glassner (2018) has argued that politicians have long promulgated fears, such as of crime and drug use (read: among people of color), for the sake of ginning up votes. Yet candidates will weaponize such rates of crime and drug use *even when said rates are in decline*. In another apt example, the Trump Presidency successfully whipped up fear of immigrants—namely Mexican and Muslim ethnics, but elaborated beyond—so as to secure office; yet immigrants and refugees commit much fewer crimes than native-born Americans (Rumbaut et al. 2006). Glassner further ties emotions to top-down power by stressing how media corporations rake in the dollars by overrepresenting drugs and crime as our country's biggest epidemics (see Dixon and Linz 2000) while underrepresenting the real problem: deepening social inequality. "The culture of fear," therefore, hinges on powerful social structures instilling misguided fears into the hearts and minds of Americans for "profit," in turn neglecting the social problems in dire need of attention, such as the climate crisis. Glassner finds Trump's fearmongering particularly resonant, in part because he did so at a time when three out of four Americans claimed they were more afraid than they were a couple of decades ago.

In studying the immigrant mega marches that overtook cities across

America in 2006, Zepeda-Millán (2017) found that fear operated among the powerful in another way. In the words of a D.C. immigrant rights advocate: "Politics, I've come to realize, runs on fear. Ultimately Congress was afraid to pass Sensenbrenner and they were afraid to pass comprehensive immigration reform. Only when they are afraid not to will they get it [reform] done" (182). In other words, politicians belie all manner of rosy rhetoric by voting and legislating out of fear of facing strident opposition or being booted from office, *not* to correct social problems or serve the people. In effect, politicians can often fear their own fear-mongering.

EMOTIONAL COOPTATION AND DISCOURSE FROM THE STATE

Concerning environmental justice, one of the most deleterious processes of state engineering is the cooptation of the movement itself, what I like to call "coopting care." That is, one of the primary forms of cooptation is the use of emotive language of care while, in effect, physically assaulting marginalized bodies by letting them die and emotionally assaulting by dismissing "lower people's" feelings. Pulido cites that cooptation also takes place through a "neoliberal multiculturalism" and organizations such as the American Legislative Exchange Council (ALEC). ALEC's mission is to bring together big business and congressional leaders to write neoliberal legislation, such as on "Energy, Environment and Agriculture." Even writing its own "Environmental Justice Principles" and passing a "Resolution on Environmental Justice," ALEC has written over seventy bills (Pulido 2017b:21). Pulido writes,

> The Principles state that everyone should be treated equally, while also rejecting any additional regulations. "Existing federal, state, and local regulation, properly implemented and enforced, are sufficient to assure protection" (Center for Media and Democracy n.d.). . . . Of course, this is contrary to the essence of EJ—the idea that some communities are disproportionately impacted. But it exemplifies neoliberal multiculturalism by affirming equality, assuming the market is the best solution, and evincing completely deracinated language. Race is no longer a power relation, indeed, it is not even mentioned. By adopting EJ language, while simultaneously blocking any meaningful change, ALEC is ensuring that vulnerable communities will continue to be polluted, sickened, and die. (ibid.)

In this context, corporations and government agencies coopt the language, ethos, care, and concern of the margins who fight environmental injustices and, as Pulido noted, do so by deracinating (and I would add, declassing), a problem that is caused precisely by racism, capitalism, and classism. As corporations, government agencies, and ALEC have been operating in a context of "global warming" and in the post–Exxon Valdez and BP Deepwater Horizon era of oil spills, they have to coopt the language of the environment and, given the communities around toxic facilities and "hot spots," coopt the concerns of the environmental justice movement. I turn to official government and corporate discourse to demonstrate how they are "coopting care" as well as the work, or emotion work, that it performs. Consider California's Department of Transportation (Caltrans), the agency hoping to expand the I-710 freeway despite communities' protests over the premature death it brings. Here Caltrans seeks to prove their civic and social responsibility bona fides by highlighting their strong accountability to "Project-level Air Quality":

> The Federal Clean Air Act . . . , the California Clean Air Act, the National Environmental Policy Act (NEPA), and the California Environmental Quality Act (CEQA) require transportation planning and project development to consider air quality as a part of the environment review process. . . . The Department develops policies, guidance, and tools to conduct air quality analyses in compliance with Federal and State regulations. Caltrans also initiates and participates in air quality researches [*sic*] and studies to advance its scientific knowledge and state-of-practice on the subject. (http://www.dot.ca.gov/env/air/)

The main takeaway from the Department of Transportation is that it performs due diligence. As a case in point, Caltrans "initiates and participates in air quality researches and studies." As per the dialectical relationship between top-down institutions and bottom-up resistance, however, this state agency coopts the environmental justice movement by excising its race-class talk while being sure to appropriate its discourse of care; as per the subtext of their website, the agency *must* care because expending great effort to protect the environment and affected communities presupposes it.

The main regulatory body with which the informants of my study engage is the South Coast Air Quality Management District (SCAQMD), the localized branch of the federal AQMD that covers Los Angeles County; it writes that it is "actively conducting exciting and comprehensive community-based efforts that focus on improving air quality and public health in environmental justice communities" (http://www.aqmd.gov/nav/about/initiatives/environmental-justice/ab617-134).

In its "Background" section the SCAQMD specifies,

> Assembly Member Cristina Garcia authored Assembly Bill 617 to address the disproportionate impacts of air pollution in *environmental justice communities*. The measure requires local air districts to take specific actions to reduce air pollution and toxic air contaminants from commercial and industrial sources. . . . [There is also legislation] to fund . . . clean vehicle and [clean] ports investments. . . . SCAQMD will conduct extensive outreach to residents and other stakeholders to describe the program and seek input on how to implement it. (emphasis added)

As an institution that is specifically designed to monitor and address air quality issues, SCAQMD says that it does everything that it is supposed to in order to "address the disproportionate impacts of air pollution in 'environmental justice communities.'" I have long been struck by this nomenclature for communities such as Carson, Wilmington, and West Long Beach. They were *fighting for* environmental justice but they were not communities *getting* environmental justice, otherwise, they would have no reason to continue fighting for it. As well, these agencies would never have this language were it not for the local environmental justice movement and the need to contest the hazards unleashed upon them (Pulido 2017b), attributions one never sees in public relations script.

The California Air Resources Board (CARB) is another arm of the state bureaucracy tasked with regulating industry. On its official site, CARB writes,

> California has made significant progress to reduce our exposure to harmful air pollutants, the result of regulations and programs based on sound science. *These achievements reflect a collective and bipartisan effort* over the past half century that involves the Legislature, air districts, regulated industries and the public. *We have come a long way but many in our state still breathe unhealthful air*, and childhood asthma rates are above the national average.

> There is far more work to be done. CARB stands ready as it enters its next 50 years to build on this strong environmental legacy and ensure that all Californians will breathe clean air. (https://ww2.arb.ca.gov/our-work/topics/environmental-justice)
>
> A clean and healthy environment is a fundamental right for all California residents. . . . The California Air Resources Board is committed to prioritizing environmental justice in everything that we do. This is supported by engaging with community members to provide them with the best possible information about the air they breathe, and working with them to improve air quality in their communities (emphasis added). (https://ww2.arb.ca.gov/homepage)

As their language reveals, CARB is the only agency that addresses the history of environmental redress to account for poor air quality in the Los Angeles basin, yet it does not grant original credit—or even the lion's share of it—to the people of color, immigrants, and low income who forced CARB to make progress. Rather, it is credited to a "collective and bipartisan effort over the past half century that involves the Legislature, air districts, regulated industries and the public." Hence, regulated industries are just as responsible and laudable for cleaning up the air as the less powerful "public" who devoted their lives to fighting for it, and who taxed their own resources, bodies, and emotions in the process. This cooptation is redolent of how the US (and other) governments credit themselves for the passage of such milestones as women's suffrage, civil rights laws, and pro-gay-marriage decisions, as the racial state is wont to do ("We gave America Civil Rights") (see Goldberg 2002). No gestures toward environmental justice or civil rights, however, would have been realized without decades and centuries of resistance from movements of everyday people. As the renowned abolitionist Frederick Douglass famously quipped, "Power concedes nothing without a demand."

Furthermore, CARB is certain to assure the public that cleaning up LA's air is based on "regulations and programs based on sound science," a qualifier that differentiates from the community (or "street") science that industry and the state have long dismissed as unsound. To be sure, CARB is the only agency that concedes that the state has not done everything that it needs to do—that the work ahead is considerable. In their own contradictory relationship to the state, as this book will detail, the Asian and Latin@ immigrants with whom I worked tended to favor CARB over the other regulatory agencies, yet they also knew that these overtures to care and concern were vacuous at best and Machiavellian at worst. If CARB was so concerned and not at all Janus-faced, the agency would be dismantling the system that contaminated (unauthorized) immigrants of color and the working class in the first place.

EMOTIONAL COOPTATION AND DISCOURSE FROM THE MAKERS OF BLACK GOLD

Care and concern were also the improbable leitmotifs of the oil refineries' *raison d'etre*. This is laughable to the activists, and likely to generally educated and politicized people, not out of incredulity but out of the material contradiction of oil and gas versus environmental justice, of profit versus people; few things were more diametrically opposed. Yet somehow this laughable contradiction was either lost on the corporations or they believed that they could strategically coopt the joke, this time with care. Demonstrated, most publicly by big oil's effort to give back to the community or to invest in earth's future via "cleaner" fuels, all their websites spotlight the "environment" or "sustainability" in some way or form. A final thread is that *none* of the oil refineries credit the communities and their grassroots efforts for pressuring them into doing due diligence on sustainability issues. The official discourse implies that their concern and care—indeed, their performance of proper emotion work—flowed organically from corporate management. There was no strategy of "coopting care."

Shell, one of the most recognized oil companies in the world, seemed to feature the most depth and breadth with regard to their environmental commentary. While virtually none of the other oil companies (BP, Tesoro [later, Andeavor, later, Marathon]) mentioned the words "climate change," Shell not only invoked them but went further by addressing how to account for it and how to advance to newer fuels, all while noting alternative-energy-forward projects and considerations. Their site reads,

> Climate change and energy transitions:
>
> We recognise the significance of climate change, along with the role energy plays in helping people achieve and maintain a good quality of life. A key role for society—and for Shell—is to find ways to provide much more energy with less carbon dioxide. . . .
>
> We believe that, while technological developments will emerge, effective

> policy and cultural change is essential to drive low-carbon business and consumer choices and opportunities. The transition to low-carbon solutions is best underpinned by meaningful government-led carbon "pricing" mechanisms.
>
> We welcome efforts made by governments to cooperatively reach the global climate agreement and support long-term climate goals that balance environmental pressures with development opportunities. We particularly welcomed the United Nations Paris Agreement. . . .
>
> Today, Shell is still primarily an oil and gas company, but we have a long tradition of innovation. We know that long-term success depends on our ability to anticipate the types of energy and fuels people will need in the future and remain commercially competitive and environmentally relevant.
>
> Our natural gas businesses give governments the option to reduce emissions from electricity, by replacing coal, and we have an interest in a wind business with over 1,000 megawatts of capacity. We have also invested heavily in the lowest-carbon biofuel, through our Raízen joint venture with Cosan in Brazil, and we continue to explore second-generation biofuels options. In 2016 we created a New Energies business to further explore investment opportunities in energy solutions that combine wind and solar power with gas, for example, and new ways to connect customers to energy. . . .
>
> We have a number of vehicles to support investment in new technology, such as Shell Ventures. . . . We are also committed to reducing our emissions intensity and continuing efforts to improve the energy efficiency of our operations as well as ending continuous flaring [explosive release of toxic chemicals]. (https://www.shell.com/energy-and-innovation/the-energy-future/more-and-cleaner-energy.html)

Immediately noticeable about Shell's discourse is that they lift the language of the environmental justice movement of "helping people achieve and maintain a good quality of life." Shell's caring concern for average people's lives is summoned by the language of reducing carbon; supporting the Paris Agreement; investing in natural gas, wind, and biofuel, such as in developing Brazil; and by being more energy efficient and by ending continuous flaring. Yet rather than see the "transition to low-carbon solutions" as "best underpinned by meaningful government-led carbon 'pricing' mechanisms," Shell, if they were truly one with environmental justice and its systemic causes, would commit to end the world's reliance on oil and gas altogether, both major contributors to the climate catastrophe and climate injustice in the first place. Rather than abolishing oil and gas, Shell places the onus on governments and cultures to be more eco-conscious in their policy and lifestyle choices, respectively. Further striking is that Shell seems completely oblivious to the contradiction of telling the state and people on the ground to use less oil and gas when Shell admits that the lion's share of their multinational business is oil and gas. Moreover, they write capriciously that they are "continuing efforts to improve the energy efficiency of our operations as well as ending continuous flaring" while the Asian and Latin@ ethnic residents of Carson, Wilmington, and Long Beach have over the years consistently logged, and notified Shell and the other refineries of, thousands of incidents of illegal flaring—and to what avail? Furthermore, Shell's stated investment in wind and solar energy is a tiny fraction of their business practice and their extraordinary profit margins, margins that are protected by their expensive lobbyists in Washington, who constantly pressure politicians to prioritize oil and gas over the earth and average people's "good quality of life." But discourse must matter, because Shell pays good money to public relations firms and expends great effort to tell the public that they care about the inverse.

Valero, another major refinery and polluter in the area, notes its caring bona fides in the "Environment" section on its website, namely its laudable green record in the name of civic and social responsibility.

> In 2017, Valero achieved its best-ever environmental performance, achieving a one-third reduction in incidents from two years previous.
>
> Over the past decade, performance has improved by 71 percent, by focusing on enhanced incident investigations and taking corrective actions to prevent recurrence of environmental events.
>
> Valero ranked highest among independent refiners in *Newsweek* magazine's 2017 Green Rankings of top 500 U.S. publicly traded companies for environmental performance. (https://www.valero.com/en-us/Documents/SRR/2017_Valero_SRR_Booklet_Web.pdf)

Intriguing about Valero's statements of environmental concern is that there is no base from which to relativize and ascertain the company's performance—they do not provide it. Achieving a one-third reduction after, say, Valero's record of egregiously exploding, flaring, or releasing toxins into the environment is not necessarily something of which to be proud. Elsewhere on its website, Valero lauds itself for exploring biofuels, such as discarded animal fats, used cooking oil, and inedible corn oil, and for treating domestic wastewater for refinery use, "potentially saving billions of gallons of fresh water for other community and residential uses each year." The site goes onto say that the Valero Foundation strives to close gaps in four areas: "Basic Needs/Social Services" (such as food, shelter and safety for the working poor), "Health Care," "Education," and "Civic and Culture," all of which coopt the priorities of the environmental justice (and broader social justice) movements without proper attribution. And, as with Shell, Valero says nothing of the fact that the oil they extract and refine is a major cause of carbon overload in the atmosphere and thus of the climate catastrophe; no amount of animal fats and corn oil is going to change that fact if the company's key purpose and profit source is oil and gas.

The website of Phillips 66, another Carson refinery, leads with this line, "Energy and environmental issues are important to policymakers and to Phillips 66. Our vision, to provide energy and improve lives, done with our values of safety, honor and commitment, furthers our strategy" (https://s22.q4cdn.com/128149789/files/doc_financials/annual_report/2017/Sustainability-Report-2017.pdf). Noteworthy about this mission statement is its stipulated goal to "improve lives, done with our values of . . . honor and commitment." While one may make a leap from improving lives to refining oil, that link is still a leap and is not immediately clear. While refined oil allows people to *function* in their daily lives, such as driving cars or riding public transport, Phillips 66 presumes the self-evidence that oil *improves* people's lives when biofuels and electric batteries could perform the same function. Yet the upshot of oil refining is environmental degradation, deteriorated health conditions, and a planet in crisis owing to the ceaseless emission of carbon. In this way, it is not abundantly clear what (emotion-laden) values of safety, honor, and commitment have to do with refining oil.

Further, with respect to their "Sustainability Report" Phillips 66 reiterates in the same or similar parlance, "[W]e believe sustainability means we are accountable for operating excellence and strong economic, social and environmental performance. Our company is ethical and operates in a responsible manner, demonstrating our values of safety, honor and commitment." What is interesting about this statement is that these are the same companies—and the politicians who lobby on their behalf—who have long said that we have to make a choice between either "economic" or "environmental" interests; that the two are incompatible and that of course we must always choose people's jobs (putting food on the table) over the spotted owl, herons, or lakes, as Hochschild (2016) still found to be true in her recent study of the American Right.

As these websites and fieldwork moments collectively show, oil and gas juggernauts as well as the agencies who do not regulate them enough, are necessarily coopting the language prioritized by the margins who have long resisted them: "environmental justice," "sustainability," "renewable" or "efficient" energy, "social responsibility," "environmental justice communities," "quality of life," "basic needs and social services," "health care," "education," "carbon reduction" and "climate change," and similar nomenclature related to engaging with "community" concerns. These non-sequiturs of being pro-environment whilst destroying it—being pro-"environmental justice community" whilst destroying it—reveal that, by necessity, industry and enabling regulators have to humanize themselves. They index an institution's humanity by pretending to care, that is, to exploit proper emotion work in the same way that politicians and media conglomerates exploit a culture of fear. Caring emotions are politicized as cover for lies, spin-rooms, and hyperbole and for the ultimate goal of securing the social hierarchies that empower the state and corporations over people, especially those whom society deems "lower status" (see Davis 2011). Corporations are also engaging in affective "double-speak" when one imagines what they say to assuage their investors who are concerned about environmentally conscious practices depressing profits and stock values. More broadly, Giroux (2006:189) would likely deem "coopting care" to be an example of neoliberalism's avid attack on "critical education at all levels of cultural production in an all-out effort to undermine critical thoughts, imagination, and substantive agency." Although in this book we will see the organizers interpret these discursive gymnastics as mentally and emotionally infantilizing—as if the margins cannot see the machinations and manipulation—this does not mean that the omnipresence and repetition of the dominant discourse have absolutely no effect. First, the activists intensely engaged the state when it came to environmental justice concerns; doing so meant they saw some modicum of hope in it, borne out by the moments when they invoked certain elected officials and government agencies like CARB as "OK."

WHY ENGAGE THE STATE?

"It's Complicated"

Hope in the state seemed to be buoyed by its small, bit-by-bit gestures toward "caring." Although the immigrants were well aware that these gestures only came after the community organized, protested, and lobbied, which the state rarely acknowledged, various factors accounted for why they kept engaging the state. At one Corridor Advisory Committee meeting in January of 2011, for instance, a citizen worried about there being no sound barricades and walls in the Travel Advisory Committee's recommendations, to which the Caltrans representative said, "That'll be taken care of, even though Caltrans doesn't do such things." Caltrans was showing concern and due diligence, but made sure to qualify that the community should be grateful because this was much beyond Caltrans's regular job description. Although by no means a guarantee that the sound barricades would go up, Caltrans gave the activist hope that they just might, since the agency had rarely said yes to them before. At another meeting at the end of the month, when one community organizer raised concerns about the "look" of the sound barriers that would pad their neighborhoods, the Caltrans official assured, "Whatever the community wants." Rarely did the system intone with "Whatever the community wants," yet the subtext was clear: you care, so we'll make it a point to (try to) care.

Another reason for continued state engagement—that is, hope in the state—was the amicable relationship that some activists had with official state representatives, much to my surprise. A noteworthy moment happened at the same BP hearing that I introduced this book with, at which the BP officials showed no sympathy for the Japanese American woman whose husband had died of cancer after a lifelong job at their oil refinery. During BP Arco's presentation demonstrating that the oil company was doing all that it could to meet standard procedure and mitigate pollution in Carson, most of our ears perked up when the health practitioner addressed the health impacts of the refinery. He reported that emissions generally met air quality standards yet he conceded that higher rates of asthma and other chronic illnesses could be correlated with refinery contamination. That was the only time I saw some members of PCORE and some of the audience nod in agreement. That was also the first time that I ever saw the activists talk to an agency official after a public comment, laugh and joke with him, and seem to treat the political "enemy" as a friend. Out of my stunned curiosity, immediately after the meeting, I queried Cindy, Nina, and another teacher how they knew the health practitioner dealing with BP and what the nature of their relationship was. They told me, "He's one of the good ones." I wondered, too, if it was the fact that he was a conventionally handsome White man; regardless, the interaction stayed with me as I drove home. In our interview some weeks later, I queried Cindy more deeply about this complicated relationship with the "friendly" and partially supportive member of the Establishment.

CINDY: Oh no, he is really nice. I tease him and say things to him, he just laughs. . . . [I say,] "You're the only one we want in here." . . . He's an epidemiologist and he sees the research—oh, he knows.

NADIA: Do you think he is actually doing something, though, to challenge these refineries?

CINDY: I don't think so, but we were very struck by his honesty, that he acknowledged what we were saying is true, where everyone else is, "Oh, nothing bad happens to you." That's why we like him. I said, "You're the only one who says that: 'Yeah, there are problems caused by even just smelling these toxins.'"

NADIA: So some doctors would say there is no problem?

CINDY: Yeah, that idiot from the health department kept saying for two years, "Oh, . . . , there are no health effects from these slightly elevated levels of chemicals." I raked him across the coals.

The dissonance between Cindy's view of the "nice guy" and the guy she raked across the coals was resolved by the fact that those in the Establishment who at least recognized the veracity of activists' "street science" were worth forging a relationship with. I could not help but think, however, that this was the perennial good cop-bad cop maneuver that corporations often deployed to pacify protest. Yet upon further probing, Cindy did not seem to see it this way; rather, she interpreted the issue as more personal than political as she began to humanize even the "rubbish-talking" "idiots":

CINDY: Actually, I get along well with these people when we talk, but when they say something I don't like, then I've gotten upset at these meetings. *They understand it's true—it's true.*

NADIA: So you think they understand it, or are they just like, "This is rubber stamp stuff, pro forma?"

CINDY: I think they understand why I'm upset, but they're not doing anything constructive about it, and they keep telling me, if I can't isolate who's emitting all these odors, [then . . .]. [But] there are so many different companies here! And that's a bunch of rubbish and I told them that! . . . It's, you know, I told them they're incompetent; "You don't really care about enforcing the legislation [on the books]!"

NADIA: So is it that they're incompetent, or that they don't really care enough to do something?

CINDY: *I think they have some sort of compassion for what we go through,* but the culture of their agency is to not do anything. They don't enforce anything. OK, they send out these inspectors *who can't smell anything—ridiculous*! My kids and I have stood there with an inspector smelling the bad odor, and the inspector says they can't smell anything. Happens constantly!

NADIA: Do you think the inspectors are lying?

CINDY: I think they set up their system where nothing gets reported, where they can't find or pinpoint any of these companies. . . . I think it's just a sham.

Complicating the caricature of cold-hearted snakes, Cindy instead painted a picture of state officials who seemed to partly understand and have compassion for what residents like her were saying and suffering; the betrayal was that the state writ large conformed not to their "compassion" for Cindy but to corporate power. Several of the Latin@ activists also remarked that they liked the individual officials who had a simpatico understanding for what they endured (who performed proper emotion work) or who conceded that some of their street science was valid. To be sure, the next part of the sentence was usually an admission that these same officials rarely ever fundamentally worked for the community. Even Jesse, the firebrand founder and leader of Coalition for a Safe Environment, admitted that outside of the regulatory and corporate cronies, there were some "good politicians" in the State Legislature in Sacramento who fought on the side of the community. These "good politicians" also seemed more compelling in the absence of the immigrants' explicit critique of the (racial) capitalism officials were propping up; indeed, in Chapter 6 I detail my shock over some of these EJ activists' staunch support of it. Irrespective of whether they supported, rejected, or halfway believed in capitalism, these personal relationships with politicians was one of the key reasons why they continued to look to the state to resolve, in part, the environmental crises in their communities.

For "Superarse"

Besides the state's cooptation of the movement's language and concerns, the mild concessions it doled out, and its amiable, sympathetic officials, two major forces accounted for why the Asian and Latin@ immigrants continued to be in an emotionally abusive relationship with the state. First, as I began to address earlier, these immigrants labor under not just a neglectful neoliberal system, but one at its most callous and brazen summit. They were sick and dying. They did not have the luxury to leave resources untapped nor to waste time. The state still controlled where and how much pollution rained down on them and the siting of industries, train yards, and housing in proximity to ports full of diesel-burning ships. We will later see how these activists selectively spurned the state and how they stepped into the neoliberal gap by providing for their own communities' needs, but even in self-determining their own communities (Boggs 1998; Boggs and Kurashige 2011), hundreds of thousands must still rely on the state, say, for the roads and buses that take them to the fancier, faraway zip codes where they work; in addition, the impoverished rely on the state to feed their kids free hot meals and pay their teachers at school. For the mostly newer Latin@ organizers on the scene, there are no models of an environmental justice or any other social movement that has achieved most or all of its goals without making some (selective) demands on the state. And if we activist scholars cannot provide those models and alternatives, we may be capricious in expecting more marginalized immigrant communities of color to make it all happen. Regardless, we have much to learn theoretically and pragmatically about social movements, and environmental justice specifically, from grassroots actors' selective (dis)engagement of the state and their contradictory relationship to it.

For most of the Latina organizers but also the Asian American women organizers, the second key motivation was to develop one's self through politicization in a civic sphere that barred, disappeared, and marginalized them (see Shah 2011). Importantly, the premium that the women placed on self-development through politicization was never fully discrete from developing the community as well, especially for more collectivist cultural systems like those of Asian and Latinx immigrants (see, for example, Campos and Kim 2017; Chung 2016). Coll's (2010) finding that "superarse,"[3] the notion of surpassing one's previous station in life, was vital to Mexican and Central American women's organizing on immigrant, labor, and women's rights (namely, on domestic violence) and the more personalized issues of parenting and self-esteem. That is to say, while it was crucial for the women to pressure the state to protect them from immigration authorities, worker exploitation, and abusive partners, it was just as crucial that this organizing helped the women "surpass" feeling like migrant pariahs and overreproductive "animals"; they sought to move toward becoming society's agents of political change, women who deserved respect, not just recognition. Furthermore, this self-development is connected to communal development insofar as "social movements sustain themselves at the level of desire" (Gould 2009:212). Put another way, a movement "allows participants to feel their own perhaps squelched desires or to develop new ones that through articulation can become contagious allowing, or better, enticing, participants to collectively develop and pursue their aspirations for a different world" (ibid.).

The largely Mexican and Filipina ethnic women of Los Angeles also valued superarse as much as, perhaps more than, "wins" and "losses" vis-à-vis the state. One thing that all movement actors know is that victories are few and far between. The point is not necessarily the outcome, but what the process taught them and what knowledge they gained from mistakes and experience. One example of the women's development of self and community was their role as street scientists, those who would teach the state the real "truth." They proudly mapped toxic hot spots in their hazard-filled community, explained to outsiders, such as UC Irvine medical school students, about these hot spots on organized tours, and interviewed and surveyed neighbors about when their asthma or when refineries seemed to flare the most. As an example of self-referential politics, Latina activist mothers who worked for safer and less hazard-filled schools called themselves the "Mother's Brigade," in the spirit of the "bucket brigades," who went out with their proverbial buckets to measure such pollutants as water contamination or air toxicity. In addition, LBACA's "A-Team," an explicit citizen science group, was another collective of mostly women who focused on truck- and train-counting alongside the freeways and railyards, measuring deadly particulate matter ($PM_{2.5}$) in the air by way of "P-trak" devices during high-traffic flashpoints (Figures 3 and 4). Although the state and industry would often dismiss such street science for not establishing causality and pinpointing which entity was responsible for, say, Analyn's cancer, the community refused to stop. Political death, to them, was more dangerous than physical death. This owed not to their view that the state would ultimately listen or act—not at all, as we shall see later in the book. It owed to their refusal to succumb to an existence as the living dead (Giroux 2006). If one was politically agentic, irrespective of outcome, then one was alive.

FIGURE 3. "A-Team" planning for P-trak monitoring for diesel PM2.5. Source: Marta Cota of LBACA.

FIGURE 4. "A-Team" monitoring P-trak diesel PM2.5 along I-710. Source: Marta Cota of LBACA.

WHEN THE STATE SUCKS

Worth noting is that any time the Asian and Latin@ immigrants challenged the Establishment, especially if they were *sin papeles*, it was at great risk to many among them. In addition to deportation out of the country, workers of color face potential occupational blackmail owing to their greater threat of unemployment compared to Whites and to their greater concentration in nonunionized, low-skill, and low-wage occupations. People of color in the United States have constituted a large share of the nonunion contract workers in the oil, chemical, and nuclear industries and of the migrant farmworker force (Bullard 1993:23), while the predominantly Asian and Latinx Silicon Valley workers who fall ill making our microchips live in constant fear not just of cancer or deformed babies but of job retaliation (Pellow and Park 2002).

The immigrants, including the mothers, were well aware that the regulators would dismiss residents by dismissing their knowledge ("You smell something? I don't smell anything"; "Thanks for your bucket brigade information"). Not only was this a classic Foucaultian form of biopolitics, but in light of dominant institutions' emotional power ploys and manipulation, these affective structures were what the activists believed that they also had to target and unravel. In this vein, community residents would grow demoralized by the mismatch between elites' discourse and action, the cooptation which "atrophies the public imagination" and "undermine[s] critical thoughts, imagination, and substantive agency" (Giroux 2006:189). For instance, Anya was the first project manager I met at LBACA and the one with whom I spent the most time. Upon meeting her one is immediately struck by her quintessential "girl next door" American look: bobbed blond hair; cerulean blue eyes; pale, pink-hued skin; high, thin nose; and tall, lithe body—a daughter of Norwegian immigrants. This was also how a Latina representative of the Port of Long Beach would receive her on a day when she, Anya, and a prominent Latina community activist were touring the port to discuss potential deleterious environmental and health impacts. Thinking that "White girl" Anya spoke no Spanish, the representative began lying to the Latina resident about the nature of the pollution from the port, about what the port was doing about it, including, as Anya pointed out, lying about the ports having fewer cranes carrying in product when in fact they had long been bringing in many more. Stopping her mid-sentence, Anya blurted out in loud Spanish, "No es verdad!" much to the shock of the representative. Upon narrating this incident in our interview, Anya expressed mortification that any official would tell bald-faced lies to a community resident who, along with her neighbors, were being killed by the $PM_{2.5}$, the silent killer also coming out of the ports. She mused indignantly, "What if I didn't speak Spanish? There wouldn't be any accountability!"

In addition, immigrant activists felt that their physical and emotional states were being dismissed when elites demanded "proof" that their asthma and cancer were caused by emissions, a crucial power-knowledge maneuver. As Cindy shared, the common refrain of regulators and corporations at public meetings was, "We can't do anything unless you can prove that [insert oil refinery, port, railyard, freeway] caused you or your child's [insert illness, disease, or cancer]." Of course, this was a nonstarter, a non-sequitur. It is clear to all involved that air moves (as do people). There is no way to isolate one stream of toxic contamination from BP oil refinery to the lungs of little Cecilia or of her brother or parents. There is no way to discern from a cascade of pollutants what entered their lungs and to identify unequivocally which came from where. There is no way to prove that once those toxins entered the body that they irrefutably caused the asthma, cancer, chronic nose bleeds, fibromyalgia, or reproductive complications. Yet this "proof" was the only criteria that was truly actionable; if the local residents could present this proof—whose parameters are determined by "hard" or "acceptable" science"—then the agencies and companies would provide financial compensation or change their business practices or possibly change the metrics of what are "allowable" rates and thresholds of disease, cancer, and death.

To add insult to injury, the state would usually deny such proof if the community did the hard work to present it, or at least, present related data to support it. In other words, the state often refused and dismissed the margins' knowledge production wholesale. The necropolitics of "letting die," after all, is much easier to deploy when the margins are politically paralyzed or almost so—such is the point of wars over power-knowledge. Indeed, the notion of a dominant, universal science, Devon Peña (1998:5) writes, began with imperialists partially justifying their globe-trotting as the search for timeless and "placeless" truths, including that of their own superiority over the colonized. History therefore teaches us that knowledge has always been situated (Haraway 1985) and that we should practice "strong objectivity," or interrogate how each form of knowledge has been created by historical social forces (Harding 1993). Fast-forwarding a millennium, Corburn (2005:203) writes that community knowledge (or knowledge discourse, a la Foucault) has proven vital to environmental justice victories for the margins (see also Rose 2007). At the same time, many communities do not *solely* rely on street science to proffer knowledge and to resist regulators and corporations. Respected research universities that ally with these groups of color and their environmentally taxed communities conduct rigorous research, often *more* rigorous than that of the scientists and technocrats hired by government agencies (and corporations). Some examples include research that comes out of UCLA's Fielding School of Public Health and UCLA's Institute of the Environment and Sustainability. Research also comes out of USC's Program for Environmental and Regional Equity, and Environmental Health Centers funded by the National Institute for Environmental Health Sciences. At the helm of these institutions are eminent professors and contracted researchers—those centrally involved included UCLA's John Froines (incidentally, one of the infamous Chicago Seven) and

USC's Andrea Hricko, as well as Occidental's James Sadd, to name a mere handful. And yet, agency and industry would often question this research or claim to take it under advisement while reproducing their main response: inaction and mild concession.

In this vein, Corburn writes, "Professionals remain skeptical of local knowledge and will almost always find it easier to defer to the politically powerful knowledge of private-interest groups or other professional scientists" (Bunders and Leydesdorff 1987, cited in Corburn 2005:203). As my fieldwork bore out, regulatory agencies (and corporations) work with in-house researchers and medical experts to reach conclusions about mortality, morbidity, and disease rates. At countless public hearings and public comments across Long Beach and South Bay LA, very infrequently did the in-house scientists ever challenge, problematize, or overrule the established morbidity and mortality rates promulgated by the corporations and agencies. Elsewhere, it appears that Silicon Valley has perfected the neoliberal trifecta: high-tech industries poison their workers; the doctors say that they are fine ("Just rest or take an aspirin"); and then when workers find counterinformation and resist, both tell them that they, especially the women, are hysterical and imagining things, and that they or their family members will lose their jobs if they do not shut their mouths anyway; at times, Silicon Valley uses much cheaper prison labor when they want more workers (Pellow and Park 2002). Corburn (2005) alludes to the fact that cases like this do not have to be the reality:

> For "outsiders," such as planners, to effectively incorporate street science into their work, they first must understand residents' experiences, appreciate the nuances in what residents are saying, and be willing to work with residents in formulating policy responses that take account of both professional judgment and local knowledge (Gaventa 1993). This will not happen easily.

And, in my fieldwork, it never did. Given this dismissal of their street knowledge, the withering of the social services that these immigrants—especially those undocumented and of low income—relied on, and generalized government violence against them, the organizers also threw up their hands when it came to the state. In effect, they knew that they were banking on a system that was utterly ignorant about the very communities that they were supposed to "protect"—the blocks and neighborhoods that they rarely walked, the brown air they didn't breathe, and their lack of familiarity with the looming overpasses, foreboding oil refineries like mini-cities of light and metal, diesel-spewing trains, and with their cherished churches, markets, and schools. The irony was not lost on them that SCAQMD did not have to thoroughly embody a community about which they wrote body-related policies.

LBACA youth activist Miguel, in this vein, connected the impossible demand for evidence to the lack of concern (that is, he censured their improper emotion work): "They don't really care . . . they just ask for proof and they want solid proof, but how is that going to help? [They ask] 'What's causing these problems? How do you know? Like how many people . . . ?' Solid proof!" Invoking the precautionary principle, a Filipina-Mexican mother named Vega turned the argument on its head and insisted, "*They* should be providing proof to the community that they're causing all this sickness!"

At a particularly heated public comment meeting concerning the I-710 corridor expansion, for instance, Cesar, a long-time and soft-spoken influential member of East Yard Communities for Environmental Justice, approached the mic in goatee, flannel shirt, and jeans, opposite the mostly clean-shaven men in suits and pressed, button-down shirts. In a calm and studied fashion, Cesar explained why he thought the committee did not account for all the sources of diesel in the Health Impact Assessment (HIA)[4] on the I-710 expansion. Noteworthy is that this HIA was an unprecedented concession by the state to grassroots community demand. To support his arguments that rates of diesel pollution were much higher than what the agencies alleged, Cesar cited systematic university studies. The agency representatives from Caltrans, Metro Transit Authority, and the Air Quality Management District barely acknowledged the validity of his points nor did the officials expressly integrate his suggestions as possible avenues they could pursue. Accordingly and eventually, the HIA—otherwise historic, landmark, and the impressive product of community pressure—was reduced to a pro-forma rubber stamping, not the influential force on decision-making that the activists intended. Indeed, agencies almost always did not fundamentally change anything that they had already planned or started work on, a problem certainly not exclusive to environment and health, but with an impact on human bodies that could often be more grave and immediate.

Similarly, at a Metro LA study session on the I-710 expansion on August 12, 2012, the residents had a great deal to say after the Metro presentation, "Air Quality and Health Risk Background." From the audience, Jesse, leader of Communities for a Safe Environment, chimed in with, "Pollution is not only related to the freeway, so you need to show more clearly how it's linked to the refineries and the ports, etcetera. Okay, and why is [pollution from] construction not in the air quality analysis? Is it because so many causes like construction are only measured qualitatively?" In response to Jesse's community-informed thinking, the Metro LA official, Julie, said, "It's [construction is] in there, in the main part of the analysis." Jesse then asked, "Is [what you presented] the worst-case scenario of construction risk on air quality, based on all seven sections being built at the same time [or just one at a time]? And are those rates over regular AQMD levels?" Julie, the official, tersely replied, "Yes," leaving patently unclear which question she was answering. These kinds of emotionally callous dismissals were enshrined in state refusal to hear or know the community's street knowledge, and to act (expeditiously) on most of the suggestions that emerged and attended. Yet the activists plodded on, in part by remapping the way the state and industry defined pollution, measured it, and calculated mathematical formulas.

A similar burden of proof applied to the domain of environmental health. Teresa shared that the agencies were disbelieving of even physicians whose claims based on long-term treatment of the deleterious effects of air contamination did not constitute "knowledge." Maria shared, "One day I saw that they asked a doctor about the pollution of the air and the doctor said that it also contributes to obesity, and they just said that that was unbelievable to them, like 'What does being obese have to do with the air?' And they were just being narrow-minded because, first of all, when a kid is obese they need to exercise and they can't exercise when the air is polluted, and I mean it was very clear that it *did* relate, but they were like, 'What does that have to do with the polluted air?' He said that he needed statistics and numbers to prove that the pollution of the air contributes to obesity."

Without using the esoteric term "neoliberalism," Samoan American teacher Cindy invoked many of its aforementioned features in explaining why she thought regulatory agencies were so ignorant and inactive. To launch her invective, Cindy derided the agencies' market imperative at the expense of state regulation and the public good; she also derided the smoke and mirrors nature of the public meetings.

> CINDY: I can almost guarantee that for the city of Carson, they don't say anything against Shell or against BP—
>
> NADIA: What about Shine [truck-washing company]? They're a small little business.
>
> CINDY: Yeah, and then, well, they actually want Shine to move because they're going to redevelop that, build homes there. . . . They [the city and mayor] don't understand it. The mayor comes to our meetings and just talks, he stands with us, but he doesn't do anything. I said, "Well, can you revoke the permit of Shine?" [Mayor:] "Well now, you know, we can't do that." [Cindy:] "Then you can't help us! Don't come to our meetings!" . . . Don't waste our time!" I'm not into conspiracy theories, but I just really don't think AQMD is doing as much as it can. "So how can you allow all of this to happen?" . . . These regulatory agencies that are supposed to be regulating? . . . They come and hold these little meetings to just appease us, give us these samples, and then don't do anything. . . . That's why I don't need to get as upset anymore because I don't see a future for us in these meetings. It's nothing!

Cindy continued by elaborating on these meetings as an "absolute joke," and ended with, "So we're going to have to work on our own." Indeed, one of the key messages and practices of neoliberalism is to tell the average citizen, "Since the market dictates everything, you're on your own." Why? As Cindy relayed, neoliberalism ensures that precious land and space will be used for gentrification and profit (for example, the property next to her school), because there is little to no regulation of profit-making industries even if they kill people quietly, and because industries shroud their power in a "show" of public meetings (that are not always announced or at convenient times), in the constant kicking of the can down the road and in the burying of community needs under bureaucratic delays. Across countless public comments, I don't think I heard any words more than I did "delay" or "We'll get back to you on that."

THE FALSE CHOICES OF NEOLIBERALISM

As a top-down, discursive-material process of "letting die" waged by neoliberal racial capitalism and the racial state, "bioneglect" was, at times, most evident in the false "choices" that neoliberalism presented to those living and going to school in the afflicted communities. For instance, community institutions such as free or low-cost asthma clinics survived in part by taking money from the port or oil industry in order to sustain themselves, in turn allowing the latter to avoid opposition. On the issue of "being in the port's pocket," so to speak, the physician at an asthma clinic for low-income and uninsured immigrants noted that "people are not happy that I accepted money from the port [and oil industry]. But that money would've gone elsewhere, to outsiders, so *we need it.* We're about *service.* If we were just about advocacy, then okay, I get it, but we're also service." This physician believed that if his was merely a movement organization, then he could understand the backlash and criticism against him—often framed as allowing industry to "buy his silence"—but he justified it as providing a service, a service that under neoliberalism rarely came from the state or corporations. Following this line of logic, had he not taken the money, it could have gone to places or people who certainly did not need it. Again, this is what I would call the neoliberal bargain: it helped the symptom of the problem by providing the low-income Latin@ immigrants medical care that was often inaccessible. Yet by deflecting criticism of, or organizing against, the industry, it also propped up the very system that caused their health problems in the first place. Another manifestation of this problem was the doctor's active presence on community committees that gave input on the I-710 expansion—often alongside prominent local activists; in this way, he was operating on both sides of the fence—on the side of the activists and on the side of the ports and oil—that is, embodying the contradictions of neoliberalism and its tools of nativist racism.

At a meeting a couple of months later, he continued to depart from the opinions of the community organizers by declaring, "The I-710 expansion may be good because [then] we could gain zero emission trucks plus other eco options, so if we get eco alternatives, then we can deal with the health impacts. If not, then we're against it." In a sense, he was (perhaps unintentionally) painting activists into a corner. If the residents would respond that they did not believe that having more trucks on the freeway, even if some were zero emission, would improve their health and thus they opposed the expansion, they were foreclosing the opportunity for more zero emission trucks. What the doctor neglected to say was that the presence of more trucks overall (not all of which could be zero emission) would likely exacerbate their maladies. More trucks would also cause more environmental injustices such as more street traffic in their neighborhoods (owing to the reality that more lanes meant more congested freeways [Mann 2014]) and more construction, noise, and light pollution. Also worth mentioning is that the community was not guaranteed any of these eco options if they decided to support the government entities behind the freeway expansion—that the state could promise all of these eco "bells and whistles" and then later renege. The activists were very familiar with the way "the state" worked—not only did it mean that the Establishment offered false "choices" that would always uphold and empower the market, but that it could always claim "(sudden) lack of government money and resources" as a justification to renege on earlier promises for the public good.

Neoliberalism also wrapped its tentacles around public schools, which, as we shall see in a moment, also fosters false choices. Arrayed against this neglect, the slogan, "It Will Be a Great Day When Our Schools Get All the Money They Need and the Air Force Has to Hold a Bake Sale to Buy a Bomber" is not a polemic. It reflects a basic fact. In 2015, the US spent 16 percent of its federal budget on the military ($609.3 billion)—the third largest expenditure—and a mere 3 percent on education ($102.3 billion) (Bloom 2017). A Brown University study titled "Costs of War" found that "[t]he U.S. wars in Iraq, Syria, Afghanistan and Pakistan, and the increased spending on homeland security and the departments of defense, state and veterans affairs since the 9/11 attacks have cost more than $4.3 trillion in current dollars through fiscal year 2017." Disaggregated to the individual US taxpayer, s/he has spent $23,386 on these wars every year since 2001 (Brown University News 2017). Worse, the US relies not as much on federal, socialized funding of K–12 education, but instead on the local property tax base of the community; hence, schools in rental-unit-heavy working-class Latinx immigrant communities are even more underresourced. And while the rest of the world is investing more in education, the United States stands alone in reducing its spending on elementary and high school education (4 percent decline from 2010 to 2014), curious given the US economy's prosperity in those years. In contrast, the thirty-five OECD countries averaged a 5 percent increase in education spending from 2010 to 2014 despite their stalled economies in the wake of the 2008 financial crisis. To boost education budgets, these nations slashed other parts of their budgets; "[m]eanwhile, U.S. local, state and federal governments chose to cut funding for the schoolhouse. A comparable advanced nation like the UK upped its spending by 32% while Turkey spiked to 76% [2008–2014]" (*US News and World Report* 2017).

On false choices related to schools, youth organizer Bella censured corporate strategy: "They say, 'Okay, we'll give you money *and* you can fit our [plant] close to your school.' [School says]: 'Okay, we need the money now, the governor is coming down on us, okay, we need the money.' Like I mention, they can control us." One of the tentacles of social control also choked the life out of school-based organizing against environmental racism. Youth activist Tomas invoked the expulsion of Communities for a Better Environment from one of these schools.

TOMAS: CBE was kicked out of Bowdoin High School.[5]

NADIA: Why?

TOMAS: Because Bowdoin High School gets money from industries.

NADIA: Ohhh.

TOMAS: [Also the] Trucking industries.

NADIA: So that's what kept everyone quiet?

TOMAS: Exactly, to hush them. And basically what happened was that everyone [at Bowdoin] was nervous because everyone was like, "Who are you blaming?"

Like the doctor, high schools knew that criticizing and contesting industry would mean the drying up of precious industry money. To be fair, it was not just the physician who could be confusing about his allegiances and political maneuvers. Ultimately, convoluted, opportunistic, bioneglectful politics seemed most culpable. Consider the fact that two of the most strident and vociferous community organizers, Jesse of Coalition for a Safe Environment and former Communities for a Better Environment and Tomas noted that, at times, they were in the awkward position of praising and supporting their political enemy when the "enemy" could or would give them what they wanted, such as clean trucks (electric or compressed natural gas).

TOMAS: And I said, "We're on the side of the Port of LA. We're backing up the Port of LA because they're doing a good job."

NADIA: Wow, you said that?

TOMAS: Well, it was true! . . . But we want to hold the Port of LA accountable still. Our people, even Jesse Marquez, was suing the hell out of the Port of LA. But Jesse . . . was also like, "Kudos to the Port of L.A." Yeah, people that were suing, or at war with, the port joined forces to get the clean trucks program.

NADIA: Was it politicians responding to organizers?

TOMAS: Yeah, it was actually the Port of LA and the Port of Long Beach who came together in 2006 to come out with a cleaner [truck] action plan. . . . It was the first time since World War II that the Port of LA and the Port of Long Beach had a joint agreement.

Again, low-income communities of color under a bioneglectful assault learned quickly that, whether it was intentional or not, the state could be both friend and enemy.

Another form of neoliberalism with which the immigrants engage concerns health care. Speaking of an increasingly neglectful world, Maria and Eva invoked the federal government's slashing of health care programs, such as Medi-Cal, Medicare, and children's care. Eva opined,

> Right now with so many kids and the whole medical insurance debate that's going one way or the other, I think that the politicians should never leave those kind of things [health, sickness] to our own fate . . . for a long time now, Medi-Cal and Medicare for the children and the old people, have just not been enough.

Also about the health care system, Carmen discussed how careless and uncaring doctors often were when the Latinas would bring their asthmatic children in for treatment. Carmen's utter dissatisfaction with what she considered substandard medical care led her to her grassroots community work with the organization Community Partners Council (CPC).

> It was a very difficult time in terms of the health of my boys, and I said to myself, "I'm going to advocate for my kids and . . . advocate for other kids too." . . . We got the doctors to get training. The doctors would just come in and say, "Oh, asthma? Albuterol [medicine], blah blah!" Then they would turn around and walk out. That's *not* what we wanted; we wanted the doctors to sit down and explain to us what asthma was in their medical terms so that we could go and investigate more. But we got the doctors to sit down and take the time and patience to look at the child calmly; we know they have a lot of patients, but they [finally] took the time to talk to us, the parent of the child. *We achieved that.* Another thing is that now when I go to the emergency room, after we advocated for these changes, . . . they don't wait to fill out the paperwork, they just take the temperature and send the patients in. *It's been a great change!*

Carmen made clear that she and the other mothers would not take the (bio) neglectful and nativist racist practices of the health care industry sitting down. Rather, they would get the doctors to sit down, talk to them, and take care of their children properly—until they were no longer neglected.

THE STATE ENGINEERS SELF-SABOTAGE

What are the broader implications of the top-down, or repressive, flow of bio-neglectful power? In addition to the dismissal of subaltern knowledges, such as street science, the state generated avoidable population-level problems and then barely responded to them, turning them into crises for "environmental justice communities" that were unbeknownst to much of the rest of society. In this way, bioneglect departs from Foucault by moving the focus away from the state merely reacting to often-unexpected populationwide health crises (such as the plague, or grain scarcity) toward the state germinating populationwide health crises (especially involving disease and death) as well. In arguing thus, I emphasize that the state often does not care if even segments of the dominant population are healthy and, in fact, it actively makes them unhealthy. A case in point is how communities of predominantly Whites, the dominant racial group, are also contaminated under this system.

Asthma, for instance, is a populationwide health crisis engineered by the US state. Although asthma is one of the fastest-growing diseases and thus a funding and resource drain on the government (Centers for Disease Control, 2011), there is no federally directed effort to monitor and address asthma that afflicts disproportionate numbers of people of color (Brown 2007) (and now in the era of COVID-19, such a crisis is even more problematic). Yet the following text straight from the CDC website shows that the state does not concede inaction; its discourse reveals no impulse to identify the true culprits to be state and industrial preference for profit, goods movement, jobs, and the race-class privilege of affluent White communities. As the state (via the CDC) tells us, asthma is an individual problem that requires "personal action plans." In other words, the best way to combat asthma is for people to be more educated on the disease and to have their inhalers and medications at the ready—a supreme form of individualized Foucaultian discipline. The site reads,

> *Better asthma education is needed.*
>
> - People with asthma can prevent asthma attacks if they are taught to use inhaled corticosteroids and other prescribed daily long-term control medicines correctly and to avoid asthma triggers. Triggers can include tobacco smoke, mold, outdoor air pollution, and colds and flu.
> - In 2008 less than half of people with asthma reported being taught how to avoid triggers. Almost half (48%) of adults who were taught how to avoid triggers did not follow most of this advice.
> - Doctors and patients can better manage asthma by creating a personal asthma action plan that the patient follows.

In fact, rather than stop at advising individuals on how to prevent asthma attacks, the state admonished the forty-eight percent of adults who did not follow their advice. Such dominant framing also reveals that the state has learned very little from the environmental justice movement, whose knowledge discourse has long argued that asthma must be understood not as an individual problem but as the product of social injustices ranging from racial capitalism to residential segregation. More important, doing nothing structurally about asthma will perpetuate this engineered asthma crisis.

As was often true of the youth activists, Miguel put state self-sabotage plainly but poetically when I asked, "You have a long history now—CPC,

LBACA, other organizations—going and talking to city councils, Sacramento, and telling them about this stuff constantly. Why do you think they haven't made any fundamental changes in the air quality?"

MIGUEL: Probably because they see that it will cost too much to actually fix the problems.

NADIA: So you mean instead of fixing the problems and making people . . . healthier, they'd just rather let the people get sick, even die, from some of these conditions?

MIGUEL: Yeah! But then, at the same time, that's a problem, too, because then people get sick . . . they go and use the free health clinics and that ends up costing the state money, so no matter what, it's a lose-lose situation. If they don't want to fix the problem they could save themselves some money, and if they don't fix the problem they're still going to lose money.

NADIA: Do you think that they think long term like that?

MIGUEL: I doubt it.

Not only is Miguel astute enough as a youth resident to indict a government for refusing to underwrite social services, he is correct in saying that government also loses out (and loses profit) by doing so. Miguel is lucid and logical when he argues that if the industry and state did not environmentally dump on communities of color, then so many of them would not be so sick and demand so much in medical care and costs. But elite institutions make clear that withering the welfare state is not always a long-range, big-picture calculation; it is also presupposed on short-sighted impulses, akin to the seduction of laziness.

Maria of LBACA and CPC shared this notion that politicians, such as Arnold Schwarzenegger, were the ones who caused immigrants so many problems, which in turn, caused so many societal problems:

Well, what I haven't really liked is what Arnold has been doing, because it's really sad to see the people who are really poor be trampled on. And it's not that I just speak of us immigrants [Latinxs] but there are also other people from other countries. For example, instead of helping the [immigrant] people here, he did the opposite and took ten percent of their paychecks. *I say that the country is in deficit because of the bad organization of the politicians and not*

> *because of the [immigrant] city.* (*El en lugar de en verdad luchar por que este la gente, yo digo que si esta el pais en deficit y el pais tiene deudas es por culpa de su mala organización de ellos no de la ciudad.*)

Millennial PCORE environmental justice coordinator Ben was even more incensed. He made plain that the state and industry were not just making health crises, they were making death. Declaring race-based contamination as running afoul of human morality, he moved beyond corruption and bribery to accuse the healthy wealthy of the crime of murder:

> I think that it's *criminal,* basically, for these communities to have all these health effects that are going on in these communities and, you know, these industries are responsible for tens of thousands, if not millions, of deaths every year and the majority of them are people of color. *It's murder*. They [industries] *can't not* kill people, so they shouldn't exist.

In Ben's account, then, one could conceive of environmental racism not just as Foucault's "letting die" or Giroux's "biopolitics of disposability" but as the crime of premeditated murder, full stop. This raises the question, however, What exactly is good or expansive about a society that murders its own citizens? According to Foucault, Agamben, and Mbembé, it produces the life of the ascribed "superior" and "worthy" peoples, but shouldn't dominant elites also be asking themselves, How is this not also a form of state self-sabotage? Without implying the merits of nation-states existing at all, the point remains: a society that lops off a considerable portion of its population ceases to be a society or, more precisely, a nation-state. Nation-states cannot exist, let alone thrive, without a booming population and without immigrants. One need merely look at how rates of low fertility and rapid aging have South Korea, Japan, and even the United States now wringing their hands about how they will sustain themselves (assuming they keep demonizing and barring immigrants), while an ascendant China boasts roughly 20 percent of the world's population and casts a pronounced imperial shadow. Even if we follow the logic of racist and classist power, for instance, how can one claim race or class superiority if there is no one left to be superior to? As these examples attest, self-sabotage just makes society more ephemeral.

If we return, however, to the case of environmental racism, we cannot ignore the tragic fact that even as states and industry self-sabotage by exacting suffering on much of their population (especially the non-White, the immigrant and refugee, the poor, and the like), they scapegoat the very people they kill for the problems government itself created: lack of college affordability and terrorism, along with underresourced K–12 education, health care, housing, and disaster relief. In this way, the state and industry at once self-sabotage and privilege themselves. As a related point, governments often declare a "state of emergency" to justify racist and classist biopolitical responses, such as the Jewish genocide in the Holocaust (Agamben 1998) and Black genocide in Hurricane Katrina. Yet the state no longer needs a state of emergency to control populations or to treat disadvantaged populations as the socially dead. It merely needs to normalize the neoliberal dereliction of duty, such as weak regulation of hazards, as normal, pedestrian, and unremarkable.

Trump's ability to tell a good story, for instance, galvanized an American movement and fascist apparatus that assault the physical and emotional health of Mexican migrants and Muslims in particular. As the emblem of an increasingly Alt-Right world, not only is the Trump Era sabotaging the country's capacity to function and thrive, he harmed White Americans' capacity to think and feel. Yet the fact that a White "nationalist" movement feels no compunction about embracing the unabashedly racist story of their big-government-hating Robin Hood reflects philosopher Charles Mills's contentions about White ignorance:

> I want a concept of white ignorance broad enough to include moral ignorance—not merely ignorance of facts with moral implications but moral non-knowings, incorrect judgments about the rights and wrongs of moral situations themselves. For me, the epistemic desideratum is that the naturalizing and socializing of epistemology should have, as a component, the naturalizing and socializing of moral epistemology also (Campbell and Hunter 2000) and the study of pervasive social patterns of mistaken moral cognition. Thus the idea is that improvements in our cognitive practice should have a practical payoff in heightened sensitivity to social oppression and the attempt to reduce and ultimately eliminate that oppression. (Mills 2017:22; see also McIntosh 1989)

In accordance with Mills, White societal ignorance stems from socialized cognition but, perhaps more important, was tantamount to personal moral bankruptcy as well as state self-sabotage. The only way through these social problems was "heightened sensitivity to social oppression and the attempt to reduce and ultimately eliminate that oppression." The alternative, after all, would only be the self-sabotage of society to the point of societal death.

On balance, given the clean air organizers' keen awareness that the state could be nonsensical, coopted their movement, deployed smoke and mirrors, dismissed their power-knowledge, and exploited them with false and limited choices, it might seem that they would repudiate the state whole cloth. Yet the fact that the lion's share of social movements has engaged the state, that the LA immigrants did not see alternative systems to tap, that those with sick and dying loved ones felt compelled to tap every resource, and that politicians at times made concessions, meant that they kept themselves in the throes of the state. To be certain, this was a complicated, contradictory relationship. The next chapter explores the various forms of emotional domination used by state and corporate institutions to resist the push back from the margins.

CHAPTER 2

EMOTIONS AS POWER

THERE WERE NUMEROUS instances in the field when the singular axis of class just did not seem to fit the social situation. Rather, the excesses of race—albeit interrelated with class, as well as legal status and language—would spill over onto the scene and release their pungent stink. We wrinkled our noses at the familiar odor at one Community Action Committee meeting for the I-710 freeway expansion. In the emerald-walled room with the dark of night flooding through the wall of windows awash in fluorescent glare, I heard the usual presentations and reports by transportation authorities and the AQMD. When the public comment session began, the activists and community allies came armed to condemn what they deemed a very truncated time period to read the encyclopedia-thick Environmental Impact Report (EIR) translated into shoddy, confusing Spanish—a bilingual effort for which they had previously fought a contentious, protracted, and now seemingly futile battle. The initial mood of tense formality soon graduated into one of mutual disquiet and discord. Many of the women stepped to the mic and shouted angrily in Spanish that fluent English speakers could barely comprehend jargon-filled, phonebook-sized EIRs, so might the officials imagine the struggle of non-English-speakers to grasp the report through its sloppy

Spanish-language summaries? What then brought the contention to a feverish pitch was a dismissive comment by a White American male state official on the committee who declared from the podium, "Come on, folks. Let's talk about the real issue here, which is that the committee gave everyone plenty of time. The truth is that everyone procrastinates, including me. It is human nature to procrastinate. And that's why folks haven't had enough time to finish this. I'm sure no one opened up the EIR as soon as it came out." A collective gasp was heard throughout the room, followed by mutterings of disgust and disagreement. After a few community residents amplified their displeasure at the mic in English and Spanish, the moderator officiating the meeting spoke up in a tone of measured indignation to condemn his fellow committee member: "Stan,[1] with all due respect, I actually agree with them that your comments are inappropriate. I think it's a real problem to tell them that the reason they're upset is because they're procrastinators. I know you didn't mean it that way, but it does sound condescending. I think we can be fair and reasonable in how we speak." Stan quickly retorted, "But I wasn't being condescending, I was talking about myself too! We all procrastinate, that's human nature!"

Striking about this moment was how unaware Stan—a middle-class White male citizen—was that he had just stereotyped as procrastinators an audience of mostly immigrants of color, many of whom were working class, were unauthorized, did not speak fluent English, and were ill and disabled. To be sure, using himself as an example, he derided all humans as guilty of the bad habit ("human nature"). Yet only someone with the privilege of entitlement would deem himself fit to speak on behalf of *all* people, to proclaim his personal proclivities to be a reference point for humanity. His inability to see his sense of entitlement even after he was chastised by a fellow White male agency official was further testament to his political myopia. The audience muttered in agreement with his colleague, especially about how they never had the luxury to procrastinate—that every minute of their lives fell under the weight of counting pennies, constantly seeking work, waiting for buses or car rides, not understanding basic signage or bills, or caring for others' children in addition to one's own—something Stan did not acknowledge. Needless to say, the audience's deep indignation revealed their impatience with Stan's racist ignorance that seemed an all-too-familiar experience in their own daily lives. This fieldwork moment emblematizes the emotive processes as well as the intersectional dimensions of nativist racism and classism (and even sexism) that are often missing in empirical studies of immigrant organizing.

This chapter extends from the previous chapter's introduction of the emotive structures used by *dominant institutions*, those that are fundamental to political processes but that are underappreciated in scholarship on emotions or affect and on social movements. This chapter will also address how the community's fight for environmental justice, school reform, and immigrant rights affirms as well as contests systemic racism, classism, and sexism. In this context in which the immigrant women of color suffer the state's project of "letting die," I address three political strategies that elite institutions used most commonly and forcefully to emotionally manipulate and wield power, and to pacify the activists' resistance: (1) apathy;[2] (2) disbelief, annoyance, mockery; and (3) guilting (often by way of condescension). The second part of the chapter addresses how the immigrants contend with this affective economy, in large part by strategizing their own emotive responses and displays. This chapter also analyzes gender by way of the women's more heightened expressiveness about, and the higher premium they placed on, elite emotive strategies (in comparison to their male activist counterparts). As feminist and intersectionality scholars have deftly shown, environmental problems have been borne differently by women than by men (see Voyles 2015:6), in large part because gender ideologies and roles have positioned women to be caretakers and to be more likely to suffer poverty, hunger, and toxic exposure through domestic activities and the link between "industry and home" (7). Finally, the chapter conclusion will identify the specificity of emotive dynamics for the neoliberal state, for the organizers themselves who reinvent and respond, and for racism and sexism more systemically—in so doing, I deem emotional power to be central to bioneglect and theorize resistance as vital to understanding biopower.

RELEVANT EMOTIONS

The extant literature on the emotional dynamics of the dominant groups and the margins significantly inform this chapter. As Bonilla-Silva (2019) writes, we social scientists know little about the affective structures of institutional systems, in particular a "racial economy of emotions" that runs on racialized emotions. Yet, social scientists have paid sparse attention to the race-based dimensions of emotional life (Mirchandani 2003). Yet beyond clarion calls and theoretical treatments, this chapter empirically examines a racial, and intersectional, emotional economy with respect to clean air activism and, more specifically, to political processes *from the top-down.* Although Bonilla-Silva does not provide an explicit example of how White supremacy uses racialized emotions to marginalize APIDAs, the one group he excises, *Refusing Death* spotlights the predominant Whiteness of the state and industry officials vis-a-vis the Asian, Latin@, and other of color activists within this racial economy of emotions (even more important in the wake of anti-Asian knifings and beatings per coronavirus racism). In this context, the dominant racial group's emotions reach proportions of "hegemonic emotional domination" (Matias 2016), indexed against the foil of the so-called inappropriate emotions of the margins. In my empirical examination of what has mostly stayed in the purview of theory, this LA-based clean air movement requires an intersection of race with gender, class, and citizenship given that these are the main axes that hierarchize the officials relative to the residents. Studies such as Mirchandani's (2003) and Padios's (2018) on the racial abuse and callousness that First World customers unleash on, respectively, Indian and Filipinx call center workers, reminds us that we must also interrelate nation, or what we might call imperial racial formations (N. Kim 2008b), in this matrix.

From the bottom up, students of collective mobilization have taken up the mantle of emotions, elaborating on the foundation laid by the sociology of gender and work. Sociologists have made clear that few can address movements without in some way engaging questions of emotions and related forms of storytelling, narrative, and identity. For instance, in her book *Moving Politics*, Deborah Gould (2009) studies the AIDS activist group ACT UP's organizing in the 1980s, the early years of what she called the LGBT movement, and provides a comprehensive, searing analysis of its emotional politics. ACT UP organizers let their emotions erupt within a dominant culture that has generally portrayed much emotion as "chaotic and irrational." As one of the most common emotions in contested political environments is anger, Gould aptly demonstrates anger not as irrational or knee-jerk, but as productive (2009:252; see also Lutz 1988:180). Moreover, "anger is often seen as an antisocial emotion" because it can involve protest against norms and institutions deemed necessary for social order and harmony (Lutz 1988:180). Lutz notes the complexity of this dynamic, as America's individualist ethos also affirms bucking the Establishment, with only the dominant and privileged (such as White men) being permitted to express "righteous anger." I underscore, then, that angry women and people of color are especially censured.

As emotions like anger are inseparable from movements, Gould concurs with anthropologist Clifford Geertz (1973:449) that collective mobilization is "a vocabulary of sentiment," a "sentimental education." She writes, "More than manage emotions—a term that implies a preexisting emotional state that then is amplified or dampened—the emotion work of movements frequently generates feelings" (2009:213). Similarly, James Jasper (1998:294) writes that groups are shaped and strengthened when they share reflex emotions in response to events; this holds true for *negative* emotional responses, such as fear and anxiety (Eyerman 2005:43). Berezin (2001) also finds that positive affect, such as love of the group, is crucial to securing a collective identity and loyalty. Asthma, for instance, has been found to leave people of color feeling *powerless,* an emotion that has galvanized women, immigrants, and other people of color to the front lines of environmental justice fights (Brown, Mayer, Zavestoski, Luebke, Mandelbaum, McCormick. and Lyson 2011). Love for the group and unleashing old and new desires, such as for a new selfhood and reality, are also galvanizing agents (Gould 2009).

LINKING BODIES, EMOTIONS, AND ACTIVISM

In her ethnography of Asian immigrant women and New York nail salons, Miliann Kang (2010:18–21) argues that much of the emotional labor research has not sufficiently theorized the body and embodied processes. She argues further that the emotional labor research has not centered women who are disadvantaged by race and immigrant (and class) status given its long-standing focus on native-born White American women. These very intersections, however, mediate the body labor (holding hands to paint nails, massaging others' feet) and the emotion labor (listening to others' problems or to angry, prejudiced customers) performed by her Korean immigrant informants; she also finds that body and emotion labor are not discrete but dovetailed. In related fashion, I contend that emotionality is a form of embodiment precisely because, as Kosut and Moore (2010) remind us, Foucault and other scholars did not take seriously the fact that the mind is part of the corporeal body. We therefore "enliven" bodies when we recognize, as have many psychologists (for example, Forward and Buck 1989; Levine and Heller 2019; Thoits 1989), that our emotions are largely shaped by our mind's thought processes. Living in a body and enacting embodiment necessitate emotion.

In addressing the relationship between the body and emotions, Johnson (2017) notes that hierarchical social systems tend to be dissociative insofar as they disconnect subjects from a felt sense of their body. Subjects are discouraged from feeling themselves from the inside (for example, pleasure is unseemly) and encouraged to identify with the outside of their body. She further underscores that as activists become more comfortable and effective in their bodies holistically—that is, activate embodied forms of knowledge—they enact more authentic forms of leadership. Similarly, we underestimate the body's power: "Bodies and bodily performances—including physical stature, features, stance, gestures, and voice—are central, yet ignored, elements in the accomplishment of leadership" (Sinclair 2005, cited in Fonow and Franzway (2016:9–10). In concert with the previous chapter's focus on the broader emotional violence of neoliberalism, this chapter spotlights the body and emotion language of the representatives of elite institutions. Together, these constitute the processes of an underappreciated form of power, one that a transcorporeal lens exposes as hierarchizing bodies—and I would add, hierarchizing emotional life—in relation to nature (air, soil) as well as "built nature": homes, freeways, and refineries. At the same time, studies of political process are not complete without examining the dialectical relationship between agents of monopolized state and corporate power and the disadvantaged; we must therefore equally integrate how the disadvantaged politicize their bodies and feelings to push back. Few studies of emotionality or of Asian American and Latinx movements foreground this dialectical process or its multilayered and intersectional character.

TOP DOWN, BOTTOM UP, AND THE EMOTIVE DIALECTIC

As most of the women articulated, the key reason they joined movements, stayed in them, and gave them more time and energy than they could afford was the empathy from fellow activists and community-based organizations. Indeed, the empathy was largely remarkable to them *because* of the foil of state and corporate officials' structures of *apathy*. Not only did the officials lack emotive expression, they violated other forms of "emotion work," or the set of rules governing the emotions that people involved in social situations "should" experience.

Across countless meetings about the freeway expansion, for instance, the repetition of the emotional power dynamics would send me into déjà vu. At the largest public comment against the I-710 expansion, in August of 2011, Blanca, a Filipina American mother, railed into the mic, "How much more cancer will you accept? If you had to live next to it, you'd never do it!" In that same moment, I witnessed a male official in the front (either White or White-passing Latino) perform a very elongated and obvious eye-roll. He chose not to respond with verbal language, but with body language, unmistakably communicating, "You're being dramatic. I don't care." Then, to naturalize his emotional expression as "normal," he, as many state officials were wont to do, began his technocratic talk of "data" being under the disease threshold. In doing so, he seemed to render community organizers like Blanca as emotionally outsized, unprofessional, and disqualifying.

Many of the Latin@ informants invoked language-based racism when they addressed the racist apathy among the officials, whether they did not speak English or only broken, accented forms of it. First-generation immigrant Laura, who was not English-fluent, conveyed that even the young change-makers suffered racist apathy despite their English fluency and other markers of "(White) Americanization." Laura began the narrative by answering the following about youth organizers:

NADIA: Do you think the politicians would take them more seriously than someone who has an accent or speaks less English?

LAURA: Yes and no. *Yes,* because politicians are more confident that the youth are correctly and clearly delivering their message. With us, they may think that we don't even understand the question we're supposed to be answering! And, *no,* because I once saw a student testifying at City Council and the mayor just stood up and left.

NADIA: You mean, because it was a young person?

LAURA: Well, I suppose they would pay attention because the youth speak the language of this country, but *I think it's simply because they don't care about us.*

Laura makes clear that it is not merely the fact that elected officials prioritize English fluency, it was simply that they just did not care about people like

Laura or the youth who looked like her. More than language, apathy ruled the day in a racist society.

Even with their English fluency—or perhaps because of it—those of the younger Latin@ generation concurred with the first generation's interpretation of repressive apathy. Twenty-one-year-old Bella, a youth organizer and daughter of an activist mother, shared the following:

> And I remember one time that I went to testify . . . one person in front walked out talking on their phone. Yeah, that was really rude. . . . And [when] there was a [community] person who did not know how to speak English . . . They discriminate! It doesn't really matter whether you're Hispanic, African American, it doesn't matter; if they feel they're not interested in something, then *they show you*. . . . Some of them may . . . say that, "I'm here, I'm still listening to you," but you can tell by their body language that they're not interested.

Striking is that Bella considered not verbal language but *body language* to prove the veracity of the officials' intentions, which in her mind were racially discriminatory. Youth leader Tomas echoed the same upon my asking him if he thought that officials were more biased or condescending toward first-generation Latinas who had accents or needed a translator. Without missing a beat, Tomas retorted, "I think they [the women] are immediately dismissed. I think as soon as you hear an accent or they need translators, there's automatically a disconnect. [The officials think to themselves,] "She's not speaking my language and that's some community that I never go to anyway."

Another frequent process of emotive bioneglect I identified was "Disbelief/ Annoyance/ Mockery," as we witnessed earlier with the male official's dramatic eye-roll. Redolent of Matias's (2016) "hegemonic emotional domination" for the purpose of making dubious the immigrants' emotionality, dominant officials dismissed the movement actors writ large, but especially the women of color majority. Gwyn Kirk (1998:182) found that in the environmental justice movement officials often ridiculed the women and their expressed emotionality as being "hysterical housewives" and "trivializ[ed]" their street science research as "emotional and unscholarly." I saw this echoed at meetings at which mostly Anglo male officials seemed disaffected and unwilling to suspend disbelief whenever the immigrant women (and men) passionately enjoined the officials to act. For instance, disbelief, annoyance, and mockery were on full display at the same public comment on the freeway expansion at which Blanca had spoken. Since this was the largest meeting, complete with the activists' organization of a loud block party just outside the building (an ode to community that I was not expecting), I had noticed many more White Americans in attendance. One White woman wearing a scowl lambasted the officials with, "Let's be honest and call this what it is; this is institutional racism, plain and simple!" The audience erupted in such cheer and piercing whistles that it took the moderator several minutes and many stern pleas to calm the audience down. Despite White support, the elites maintained their strategy of annoyed disbelief by not acknowledging the community's facts at all, let alone whether they were convincing or not. The elites also betrayed visible irritation when they lost control of the fired-up crowd (annoyance) and when they dismissively shook their heads (more disbelief), particularly when people of color angrily stepped up to the mic. But I also noticed that even when residents were sad and soft-spoken, the officials seemed more irritated than empathic or believing.

Thirty-four-year-old long-time community leader Carolina conveyed the elites' version of emotive disbelief and annoyance this way: "Well, when I was testifying I couldn't see anything, but when someone else was testifying I saw the [officials] that were listening make a gesture, like saying, 'What fault do I have in this?' They were acting, like, ironic." Fifty-six-year-old Teresa remarked on the emotional mockery her group suffered when she said, "Our *pueblo* is speaking for what it needs. A lot of the time the people who are supposed to be listening, helping the community, they listen and they just laugh." Striking about Teresa's narrative is not only the elites' "feeling rules" of entitlement, which they expressed through mockery, but her choice to use the word "pueblo." Much more than a mere neighborhood or community, "pueblo" evokes family and the loving ties that bind.

At a meeting of the EIR/EIS Project Committee on January 31, 2011, the dynamics of apathy and Disbelief/Annoyance/Mockery were palpable, as the discussion between the officials on the committee and the audience grew tense. To set the scene, these meetings were almost always at 6 p.m., a time when community residents were supposed to be having dinner with their families after a hard day of work and school. When we arrived at the emerald-green meeting room, one that always reminded me of a library, we were immediately met with the wafting aromas of hot food from the warming stations arranged along a long banquet table (apparently, the EIR/EIS Project Committee had met earlier to prepare for the meeting and had ordered in). The presence of dinner reserved only for the Project Committee officials without any offer of food—or of the abundant leftovers—to the rest of us, at dinner time no less, is a categorically political matter, especially to these Asian American and Latin@ Angelenos, who I noticed rarely had meetings without some kind of meal. In fact, they would even offer meals during off-times. Not only was this a way to recruit residents to the struggle, but food is political or "revolutionary": that is, low-income people rarely take food for granted, food nourishes bodies made sick and hungry, and eating is a form of communal bonding. I myself was salivating with a grumbling stomach as I had just driven over an hour in rush hour traffic to make this meeting after having worked a long day, picked up my daughter from her care provider, and handed her off to my partner—all without time to grab even a small snack to eat. I was frustrated that the officials had not even bothered to acknowledge the political and contradictory nature of the long table full of fare emitting seductive food aromas right next to us nor did they even apologize for the bad optics. At the same time that I contemplated dishing some food from the steaming hot plates and gesturing for everyone else to follow suit, one of the Latino youth, clad in flannel and jeans, boldly walked over to the buffet table, helped himself to a Coke and a handful of snacks from the table, and grinned from ear to ear as the officials looked on; we in the audience smiled and nodded in silent understanding. In the young man's mind, their 6 p.m. meeting time and denial of food were political acts, hence, his grabbing of their food without their permission was equally one as well.

The state officials' treatment of the food was a microcosm of the political nature of these meetings altogether. That is, if, when, and where public meetings are held have long been political issues for social justice movements. In the first place, community residents often bemoan the fact that state and corporate entities rarely hold meetings for the public to weigh in on decisions about, say, where railyards and power plants are being placed or who is overseeing their practices (Brodkin 2009). When elites decide to announce meetings, community members have sometimes found them obscured in a small corner of a local newspaper or hidden on web pages behind multiple links.

The meetings are sometimes held at times that residents, especially working-class people who work multiple jobs, cannot attend; as we witnessed, they often do not provide meals or childcare. For families who cannot easily afford the prohibitive cost of childcare, the lack of childcare provision was particularly class-biased. On multiple occasions, grassroots leaders have noticed that the meetings are held in locations that are difficult for residents to access even by way of public transportation. These meetings, their existence at all, are therefore a political phenomenon.

At this particular dinner-time meeting with no dinner, we were also agitated by the fact that the facilitator kept referring to the audience as "they," talking about us in the third person as if we were not there—as most facilitators would usually say, "You guys in the audience." One could not help but feel that this was a passive-aggressive form of mockery. In this particularly heated context, one of the male leaders of East Yard Communities for Environmental Justice was met with disbelieving annoyance and hostility from one of the officials. He addressed how the committee could be exploring multiple public-private partnerships to come up with more options other than expanding the I-710 freeway, or at least more ideas on how to do so in a manner conscious of community health. He remarked that the Project Committee's one extra study on a public-private partnership was "just one approach." A female representative from the committee retorted brusquely, "What's another approach?!" When her fellow committee member, a male official, chimed in, "There are other public-private partnerships out there," the woman queried in an annoyed, disbelieving tone, "Where are these studies coming from? How relevant are they to the 710 project?" After tabling that discussion for the moment, a Communities for a Better Environment (CBE) researcher stepped up to the mic and said, "The HIA [Health Impact Assessment] inclusion into the EIR/S was a wise decision" (it was included because community leaders pressured the committee to do so). He continued, "I need a response from Caltrans or someone else on whether you'll include the HIA or not [into your decisions about the 710], because you equivocated recently." In agreement, indignant activist Marta, a long-time LBACA community leader, inveighed in Spanish without requesting any translation as per usual protocol: "We shouldn't have to wait for Caltrans to approve it! We need to present all evaluations on the HIA, in multiple languages, and send it to every affected community through your website. I'm involved in the community but I never received any invite to these meetings; think of all those people with properties in that area!" In response to both, the Caltrans male official replied, "The legal team said we can't say anything until we get results and info on what's relevant." Bothered by the apathy and the use of a legal alibi, Mark, a CBE youth leader retorted combatively from the audience, "What's irrelevant?!" The Caltrans official simply replied, "I can't comment." In this negotiation over what Foucault would call proper power-knowledge, CBE's staff researcher implored yet again, "We think this debate should be had, even if you don't want to—if this expands collective knowledge, then the public should know; we have decades of experience and knowledge on EIR/S. Caltrans is being disingenuous by saying that first, 'We'll look at what the HIA says, then, we'll include it in the report.' No one does analysis this way and, frankly, the EJ community is sick of it!" He was implying that the officials were condescending to, and infantilizing, the residents by conducting research in a backwards way. Furthermore, the possible unwillingness to consider the health impacts of the freeway was not in service to the community but in hopes of removing any barriers to the freeway's expansion, and carrying on as if the community had no idea what Caltrans was up to. Another common emotional tactic among the officials—that of guilting and shaming the activists, and often by way of condescension—occurred at one of the smaller meetings on the I-710 expansion. Many of the officials were tiring of the residents' testimonies about all the illness in the community and, ultimately, how it evidenced the government's dereliction of duty. Some of the speakers' voices broke, tears spilt, and faces reddened as they narrated emotionally charged stories of their struggles with their children's asthma and of their neighbors' affliction with cancer, some of whom had died. One of the officials, whose racialized background could be deemed ambiguous but whom several of us received as Anglo, interjected with exasperation, "You know, I had cancer for many years and it was very difficult for me and my family too. You guys are not the only ones who get cancer; and cancer is not just caused by air pollution!" Suddenly slack-jawed, most of us gasped. Although to some extent we could see where he was coming from, his empathy deficit, frosty delivery, and poor timing—all of which seemed to guilt the residents into no longer sharing about *their* cancers because theirs were not as worthy as his—made the unmistakable emotional manipulation chilling. In brief, he was guilting the activists into shutting up, if you will, about their cancers. He left the same feeling that Stan left when he patronized the immigrants of color for ostensibly "procrastinating" on reading a huge report and concluded that the community's request for more time was baseless.

Emotion as Strategy and Superarse

Turning now to the emotion work of the organizers themselves, in my fieldwork I witnessed many crying women; many staid, confident women; and some shy, soft-spoken women—in other words, they valued and were agentic about their bodies and feelings as political acts (Johnson 2017; Fonow and Franzway 2016) and as being crucial to the role of leadership (Sinclair 2005). In so doing, the activists—namely, the women—were also partaking in a "sentimental education" by engaging in conscious (and, at times, unconscious) feeling strategies. By strategy, I refer to their practice of conveying their lived reality to the powers that be, but also their belief that *how* they said those things was a matter of craft. For instance, at the LBACA workshops on public testimonies (see Figure 5 for a flier for one of these many trainings), it was not always about all the technical and know-your-rights information; a good amount of time was spent on the affective nature of the delivery, for instance, needing to connect their personal story to the political as well as being genuine, heartfelt, and confident.

In this way, the women were responding to the state's callousness and to its mostly (more affluent, citizen) White male representatives, whilst also generating their own emotional economy (Ahmed 2004) by way of their efforts and leadership for the movement (Gould 2009; Jasper 2011; Berezin 2002).

Of all the emotional assaults on the part of officials, foremost in the immigrants' rendering was the elites' general apathy, no matter how many "good guy" exceptions there were to the rule. As we heard, "They just don't care" was the most frequent refrain among the activists. The "they" were not just state and corporate officials but also the doctors and hospitals who were indifferent to their (and their children's) physical suffering. Indeed, doctors are often hired by industry to toe the corporate line, even when evidence abounds that workers are being slowly poisoned and killed for doing their jobs (Pellow and Park 2002). In response, the women chose to negotiate the elites'

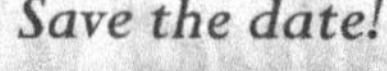

FIGURE 5. Flier for Health and Housing Meeting. Source: LBACA and CPC.

empathy deficit in varied ways. Some drew on the long and storied tradition of maternal politics wherein an emotional, sometimes tearful, delivery has long been a strategy, genuine sadness and frustration notwithstanding. It is a strategy designed to tug at the officials' and the public's heartstrings and thereby shame the elites into action. Lois Gibbs, for instance, was successful in appealing to the wider public for support and in shaming state-corporate entities into action by highlighting the plight of mothers like her who were just trying to keep their babies alive and their families intact (Hay 2009). This was also the strategy of the Mothers of the Disappeared in Argentina—Las Madres de la Plaza de Mayo—against the US-backed military dictatorship during the Dirty War (1976–1983), mothers who demanded answers about their disappeared children (kidnapped, tortured, and presumably murdered). Donning white scarves and circling Buenos Aires's famed Plaza de Mayo in protest, they garnered world-wide attention for their tireless, heartbreaking, unapologetic, and emotional demands for justice for their children (and later, their disappeared grandchildren) and for justice under the military junta. If they could not get the dictatorship to care, they would get Argentina and the world to care and thereby force the uncaring regime's hand. In demanding an end to a prison and an oil pipeline planned for their working-class Latinx neighborhood, the renowned Mothers of East Los Angeles of the 1980s waged an environmental justice campaign that took a page out of the Argentinian mothers' playbook by appealing to the primacy of family and community, but also by rejecting other virtues associated with femininity and maternalism (Pardo 1998).

Carolina of CPC and LBACA chose to highlight the virtue of the child—and of the difficulties for her as a mother—when testifying in front of the officials.

> I have taken my kids when they were younger and I would say, "Look, he has this and this disease. Look at my son, he is autistic" and I tell them my suffering: "I struggle with children who have autism." *It is so it can touch their heart* by saying that they're autistic and that I have to fight for them—to have a disease and to have asthma is very difficult. *But, it does not interest them.* (*Si yo llevo mis hijos cuando sean mas chiquitos y le dicean mira el tiene estoy y el tiene esta enfermadad. Mira mi hijo el es autista osea yo les dice mi sufrimiento. Batayo con los ninos tienen autismo. Osea para que se conmovia su corazon de que pesar tenia autismo y tenia que luchar por ellos. Trae una enfermedad mas tiene el asthma. Que era dificil. Pero no les interesa.*)

Although Carolina would not always cry during these testimonies, I witnessed many other crying women. In these situations, the women could be accused of turning the "faucets on and off," as revealed by Carolina when I inquired about those specific moments:

> NADIA: When people cry up at the mic, do you think they feel more for all of you?
>
> CAROLINA: Well, yes, but then, no. Because they think that it is theater and one does it for attention. (*Pues si pero pienso que si pero a la vez no. No por que cren que es teatro de uno que uno lo hace por llamar la atencion.*)

Carolina implies that the tearful and other emotional forms of delivery are, in fact, not acting, "not theater." In some ways, the very fact that these women could cry instantaneously meant that their emotion and lived reality were coeval: that is, suffering and tears were often bedfellows. Recall that I started this book with the vignette from Latina immigrant Tanya who believed that perhaps the only way to tug on the elites' heartstrings was to show gory pictures of dead bodies, lives taken by the toxic poison in the air that the elites allowed. People do not conjure such macabre thoughts if their reality did not point them there.

To be sure, the political plane animating these emotional strategies was also horizontal, not just vertical. Seeing as how embodied citizenship is precisely about politicizing, helping, and emotionally supporting the embodied community, which I elaborate on in Chapter 5, the female organizers stepped up to the mic not just to convince officials from City Council, SCAQMD, Caltrans, or Valero refinery, but to convince their own. Worth noting is how those, such as Ben, PCORE's environmental (health) justice facilitator, bore frequent witness to the Asian American women's and Latinas' public testimonials. Our discussion of his interpretation of their emotional strategy, and its efficacy, is revealing:

> NADIA: Do you think they [the women] ever do tugging at heartstrings as a political strategy, or no?
>
> BEN: I've seen that sometimes, yeah. They give a lot of real personal stories; you have to be made of stone not to care about them. . . . It's a tactic also *because it connects more with the audience, so maybe it can encourage the audience*—and the solidarity within them—to really fight harder, and *realize what they're fighting for with people who are . . . also fighting for the*

> *same thing.* With the council members it's hard to say with something like that, it might speak more to their interest if you talk about like, economically, this [request] will be good because it'll bring more jobs or whatever. *But I think it does work towards the general community.*

These Angeleno change-makers, as the Mothers of the Disappeared and the Mothers of East LA did before them, had to be perpetually conscious of their emotional strategies on multiple scales and to multiple audiences at once. Their frequent expression of emotional exhaustion stood to reason.

Indignation and Anger

Delivering remarks that were firm, unapologetic, and angry, however, was often the women's method of choice, as exemplified by PCORE's Cindy unleashing against BP Arco at the outset of this book. In their words, the first emotion they felt when they conjured up their engineered lot in life was anger. As the narratives in this chapter and in the remainder of the book show, their anger (at times, rage) owed to their keen awareness that, if the Establishment did not originate so much racism and classism, their communities would not have to suffer to such a physical and emotional extent. In the name of "sticking it" to the system and forcing concessions from it, then, the immigrant women did not think twice about violating "feminine" norms of emotional performance, indeed, flouting all manner of gendered softness, docility, deference, and nurturance. Indeed, they were much more willing to do this than the inverse: male activists willing to break masculine norms by "effeminately" crying, for instance. I was witness to this type of female moxie especially at the public meetings with the mostly White male state and corporate officials. Spending what seemed like many slow (albeit intense) hours at these meetings, my periodic descent into a daze owing to sleep deprivation, "food coma," or daydreaming would be halted by women "raising hell" at the mic. Typically, these women were casually dressed in jeans, could not speak English, and took up much less vertical and lateral space than the mostly formally dressed Anglo men—yet their words and spirit loomed large.

On the basis of my many wide-eyed moments at these public comments, I pointedly asked the women about what emotional delivery they considered most effective. They usually explained in a manner akin to Cindy, the Samoan

American teacher. About her general emotive tendencies within movement work, she shared,

> *Okay, I blow up*. . . . For the first two years that we had been having these cordial meetings with these groups . . . all different agencies, I would get so upset; I'd get emotional, I'd get angry. *And one meeting, the former director of the Office of Environmental Health and Safety for the district, school district, he had to tell us—after I'd just got into it—that we need to be more respectful, or something to that effect. I thought, you know, I'm not going to sit here and take more of this rubbish!* I generally am the one who gets upset in meetings!

Cindy contends that demands to be "more respectful" were coterminous with elite officials' silencing of residents into submission, into taking more "rubbish." In this way, the institutional representatives could proceed with business as usual, which, more often than not, was the "business" of doing nothing.

Anais of CPC and LBACA remarked how she was impressed by her friend who emoted much more anger and aggression than she:

> Like, I have one friend, like she speaks so much, and *she's angry*, because someone [the official] do this [makes exasperated face and sighs]. And she responds, like, "Why is your reaction like that?! It's because, it's not your problem!" . . . Then when that happened, she told me like, they stay quiet, they don't make any more faces, you know.

In this case, Anais and her friend realized the power of anger in getting them to show some attention and respect. Another strategy in the spirit of maternal politics was "to shame the hell out of the officials." Respected LBACA community liaison and leader Marta was especially skilled at shaming. When, for instance, an official pretended that she knew just as much, if not more, than Marta about her community, Marta made sure to impart her street science—her power-knowledge—as the embodied "reality" that could only be known by living the community's reality.

> When I recently went to Sacramento and I was talking to somebody, a representative of one of the legislators, and she was talking really charismatically that we were already going to have clean trucks. And I told her, *"What do you think clean trucks are?"* She said, "Oh, that we are going to have less contamination."

> *"Are you aware of the contamination that is in Long Beach? Do you think only the trucks contaminate?"* "Oh yes." So I told her, *"No, the trains also contaminate, the ships also cause contamination, and that's why a lot of the proposals that we have for you to support make changes on that front."* I told her, *"But I'm going to ask you another question. Do you know who buys those trucks?"* "Mhm, I know, the drivers." I told her, *"Do you know the significance of the drivers buying the trucks?"* She said, "No." I told her, *"So then you don't know the needs of our community. . . . You don't know that the truckers [are not] going to buy a truck when they're earning eight dollars an hour and they don't have insurance and they don't have benefits."* She became more pale than she already was and she told me, "You know what? I didn't have that information." So they act naïve, or they really don't understand the community as much as they think they do!

Not only did Marta "school" the official on all the sources of pollution and illness, she also made clear the labor injustices that disrupted the simple, linear picture of truckers buying cleaner-burning vehicles and thereby resolving the environmental health crisis. Marta was also the Long Beach resident pictured in a full-page spread of the *Long Beach Press-Telegram* captioned in big letters, "Shame on you, Bob Foster," to draw attention to Mayor Foster's acquiescence to industry over the needs of the people. Thereafter, Foster met with Marta and LBACA, although the changes she was demanding have yet to be realized.

To be sure, some did not conform to the strategy of indignation. Longtime activist Eva was soft-spoken and reserved, yet of strong conviction. It is no surprise that she combined those attributes in her more staid but equally forceful deliveries:

> EVA: No, I don't think I have to be aggressive. I just have to be firm with what I believe, and remember that I have rights, and things can be done.
>
> NADIA: What if they're really angry and rude? I mean, how do you think you have to respond?
>
> EVA: Well, I wouldn't be aggressive. I would just let them know that I am a person just like them, and that I have the same rights they do. (*Pues muy agresivo no pues nomas decir que soy una persona igual que ellos y que tengo los mismos derechos que ellos y estoy allí.*)

Maria, whom I interviewed together with Eva, chimed in,

> You get a rush of adrenaline. But sometimes when you go to speak, like in City Hall, they can be disrespectful when you're trying to give your opinion. . . . And, for example, they show the channel on TV and they never show the Latinos on TV; and you think, why is that? They . . . only show Anglo Saxon people on that channel. (*Pero nunca pasan cuando pasa la gente Latina nunca la pasan en la tele entonces hay cosas que tu dices como son. Allí pasan la gente cuando en ese canal pasan a la gente que pasa a testificar y nomas pasan a puro Anglosajon osea puro Americano.*)

Not only did Maria explain that sometimes activists like her exuded some nervous energy ("adrenaline") but that the government erased Latinos altogether. Apathy, therefore, did not just manifest in officials sleeping, walking out, or texting on their phone while residents spoke, or in annoyed sighing and eye-rolling, or in ultimately doing nothing; it also meant erasing the presence of Latinos altogether. In Maria's mind, if the government did not care about Latinos during the actual meeting, why would the government care about televising Latinos to the world?

To be sure, there was a small minority who believed that there was no strategic place for anger or negativity. Yolanda of CPC and LBACA revealed that her own efforts at positivity flowed from her gendered perspective on the power of normalized femininity.

> You know, I think the women have the big *arma,* weapon. Because when I go to the City Council, some man is talking, and don't put [their] attention [on me]. And so I showed my face, I gave him a big smile, and he turned his face and he start[ed] to hear. So I think that one can use, maybe, the smile. I think that the woman has, like, this special tool.

While Yolanda believed that women could compel men to listen with the *arma* of a smile—of feminine warmth and kindness—others more often conceded that one had to deploy a combination of both affirmation and criticism. Cambodian immigrant and LBACA staff member Tina shared, "I like to let people know if they're doing good and let them know if they're doing bad, so if you're going, like, negative and negative all the time, it's not going to be effective." Others tried to enact "female nice" so as to curry political favor while they quietly seethed under the surface. When, for instance, I queried

Laura about her opinion of the Air Quality Management District, the exchange went as follows:

> LAURA: My opinion is that they're not doing a good job.
>
> NADIA: Do they care?
>
> LAURA: No, they don't care, . . . or maybe they care, but it's like the same thing: they care more about economics.
>
> NADIA: Do you feel like you have to be nice to them to get what you want from them? Or angry, or some other treatment?
>
> LAURA: Not angry, yeah. . . . Well, actually, my only feeling is strong, and *frustrated, and angry. So it's hypocritical* (*hipocrita*) . . . when I say, "Oh, hello" (gestures a forced smile), actually, I feel bad [for being fake].

Laura's conflicting thoughts about the government are apparent here. At first, she seems to state unequivocally that the state regulator of air pollution, the SCAQMD, does not care, but upon second thought, qualifies, "or maybe they care [but] they care more about economics." In turn, she says her emotional delivery during public comments is "not angry" but then says that she, in fact, is angry—that her hypocrisy makes her feel guilty. In light of the complex emotional power dynamics between state-corporate institutions and marginalized immigrants on the ground, it is no surprise that activists demonstrate internal conflict—conflict over condemning the state (as "evil") or having hope in its acquiescence (they have some "good guys"), over whether to perform "female nice" or righteous anger, and over whether women should feel guilty for feeling so much rage.

Men in Their Feelings

While the women constituted the vast majority of the membership of the CBOs, more of the founders and formal CBO leaders were Asian American and Latino men. Although this is a relic of a patriarchal past in which men predominated over social movements, men still have to negotiate with the women, lest they lose all of their community soldiers. As it was mostly the women, not the men, who chose to fuse emotions and politics in varied ways, the women indelibly influenced the men (see Pardo 1998). To be sure, sometimes the women conformed to traditional masculinist forms of leadership, such as Kelly of PCORE, a Black American woman and teacher. To this point, she noted, "They [the officials] don't really listen, they seem more driven by money. I guess we kind of have to be nice, but I don't really like doing that. I think PCORE [which had a female leader at the time] needs to be more in your face and stand up to those folks stronger, like Coalition for a Safe Environment does [whose male leader is known for railing at the officials]." Despite the predominant view of masculinist righteous anger as wielding the most influence, it was the Asian and Latina immigrant women who taught the men how important it was to express alternative emotions—albeit alongside anger—at public comments. That is, compelled by the searing, heartfelt testimonies of the women, the male organizers, learning by their example, began to wax eloquent about the emotional toll of being sick and of shouldering the burden of having to prove oneself sick to the powers that be. For instance, at a Metro LA study session in August 2012 in which Metro compared all the possible I-710 expansion alternatives to doing no expansion (the "No Build" option), Jesse, the outspoken male leader of CFASE, interjected, "All of what you said is based on the HRA [the Health Risk Assessment], which are projections, but you didn't do any baseline studies, you don't have any raw data, you didn't do a public health survey, you chose not to do a Health Impact Assessment [this was before Metro LA conceded this]; where do my friends and nephew fit into all your calculations?" Invoking his loved ones—friends and young nephew—was an emotional strategy straight out of the playbook of historic maternal politics and the gendered politics of the women who fought the good fight with him.

Youth leader Tomas was also highly attuned to the women's emotional labor and how crucial it was to movement building. He shared some of the emotional labor he performed that many of the female activists typically took care of.

> I'm very proud of the youth and very proud of the students. And it was also my commitment to them. If they needed a ride, I'd better be there. If they needed food—'cause some students weren't eating—I'd be like, "Okay, let's get a burrito." Some students were having challenges with relationships, like, you know, I'm no one's therapist or counselor, but I think sometimes we just have to listen to the youth and let them vent. Let them be creative.

Both Jesse and Tomas demonstrate that they are much beyond one-note emotional actors—in other words, they are exemplars not just of the angry or militant revolutionary man but of the multifaceted movement man. Without my specific prompting, for instance, Jesse began waxing poetic about his existential philosophies on life and how he expressed them in a manner much beyond political frustration, resentment, or rage.

> These are universal concepts that I've learned from my Buddhism, from my Taoism, from my Islam (laughs). I have [my writings] on family, in politics when in Mexico they went in and massacred all these males that were protesting, you know. And Chiapas: when I read the [news]paper and had the pictures of all the Indian mothers or wives or sisters with the caskets, you know, it just hit me! And so I write things. I write poetry and prose.

While Jesse most often emoted vexation and rage when he challenged state-corporate entities, he cast into relief that he was by no means emotionally singular when it came to his politics.

Some of the male environmental justice leaders, however, also detected the ways in which hegemonic femininity (Pyke and Johnson 2003) might bear costs for the women in ways they did not for the men. Unequivocal about the gender order at play, PCORE leader Ben—who earlier said that the elites would have to "be made of stone *not* to care about" the women—identified the gendered double standard in public testimonies with crystal clarity. Here, Ben explains why the women would ultimately be ignored, even discriminated against, because they spoke a political language that the mostly male officials derided and an ethnic language that elites deemed inferior, foreign, or both: Spanish or Asian-accented English.

> I think for the most part they don't really listen to women, I think especially if they're not speaking their *language of business* or just their like *capitalist language.* But I think maybe women have a stronger tendency to speak more about, you know, not necessarily business language but business affecting my family, business affecting my community. . . . It has a lot to do with organizing because you have to actually listen to the community and connect with people on a one-on-one [basis]—like, you actually have to care about people—whereas if you are a man in a patriarchal society, that's considered a weakness. You know, you [a male] might be militant, you know, you might want to bring down the system per se, but that is still a violent way to necessarily connect with people. . . .

He traced such top-down response patterns to the women's centering of feminized language of personal and familial struggles over the masculine-speak of business and money (and "hard" science and technocracy, I would add). Relative to men, the women were discreditable as too "female" and "soft." He ends this interjection by critiquing male activists such as himself for identifying with, and enacting, a masculine politics of militancy and violence over that of vulnerability, pain, nurturance, family ties, and prioritization of community ties. Of course, not all of the men valued militancy and violence and not all of the women valued personal relationships and cooking, yet such is the patterned product of gender socialization under patriarchy. At the same time, most of the women's preference for anger as their strategy of choice roundly rejected feminized stereotyping and convention. As their more profound influence on US politics than their husbands attests, these were by no means "typical women."

Fear among the Fearless

It is important to emphasize that many of the women did not immediately realize their capacity to tell the government and corporate America their truth, whether that was through tears, pointed fingers, or clenched smiles. Owing to the power ploys of the state and big business—much of which were predicated on "hegemonic emotional domination," passive-aggression, and borderline manipulation—the system often stoked acute fear and insecurity in the cadre of community organizers who tended to be more reserved, shy, and inexperienced. Of course, such emotional hegemony could never be divorced from the White supremacy and nativist racism, capitalism and class inequality, patriarchy, and ableism that propped it up. Upon my querying Laura, for instance, whether she had involved her children in her organizing with CPC and LBACA, she replied as follows:

LAURA: They just say, "Mom, I don't want to be there. I don't want someone to ask us something!"

NADIA: Oh, because they're afraid that someone will ask them something they don't know the answer to?

LAURA: Mhm.

NADIA: Are they afraid to speak in public, in front of a group?

LAURA: Yeah.

NADIA: Even though you're doing it? *You're* doing it.

LAURA: Yeah, but *I'm afraid. I'm still afraid—*

NADIA (surprised): Really? And what do you wish the young generations would do on these issues of health and environmental contamination?

LAURA: Well, I want them to fight for it. . . . They have the opportunity. *They are from here—sometimes because of language, I hold back*—but they have a future and they can do it. *They have more education.* . . . Because there are times when *I want to say many things, but I'm afraid that I will be questioned and I won't know how to respond.* So, I wish I had the capacity to do it well. *Sometimes I can't do it.* Also, for example, I am not afraid of someone because they're influential or wealthy and I'm not; that isn't why. *I'm afraid because this person is highly educated and I'm not.* For that reason, I feel like I can't win when we are debating. I wish I knew more . . . knew all the language and technical stuff.

Laura's comments shocked me. Laura probably knew more about the environmental injustices in her community than anyone I had met. Certainly, she could not speak English fluently, but translators were almost always available at public comments owing precisely to the demands of residents like her. While, to be sure, Laura was soft-spoken and more genteel in her affect, to hear her say that she was always afraid to speak because she felt so much less knowledgeable than the officials was nowhere close to actuality, in my view. No one knew the residential area and the pollution sources, hot spots, and types like her. Yet Laura's self-silencing was precisely a product of the biopolitical state suffusing its own discursive knowledge with the authoritative, normalizing, and disciplining tendencies that, in turn, marginalized Laura's own discursive knowledge. To them, her "street" power-knowledge was more embodied, amateur, and emotional than the numeric, technocratic, scientist-endorsed data of the elites. She is quick to point out that their wealth and her working-class poverty were not what struck her with fear, it was their *knowledge*. And knowledge was always raced and classed, which Laura invokes by using her children to summon the wages of approximate White Americanness and (upper) middle-classness: they're from here, they speak English, they're more educated—so they can and I can't.

On an affective scale, Laura was also saying that those "who can" should lack fear, while those "who cannot" tend to inhabit it, no matter how divorced from reality is the "cannot" (Laura's deep well of knowledge). Yet add the layer of adolescent inexperience and immaturity to systems of nativist racism and classism, and Laura's children were themselves silenced by insecurity and fear. Not only did Laura's children mute their own voices—"I don't want someone to ask us something!"—but it weighed heavily on the minds of even seasoned, committed youth leaders. Bella, for instance, narrated similar feelings from early in her activist career:

BELLA: I remember the second time there were a lot of people and I was just kind of nervous and I was kind of shaky, but I noticed when someone else went up and they sounded really, really afraid and shaky, I didn't want to do that. So, I just went up, and looked up, and said, "Okay, I'm going to say this and I'm going to try not to be scared—

NADIA: What do you think the agencies do when they see some of you guys shaking? (chuckles)

BELLA: I don't know what they think. But they might think, "Okay, they're nervous and they don't know what they're saying." And then, one time, this [young] guy lost his train of thought and he was like, "Uhhhhhhhhh—uhhhhhhhhhhh—ummmmmmmm." And it went on for about a minute! . . . I was like, "*Someone please help him.*"

Not only did elite discourse strike the fear of God into Bella, but she was consumed by the embarrassment and tragedy of another teenager from her neighborhood stammering nothing but "uh—uh—ummmm" into the mic for what felt like an eternity in front of a group of largely (upper)-middle-class White male US citizens who likely recycled stereotypes of working-class Latino male youth in their heads as he failed to articulate. Miguel, Bella's brother who fought the good fight alongside his sister, also shared a rather dissonant moment in which he was so nervous about his own power-knowledge that he nearly ran out of the room right before they called his name. Yet toward the end of the exchange below, he repeats what he had said to the suited representatives and as I listened, I could not distinguish between his words and those of the sixty-year-old organizers who had been at it nearly their whole lives.

MIGUEL: I was nervous. . . . The first time I was like, "Oh my God." One time I flipped out: I was, like, I'm not doing it. Then once I started talking, it comes out and then after, I feel good about it, because they were actually listening to me, and at the same time, you hope they actually take it in and not just ignore you.

NADIA: Yeah, well, first, what did you say to them, if you can summarize briefly what you said?

MIGUEL: [F]or the clean air, . . . I would tell them that every time we look up, there are refineries next to [us residents]. Then they are trying to do the railyard extension and that's going to be worse: fuel-burning trucks are going to stop by here more often, and it's going to pollute the air. There are a lot of people with asthma there, and one of my cousins ended up being diagnosed with cancer. . . . It was a scary thing.

Taken together, the politics of emotion that these grassroots organizers laid bare involve sadness, depression, anger, disgust, resolve, passion, fear, self-doubt. One may quip, But aren't these feelings just individualized, visceral, and ephemeral? Hochschild (1979) and Ahmed (2004) say a resounding no. Emotions, instead, are always social structures that connect individuality to the collective and are structures of power embedded in social systems, institutions, and cultures, not mere ephemeral forms of visceral embodiment. The activists whom we have met thus far point to why emotive structures matter in the political sphere at all.

In March of 2018, four-and-a-half years after I left the field, I was stunned to learn that, regarding the I-710, LA Metro had decided to punt the $6 billion decision of "to widen or not to widen" indefinitely. Certainly, community pressure from the AAPI and Latin@ immigrants was a potent factor. At the same time, one could argue that LA Metro, the Air Quality Management District, and corporations have done little to mitigate the fundamental problems in (low-income, undocumented) communities of color like theirs (such as the disproportionate placement of freeways and oil refineries within). Sparing them a freeway expansion that would simply worsen their lot in life did not seem like a major victory, though the delayed decision-making about it is certainly a laudable one.

* * *

The dialectic relationship between dominant and subordinate emotional structures has not been sufficiently studied. Although emotional life is a key form of embodiment—as thoughts shape and frame our emotions—Foucault himself did not center emotional knowledge, power, and politics in his framework. Although he addressed it as an outcome (or incidental part) of discursive processes, the activists show that it is *a driver and anchor of biopower contests.*

The Angeleno immigrants here revealed that the institutionalization of emotions in EJ fights seemed to help perpetuate gender, race, and class ideologies; discourse; and discrimination as well as justify policy decisions that, too, reified systems based on these axes. Beyond the elites' "feeling rules" that marked the women as too emotional and irrational, the elites could have easily deemed the Asian American women as "effeminate," "moms," unentitled, and "model minorities." In other words, the crying or soft-spoken Asian-descent female (or male) activist extends from the put-your-head-down, passive caricature of the model minority mythology (Espiritu 1997); as a passive caricature, "model minorities" have also been rendered invisible in the political sphere (see Lien 2001). Sans the model minority mythology, the elites seemed to have similar biases against the Latina activists as "effeminate," "moms," and unentitled (Pardo 1998). It was also the Latin@s' unauthorized and working-class immigrant status that crystallized their "effeminacy" and their unentitled status (ibid.).

At the same time, the women's other marked form of emotional delivery—anger—could affirm (White) America's prevailing masculine "dragon lady" trope of the angry Asian hothead and the long-standing view of Asian ethnic men as brooding patriarchs (Espiritu 1997). Similarly, the angry emotional delivery of a Latina ethnic affirmed the masculinized "fiery Latina" stereotype while that of a Latino man was redolent of "hypermasculine" machismo (see Chavez 2008, 2017; Gutmann 1996). In the same vein, the passive male activists became the well-worn trope of the effeminate, emasculated Asian man (Espiritu 1997). And, per the yellow-brown peril, both Asian American women and men could be *masculinized* by mainstream race-gender discourse (see ibid.).

Just as gender is a key dimension of emotive processes along the vertical axis—between the corporatist state that monopolizes power from above and the marginalized communities who fight for power from below—it is of signal importance along the horizontal axis as well. That is to say, gender did not merely figure in when the vast majority of community organizers were women and the majority of the elites were (White) men, it was also horizontally salient insofar as many of the male (co)founders and leaders of the CBOs were (coethnic) men. Although in Chapter 5 I will address some of the fissures among Asian American women and men and among Latin@ women and men, here I seek to underscore that the women were much more variegated, nuanced, and strategic when it came to their emotional presentations. While men were admittedly more limited or singular with respect to emotional life, they paid attention to, and learned from, the women the value of deploying emotions into political processes as well as marshalling them to recruit for the movement and to build community by stepping into the empathy gap.

By broadly analyzing the emotive *dialectic* between top-down and bottom-up political actors, I introduce a dynamic that is rarely studied but of enormous social consequence nonetheless. By reproducing the emotive dimensions of power, the elites reinforce one of the tenets of institutionalized racism: that people of color are more embodied and emotional; White America, by contrast, is more mental, "rational," and thus civil—a hallmark of race superiority (Collins 2000). By virtue of the mind-body split that originated historically in the Enlightenment and that has served power well since, the mostly White male politicians, agency officials, and corporate representatives construct themselves as calmly rational, even when they are emotionally aberrant or inappropriate per norms of emotion work ("You're not the only ones who get cancer!"). What is more, the officials couple their "non-emotionality" with their discursive power-knowledge, the "superior" mental state legitimized by scientific studies from in-house or contracted researchers and from other forms of technocracy (read: *not* "emotional stories"). Hence, such a false dichotomy (Moore and Kosut 2010) has also calcified White male superiority. In other words, the split justifies the frequent policy decisions of inaction and minor concession-making endemic to racism and sexism, whether it concerns the environment, housing, education, or health care. To be sure, concessions are also the product of state regulatory agencies and corporations not wanting to be forced to go all the way.

At the same time, this dialectic of emotional power afforded resistance from the bottom up, especially from those whom the state sequestered and refused to offer legal peace of mind. As Zepeda-Millán (2017:17) contends,

> [W]hen broadened and racialized, legislative threats against disenfranchised undocumented immigrants can provoke a political backlash—on the streets

> and at the ballot box—against those deemed responsible for the attacks, not only from people without papers but also electorally armed naturalized- and U.S.-born citizens. Depending on the type of threat and the degree to which they feel under attack, activists can rouse racialized immigrants and their descendants to use nativist actions as a heuristic that prods increased political participation.

This chapter sought to center the emotional dimensions of this backlash. As the deliberate emotional strategies of the Asian Americans and Latin@s bear out, their demands for normative emotion work, such as empathy and respect, poked holes in top-down emotive strategies. The women's affect and demands also showed that they are not bound by the anti-emotion and anti-anger ethos of, and binarization of emotion and rationality in, American society (Gould 2009; Fonow and Franzway 2016; Johnson 2017). Therefore, it would be remiss to underappreciate the activists' emotive strategies as a form of resistance. When the women and children in particular make the elite officials look like heartless people made of stone, the officials are aware that they have to save face so as not to look like "racist xenophobes" and misogynists per post-1970s liberal discourse. When the residents yell in frustration at the officials, they are genuinely enraged over the fact that their lives could be free of the assaults of environmental injustice if the powers-that-be would just stop oppressing. The subtext of their angry testimony is typically, "You may not respect what I say, but you will respect me." They are unapologetic about their Asian and Latin@ (female) racial uniform, their Asian-accented English or their Spanish, and their perceived weak (or nonexistent) political legacy in the United States. They operate on the belief that, just as most people have to begrudge some respect to those who respect themselves, so must the elite officials begrudge it to them. After all, the officials *do react, even if the reactions are eye-rolls and justifications for inaction.* As this chapter sought to show, we are in dire need of more studies on these dialectical kinds of emotive and embodied dimensions of collective mobilization and political process, in part so that immigrants everywhere do not have to shoulder the (emotional) burden of fighting the power alone any longer. In the next chapter we turn our attention to how, among the Asian and Latin@ immigrant change-makers, environmental justice has profoundly informed conceptions of the body and embodiment and has textured emotionality.

CHAPTER 3

EVERY BODY MATTERS

LILIANA: I used to have pain, since I was a little girl. I remember the first time that I got sick; I think the emotions have a lot to do with [being] sick. . . . And I remember the time that my father was drunk, and he was trying to wield a weapon, trying to follow my mom with a gun. My mother ran away, and he was like throwing chairs and everything. And I remember, since that time, I was sick. I had stomach pain and I was really constipated. And that's the first time I got pain in my colon. I was like, maybe, seven.

NADIA: Oh, I'm so, so sorry—

LILIANA: It's okay (voice breaks). And um, the next time that I had [health] problems was when my family was murdered [by a family enemy], and also the thing [the sexual assault of me] happened. And then when we came here [to the US] in 1997, I got pain, I don't remember why, all I remember that I was really stressed because there was a lot of raids, immigration raids—

When Liliana said, "I think the emotions have a lot to do with [being] sick," not only was she prioritizing emotions and the body, but she was interconnecting them; one's emotional state reared itself in the physical health of one's body. Also worthy of note is the litany of tragic experiences to which she attributes her pain—physical and emotional. Although her effort to maintain emotional calm prevented her from filling in the details—and thus my understanding of her hardships were murky at best—she lists the causes of her chronic stomach pains, which she would later discover, once she finally accessed health insurance, to be Crohn's disease: her alcoholic, abusive father, the violent murder of him alongside her uncle and cousin, the sexual assault that was too painful to name ("the thing"), and the intensive INS (Immigration and Naturalization Service) immigration raids that greeted her after her arduous migration trek north. It was not lost on her that the personal and political dimensions of her life were never separate, just as her emotions and her body were not: she vehemently opposed the patriarchy she and her mother suffered at the hands of her family and Mexican society, an oppressive system that also socialized a man in her life to sexually assault her. And, as we will discover throughout this book, nativist racism such as INS raids consummately worried immigrants like Liliana, who plainly remarks that they stressed her out so badly that she spoke of them in the same breath as her chronic pain. Scholars such as Martinez, Ruelas, and Granger (2018) validate that nativist racism indeed causes illness, as they found that fear of deportation increased unauthorized immigrants' propensity for chronic disease. In an inverse statement of the famous mantra, the political is the personal.

I was similarly struck by an embodied analogy that youth leader Tomas offered to describe his Long Beach and Wilmington community. Articulating in intensely embodied terms, Tomas conveys the defeatism and cynicism that pervade an oppressed community to the point of fear, inaction, apathy, and keeping others down. Waxing poetic, Tomas remarked,

> There's a lot of youth out there, especially teens of color who walk with their heads down, that are scared—scared because mom is undocumented or dad is beating up on mom . . . or we're "criminals" and we're "mules" because we're illegal, we're demasculinized, desexualized, we're [de]humanized on all levels. . . . Because the air is so bad and the pollution is always there, the fight is always there—really, just finding those ninth and tenth graders, and helping them develop leadership and radicalism and getting them agitated, because a

> lot of the cynicism [is there], I call it *"the cancer of the community"*; or sometimes those parents who are just like "¿Para qué?," you know, "For what? We're all going to die [anyway]. Oh, Maria or Mary, what do you think you're going to do? Change the world?" like that cancer: *the crab in the bucket where one is trying to get out and the other pulls them back in.* . . . We have to protect the youth from that *cancer* of negative cynicism and fatalism.

In this analogy replete with embodied references, Tomas invokes Latina bodies being domestically abused and Latino bodies being emasculated, desexualized, and dehumanized. He proffers a transcorporeal metaphor of a cancerous body to denote how cynicism and apathy kill political progress and a chance at social justice. Specifically, he sees a defeated community in the sentient workings of a crab who ensures another's death by pulling it back in the bucket, just as a cancer kills the body and, metaphorically, the communal body. In other words, cynical and fatalistic immigrants of color not only immobilized themselves politically, but immobilized others.

Although this chapter focuses on the body, Liliana's tragic story and Tomas's analogy are emblematic of how important the body and emotions are to the activists in identifying the causes of environmental, immigration, and education injustices: in their eyes, the ultimate culprits being racism and/or classism. How day-to-day experiences of neoliberal bioneglect inform this kind of embodied thinking is the focus of this chapter. Tomas's eloquent analogy on the embodied nature not just of racism but of sexism and sexuality, at times through animal metaphors (such as crabs), is a lucid example. The focus here on the "everyday" of bioneglect and how this fosters an embodied discourse sets up the rest of the book's focus on the immigrants' resistance movement for breathable air; more specifically, it is an introduction to their insistence on a political boundary of "embodied community" and a political strategy centered in "embodied citizenship"—and why these were their politics of choice. More broadly, what I seek to show in the pages that follow is that top-down and bottom-up processes are not fixed and discrete but are perpetually maneuvering with, through, and around each other.

The interplay of materialist dominance, the subjectivity of the margins, and resistance movements—all underappreciated by Foucault—frame the narratives that we are about to engage. Namely, the immigrants demonstrated a hypersensitivity to embodiment, not just in terms of the maladies their bodies carried, but in how their bodies were immobilized, rendered unattractive and unprofessional, and not cared for in the aftermath of disease and cancer; as we shall see later in the book, this suffering and sentiment animate why the activists place a premium on taking care of each other's neglected bodies. To understand what exactly they and their (extended) families are embodying and thus rendering as "community," it is imperative that we hear their stories and their own interpretations of how environmental injustice (as well as education injustice and immigration surveillance) are intrinsic parts of their daily lives and those of the children they love and teach. In other words, in order to grasp the subjects of this study and their lived experience, we must ourselves try somehow to embody what these immigrants of color embody. After all, the racing, gendering, sexualizing, and classing of their bodies has been the bane of their existence for all of their lives; thus it stands to reason that they would start with embodiment as the source of their pushback, subversion, and political resistance.

A SELECT HISTORY OF ASIAN AND LATIN@ EMBODIMENT

In the case of Asian Americans, Nayan Shah (2001) demonstrated that racist views of the Chinese body were the fulcrum for state denial of Chinese entry into the ports and bounty of 1800s America. State denial hinged on health inspections that presupposed Chinese bodies to be infected with the animal-like diseases that foreign, exotic bodies like theirs "naturally" carried. Raced, gendered, and sexualized discursive tropes undergirded federal immigration bans, such as the 1875 Page Act that forbade Chinese women entry for being ostensible "Mongolian prostitutes" sullied by sexually transmitted "diseases" and the 1882 Chinese Exclusion Act, which barred the mostly male Chinese laborers who would get infected by, and reproduce with, these supposedly throwaway women.

Extending from Natalia Molina's (2013) argument that Asian and Latin@ ethnics were, at times, racialized together in the service of hegemonic White supremacy, both groups were also subject to the terror of medical racialization. Per the 1875 Page Act, the 1882 Chinese Exclusion Act, and an 1891 law stipulating that immigrants carrying "a loathsome and dangerous contagious disease" were "likely to become a public charge," Asian and Mexican immigrants became justifiably deportable. The late nineteenth- and early twentieth-century zeitgeist was that "good American citizens" were wholly independent while racialized immigrants were dependent, especially those seen as diseased and thus ineligible to belong, even with legal papers in hand (Molina 2013:119).

Historically, Asian Americans have occupied a unique position in this racial project, as White America defined them as more embodied than rational up until the 1960s, when Asian Americans, namely those of South and East origins, were popularly redefined as intelligent "model minorities." Yet alongside and mutually constitutive of the model minority mythology is the racialized foreigner positioning of Asian ethnics (when the Asians become too model at what they do, that is when we act on our perceived threat: beat up, exclude, deport, and kill those model bodies [N. Kim 2008a, 2008b]). Furthermore, the model minority mythology kills softly when preexisting notions of Asian Americans' nonracialized existence (as the "good" minority) and a growing transnational elite class of Asian professionals delegitimize Southeast Asian refugees' need for public assistance; more dangerously, it hides the dominant American discourse that Asian "foreigners" are undeserving of it.[1]

To highlight body politics against the Latin@ population, here I focus on the sterilization campaigns against Mexican immigrant women in the United States. In line with modern biopolitics, Gutiérrez (2008:11) writes in *Fertile Matters* that "the concern about the fertility of Mexican women was wholeheartedly adopted by those associated with eugenic efforts." The significance of the eugenics movement in the racist treatment of Mexican ethnics and all people of color, especially the sterilization of women and even men, cannot be overdrawn. Historian Alexandra Minna Stern found that laws enforcing sterilization were the product of the joint efforts of medical superintendents, legislators, and social reformers affiliated with the eugenics movement emergent in the early twentieth century. She also found that sterilization was buoyed by the Supreme Court in its 1927 *Buck v. Bell* decision whereby thirty-two US states had passed prosterilization laws between 1907 and 1937, with surgeries reaching their highest numbers in the later part of those years. Capitalizing on empty, sinister theories of the wholesale inheritance of traits such as congenital feeblemindedness, pauperism, mental disability, sexual promiscuity, criminality, and dwarfism—often racialized to target immigrants and people of color—sterilizers targeted mental institutions (Stern 2015). Most of these operations took place until the 1960s and in the state of California, where one-third of the sixty thousand sterilizations in the United States occurred (ibid.). Stern's dataset of nearly twenty thousand patient records revealed that the majority of those sterilized were the sons and daughters of Mexican, Japanese, and Italian immigrants, typically those with parents too destitute to care for them. During the peak decade of operations—1935 to 1944—Spanish-surnamed patients were three-and-a-half times more likely to be sterilized than patients in the general institutional population (ibid.).[2] This owes in part to proponents of the Americanist agenda (1915–1929) focusing their efforts on assimilating Mexican immigrant women and their children into (White) American culture (Ruiz 1998:38, cited in Gutiérrez 2008); those who did not fit in this frame were undesirable. As with most "controlling images," a large, complex, diverse group—in this case, Mexican women—were defined by one role: "[a]n exaggerated 'super-mother' figure: . . . the unceasingly self-sacrificing, dedicated, ever-fertile woman totally without aspiration for self or initiative to do other than reproduce" (Andrade 1982:229, cited in Gutiérrez 2008:12).

Beginning in the 1970s, state legislatures began to repeal the sterilization laws owing to charges of discrimination, particularly against those with disabilities; that would not be the case for Mexican-descent women, however (Stern 2015). In fact, it was the early 1970s when another wave of sterilizations would target Mexican American and other women of color—native-born and immigrant. Besides racist ideologies of the reproductive excess of Mexican women's bodies, structural factors facilitating coercive sterilization involved physicians' free license to perform illegal procedures without any monitoring or oversight, increased federal funding for sterilization procedures, a low-income non-English-speaking clientele, and medical professionals' exploitation of demographic research that found the national population to be growing because of Mexican ethnic women's "high fertility remnants" (while "Anglos and Jews" were reproducing at replacement level) (Gutiérrez 2008:51).[3] Worse, mass media news reports often depicted Mexican-descent women as devious, calculating, and dishonorable, the "foreigners" who abandoned their newborn babies on the US side of the border or falsely registered them as US-born ("False Registration"; "Born on Border"; compare Gutiérrez 2008:53).[4]

The case of *Madrigal v. Quilligan* involved systematic, premeditated practices of the LA County Medical Center (LACMC) aggressively pushing IUDs onto the women immediately after birth, who would in turn have to forego their postpartum checkups or their questions about their baby and health given the IUD procedure.[5] The coercion techniques to rope the recovering mothers into signing the sterilization orders were also legion. As Gutiérrez (2008) writes, "The doctor would hold a syringe in front of the mother who was in labor pain and ask her if she wanted a pain killer; while the woman was in the throes of a contraction the doctor would say, 'Do you want the pain killer? Then sign the papers. Do you want the pain to stop? Do you want to have to go through this again? Sign the papers'" (44).[6] Gutiérrez also found that in a San Diego hospital, "one resident would be so furious if a woman declined (sterilization) that he would say, 'We know you're here illegally and if you don't consent to have a tubal, we'll call the feds [immigration officials] and get you deported'" (58). Boys were also sterilized. As Stern (2015) found, in 1943 a fifteen-year-old Mexican American boy was committed to the Sonoma State Home, an institution for the "feebleminded" in Northern California, after he was picked up by the police for a string of minor infractions. Stern found that he was sterilized for his "borderline" IQ score of 75 and record of delinquency.

CONNECTING TO THE BODIES OF MORE RECENT HISTORY

For Asian Americans, White America's primary concern was with their physical bodies until the racialization of Asian-descent people as smart and potentially smarter than Whites ratcheted up concern about their mental capacities. Per the discourse and institutionalized racism and sexism of the advanced West, the state's fear of the "Asian mind" manifested both in Britain's and the United States's concerns over China's potential global prowess in the Opium Wars and in uneven trans-Pacific trade; the potential power of the "Asian mind" spawned America's fear of Japan's ability to paint the world yellow with its "Jap" empire. This accounted for the fear of Japanese Americans being smart enough to help the emperor nation thousands of miles away in its imperial endeavors—hence, the United States government chose to mass incarcerate the Americans of Japanese descent as wartime enemies (though, not Americans of German or Italian descent), all without due process and probable cause. In the same vein, the US fomented the fear of a Japanese takeover of

America's vaunted car industry, as expressed in the "Buy American" campaigns and in 1980s scenes of "real Americans" each taking a turn bashing a Japanese car with the same speed and force that two White male Chrysler employees bashed in Vincent Chin's brains on a fateful summer night in Detroit. Although fears of Asian-origin people as viruses and infections have never gone away, the fear of the "superior" Asian American mind culminated, of course, in the journalistic rollout of the model minority mythology around the 1960s[7] and its popularization by the Reagan administration in the 1980s, in large part to discredit the claims of institutionalized racism by Latin@s, first nations, and Black and Asian ethnics, expressed via the Brown Power, Red Power, civil rights, Black Power, and Yellow Power movements. Fear of Asian ethnics using their "too model" minds was also manifest in the illegal weighting of Asian American applicants' verbal standardized test scores by elite universities such as Brown, Stanford, and UC Berkeley to keep their campuses predominantly White (Takagi 1993). It reared its ugly head when, absent of any basis or evidence, the US government feared nuclear physicist Wen Ho Lee's smarts were being used to benefit China and not the Stars and Stripes (never mind that Lee was Taiwanese). It is precisely a testament to the power of racialization and racial scripts that elite institutions can condemn the part of the body below the head and then switch to what is in the head whenever it feels that racial projects necessitate it, or whenever they simply feel their racial power and standing are threatened.

Throughout Mexican Americans' time here, White America's fixation has been on their bodies below the head. As an example, Seth Holmes (2013) conducted an embodied anthropology through which he crossed borders illegally, picked strawberries, and languished in jail cells with Mexican labor migrants, noting that US agribusiness, the US government, and the US health care industry naturalized the breaking of their bodies. Although these very workers fed California, the nation, and the world, nativist racism culminated in the 1990s when Governor Pete Wilson ginned up hatred of Mexican immigrants, women especially. Taking a page out of history's playbook, one of Wilson's signal demagogic weapons was a dubious 1991 report alleging that two-thirds of newborns at Los Angeles County hospitals were born to undocumented women; Mexican and Central American women became his "Willy Horton." Amplifying racist and sexist nativism, Wilson also charged undocumented "hyperfertile" Latinas with abusing and overextending an ostensibly generous welfare system (Fujiwara 2008:7), never mind the much higher price for corporate welfare or the fact that federal programs (with the exception of emergency health care, immunizations, WIC [nutritional assistance for poor women, infants, and children], and education) have never been available to undocumented immigrants (see Chavez 2008, 2017). Facts did not matter when they could be supplanted by images of Latinas crossing the border to have their children on the US side, receiving US taxpayer-funded medical care in the process and being dehumanized as "dangerous waters" who would wash out Anglo culture and dominance (Santa Ana 2002, cited in Fujiwara 2008). Indeed, this race- and gender-baiting enabled Wilson to get Proposition 187 on the ballot and to convince California voters to pass it, effectively denying nonemergent health care (including reproductive services), education, and public benefits to the immigrant population that kept California and the nation running. Finally, Chavez (2008) highlighted a less-known but chilling controversy over an unauthorized Latina immigrant who was unable to receive an organ transplant: rather than the American public expressing compassion for the patient and her family, many expressed outrage that an "illegal" was in line to get an organ at all. These emotional battles over who is entitled to an "American" body part are tantamount to questioning who can be an American citizen to begin with; Chavez thereby addresses the emotional side of citizenship in a way that race and immigration social scientists rarely do. The biopolitics of the undocumented immigrant body are also evident in the medical repatriation of these immigrants when they are unable to cover the cost of medical treatment (ibid.). After three decades of potentially the most anti-immigrant policies since the 1980s era in US history (Chavez 2017), the "Latino threat narrative" (ibid.) manifests still today in the threat of the big non-White family and the specter of [White] race suicide; in Trump's epithets that if you let one in, then you have to bring over their mom, dad, aunt, cousin, and so on; and in the bogeyman of the Mexican rapist, the strawman of Trumpian demagoguery.[8]

To be sure, when biopower in the form of sexualized and gendered racism rears its ugly head and razor-sharp scalpels and baseball bats, the margins, like the immigrants of this book, tend to rise up. For instance, when Chinese immigrants experienced medical racism at Angel Island and in San Francisco

Chinatown, the Chinese YMCA protested the laws and, in the vein of gender egalitarianism, argued for the protection of Chinese women in addition to men (Molina 2013:78).[9] As well, the antisterilization movement led by social justice warriors such as Esther Talavera sued the LACMC hospital and conducted an educational and public health expose to Latin@ communities, a campaign Talavera deemed vital to the uplifting of the entire *raza.* In her article "Sterilization Is Not an Alternative in Family Planning," published in the National Council of La Raza's *Agenda* (1977), Talavera wrote, "Someday we may have as many children as we want when we want to have them, for that is an integral part of our decision to determine our destinies." Hers was an analysis connecting sterilization to broader human rights and social justice and a galvanizing cry for other Chicana efforts to promulgate sterilization regulations.

Attuned to the relational specificities of Mexican-origin women's social locations (see Moraga and Anzaldua 1981), Chicana feminist scholars have shown theoretically that not only do the women hold complex definitions and identities concerning motherhood, but as sexual beings they interpret reproductive matters variously. The nativist racist assaults against Latina female bodies as "overreproducers" and the navigation of multiple, complex notions of motherhood in that context were apparent among the Latina immigrant women in my study. For one, the nativist racism made them more unapologetic and prompted them to hold their children (and families, neighbors) closer. And, unlike popular depictions and much of the maternal politics scholarship, the women's politics in LA were not always animated by their mothering.

In the wake of the infamous case of Vincent Chin—a Chinese American man being bludgeoned to death for being mistaken for a Japanese ethnic and for being "responsible" for the entire Japanese auto industry—Asian ethnic groups felt the inexorable need to intervene politically and to do so as a panethnic, pan-Asian collective. Chin's murder at the bloody hands of Ron Ebens and his stepson Michael Nitz, who blamed Chin for Nitz's layoff by Chrysler (which itself blamed Japan's auto industry), galvanized Asian Americans. From Chinese and Japanese to Filipinx and South Asian ethnics—from Detroit and Milwaukee to New York and Los Angeles—Asian ethnics drew on their lifelong struggles to recognize their vulnerability to being murdered for embodying a foreign competitive threat and a non-White economic scapegoat. Thus was born the major wave of Asian American organizing after the revolutionary movements of the 1960s and 1970s.

At the same time, Rachel Lee (2014) critiques Asian Americanists' theorizing and treatment of agency as if it were a "sovereign-like" power. The concomitant move away from "teleological certainties" of a post-revolutionary utopia applies well to the Asian Americans (as well as Latin@s) of my study. Precisely because of these immigrants' marginal standpoint and their weak political power and visibility (and for the "illegal" Latin@s, lack of formal inclusion), neither group had any delusions about politics being monolithic at the top or at the bottom; nor were they illusory about issues of justice and injustice taking on sovereign-like proportions. Rather, they were often at their most comfortable, as we shall see, living in political contradiction and complexity.

THE HISTORY OF LA'S ENVIRONMENTAL (IN)JUSTICE EMBODIMENT

When in 1982 the band Missing Persons crooned "Nobody Walks in LA" it spoke to Angelenos (and those in nonwalkable cities everywhere) for good reason—it was essentially their embodied reality, except perhaps for Angelenos whose clean, available, wide sidewalks in their safe or gated communities afforded jogs and strolls in leg warmers and trendy sneakers. On the whole, not only is Los Angeles marked by its exclusive neighborhoods but also by its imposing octo-legged freeways, inadequate public transportation, the attenuation of genuinely public space, fortress-like malls and public buildings, and, in the words of Mike Davis (1990), "sadistic" street life for the houseless and the poor, a sadism much more severe today than Davis could have imagined in the 1980s. If a city could represent limited mobility for the carless, Los Angeles would be it. At a LBACA (Long Beach Alliance for Children with Asthma) meeting in summer of 2011, the meeting facilitators made sure to offer a history of being made sick and of blocked mobility, physically and socioeconomically—that is, of the embodied inequalities that had long plagued the City of Angels. For instance, at one of LBACA's many presentations to the community on the I-710 freeway expansion, it began not simply with the I-710, but with the not-so-subtle polemic, "History of the Lack of Input from Those Most Impacted." The "lack" of community "input" addressed the Urban Renewal of the 1950s and 1960s, which grew out of a top-down movement of federal housing acts that offered aid for the clearing of "urban blight." This meant clearing and pushing out the "blight" of six thousand segregated, low-income public housing residents, such as "Negroes" and Latinxs (many senior citizens), and replacing them with middle-class residential communities such as the "Bunker Hill Redevelopment Project" in which no monied person wanted to live anyway.[10]

LBACA also highlighted the infamous case of anti-Mexican racism in Chavez Ravine. The state had planned to turn this segregated low-income neighborhood into public housing for the Mexican Americans who lived there. Per land developers' stoking of antisocialist fears of government-funded projects (like housing) and their desire to plop Dodger Stadium on top of Chavez Ravine, they exploited the state's eminent domain clause to renege on the public housing project; instead, they razed the entire Mexican American community despite the protestors who stared down the bulldozers, until the police violently removed the residents' defiant bodies from their beloved homes and neighborhood. The Mexican Americans' last weapon, their resistant and flailing bodies, were not enough in the end.

LBACA then proceeded to the "Freeway Building Years" during which the most congested freeway exchanges were placed in low-income communities of color like theirs, hence LA's freeways being among the most racist of monuments; the city had also built the new I-105 freeway to Norwalk, California, which sparked protests, movements, and lawsuits, as most of the areas in the freeway's path in the 1970s (and thus slated to be demolished) were predominantly Black American. Community activists and their supporters, drawing on resentment from previous freeways that ran through Black communities, were able to significantly modify the original route.

Another watershed historical moment that LBACA covered was the Bus Riders Union lawsuit against LA's Metropolitan Transportation Authority (MTA). In 1992, under the leadership of Eric Mann and Manuel Criollo, the Labor/Community Strategy Center formed the Bus Riders Union to organize around what they considered the racial (and class) inequality at the heart of MTA transit policy, in other words, "transit racism." While at the Labor Center, both Mann and Criollo realized the impact of these inequities through their organizing against environmental racism, namely, the pollution from local oil refineries and from vehicles and freeways, and especially the problem of working-class people of color having to travel two to three hours from places like Wilmington to work in glitzier Los Angeles. Criollo noted, "That was a transformative moment for us. . . . The buses would have forty people sitting and forty people standing, no air conditioning, completely messed up. . . . And on Metrolink [which was reserved for affluent areas], people were riding like Disneyland." The Bus Riders Union was able to gain a court order injunction in 1996 that required the MTA to reform its bus service by devoting more funding to better bus service in communities of color. Since that time, MTA has purchased a new fleet of cleaner-burning natural-gas-fueled buses and established a "Rapid Bus" program. In line with this environmental justice history, LBACA made sure to include the other victories of the community, such as stopping the planned demolition of hundreds of houses, parks, schools, and other community assets (having learned from Bunker Hill).

At the end of the meeting, the leaders brought the presentation back to the present and invoked embodiment when they conveyed the connection between pollution and the physical-emotional states of the residents in the room. "Pollution causes stress," they noted, such as when increased noise pollution "causes stress, which then causes health problems." The same argument was also found in a flier that I had acquired from the local environmental justice coalition, which forged the connection between noise pollution and disease (as well as unhealthy conditions like stress). In various ways, the immigrants with whom I worked insisted that not only were their lungs, nostrils, eyes, and hearts hurt by disproportionate contamination, but so were their mental and emotional states. Worth noting is that over nearly three years of attending public comments, I never heard the words "stress and sensory overload" escape the lips of state regulators or corporate representatives. The community had to produce this embodied, discursive knowledge and vocalize it into the ether on their own. As testament to how all of these dimensions are related, the weak access to (good, regular) health care among the unauthorized also circumscribes their movements because they remain sick, often get worse, and literally have nowhere to go for solid medical help (or do not want to deal with the racial, cultural, anti-environmental bias of mainstream physicians [Gálvez 2011; see also Sims 2010[11]]). And sick people are not going to go outside into dirty air or where there are few places to walk, which can, in turn, be deleterious to good health.

Another focal point for LBACA and the Latin@ residents was their belief that the disproportionate contamination and underresourced schools in their communities were not just a product of being people of color. Long-time community leader Liliana, for instance, immediately invoked class bias when I asked her whether or not she thought political and corporate officials had stereotypes about Latinas like her. Liliana reasoned, "Why they do all the bad things [they do] is [because] wherever lives the low-income people, they [the officials] know they [the low income] don't know that much. Low income means the less money you have, I think, the less education you have, because it's hard for someone that doesn't have any education to send kids to college and make income." When I asked Celia whether she thought class- and race-based discrimination explained the numerous railyards, freeways, and refineries next to their homes, she replied by singling out class:

> In part it could be that they choose these areas where there are people of low income because they think that these people do not know their rights. On that basis they say that they are going to put this [air-polluting site] here and then they will just tell the people [that] they will put filters in the schools and then [supposedly] that takes care of the problem. . . . It can be because you can see, like, if I look at what classes are being offered at the local park, I'm not going to see guitar, piano, and ballet around here. They don't offer those classes. But if we go to wealthier areas . . . , there they do offer those classes.

Keenly concerned with her children's education and cultivation of talent, she lopped off the language of race to couch her views in terms of the "low income like herself" who are targeted for industrial contamination and excluded from the learning privileges of the higher classes. Education mattered most to her, as she considered academic achievement to be her child's ticket to overcoming the boot on the neck that is poverty, nativist racism, and unauthorized status.

Such a sensitivity to class (albeit not capitalism) was also learned from the discourse of the CBOs and grassroots leaders. Consider the following East Yard Communities for Environmental Justice (EYCEJ) flier:

> People with lower incomes have higher risks than people with higher incomes for poor health and premature mortality, for giving birth to low birth weight babies, for suffering injuries or violence, for getting most cancers, and for getting chronic conditions.[12]

In other words, in addition to racism, classism also explained why their community was sick, dying, more susceptible to violence, and birthing less healthy babies.

EMBODYING ILLNESS

At its broadest and most basic, embodiment is living in, and through, a body. In order to "not die" one must breathe air. It is imperative to belabor what seems obvious here, as it reminds us that the most fundamental unit of living—of embodiment—is something that the Asian and Latin@ residents could never take for granted. For many of these residents, breathing hurts—it is labored, not guaranteed. The grassroots change-makers and CBOs with whom I worked primarily articulated embodiment in terms of the pollution and sickness that the community carried in its bodies (see Figure 6). Their fliers reinforced this point by making clear that these maladies—and health in general—were not the product of genetic transmission (that we get what our parents give us) or of our own (bad) habits and lifestyle choices. Rather, per the aforementioned EYCEJ flier, "[M]ore than 50% of our health is determined by the environments where we live and work, so the effects on health should be thoroughly reviewed in land-use decision-making." The activists back this perspective with research studies on the impact of land-use decision-making on the bodies of the marginalized residents. The key word is *decision-making*. In other words, illness and death are societally and institutionally *manufactured* and, therefore, preventable, senseless, and mal-intentioned, as bioneglect highlights about the politics of the body and health. The fliers codify the following forms of knowledge, for instance:

- Respiratory illnesses: kids living within 500 feet of busy roadways have increased risk of asthma and other respiratory problems.
- Cancer (California studies): 85% of the rise of cancer from air pollution comes from diesel exhaust alone.

Regarding cancer, the fliers often make clear that the *raison d'etre* of environmental injustice is diesel, the key beast living inside the community's bodies. Again, asthma, respiratory disease, and cancer were "not natural" and not just "what happened in life," as some residents were conditioned to think. To drive the point home, one of the fliers, titled "Asthma and Diesel" and written by the environmental justice coalition the Green LA Port Working Group, emphasized that the state of California is well aware of the health risks of diesel exhaust, yet it fails to sufficiently publicize that *diesel in fact causes asthma*. The activists write to the public, however, that "California has formally recognized diesel exhaust particulate (DEP) as an air toxin" and that in 2001, the "Office of Environmental Health Hazard Assessment found DEP [to be] one of the 'top five' outdoor air pollutants of concern to children's health." The flier refuses to stop there, however. It explains,

- Exposure to DEP can disrupt the immune system (it increases a sensitive person's risk of having allergic reactions to other things in the environment).
- Particulates and ozone from traffic causes cell damage to lung lining and through inflammation.
- Fine particulates can get into children's narrow airways and lodge deep within the lung, where they are more likely to stay and be absorbed.
- Kids also have higher breathing rates than adults, which can increase their exposure to air toxins per unit of body weight. . . . Kids raised in heavily polluted areas face reduced lung capacity and prematurely aged lungs.

The fliers also zeroed in on the I-710 freeway expansion, an eighteen-mile stretch from the Los Angeles/Long Beach Port Complex all the way up to the 60 freeway, cutting through fifteen cities and involving an estimated thirty to fifty thousand daily truck trips. The coalition stipulates, "High traffic congestion from goods movement activity has led to levels of pollution in the area that exceed many areas in the county and across the state" and that [freeways, railyards, ports] are "in close proximity to schools, hospitals, daycare and senior centers. This [freeway expansion] is one of the largest public works projects in the nation and therefore of vital importance that this be an improvement project to benefit the health and safety of local residents." Not only did the coalition uphold that community institutions are vaunted institutions—hospitals, daycare and senior centers, where the young and old proliferate—but that the residents wanted an "improvement" project, not a "freeway expansion" project.

A flier by EYCEJ minces no words about how embodiment is not just an issue of being sick but of lacking full mobility. That is, disproportionate

FIGURE 6. Educating about diesel pollution. Source: courtesy of the author.

pollution impedes *people's ability to move*; therefore, the politics of embodiment were also the politics of movement:

> **CONGESTION and MOBILITY** on the I-710 and on arterial streets in local communities could impact pedestrian safety, walkability, bikeability, and accessibility to schools, retail, and public services. . . . [Residents reported] traffic density on the stress of residents.

If one cannot move—whether that means walking, exercising, biking—and if one does not even have parks or other forms of green space to walk to and walk in, then one cannot be healthy and mobile; indeed, the two go together. Other fliers supported these notions of mobility. As [one] writes about "physical activity:" "Access and proximity to places for physical activity, including parks, are significant predictors of physical activity levels." Recall from the previous chapter that environmentally aware doctors associated obesity with the lack of parks. The same flier spotlighted the deleterious health impacts of "noise exposure," a social problem most class-privileged communities perhaps only think about when concerts in nearby fancy venues, such as the Hollywood Bowl and the Greek Theater, break their 10 p.m. curfews. As even "moderate levels of ambient noise can he harmful," residents in the port-industrial belt's "long term exposure" to loud noise is of considerable consequence.

Furthermore, the activists were also clear that their embodied politics never separated environmental justice from economic justice. The aforementioned Labor/Community Strategy Center and the Bus Riders Union realized this upon listening to working-class residents. Not only did they become aware of the limited mobility to the nicer zip codes where they worked, but that the neighborhoods they called home were making them sicker by the day, and the immigrants could not take it any more—they wanted justice.

In Yolanda's telling, she narrated how living in the United States was precisely what made her and her family sicker. In this way, she is one of the many data points in the social science research that proves that immigrants get sicker the longer they live in the United States (Gálvez 2011; Lee, O'Neill, Ihara, and Chae 2013). Addressing the rural, open-air hometown from whence she came prior to El Norte, our exchange went as follows:

> YOLANDA: There's very little people with asthma in Mexico. It's very interesting. Over here there is a lot of people with asthma. . . . When I came here she [daughter] can't breathe sometimes. It's no good.
>
> NADIA: You can't breathe also?
>
> YOLANDA: Yeah.

In narrating thus, Yolanda defies the nativist racist discourse that Mexico is a pathetic country of decaying bodies while the United States is superior and peopled by healthy, happy bodies. Some of the youth activists defied this racist nationalism by conveying how smothered they felt by oil refineries when they were coming up in the City of Angels; indeed, they shared how they could not separate industry from their biographies nor from their individual thought patterns and feelings. Ben, the EJ coordinator for Filipinx American PCORE, remarked on the omnipresence of the oil and defense industry behemoths when he played in the streets of Torrance and scanned its horizon. Upon my asking what inspired his life of activism, Ben replied,

> I think, maybe just growing up in the South Bay, because there's the refineries, there's Torrance, Carson, just everywhere, and whenever you pass—I moved [to a place] pretty close to the refinery—that influences [you], you know; just being aware of it and having to look through your windows every time you go down the street, and just knowing that something like that is in your backyard. And then there's also the other main industry in South Bay, the defense industry, so it's like the defense industry and oil industry.

Another undocumented youth activist, a young Filipina named Lily whose entire family lacked papers, expands upon Ben's claim by sharing her frustration over her and her friends' inability to escape their refinery "neighbors;" in other words, their limited mobility influenced their emotional state. In Lily's case, it was frustration.

> LILY: It wasn't until high school, like, I started going to peoples' houses, I started hanging out with people and I would see that where they would live [was] right next to a refinery. Like *all* my friends lived next to a refinery (laughs). And I remember, like, *it was frustrating*. . . . Like as a child, I remember when they would flare, *I actually believed that that's how you made clouds*!
>
> NADIA: Oh, really? (both laugh)
>
> LILY: I would look at them and tell my mom, "Oh, look! There's my cloud!"

Striking about Lily's understanding is how the omnipresence of oil refineries made them seem as if they commanded nature. That she thought nature's cumulus clouds were made by oil refineries marks how she not only embodied oil pollution in her body but embodied a community that had different kinds of clouds. Lily's story is precisely the transcorporeal place-based lens that helps us grasp why she connected her health, emotions, and nature to deem oil's omnipresence and cumulus clouds as a source of frustration.

In a similar vein, youth activist Monica relayed her family members' inability to go outside without being poisoned to the point of immobilization.

> MONICA: When my mom and her sister were growing up, they grew up in an area near "Sare refinery." I'm not sure if it was air quality but maybe it was. . . . So they'd faint when they would go out.
>
> NADIA: They would what?
>
> MONICA: They would *faint*! So they would just like pass out, and they didn't know why!

In Wilmington, Alisa, an energetic Communities for a Better Environment (CBE) youth activist and cofacilitator of the Wilmington "youth EJ" program, described the dark side of community embodiment upon my asking how she and her mother had first gotten involved with CBE:

> ALISA: So I lived next to *Warren E&P*[13] [oil and gas company] and . . . so, they [my parents] had been there like three years already in that house. . . . And one day, just something popped out [of my eye], you know, . . . my parents didn't really know what was going on. . . . It was [a hot] summer so I was sleeping with my windows open and, um, yeah, apparently, stuff went into my eyes.
>
> NADIA: [Gasps] From the drilling?
>
> ALISA: That's what the doctors told me. . . . And they were like, well, sometimes your windows may be black and that's because of . . . , you know, all the pollution in the air, all the dirt, all the filth, all the toxic stuff in there. So my eyes were swollen and I could *not* open them. . . . And, um, . . . it was *hideous*! . . . (pause) It was really ugly. Um, I remember like taking pictures of it because people wouldn't believe me. And I wasn't allowed to go back [to school for two weeks]. . . . And my mom and my sister, after that happened, literally within like a couple of months, . . . were like, "Hey, there is this [political] meeting that somebody told us to go to," [where] they're talking about things that were happening—a lot of kids had what I had [non-opening eyes] in the neighborhood. . . . I believe it was outreach in my neighborhood. . . . [And] I was just like, "I know I can't sleep with my windows open, but I definitely felt like a prisoner within my own house."

In chilling terms, Alisa conveys how the extreme toxicity of oil and gas companies shut her eyes so she could not see; left her immobilized in her own body and in her own home; and left her unable to go to school, learn, and help her family move up socioeconomically—another kind of mobility—for which most working-class Mexican immigrant families aspire (Hochschild 1996; Telles and Ortiz 2008). To be sure, suffering this kind of bioneglect is also precisely what got parents, namely mothers, and youth like Alisa to their first political meetings, to eventual political consciousness, and to grassroots community work and leadership.

Regarding the interplay of the built and natural environments, a middle-aged Filipina American activist named Pia described her Southern California summers—much against conventional wisdom and Hollywood stereotype—as "horrible."

> PIA: I have allergies.
>
> NADIA: Do you think it's worse by BP [refinery]?
>
> PIA: Yeah, it is worse. Every time it's summer like this, it's crazy, it's too hot. So we would like, the other day, I had nosebleeds. So that's why I try as much as possible to stay indoors. Because in the summer you really need to stay indoors. It's horrible.

Pia lamented how much heat and allergens the BP oil refinery produced, ruining a Los Angeles climate and season hailed as the best in the country and ultimately rendering her significantly less mobile by keeping her indoors. In another instance, Tina, a Cambodian American community health worker on LBACA's staff, shared her horror when, from the coastal city of Huntington Beach, she scanned the horizon and saw two separate, uneven worlds. Indeed, it was Tina's day-to-day life in grey Los Angeles that inspired her to go beyond her public health work of educating people about asthma to organizing against the polluters who caused and worsened it—a new goal and aspiration.

> TINA: It's such a bad environment in this area [Long Beach].
>
> NADIA: Why is it so bad here?
>
> TINA: I just think that, you know, the air. I was at Huntington Beach one day and, so I was looking, and I turned to my left which is going to Laguna

area—nice, beautiful, clear blue sky! [chuckles] And I turn to my right, dark as night! You could see it! The smog is so black.

NADIA: It's that dark, huh?

TINA: Yes, it's that dark. So I (pause), it's just like day and night! And I'm like, Oh my gosh!" And the other thing is, my husband has allergies. . . . And we used to live here by the I-710 freeway and my son, at that time, he was about one year old. So he always sounded very congested, and coughing a lot, hard to breathe. And he wasn't diagnosed yet with asthma. And my husband would be taking allergy pills all the time. And then we moved to the east side in Long Beach, so it's away from the freeway and all that, and we've been there for ten years and the condition there was so different. Day and night!

The fact that the oil refineries had caused Alisa and her neighbors bodily harm and, for Tina, created an unequal sky, attests to the kind of embodiment of one's community that those in Huntington Beach, Beverly Hills, or Malibu rarely had to think about. Activists could never not fixate on how environments made bodies; activist bodies would therefore have to remake the environment.

The West Long Beach Latina activists, many of whom had cleaned rich people's pretty homes (and nannied their children), agreed. Teresa, for instance, was becoming more fearful of the soot that had increased in recent years on the exterior of her rented unit under the foreboding West Long Beach sky.

TERESA: Before, I just used to hose down the dust on my house. Now when I hose it down, it just stays! It's sticky.

NADIA: Is it black?

TERESA: It's black. All the smog is just sticky. *And we are breathing this!*

Taken together, the activists made clear that those who live in West Long Beach know that they are trapped in plumes of diesel and other chemicals, because the evidence either dusted their house or stuck to it in the form of black gook that never came off. In fact, they felt that their air quality was so poor that Marile, one of the millennial staff coordinators of CPC, was surprised that I would bring my bouncy, chubby five-month-old firstborn to meetings with me (but there was no way I could conduct this fieldwork without combining work and parenting).

As we have seen, one of the other major ways that the activists foregrounded embodiment was by framing it in terms of mobility. Here, it takes on a different cast if we connect it to gender. From the transnational optic of the women, their ability to be spatially mobile in the United States marked a welcome departure from the sexual shame imposed on them in their Mexican villages if they appeared too often "in the street" (Hirsch 2003; Zentgraf 2002; Milkman and Terriquez 2012). When we connect the mobility of bodies to immigration, we find that the unauthorized Latina activists often lamented the surveillance and the fear of deportation as making them "sick;" therefore, embodied racism caused illnesses other than those from environmental contamination. Embodied racism literally stopped or circumscribed people's ability to move their bodies, that is, to move through life. For those who are detained and imprisoned, they fall into the vortex of immigrant detention—the fastest-growing segment of the prison industrial complex (Cisneros 2016; see also Golash-Boza 2018). Once immigrants are deported back to their sending countries (for undocumented youth, to countries they barely or don't know), the lesson is that you may no longer place your body in the United States. Doing so is tantamount to a crime, and criminals are not allowed to move in public space. The body is the crime.

EMBODIMENT AS THE POLITICS OF BODY ADORNMENT

In the domain of social justice struggle, the Latin@ activists articulated embodiment in another way that I did not expect. When asked about her favorite parts of grassroots community activism, if any, middle-aged mother Dalia noted her favorite gatherings were not the organizing meetings but the workshops for "Healthier Cooking and Living," "Healthy Families," "Public Speaking," and "Dressing Professionally." Dalia was certainly not alone; as I conducted more interviews, her answer became a familiar refrain. To be sure, studies have established that Latin American women's social movements have long had a tradition of training poor, rural women to make food and learn other skills as part of cooperatives for economic survival; not only do these raise money for social justice causes but they serve as group therapy and an emotional support system (see Safa 1990). Clearly, LBACA offered myriad presentations on Asthma 101, on issues related to housing, and on how to deliver sound public testimony, but I was a little puzzled as to why the women would spend so much time and energy investing in "dressing professionally." Sometimes I wondered if we were not better off spending those hours directly organizing against the state agencies and corporations, or at least securing more meeting rooms, recruiting more members, or something to that effect. Despite feeling a bit skeptical and perplexed, I was trying to keep my mouth shut to avoid interfering with the general, regular flow of the Latin@s' day-to-day organizing and so as not to make them uncomfortable with me. The women's emphasis on these seminars rooted in embodiment—from "dressing professionally" to "how to do hair and make-up"—went from throwing me off to making perfect sense. These women of CPC and LBACA made me see that if endeavors such as line dancing, *danza Azteca*, aerobics, and cooking classes were in the service of a healthy embodiment—the kinds of bodies that the powerful perpetually denied them—then why would it not also manifest in how to adorn one's body: how to dress it, paint it, style it, and comport it? I would soon be reminded of the similarities between the LA activists' emphasis on their workshops and of the service programs that much more radical organizations such as the Black Panthers (Nelson 2011) and the Young Lords (Enck-Wanzer 2010) would offer their low-income communities, from free breakfast to free basic health care.

Recall that the Latina body has long been reduced to an undesirable baby-making and mothering machine (see Chavez 2008, 2017; Gutiérrez 2008; Molina 2013). Adorning and presenting it differently was therefore not peripherally political, but *intensely* political. Initially, I thought the women might be doing apolitical "feminine" things with each other and possibly wasting precious "real organizing" time—and, in my critical view, unduly prioritizing assimilation into White (female) middle-class standards of "professional" appearance, speech, and affect. Rather, the Latina activists taught me that they were performing a strategic subversion of class (and other) biases. That is, by dint of bucking society's race, class, and gender caricature of the shabbily dressed, uneducated Latina breeding brown babies, she already disrupted the very expectations that had conditioned the officials not to listen to her long before she opened her mouth. Therefore, standing before the mostly White men in suits in attire and make-up redolent of professional white-collar women, the Latinas at the very least jolted them out of their taken-for-granted bias and got them to pay attention—that was, after all, a major part of the battle, making them look up, open their eyes and their ears, and pay attention to the non-White female body standing in front of them. In this way, a noteworthy change of clothes might force the elected and corporate officials to perceive the "Mexican moms" in a new light. Although political acts can be read in myriad ways, and may be hegemonic and counter-hegemonic at once, what mattered most was that the women felt buoyed—politically and emotionally—by the act of adorning their bodies in unexpected ways. And it showed when they faced intimidating White men at the mic but with renewed confidence, vigor, and purpose. After all, they were not just representing themselves; they were representing their community.

Another reason for the premium the women placed on "feminine" activities such as getting advice on how to look flowed from the intense desire and need for community and for the emotional support within; these desires and needs were especially amplified given the tyranny of living as an unauthorized person in the United States. A primary strategy, therefore, was to organize seemingly fun social events that were, in their eyes, also *political* events—political because they were *politicizing* events. As LBACA staff community activist Marta explained, "One thing that's important, if you don't have the contact with the people, if you don't know them and what's going on, they're not going to believe in you (*si tu no tienes el contacto con la gente si no conoces lo que esta pasando ellos no van a creer en ti*)." For instance, through Latinos in Action, Marta invited me to a fundraising banquet at which, as a culmination of the Latinas' participation in political and "dress up" workshops, we were to get dressed up, sit down for a three-course dinner, and take photos on the make-shift red carpet. I had never seen the women be so buoyed by feeling glamorous and like the rich and famous. In essence, the cake-baking, floral-arranging, personal grooming tutorials, and rare banquets were equal parts befriending one another; feeling useful, productive, respected, and beautiful; offering emotional support; and gently pulling people out of the shadows of fear and self-protection to become part of the struggle. As Marta declares, if no one knows her, no one trusts activists like her, and then, of course, no one joins the movement with her. Thus what appeared initially on the surface as women just doing apolitical sisterly things with each other was strategically about how to engender a critical mass—one person at a time—the major ingredient for swaying elected and corporate officials to back down and dole out.

OUR EMBODIED (STREET) SCIENCE VERSUS YOUR DISEMBODIED SCIENCE

One of the most common charges the activists leveled at elites was that those who did not embody their community in some way or form had no authority or license to make decisions about it. To these embodiment-framed charges that residents leveled at meeting after meeting, the officials often responded that although they might not know the affected community like the back of their hand, some of them had come from humble origins and had grown up in neighborhoods "like yours," or they would note that air moved and that their (nicer) neighborhoods would, too, get hazy, smoggy, and rancid drift from time to time.

This embodied philosophy is what guided the activists to reshape the discourse around the I-710 freeway not as an "expansion" but as an "improvement" project.[14] Despite knowing the state would likely not accept it, an environmental justice coalition proposed their own alternative project.[15] While they could not stop Chinese-made goods from flowing from the ports to the rest of the country, they sought to show the community that they could try to temper the deterioration of their health conditions in the process. In the CBOs' overall assessment of the highly technocratic proposals (or "alternatives") for the freeway expansion, their biggest grievances were as follows:

> While some aspects of the reviewed alternatives are promising, as presented, the alternatives are problematic because they will have a negative impact on air quality, will cause displacement of homes and business, pose an ecological danger to the Los Angeles River and the species it inhabits. All alternatives show a reduction in Particulate Matter and other pollutants, however, some alternatives show increases in these pollutants along certain areas along the I-710 freeway.

For the alternative improvement project, the coalition (led by EYCEJ) did not just want a corridor for trucks and freight that would be completely electric (zero emission). They also demanded the following:

- No I-710 widening
- Comprehensive public transit element
- River improvements
- Comprehensive pedestrian and bike element
- Community benefits: local job hire, expanded open space and other community enhancement

Notice that the community's alternative made sure to center an embodied politics, for instance, in terms of increased mobility and accommodations for low-income and disadvantaged people, such as a comprehensive public transit, pedestrian, and bike elements. Such a transit element is not just premised on the hope that the buses could run on electric energy or compressed natural gas, but that disadvantaged community residents would not suffer discrimination in terms of urban and spatial planning as well as land use, such as the difficulty that low-income people face traversing from their "undesirable" zip codes to work in more coveted ones (hence the request for "local job hire"). Per the emphasis on environmental justice as also economic justice, the logic was that if one could not work, then one could not afford to live; if one could not afford to live, then one could not afford good health care. As the old adage goes, everything is connected.

The other community benefit of "expanded open space and other community enhancements" is indelibly connected to the "pedestrian and bike element" they prioritize. The aesthetic of the community is also crucial to the activists—one does not want to walk, exercise, or socialize in a community that is aesthetically unpleasant. That is why cleaning up and beautifying the river and protecting its animal life are central to the alternative. The cleaner and more desirable the community, the healthier and more mobile are its bodies—physically, mentally, and emotionally. In these ways, the community's prioritization of rivers, parks, and other open space is not a sign that their movement is less radical, as has, at times, been the case (Pulido 2017a, 2017b), but that their ecological—material and cultural—reality values a mix of the natural and built environments. The transcorporeal manner in which they related the body and emotions to their ecology demonstrates that having access to and enjoying nature, such as trees that could help clean their air, was a matter of social justice; indeed, neoliberal racism and classism did not care if they had anything pretty in their neighborhoods. Roughly three decades earlier, the Mothers of East LA's environmental justice movement against the siting of a prison, waste incinerator, and oil pipeline in their neighborhood was similarly animated by the pride they had in an East LA that Anglos insulted (Pardo 1998). These activist mothers let Anglos know, in no uncertain terms, of their working-class Latina pride when they fought Hollywood film crews that graffitied surfaces and threw fake trash around to make East LA look more "ghetto," or fought back when Hollywood directors yelled at them for beautifying their own community (ibid.).

WHY AREN'T YOU SCHOOLING US? LIMITED PHYSICAL AND SOCIOECONOMIC MOBILITY

Embodiment politics also reared their head in educational settings, not wholly unexpected as the history of Latinx and Asian embodiment often played out when White nativists justified exclusion and deportation laws by emphasizing that their White daughters would be sitting next to "Japanese boys" at schools or that they would be overrun with "Mexicans" (Molina 2013). Although environmental justice was the activists' key campaign, their focus on schools stemmed from the high value they placed on education and socioeconomic mobility. As Hochschild (1996) has shown, Latinos and Black Americans value education just as much as White Americans do (as do most Asian ethnic groups [Louie 2004]). And these activists and residents are no exception. Yet the Latina change-makers are indeed the exception insofar as socioeconomic status is a key determinant of school participation (Verba, Schlozman, and Brady 1995; Terriquez 2012), yet these low-income women buck the trend by being as active and enterprising as middle-class mothers, albeit about concerns tied to disadvantage.[16] Without the Latin@ children acquiring an education, for instance, the activist mothers believed that there were very few avenues for their unauthorized, working-class family to surpass their current station in life. While both the Asian and Mexican American activists deemed education sacrosanct and the key to their family's success, the Asian ethnic activists invoked their middle-class view of education as the cornerstone of socioeconomic success while the Mexican ethnic activists had to fight within the broader reality that educational outcomes worsened with each succeeding Mexican generation (Telles and Ortiz 2008) and that school officials were biased toward wealthier mothers (Reay 1998). School was thus not just an emblem of health and physical mobility but of *socioeconomic mobility*, a symbolic form of mobility, and therefore a symbolic form of embodiment.

Education was in fact the primary reason that many of the Latina women first joined Community Partners Council: CPC provided a great deal of information and resources concerning schooling and was also a site for organizing for educational reform. CPC would host workshops and discussions on how to ensure that the children studied; how to raise them properly; how to avoid gangs,[17] drugs, and teen pregnancy; and what the dangers were of corporal punishment on one's children. Advocating as parents on these issues was even more important given the few counseling services offered by California public schools (Rogers and Terriquez 2016); in fact, the Golden State ranked last in the country in terms of counselor-to-student ratios (Rogers, Bertrand, Freelon, and Fanelli 2011). Contrary to racial stereotypes of disengagement, then, the Latina mothers redress underresourced schools by being engaged as much as White American mothers irrespective of legal or citizenship status. As CPC spawned groups such as The Mother's Brigade, which advocated for their children's education, it exposed the mothers to policies and politics related not just to public education but to environmental justice issues at the school, thus training them civically and expanding their political profile (see Terriquez and Rogers 2011).

One of the mothers' biggest concerns was the health hazard that school posed (Figure 7). Not only were youth being killed quietly at school, but they could not study or move up socioeconomically. As this was coupled with the paucity of counseling services—whether to improve students' grades, social skills, or mental health—the immigrant mothers knew that the odds were stacked against their children. In these ways, environmental justice was never separate from educational justice. This transcorporeal perspective was afforded by the specificities of place (Peña 1998) but also by the latitude and inventiveness afforded by living at the interstices and margins of politics, especially for the unauthorized; it was also informed by gender, by the mothers being tasked with the lion's share of responsibility for the children's schooling but also their desire for superarse. Taken together, these processes informed why the largely Latin@ and Asian American activists dovetailed their organizing for school

FIGURE 7. Suva Elementary (Bell Gardens, CA) next to chrome-plating facilities, which caused twenty-five cancer deaths and deformed, miscarried babies. Source: Communities for a Better Environment.

reform and clean air in a way that I have not seen in environmental justice movements (Figure 8).

Filipina American mother Roselie, for instance, was more active in school reform than in the clean air fight despite her passion for both. At the time of our interview, she was in the process of founding a nonprofit for youth development with an eye on teaching them to be "citizens of the world." She described her nonprofit as follows:

> ROSELIE: [F]or the kids, [so] that we can support them and empower them; and through the experiences . . . if the community offers it, it enables them. And also . . . , like in my community, you don't finish school until you graduate college.
>
> NADIA: [A]nd they can accomplish that in the Philippines too?
>
> ROSELIE: Yeah. They . . . make a way for you to finish college. It's more of a priority that you have to finish college. . . . If you don't finish it [we can't be] citizens of the world.

HOW PROTECTED IS OUR CHILDREN FROM POLLUTION SURROUNDING OUR LOCAL SCHOOLS?

People's Community Organization for Reform
and Empowerment
(People's CORE)
Presents:

COMMUNITY HEALTH DATA GATHERING TRAINING

COME AND BE TRAINED IN SURVEY GATHERING...

PARTICIPATE IN CONDUCTING COMMUNITY HEALTH SURVEYS...

LEARN WHAT WE AS THE COMMUNITY CAN DO TO PROTECT OUR CHILDREN FROM POLLUTION...

HELP US FIND THE ANSWERS TO QUESTIONS REGARDING OUR CHILDREN'S ENVIRONMENTAL SAFETY...

LOCATION: 22328 MAIN ST. CARSON, CA 90745
ROOM # H4

TIME: FRIDAY DEC. 11TH 2009
4:30PM–6:30PM

CONTACT:

FIGURE 8. People's CORE training flier. Source: People's CORE.

Yet education justice as environmental justice, and vice versa, was the way most approached the problem. For one, the state often located the goods movement apparatus right next to schools: in West Long Beach the Southern California International Gateway railyard is right next to Elizabeth Hudson Elementary and Cabrillo High schools in Long Beach (and to a houseless shelter) and the Union Pacific Intermodal Container Transfer Facility railyard is right next to

Webster Elementary and Stephens Middle schools. This proximity to railroad and diesel exposure causes fourteen hundred premature deaths annually, according to LBACA. Freeways could also double as school playgrounds; for instance, Elizabeth Hudson was a mere four hundred feet from the 103 freeway that connected the port to side streets—all so that trucks could bring as many goods to middle-class America as it could buy.

As a lived reality, community leader Laura introduced me to the ways in which school also caused her daughter—who contracted asthma—to fight for breath:

LAURA: My daughter, every night and morning, yes, she was coughing a lot. I felt so frustrated.

NADIA: Yeah, when did this happen with your daughter? When did it start?

LAURA: Uh, I think she was, like ten or eleven years old . . . because, um, my daughter's school is Hudson, so it's next to the freeway. And sometimes she came and said, "Oh, mommy, today we were outside playing and then the principal would say, "Go to your room because the air is, um, bad." But I didn't know why, I just said, "Oh, ok."

NADIA: But then, when you went to LBACA—

LAURA: Yeah, I learned.

Referring to a similar struggle with the elements for her son at school, activist member Yolanda responded thus to my question, "What is the air like in your community?":

YOLANDA: Mmm, it's very bad . . . especially for the, I don't know what you say in English, when the gas company— (trails off)

NADIA: Because it all goes in the air?

YOLANDA: Yeah, because I remember two years ago . . . in every [part of] downtown [we'd] smell gas. It's very bad. Because you come out of the street, and gas [is] on.

NADIA: Like a strong gas smell?

YOLANDA: Yeah, very strong.

NADIA: Do your children complain about the smell?

YOLANDA: Yes, and I especially told my son [who] goes to the Cabrillo High School [because] it's [a] neighbor to the gas company. And one time after this, they had other explosions, little explosions. . . . And it's very hard. My son has headaches and pain in the ears. So it's very hard and I tell him, "Be careful, when you see this [smoke, and so on], don't go outside the classroom. And explain to the teacher, "This is no good for me and no good for the students."

NADIA: Do the teachers know? Do they keep them inside?

YOLANDA: Yeah, no, no, they keep them inside.

In Yolanda's telling, not only was their community a toxic open-air chamber, but their schools were among the community's toxic closed chambers. She remarked that this senseless reality was what prompted her to protest for her son who sat for hours in classrooms each day next to an oil refinery known for dangerous explosions. It certainly raises the question, How can our low-income youth of color (many from unauthorized families) learn and succeed academically if they cannot even get fresh air or cannot avoid noise pollution at their campus or cannot sit in a classroom without their bodies being hurt? Furthermore, doing well at school also involved thriving at physical education and taking breaks from the books to run around at recess, a form of physical mobility that students in these cities could never take for granted. What kind of socioeconomic mobility does any of this guarantee for students like Yolanda's son and for their larger family?

Indeed, these conundrums inspired the women's interrelated organizing by pressuring schools to account for poor air quality as well as its most toxic flashpoints. In addition to the crumbling buildings, vastly underpaid and overworked teachers, old textbooks, and unceasing pleas to impoverished parents to pay for this and that, perhaps the most damning indicator of bioneglect was the lack of air filters in schools. Per this hyperpolluted and dangerous learning environment, mothers also organized to ensure that cars did not idle for long periods in front of the school where their asthmatic children waited to be picked up. Sometimes, the Mother's Brigade had to fight for basic resources for basic safety, as in this example:

ANAIS: Mother's Brigade, we focused on what the school needed, but now we want the people [crosswalk guards] close to the kids on the street . . . but the principal told us the state don't have the money . . . to pay for cross[ing] the street.

NADIA: Oh, a crosswalk guard? They don't have the money to pay for a crosswalk guard?

ANAIS: They say it's too expensive to pay somebody. I say, why does Edison [another primary school] have it? Two cross[walk] guards . . . ; they have a freeway [nearby], yes, but we have a freeway too! So we really need it because . . . , in September there was an accident in the parking lot in the school because one car accident took out, like, another car.

Although crosswalk accidents were less common (albeit important), the dearth of something as basic as air filters seemed particularly callous. Perhaps even worse was the schools' lack of pushback against surrounding industry because of the funds they received from industry to "buy them off," as discussed in Chapter 1. The paucity of air filters in our nation's most affected schools owes, as well, to the unwillingness of government agencies and billion-dollar corporations to spare the easily affordable expense of buying them, never mind the will to decrease the amount of refineries or goods movement that was polluting people of color's lungs.

Teachers who taught in these hazardous school settings also got involved. Black American teacher Kelly maintained the stance that the school was killing her and her co-workers quietly. When I asked Kelly how she got involved in grassroots efforts for environmental justice, she instantly replied that it had to do with teachers, students, and staff "getting sick." She explained, "Because we're mostly in bungalows that are lower to the ground, we're exposed to the worst air. That's why the teachers on the higher floors in the taller buildings don't get what we're talking about, and they oppose us. But we're not going to stop holding meetings, we're not going to stop trying to convince parents through our leafletting, through the PTA stuff. We're applying now for worker's comp, but there's lots of red tape—it could take years." Not only were the activist teachers and students fighting for each breath, but the teachers were fighting polluting industries, government bureaucracies, and even their own co-workers. In fact, the bulk of the community activists in PCORE were Carson teachers, all women of color. Their school, Dolphin Elementary School in Carson,[18] was right next to Shine Truck Washing Company, prompting the teachers, alongside parents, to ask PCORE to help them fight the spillover of oil and other toxins onto the grounds of their school. Although PCORE happily obliged, the campaign would quickly dissolve owing to the many other EJ- and labor-related battles the women of color teachers had to fight.

One of the most ironic, striking, and tragic issues at the nexus of the environmental justice and school justice movement pertained to the cruel lesser-of-evils choices imposed on marginalized communities. Akin to neoliberalism's "false choices," Molly, a White female and former LBACA project manager, relayed to me the mothers' political conundrum over whether to choose health or mobility. Molly shared that LBACA, per standard practice, had decided to protest a new school being built right next to the I-710 freeway, thinking it a no-brainer that the activist mothers would agree. Instead, much to Molly's and LBACA's shock, the mothers *opposed* the school being sited somewhere else because they absolutely needed a school within walking distance, even if a freeway imposed on it. As low-income and undocumented people, the activist mothers and their families often suffered the dual burden of having no cars and no driver's licenses. The school's convenient location would prove to be the lesser of two evils, as the mothers were risking their young children's contraction or triggering of asthma, other lung diseases, and possibly cancer from spending hours trying to learn amidst freeway's choking diesel clouds. But at least the parents could get the kids to school so they could learn and so they could carve a successful future for themselves that would, through their children's academic leap-frogging, elevate their working-class families into middle-class security. Needless to say, LBACA was utterly thrown by the mothers' choice, but gradually understood it. What other choice did the Latina mothers have? An Asian American teacher named Lana also invoked this conundrum when she referred to her activism against schools being built so close to freeways:

LANA: The one thing that we thought that we could get possibly passed . . . was a rule about [not] building new schools within a thousand feet of the freeways. And they had to think of that with all of the pollution from the freeways and from like BP [refinery], for example. But [the ordinance is] for new schools, and so if you take that to the old schools, you'd lose all the old schools.

NADIA: So what are they going to do?

LANA: They haven't [done anything]. That's one of the things that had us

> getting into that. And you don't want to get rid of all the schools that are by the freeways, because this is an issue of accessibility and parents want their kids to be nearby. They really want that—it's a sense of security. But they could provide safety at the same time, you know?

Although the Latina activists were able to change LBACA's stance, these lesser-of-evil choices cast into relief that no amount of ecological "street science," multipronged organizing, or looking out for each other through communal citizenship could grant the women full self-determination over their own neighborhoods.

In addition to having to worry about whether they had a school close enough to walk to and whether their kids could learn without falling sick, the Asian American and Latin@ mothers worked to ensure that their children were not being racially tracked, surveilled by ICE, or otherwise discriminated against in the school. Liliana narrated an event in which a Compton school principal weaponized the unauthorized status of a family who had lodged a complaint about the school discriminating against their child.

> LILIANA: And so they want to switch to another school. When they tried to do that, the principal started telling them they're going to call immigration. . . . And, then, the [mother] . . . called [a community advocate named] Fernando [who] gave everybody the idea to call [the principal] on the phone, and get the [email] address of the principal of the school, to say "You need to STOP. That is wrong." She [the principal] did!
>
> NADIA: She did?
>
> LILIANA: Yes! That's why I'm telling you: whenever you're a victim, you can do more.

The schools' institutionalized racism represented another "boot on the neck" of Latinx youth and families who were trying to move up the racialized socioeconomic ladder. In response, Liliana, one of the residents who was first politicized by volunteering in schools, found her superarse by realizing that they were not categorical victims, that they could "do more" and win. She also began offering programming for high school teens who were struggling with racist tracking and profiling at school (as well as mental-emotional struggles, problems at home, and so on); that is, rather than helping the youth, the schools—in the vein of the "school to prison pipeline"—were criminalizing them. Considering her volunteer work to bring healing—or what she called "medicine"—to the criminalized students, Liliana shared this about her politicization:

> So I think I did become an activist when I was going to give medicine to the kids [at the high school]; they needed this and wanted this. Instead of going to the police department [with the students]—they're not criminals, they're kids!—the school needs to help. They need help. And I think, then, I became an activist.

Another element of youth education was afterschool programs, which themselves depended on the presence of parks and playgrounds to be mobile within and to enjoy a reprieve from the concrete that dominated their urban community. For CPC in particular, in conjunction with LBACA, one of their biggest programs was to ensure that youth had options beyond gang-banging, drug dealing, teen pregnancy, and the like—parks and recreation programs were often the only other alternative. CPC was heavily involved in "Summer Night Lights," a city-sponsored program designed precisely for that purpose: to offer activities like free sports and recreation and camps, and to rid parks of criminal activity. Indeed, an embodied community could not exist without a place at which their bodies could gather.

WHY SCHOOLS HAD THE ENVIRONMENTAL SOLUTIONS

Owing to the mothers' and teachers' fusion of the school reform and environmental justice movements, they could not help but fuse the two when they proposed solutions for cleaning the air and how younger activists could play a crucial role. Teresa, a Mexican immigrant activist with CPC and LBACA, responded thus to my question of what she wanted the youth of her community to do:

> Something specific they can do is find a teacher who is going to help them organize and get together, and find a kind of project in the community they can work on, like, going to a [health] clinic or being a mentor at an afterschool program, or something like that. But the youth need to organize, though, they should do that with the help of a teacher *within* the school so they could be formally organized, so they could keep to it. It'll help start the trend of helping out with little projects, here and there, around the community.

Teresa had the thoughtful idea that youth who did not know how to start getting involved in organizing would be best served by germinating their politics within the institutional setting where they spent most of their time and that they knew best: school. She implies that, as with many first-generation activists, youths' path into environmental justice was to volunteer, such as "going to a [health] clinic or being a mentor at an afterschool program," and as with most of the activists throughout this book, Teresa's suggestion bespoke her belief that one could not draw a thick line between social services and formal organizing. Indeed, Teresa believed that these "apolitical" youth programs and youth centers would foster politicization and environmental justice activism. Under the guidance of one of the many teachers who supported the community's struggles (though, not all did [see Brodkin 2009]), youth would also have the advisorship to help them "keep to it." From her own experience trying to organize her neighbors, Teresa knew how easy it was for people to lose political momentum when the infrastructure was absent or lacking. At the same time, in the following exchange long-time Mexican immigrant leader Marta stressed the importance of community youth seeing environmental issues as political, as a movement, as a realization of justice, not just as resume filler.

NADIA: So what do you think the young generation should be doing in general?

MARTA: Oh, besides studying?

NADIA: Yes, in terms of organizing—assuming you think they should, too.

MARTA: The ideas I give to the [environmental justice] coalition—so that the youth start doing what we're doing as adults—is that we need to take them to the places where these situations are happening. One of the points I make to the youth who are going to [LBACA, CPC] meetings is not to see it as hours of service, but to be conscious that we need them to make changes in their communities. The first idea is to take them on a tour in the middle harbor on a boat so they can see what's going on. The second recommendation was that when the A-Team group [mothers' street science team] makes an assessment, to have them go with us to the west side [of Long Beach], to Hudson Middle School, for them to see how many trucks pass on the 103 freeway, to see the cancerous particles that

> come out of these trucks. So the thing with the young is that you can tell them what's going on, *but they need to see.*

Not only does Marta reveal her fierce eye on education ("Besides studying?"), she implies that community youth were not mobilized enough. As an activist in a movement that saw racism and classism as embodied, it made sense that the only way to politicize youth, in her eyes, was to make sure that they embodied the community's pollution (saw, breathed, smelled, measured it). Anything short of that would dampen youth politicization and recruitment into the movement.

Tomas, fully cognizant of the power of youth and taking a page out of his own mother's playbook, had achieved years ago what Marta was imploring. He begins the narrative with how exactly he was able to corral the students to show up—he visited his old teachers and told them,

> "Hi, I'm a former alum of class of 2002 from Banning High School. I'm back and I'm doing this project on environmental justice and labor rights." And they were like, "Oh, okay cool, yeah, you used to be my student." And I met up with the ecology students and recycling club, whatever, . . . also with social science teachers who were very much like, "I feel you." I worked with Cabrillo High School and Cal State Long Beach [with a professor there] . . . also getting his university students out there in the harbor. So we created this idea. . . . "Harbor Ride Along": we took the youth, the community, we took parents to the port to meet truckers and to see the environment from the pollution they're breathing, but we wanted them to hear the stories from truckers. And truckers were sitting down with high school students saying, "I have diabetes, I have no health care, this is the truck I have to drive to support my family. I breathe in the diesel pollution directly right into my lungs. And I'm sorry about this whole thing. I want clean air and I want a clean truck, but I'm sorry, I can't afford it." And some [truckers] would be like, "Don't end up like me! Stay in school."

Not only did Tomas believe that high school eco-clubs should be more justice-oriented, he made that happen by bringing students face-to-face with the ports and the truckers who moved all the product. In this way, Tomas was coalescing environmental, school, and labor justice issues. The truckers underscored this trifecta as well. First, they highlighted how they embodied economic and physical suffering from their jobs, and how apologetic they were that they were polluting not just their own lungs, but the youth's. A product of a neoliberal economy that allowed profitable trucking companies to shirk responsibility as employers (re: wages, benefits) by treating truckers as "independent contractors," the men underscored labor injustices by making clear that truckers cannot buy their own trucks on poverty wages, let alone those that run on electricity or compressed natural gas. Finally, invoking education, the truckers advised the youth that the solution was to stay in school.

THE TRANSCORPOREAL EXPERIENCE OF CONCRETE, OCEANS, AND OWLS

Interestingly, youth activists like Bella affirmed how much they loved nature independent of community aesthetics, such as her expressed love of dolphins and her passion for beach cleanups. As further testament to these urban warriors' appreciation of the natural environment, Jesse Marquez of Coalition for a Safe Environment had pulled me into an animal rights campaign that I did not anticipate. Amidst all his countless hours spent going after big oil, the ports, Caltrans, and train yards, he somehow found time to start the "Save the Burrowing Owl Committee." He originated this group to prevent the endangered owl's habitat from being destroyed by additional airstrips that the City of San Diego sought to build at Brown Field Airport in Otay Mesa. When he told me about it and asked me to be the campaign coordinator, I was immediately compelled. After we sent a letter to the city, we buttressed our campaign to save the owls from mass murder by driving four hours down to the airport in early July 2011. There we would count the number of owls and habitats, scan and take notes about the grounds, and take photographic evidence; these were, after all, the last remaining large colony of western burrowing owls in San Diego (Figure 9). Our efforts made me think of what it might have required for conservationists to secure the long fenced enclosure around LAX to preserve the beautiful, endangered El Segundo Blue butterfly. As we walked around the nondescript dusty, rocky airfield under the baking sun that day, I, an animal lover, thought about how I was embarrassingly biased toward "charismatic species" such as endangered elephants and dolphins; of course, I also loved puppies and kittens, too, but owls? I knew they were

FIGURE 9. Western burrowing owl, Brown Field Airport. Source: courtesy of the author.

skilled hunters, but I had never before established a connection—that is, until we got up close and personal with them and their babies. They were simply majestic, haunting, mysterious, and fascinating. I could not believe that these flying birds could burrow a hole and tunnel underground, hang out there, and call it home. When I locked eyes with theirs, I finally understood why, for many people, owls are sacrosanct. Jesse and I were thus heartbroken to learn a year later that a good number of the owls had been poisoned to avoid the hard work and expenditure needed to carefully relocate them and their habitats. By the time Jesse had finalized the lawsuit against the City of San Diego in late 2013, I had just left the field to finally start writing the book and start planning for my second baby. When I finished my field notes on the experience, I noted how grateful I was to him, an urban-minded activist, for introducing me to these creatures. Despite my love of nature, I highly doubted I would have met them otherwise. I also noted how impressed I was with Jesse's ecological commitment not just to air quality but to the quality of animal life, and to urban communities' priorities not just of parks and trees, but of animals, beaches, and oceans. The immigrants were profoundly shaped by an ecological and transcorporeal experience of what they deemed a blended built-natural environment, of living at once amidst the concrete and stunning nature of Southern California. Both were under assault by similar forces, and I myself was transcorporeally transformed.

* * *

After reading the history of nativist racism and citizenship injustice against Asian Americans and Latin@s from a body- and emotions-centered perspective, we can see that Liliana's story with which the chapter opened takes on a slightly different cast. Not only do we recognize that she was very much in her body and in her feelings, we realize that she was given no other choice but to be so. And that is precisely how inequality works. As a young girl, she watched her mother be regularly beaten, and almost killed, by a father whose mental and bodily faculties were compromised by alcohol; as a young woman she was sexually assaulted by a man and lost her family members to gun violence; as a US immigrant she was made ill by INS's raids to deport the bodies of Latin@s like her. The gravity of her suffering was marked by how much she wanted to divulge her struggles to me, someone with whom she was not that close. Importantly, the subtext was that her bodily and emotional states were coterminous. Like Liliana, the immigrant women fighting for cleaner Angeleno air made plain that they were rarely able to take their bodies for granted in the way that privileged "American" bodies could and did each day.

Historically, for instance, Asian and Latin@ immigrant women have descended from generations of those whose bodies had long been marginalized as undesirable, weak, sexually excessive, hyperfecund, unintelligent, threateningly intelligent, inscrutable, and simultaneously hypereffeminate and hypermasculine. Because the women lived day-to-day at the historical and present-day nexus of race, gender, class, and citizenship, their transcorporeal knowledge was premised on the embodiment of illness, mobility, and inequalities in the built and natural environment. Although the day to day may seem unremarkable and unworthy of note, it was precisely what allowed the Asian Americans and Latin@s to grasp race and class injustice, and more specifically, the body inequalities endemic to both. Spending years with the immigrants in port-industrial LA, for instance, I would learn how out of momentary fear for their children's lives, the mothers would often have to rush their kids to emergency departments for violent coughing, gasping, or black accumulation in little noses. At times it was to entrust ER doctors with the chronic symptoms of fibromyalgia, lung disease, or cancer, as most unauthorized immigrants without health insurance must do. The Latinas taught me that their choice was between having a close-enough school that would make their children sick or a school that would be difficult to get to but would have cleaner air. The Asian American teachers taught me that they, not just their students, were also sick from the freeway or industry next door, yet detractors would derogate them as complainers while workers' compensation would elude them. It is this daily grind of bioneglect that compelled these women to see the big picture—that is, racism and classism—as thoroughly embodied.

When I read the fliers, spent more time in the field with the organizers, and spent countless hours interviewing them, I noticed that embodiment went much beyond their bodies being asthmatic and cancerous from pollution. In fact, they showed me that one of the most significant vectors of embodiment was the ability to be mobile (or not)—not just physically but socioeconomically. The Asian and Latin@ immigrant mothers' focus on academic mobility translated into an inventive and nuanced linkage of the school reform and environmental justice movements (while enterprising youth leaders would also integrate labor). In addition, the women prioritized embodiment in terms of the politics of appearance and impression management: make-up, hair, and clothing. It was also a touchpoint for superarse, a much-needed female bonding experience and reprieve from the emotional and physical toll of house and family work and of movement organizing. Departing from Foucault's typical treatment of bodies as entities that are written and acted upon, then, the women demonstrated how they embodied an enlivened corporeal and political body. One of the choices that they made was to do what they could to forget, and compensate for, their life of bioneglect, one in which states and corporations sickened, undereducated, surveilled, and deported low-income ("illegal") immigrants of color like them. Although they suffered labored breathing, sickness, and limited mobility, they did their best to renounce the reality that their lives, in effect, did not have to be so hard.

CHAPTER 4

"OUR COMMUNITY HAS BOUNDARIES"

Race and Class Matter

WHEN I WALKED into the small room set off from the raucous public comment meeting, the contrast between the two was tangible. The crowd, the amplified din, and the sheen of bright florescent lights gave way to a hushed, dimly lit room dotted with a few people sitting in front of a row of outdated computers—some typing, some ruminating. I found one of my favorite people there, Laura, the staff community liaison and widely adored activist of the nonprofit Long Beach Alliance for Children with Asthma (LBACA), standing nicely dressed in her typical poised manner, supervising the computer process. "What are the people doing in front of the computers?" I asked. "They're typing in their comments instead of going up to the mic. Are you going to speak tonight? Why don't you go up to the mic?" Her question surprised me, given that I was still ruminating over the emphasis that the Mexican immigrants like her had placed on poverty as defining membership in "the community." I completely missed the fact that she actually wanted me, a middle-class Ph.D.-holding professor, to step up to the mic—that my social class (and even perhaps my non-Latina) status might prompt the South Coast Air Quality Management District (SCAQMD) officials to *hear* me in a way they did not her and her neighbors.

Thinking that I was in fact respecting her self-described community boundaries and thinking that I was showing reflexivity, I replied, "Oh, I don't feel right about going up there when I'm not a member of the community, taking time away from others who actually live here." In her typical measured calm, she betrayed no disappointment but remained persistent, suggesting, "OK, why don't you write your comment on the computer then?" Satisfied that a viable alternative existed, I replied, "OK, great!" It would not be until the end of my fieldwork some years later that I saw this moment anew, with 20/20 vision and fresh perspective. Immediately, the warm blood of embarrassment and regret rushed through me. In the moment, I had not sufficiently oriented my mind to the fact that Laura had a multidimensional view of class. Therefore, I did not intuit her disappointment that I neglected to use my class (and other) privileges to help uplift her community in the most forceful way possible: with my body's actual voice and presence before the elites. My head was so buried in the conceptual analysis and in insider-outsider dichotomies (Merton 1972; see also Võ 2000), that I completely missed the human connection—I had no idea, in effect, that she saw me as a symbolic member of her beloved community.

The moment, and my reflection thereafter, awoke me to the types of boundaries that marginalized groups draw to determine who is "us" and who is the political opponent, and on what basis. In pursuing these questions, and extending from the previous chapter, I found that *both* the Latin@s and Asian Americans linked up morality to inequalities of the body and emotions. It stands to reason that *unauthorized* activists in particular (and those who cared about the paperless) would engage the contested terrain of morality given Foucault's belief that the criminal justice system, such as the INS and ICE, has justified itself by reinscribing nonjuridical discourses such as those of morality (Foucault and GIP 1971). Furthermore, Michele Lamont (2000) has shown that notions of morality underpin the boundaries of who is in and who is out and the valuations made of each. Where the Latin@ and Asian immigrants *differed* from each other was in their choice of the oppressive systems they deemed most responsible for their environmental suffering; as a result, they also differed in how they determined boundaries of an "embodied us" versus an "embodied them," capaciously including affect in embodiment. Applied to the case of disproportionate contamination, the majority of the

Mexican immigrants like Laura taught me that their community was the poor who had to fight the immoral "healthy wealthy"; that is, classism was the key cause of environmental injustice. The majority of the Asian Americans taught me that their community of color had to battle the immoral "White healthy wealthy," that racism was the key source of this suffering. When pursuing the question of why the difference, a transnational and transcorporeal perspective on the arc of these groups' livelihoods proved paramount.

In other words, in forging the political divisions of "we, the embodied community" against "them, the (White) healthy wealthy," the Mexican and Asian American organizers prioritized inequalities of embodiment born, respectively, from classism and racism. They were conveying, "our" bodies are relegated to poverty, made sick, or emotionally assaulted by racism while "their" bodies are healthy because of affluence and Whiteness—and usually both (see Hall 1992). By definition, this is a moral claim, as the embodied community believes that the generally healthier government and corporate elites neglect and placate them out of *the lack of empathy that wealth and Whiteness spawned.* Drawing on Michele Lamont's work on how morality underpins boundary-making, I demonstrate how transnational, contextual, and strategic reasons inform why first-generation Mexican ethnics' boundaries hinge on class, and why those of Asian Americans pivot on ethnorace, while leaving room for both.

THEORETICAL BACKGROUND: ENVIRONMENTAL JUSTICE AND BOUNDARY-MAKING

Lamont's (2000) classic work on "symbolic boundaries" and "boundary work" found that, owing to respective US and French policy differences on welfare, the US working class positioned itself as above and morally superior to the poor, while blue-collar French aligned themselves with the poor. Morality—or the capacity for self-discipline, responsibility, and compassion to keep one's life, and that of others, in order (3)—anchored these boundary lines. These lines were premised on who they were, and equally important, on who they were not. Such a conceptualization of boundary-drawing harkens back to Fredrik Barth's (1998) work on ethnicity, wherein group lines are drawn on the basis of who falls within, and without, the boundary. Applied to corporate and state entities who watch (low-income) people of color suffer the worst preventable contamination and sickness, do elites have the self-discipline, responsibility and compassion to keep *everyone's* life in order, as the mostly Mexican and Filipin@ activists of port-industrial LA feel is their citizenship calling?

In constructing themselves in opposition to others, or doing "boundary work," Lamont's US and French working classes did not see the wealthy as such. Rather, they considered moral standards to function as "an alternative to economic definitions of success" and to offer "a way to maintain dignity and to make sense of their lives in a land where the American dream is ever more out of reach." Lamont's White male working class judged professionals and managers, in this vein, "to lack personal integrity and sincerity and to have poor interpersonal relationships" (3), thereby using their morality standards to decouple wealth from moral worthiness and to position themselves above those with money.

While environmental justice research has focused nobly on the race and class causes of disproportionate pollution, it has left wanting our grasp of how the body and embodiment anchor definitions of citizenship as well as political identities and boundaries. When we make the body primary in the environmental justice and immigration sociology literatures, we more readily grasp why the Latin@ subjects did not finger racism as the main cause of their suffering despite it being integrated within, and despite it being a veritable cause. Furthermore, we should extend American studies's perspectives on immigration and environmental justice by interrelating citizenship, transnationality, and embodiment in a manner that could explain the immigrants in my study. For instance, my work (2008b) has shown that the racial positioning, identities, and politics of immigrant groups—in this case, Korean Americans—could not be understood without an analysis of the transnational nature of racialized colonialism, (neo)imperialism, and global culture. Megan Carney's (2014, 2015) work on Mexican and Central American migrant women's collective procurement of food under neoliberal food insecurity is also relevant here.

> There are constraints on the resources that nourish bodies in one setting (Mexico and Central America) that precede the movement of women's bodies to another setting (the United States), at the same time that these women's

> bodies—particularly as essentialized 'emotional' or 'affective' bodies for the purposes of providing care and nourishment—are demanded by the United States labor market [which does not guarantee them (healthy) food]. . . . In this regard, I have followed Heyman (2004) in looking at how human-environmental flows (in this case, via food) occur . . . [within] a wider range of intersecting axes of inequality and power, by conveying the experiential as well as the material aspects of these processes, and by attending to embodiment, linked to the political ecology of health (Carney 2014:15).

As with Carney, it is the aim of this chapter to recognize this embodied and affective reality as the Asian American and Latin@ Angelenos experience the transnational and transcorporeal reality of neoliberal oppression, not so much through food insecurity, but through pollution injustice.

MORAL BOUNDARY LINES AND POLITICAL CULPRITS

The Mexican immigrants construct themselves as "we the embodied community" in a way that subverts state and mainstream discourse on their group as "illegals." Similarly, the Asian Americans roundly reject the derogation of them as "inscrutable foreigners," "non-Americans," and war-torn refugees.

The activists determine who is within and without the community by deeming the *embodied community* as physically and emotionally sick by design and deeming those outside their community—particularly, those in positions of power—as the nonempathic (White) "healthy wealthy." By delineating an us-them division on the basis of who has empathy (us) and who does not (them), the Los Angeles activists underscore the following index of morality: "compassion to keep one's life, and that of others, in order" (Lamont 2000:3). Put another way, this is a morality that state and corporate elites and their systems lack. Throwing into relief such boundary-drawing, long-time community leader Laura, whom we met in the opening vignette, responded to my question about whether or not her beloved President Obama and the federal government played any role in West Long Beach's air.

> NADIA: If you become a citizen, do you think that you will be satisfied with voting for people? . . . Maybe they're more like Obama, . . . would you be satisfied with just voting and calling the senator and the representatives saying, "Please pass this so that we can have less diesel pollution in our

communities"—do you think that you will focus more on doing [that] rather than . . . your community work that you've been doing?"

LAURA: *Never. My community is first.*

NADIA: That comes first. So even if you could vote later, you will do just as much community work [as before]?

LAURA: Yeah, mhm, yeah. . . . It's because the community needs to be educated. We need to include ourselves. Also, I think that by educating ourselves we give ourselves a better future.

NADIA: Do you feel like President Obama, or like the national level, representatives, do they know local issues?

LAURA: (scoffing) Um, no. . . . They have no idea . . . because they live in places where they don't know anything about pollution.

Laura makes clear her political identity and commitment—"My community is first"—but also how she draws a dividing line between the political Other, who "[doesn't] know anything about pollution," and her community allies, who have to educate and empower themselves about living in a life-threatening environment, something they wished they never had to deal with. Not only did "they" know nothing about the majority of the community's children doubled over with asthma attacks, but they did not have to be stressed by the noise pollution of bellowing cargo ships and rumbling trucks and trains, nor of the constant noise of construction; the healthy wealthy knew nothing of the light pollution of baseball-stadium-like glare from oil refineries and of flaring that made much-needed sleep elusive, nor did they suffer the stress of being perpetually immobile because the outdoors was unbreathable, too built up with concrete, or too policed by ICE. The healthy wealthy simply did not know a life of being regularly trapped indoors, unable to work out, or left with nowhere to go. At the same time, there is a sentiment of superarse when Laura says that educating themselves helped pave the way for their better future. For, even as victims, the community gains knowledge and helps support each other through the stress when it must clean up after political and moral neglect. She is indignant and emphatic, for instance, when she remarks, "They have no idea . . . they don't know anything about pollution," imbibing the "they" not just with the privilege of ignorance but with the immorality of killing her community quietly (see Alexander 2016). This line in the sand is also what rooted her politics in grassroots community work and *not* in the voting, campaigning, or civic office of formal, electoral politics. These are powerful words from a member of an immigrant group that has long been encouraged to assimilate into mainstream politics—indeed, scolded and shamed for not doing so fast enough.

On the "healthy wealthy" dismissing people of color's suffering in a bid to profit from it, Filipina Mexican PTA mother Vega, who worked with People's CORE, painted corporate and government elites—even elementary school principals—as immorally selling their souls for the highest price. "They're crooks," Vega remarks. "They don't really seem to be in tune. They [elected and agency officials] seem to be getting paid by the corps, and I think some of the LAUSD principals are paid to be silent, to let them [the corps] pollute."

Another organizing moment with PCORE was also instantly revealing of the immigrants' boundary work and morality tropes. One of PCORE's signature events was the annual Earth Day festival, a less politically charged event organized for the community with the hopes of raising consciousness and recruiting members to the struggle. Working with Jesse of CFASE and many other environmental justice organizations in the area, the 2012 Earth Day event involved a segment of political street theater in which Filipin@ and Mexican American children held candles with the logos of all of Carson's contaminating behemoths taped to them: Shell, Valero, BP. Wearing grim expressions and in a somber tone, the Filipin@ and Latin@ youth recited the damage that the toxic chemical emissions did to their young bodies. It struck me that this was an effective visual of the way Carson residents and allies drew boundaries and disentangled morality from the upper class (Lamont 2000). The seemingly disembodied and immoral "they" polluted for profit, largely with impunity, and without concern for the less affluent bodies of color that became invisible statistics on reports. Hence, the youth organizers presented their bodies and feelings for the public to see—the bodies that coughed, wheezed, itched, suffered, and died, and the feelings of melancholy, as a result of neglect.

Here, the lower-middle-class AAPIs and working-class Mexican ethnics, akin to Lamont's subjects, decoupled wealth from moral worthiness *to position themselves above* those with more money; these moral standards functioned as "an alternative to economic definitions of success." In contrast to Lamont's US working class, however, the Latin@ activists did not reconnect class status and morality as a way to derogate the abject poor and Blacks; rather, they imbued poor and working-class people like themselves with moral entitlement and the authority to eke justice from the mostly upper-class White American men (and their institutions) who withheld it.

MEXICAN ETHNICS ON EMBODIED CLASSISM AND THE MORAL PROBLEM OF CLASS

For the Latin@ ethnics the boundary that marked who was in the embodied community, and who was out of it, pivoted on an identity politics of class and of class-based morality. Martha articulated thus while narrating the political gulf between her community and the "healthy wealthy."

MARTHA: On one occasion when I went to talk [testify] I told [the officials] that you do not understand us because you live very far away from us in the mountains [LA or Orange County foothills]. You do not have contamination. *If you live in this neighborhood where I live, where there is contamination and your children get sick, you will understand me.*[1]

NADIA: What did they say [in response]?

MARTHA: They stood quiet. They didn't say anything. They just look at each other. Like my son said, "He [that official] got mad." It's true. They don't pay attention. That is the truth: *when people have money they leave. But they have a beautiful mansion and they have a good neighbor. It doesn't interest them.*[2]

In making this statement, Martha specifies two criteria for membership in the community of which she is part: first, "we" are the impoverished and second, "we" are those who have to breathe toxic air and who thus have to care for sick neighbors and children. She conflates the two criteria, as many of the other interviewees do, since one was rarely disentangled from the other. With respect to moral boundary-drawing, she is explicit that she excludes the rich and the powerful from her community's bounds, who are too busy intentionally disengaging or living in clean air communities to feel empathy, to understand, to have compassion. They were also part of an unequal affective relationship in which the dominant get mad while the subordinate have to be sad (and mad). Particularly striking about Martha's narrative is the latter part in which she excludes the officials for their alleged use of wealth to leave or avoid overly contaminated neighborhoods and the resultant life-threatening illnesses.

I was also struck by how consistent and impassioned Martha's coethnics were about the centrality of poverty to defining their group and their politics. Early in my fieldwork, this was the unexpected response I got from Laura of LBACA, when I asked what she meant by "community."

NADIA: When you say community, do you mean the people who live in the specific area, or—?

LAURA: Not only us immigrants, no, it's low income.

NADIA: Low-income people, so class.

LAURA: Yeah, yeah, class. I'm not talking about Latinos, Black, or . . . [other racial or ethnic groups who live here].

A relatively new organizer, Myra, similarly cited class, not race, as the system's motivation for disproportionate pollution.

NADIA: Would they do the same thing [pollute] in a poor Anglo community? In a poor Anglo neighborhood?

MYRA: I think so. I think so. . . . I think it's people who are just low income, who are not educated because of it.

To be sure, in my early days in the field, I was somewhat surprised at how much the mostly Mexican Latin@s prioritized class. I had assumed that they and their activist colleagues would instead point to race and ethnicity (we Latinos and Mexicans) and/or their racialized legal status (we undocumented), yet I was asking myself, Why would race not be as important to the very group who has long been racialized, surveilled, detained, and deported as "brown illegals" and when they are well aware of environmental racism? In this way, these immigrants could have just as easily deemed nativist racism to be the main cause—or the main *co-cause*—of their environmental, immigration, and educational injustices; by extension, a racial identity politics could have been the basis, or co-basis, of their insider-outsider and moral boundary-drawing.

To unpack this puzzle, my analytical deep dive revealed that a transnational approach and framework were critical. My previous research (2006a, 2006b, 2008b) on Korean American racial formation had made clear the centrality of the premigrant context, and the ongoing transnational connections to it, whenever immigrants navigated the politics of race, nation, ethnicity, and related social inequalities in the local context. This transnational reality could not have been truer for the Latin@ immigrants' political consciousness in El Norte, for the main oppression that they suffered in Mexico was poverty. That is, the Mexican activists' transnational and dual transcorporeal positioning was as "poor people"—not as *racial or ethnic minorities*—prompting them to make class their master identity politics.

Also influential are the politics of low-wage unauthorized immigrants under globalization who define themselves in terms of immigrant (not citizenship, nation-state) rights. For instance, Das Gupta (2006) found that immigrant activists such as the South Asian taxi drivers and domestic violence survivors in the northeast United States saw themselves as vested with a "transnational complex of rights" that attended them no matter the border crossed and no matter the documents held. In the face of polluters, politicians, and government agencies, the Angelenos of my study identified first as members of the "poor" (see ibid.:19), aligning themselves with the impoverished labor migrants spawned by neoliberal capitalism and championed by antiglobalization social movements. In this way, the Mexican immigrants' preferred method was to meld universal personhood—a human rights tenet—and social group membership as the oppressed poor (see ibid.) in order to define their political center and their political selves.

As noted, another factor behind the weaker focus on race was the fact that the activists did not suffer (systemic) racism in Mexico. Their membership in Mexico's dominant, majority mestizo (nonindigenous) population meant that they were not ensnared in an ethnicized (or racialized) net of exclusion and bias; they came to the US with a weaker consciousness about race and racism or the need for it, save certain situational exceptions. Upon inquiring about their racialized cultural backgrounds, for instance, none of the Latin@s identified with an indigenous identity (nor with the less acknowledged Asian and Black Mexican backgrounds). Rather, in line with the prevailing cultural *mestizo* ("mestizaje") national identity, a substantial number had light skin and European-esque features while others appeared more mixed (see Zamora 2016).

Paralleling Frankenberg's (1993) work on White racial discourse in the United States, one of the biggest indicators of a life without systemic racism is one's lexicon; although the Latin@s were by no means White women in the United States, they were members of the racial majority in Mexico, hence, they did not cite racism as affecting their lives there, did not racialize themselves in their articulations about their lives there, did not see how their lives were syncretic with those of the racially oppressed in Mexico, and understood themselves in relation to other Mexican injustices (classism, in my study). Moreover, Latin American social desirability norms have long prompted less overt talk about race and racism (Telles 2004), whereby race and racism are often conflated and identified only in their most overt, institutional forms (Roth and Kim 2013); to make a US analogy, race and racism might come up but only in relation to the KKK or (neo)Nazis or to Republican presidential nominees who dub their migrant brethren "rapists" and "criminals" as part of the global wave of far-right populist racism targeting migrants.

Furthermore, class loomed largest in their political sensibilities because, in their transnational experience, the rich gringo country did not end up being a complete escape from Mexico's grinding poverty either. Although the vast majority of the Latin@s were not as impoverished as one asthmatic family that Tina, the LBACA health worker, and I visited in West Long Beach one day, most were well aware of the reality that some families could not afford items such as folding chairs and had to resort instead to white plastic buckets around the table, the overturned ones that Tina and I sat on next to the friendly mother and her two children in a cramped apartment unit. That moment has never left me, as similar moments never have any of the Latin@ clean air activists. Poverty was therefore a human rights struggle, one that was global and transnational, and that reached every corner of a divided world. Such a perspective was lucid in their unapologetic language. Of the countless Latin@s with whom I spoke in the field, I heard not a single unauthorized immigrant equivocate on whether their group deserved to be in the United States. It was a given that they did—a nonstarter and a no-brainer.

Some of the respondents were quite explicit about the transnational scope of their political oppression and sensibility. While Martha, for instance, was fully cognizant of and forthcoming about anti-Latin@ racism in the United States, she used the example of Mexico's politicians to prove that race was not the main reason why American politicians dismissed them. She articulated this point when I queried about the demographic background of most of the US officials to whom she testified at public comments. She initially replied, "The majority are men. Americanos [Anglos]." Upon asking whether or not she thought that the officials' status as "Americanos" had an impact on why they were not empathizing with them and fighting contamination, she remarked,

> *It is not because they are just American [Anglo] men. Over there in Mexico we are Mexican and [it's] the same thing when there is politics. They don't pay attention to us.* . . . To put it simply, they are people who are not in a lower class like us. They separate themselves from us and they don't know the people.

She believed that the gap between rich and poor ultimately explained why political elites abused their power rather than served their impoverished constituents—and the similarity between Mexico and the United States was proof enough.

Even when transnationalism did not anchor the immigrants' articulations, their lived realities between their Mexican origins and West Long Beach, USA, affirmed each other in unexpected ways. For instance, the extreme segregation and weak racial socialization of the Mexican ethnics in Long Beach meant a day-to-day existence consorting mostly with other Latinx immigrants (many *sin papeles*) in the racially segregated barrio; there, one did not have to know a word of English and largely did not have to interact with White Americans within dominant White institutions. In industrial, working-class West Long Beach (90810), for instance, Latinx compose over 53 percent of the overall population, about twenty thousand (Whites constitute only 20 percent; Blacks, the next largest group, a mere 0.5 percent). The Latinxs' removal from day-to-day interaction with White America could be analogized to what Young (2006) found in his study of inner-city Black American men who reported less racism than (upper) middle-class Blacks (see also Feagin and Sikes 1994).

The weak day-to-day encounter with White America thus boded well with the experience in Mexico of not having to think about race as members of the racial majority; it was not the master social categorization system in their US neighborhoods either. To be sure, race mattered in the United States when they politically engaged (or fought with) White America and dealt with the broader nativist racism that derogated and deported them as "illegals." Race could even matter in Mexico, albeit more indirectly, when they heard about what gringolandia was doing to their immigrant brethren in El Norte.

ASIAN ETHNICS ON ENVIRONMENTAL RACISM (AND CLASSISM)

In contrast to the Mexican immigrants, the Filipin@ as well as Samoan, Cambodian, and hapa ethnics emphasized race and ethnicity as the key boundary line around their embodied community and as the moral beast to slay. What explained the difference from the Mexican immigrant activists? The most obvious answer is the middle-class and legal status of the Asian American activists, save for a few exceptions. While the terror of illegality or living in low-income undocumented neighborhoods was something most of the Filipin@ and other Asian American activists did not have to endure, the Filipin@ activists could have put the wealthy rather than "Whitey" in the "hot seat" or equally emphasized both. On balance, however, they articulated Whiteness first. In opposition, they talked about "our Filipino community," "we minorities," and "we people of color." Certainly, they invoked language about their weaker economic privilege vis-a-vis state and corporate elites, as we shall see, but never did I hear them lead with oppression by the wealthy.

Indeed, the qualified similarities between the Mexican and Filipin@ ethnics make their divergent political identities and boundaries somewhat confounding. Both sets of immigrants hail from countries beset by colonization and neo(imperialism), including at the hands of behemoths Spain and the United States. As a result, Filipinx Americans are the "Latinos of Asia" (Ocampo 2016) and thereby navigate being Latinx and Asian American at once. Interestingly, however, both groups are racialized as threatening or exotic "forever foreigners" no matter how "American" (read: White) they act (albeit with Latinxs being markedly racialized as "illegals"). Despite both immigrant groups' racialization as non-American and un-American, however, the political difference persisted. Another potential factor was the more explicit Filipinx focus of the PCORE organization, although it avoided officially naming itself "a Filipinx group" so as not to appear as if other racial and ethnic groups, or their issues, would be excluded. Effectively, PCORE was founded and predominantly staffed by Filipinx Americans.

In comparison, the Latin@-dominant LBACA, CPC, and CFASE were less willing than PCORE to concede a racial or ethnic membership or focus. At the same time, these Latin@-dominant groups were well aware that the vast majority of the residents, staff, and community members in these movements were Mexican or other Latin@ ethnics. They were aware that outsiders who visited noticed that Spanish was the dominant language at every meeting and event. Indeed, Spanish-language translators usually dotted the sidelines whispering the romance language into devices during English-speaking segments; every document was written in the Spanish language or on one side of a bilingual rendition; the culinary spread was usually Mexican or Latinx fare; the dances were *ballet folklorico* and *danza Azteca*; and resources from Catholic churches were often marshalled. Still, these activists were not inspired to organize explicitly as "Mexican ethnics" or "Latino/as" so as to keep the floodlight on class and to be as politically expansive as possible.

Our Racially Embodied Community

While for the Filipin@-led Asian Americans class was always in the picture in some way shape or form, ethnoraciality was the decided fixture; it was the unflagging principle around which the Asian ethnics, irrespective of generation, organized environmental justice events. Given the nagging paucity of time, energy, and resources for most activists, they would often prefer to fold environmental justice issues within an annual Filipino Cultural Day (or Festival) than organize EJ events sans the nods to ethnic and racial history and culture. In fall 2015, for instance, I found myself helping PCORE's Pia, a first-generation immigrant, spread the word on Filipino American History Month. The event this year was special given the added celebration of Larry Itliong Day, formalized to much historic fanfare by Governor Jerry Brown earlier that spring.

In a perfect blend of the ethnic, racial, and environmental, Pia was leading the charge to celebrate Itliong, the often-forgotten Filipino American labor leader of Delano, California, who in fact led the 1965 grape strike against agribusiness's refusal to pay a union wage long before Cesar Chavez and the United Farm Workers had decided that striking was the organizing strategy of choice. Prior to Delano, Itliong had helped establish the Alaska Cannery Workers Union in the 1930s as well as eight-hour days with overtime pay. Pia helped organize the event's program, featuring awards for labor and community leadership, youth achievement, and medals of honor for advocacy work on behalf of Filipino American World War II veterans, all in Itliong's name.

The legacy of Itliong is more than that of labor leader, however; he was also an environmental justice organizer who fought for improved working conditions on the job, including his opposition to toxic pesticide spraying of workers and his related advocacy for organic produce (to be sure, labor and environmental justice often overlap). Although the event was principally to publicize Filipino American history, heritage, culture, and Itliong's name and legacy, Pia was well aware that none of these were divorced from environmental (health) justice. Even other organized events, such as the more politically innocuous Earth Day festivals hosted to recruit people to the struggle, would rarely close without some nod to the Filipin@ community or without an extensive announcement of future events and campaigns related to the plight of "FilAms."

Also influential was the Asian Americans' more frequent and intense engagement of White America. Citizenship status, longer US tenures, and less segregated neighborhoods afforded close, sustained relations with White America in workplaces and schools, greater access to US race discourse and movements (given greater English language ability born of US colonialism), and longer socialization by American race norms given the immigrants' average of twelve-plus years longer in the United States. According to the Census Bureau, Carson, relative to West Long Beach, boasted racial groups that were not so disparate in size from one another: the Latinx "of any race" were 38.6 percent of the population, 25.6 percent were Asian American and Pacific Islander (dominated by the Filipinx at roughly 21 percent), and both White and Black Americans constituted 23.8 percent each. Not only was West Long Beach more of a Latinx concentration, it was in the best legal interest of the unauthorized subset of the populace not to interact on a day-to-day basis with White America and its institutions.

Unlike the Latin@s, most of whom were women and mothers who did not work full time, the Asian Americans worked with Anglos in City of Carson's Parks and Recreation department and school district, the Torrance Unified School District, the PTA, in social work offices, and, among the youth, at school. The Mexican ethnics' quasi-regular interaction with White America was at the doctor's office (to treat asthma or other maladies) and, politically, at City Hall and public meetings. The small number who worked prior to committing to full-time organizing usually encountered Whites in their more affluent homes as domesticas (but even then, they would often clean an empty house).

Another stark contrast from the Mexican ethnics had to do with transnationality. Specifically, the Asian ethnics had strong transnational political histories in, and ties to, their ethnic homeland, which translated into a strong racial consciousness. That is, the Asian ethnics' emphasis on race owed in part to their pre-US activism and/or their ongoing transnational ties to progressive political movements there. Membership in such a transnational social field persistently highlighted White US (masculine) power over the sending country irrespective of the political issue at hand.

As one example, the Asian Americans' families and relatives were deeply involved in electoral politics and grassroots organizing both in the ethnic homeland and in the United States. In further contrast to the Mexican subjects, the Asian Americans also held strong transnational identities and were part of activist efforts in their national origins (or were aspiring thus). As an immigrant from the Pacific Isles, Cindy exemplified both: her Samoan family has long been active in political circles and her own sense of longing for and repulsion by her island "home" has indelible ties to that political history. The very reason that she and her family abruptly left Samoa in 1971 was a (violent) political conflict involving a village chief and her father, a public figure on the island. She described how her departure from the islands when she was age five was actually spurred by the chief's jealousy over her family's overwhelming success as a fishing business and livestock-filled plantation.

> There was a chief in the village, my mom's village where we lived, who was jealous of my parents. . . . And one day my dad went to check on the animals up at the farm and . . . someone had cut one of [the pig's] legs off! And then her new litter of piglets . . . someone just chopped them all in half! . . . And another time someone killed one of the cows. Then my dad one night—thankfully, he didn't take any of his guns—he just took a machete, he went to the home of that chief. . . . My dad swung the machete to decapitate him. . . . He didn't kill that man, but then all the young men [nearby] jumped [my dad] and beat him almost to death. . . . And our relatives started preparing to get our papers for us to leave 'cause my dad was banished from the village. And we were supposed to go to New Zealand, but my mom's auntie here told her, "Come to America," and we did.

Interestingly, feelings of jealousy and rage associated with political rivals were the central reasons not only for migrating, but for Cindy's ambivalent transnational relationship to Samoa. Roselie's beginnings in the Philippines had also been profoundly shaped by politics:

> Yeah, our family is a political family. My father was a part of the first Constitution, [an] elective official of the Constitution of the Philippines. With my father's side we are a political family; congressmen, mayors, we're always in the political field. My mom is a . . . doctor . . . so [she and her side] weren't in the political atmosphere but they were still involved . . . that's why here in Carson, it's very strong. On the Filipino vote we might not be the majority but politically we're active.

Roselie attributes the political prowess of her Filipin@ American community in Carson directly to their deep political engagements prior to migration. Pia, whom we met earlier, grew up in a village on the Philippines archipelago, immigrated as an adult, and was an engaged transnational subject and transnational activist: she boasted organizing experience in her origin and was part of a dense social justice network between the US and the Philippines. She, like Cindy from Samoa, had the added characteristic of parents and relatives who were highly active in the formal political realm and in grassroots politics.

> PIA: My dad, he was a union leader. . . . I remember my grandmother helping out in the campaign of the governor. . . . And I grew up debating politics. [Before I came to the US] . . . my political position was mainly in the student movement in the '70s [fighting the Marcos dictatorship]. . . . I was already active with the women's movement in the Philippines, in '84. I was setting up GABRIELA Philippines [a renowned NGO that defied Marcos and advocated for women's issues]. . . . *Right now, because we live in Carson, I'm more interested in the environment because I can feel the impact. . . . We got pulled into the local issues [but] it was essentially born out of the Philippine Network which [focused on] human rights issues. The Philippine Network pulled out when the [military] bases weren't there. That was 1992. When they pulled out we felt that it was necessary to put up an environment group because the human rights had gone hand in hand with the environment issue.*
>
> NADIA: Are you saying because the bases had polluted so much?
>
> PIA: Yeah. . . . And though we were wanting to do just international [military] issues, we got pulled in because Greenpeace came in and we talked about

> plastics; that they [Global North] dump plastics in the Philippines. They dump batteries, the pesticides go there. . . . They dump all the tobacco from here over there (emphasis added).

It is not surprising that Pia's movement work on environmental justice would pivot on ethnoraciality. Her family boasted varied political involvement in the Philippines for the uplifting of their people along with a transnational connection to the pollution (and other) problems in Carson. That is, her strong political transnationalism translates into a keen awareness that the Global North—namely, the United States, advanced European states, and Japan—dump their waste in the Global South, including in their beloved Philippines (see Pellow 2007). Although she and the other organizers did not acknowledge that blocking a hazardous waste incinerator or landfill in and near Carson, though commendable, might mean that these would simply be relocated overseas (see ibid.), their transnational politics does convey what scholars have been slow to address, that "the literature on racism has yet to seriously consider the ways in which environmental and natural resource destruction is embedded in institutional racism," as David Pellow (49) writes, a destruction that is also political-economic.

Many of the Filipin@ youth activists, as well, crafted an ethnoracial identification with the Philippines by way of transnational politics, along with family ties, summer trips, popular culture, and the likes of Manny Pacquiao; this connection existed although none had grown up on the archipelago or could barely recall it if they had (Figure 10). One of PCORE's signature programs was to promote literacy among the indigenous Moro of Mindanao, Philippines (Figure 11). The contrast between the Philippines and the soulless White US colonizer was not lost on either generation. It seemed that one's own political relationship to Philippine social justice networks concretized who "we" were and who we fought for in ethnoracial terms. They believed that the primary cause of their disproportionate contamination was their "of color-ness," rendering them and their cities, here and there, disposable.

Our Imagined Class of People: Asian American and Mexican Ethnics

It is important to reiterate, however, that the spotlight on race and ethnicity did not mean that class disappeared from the social justice equation. Upon

FIGURE 10. People's CORE. Source: John Harrison of PCORE.

FIGURE 11. People's CORE literacy program for the Moro People in Mindanao, Philippines. Source: John Harrison of PCORE.

asking Cindy, the elementary school teacher, about the cause of her community's subjugation, she promptly wrung her hands over the relationality of race and socioeconomic status: "America has false images of Samoans as just being *uneducated* football players." What mattered to Cindy was not merely that White America thought of "football player" when they conjured up a Samoan American, it was that they saw an *uneducated* one. She sought to overturn the notion of nonfootball-playing Samoans as working class or poor by underscoring that within her own family as well as in the broader community, "We have diplomats, we have attorneys, we got government officials—we've got everything you can think of—scientists that are relatives. So education is a part of our family heritage, our culture. There was never any option of not going to college or not being productive."

Similarly, Filipina American Pia had served as a journalist for the Philippine *labor* movement and noted her empathy and support for it, which she would link up with her organizing in the student and women's movements there. In the United States she supported the labor movement (her first protest march), as well. Similarly, from his place-based ecological knowing, Filipino American youth organizer Daniel spoke about class (and race) in direct relation to why his Carson community faced undue environmental pollution from oil refineries and the movement of goods via ports, railyards, and freeways:

> The people that are kind of high income on the hills, they don't get all that stuff or experience all that stuff. And if you noticed we're very crowded in. . . . A lot of the garages are actually converted into houses because there is too much people in the house living there . . . can't afford to buy a new house so they convert their garages. . . . And, like the ports, they're very close to Carson, Long Beach. There's a lot of people that are minorities . . . and if you go by San Pedro, that big ridge, there's also a port there, and I've been by there; *there is also the low income and the Latinos and the African Americans*. . . . It probably, really, has to do with the government, and that's where we're supposed to be put at. *And then keep the rich rich and keep the poor poor*, so that the rich don't have to experience anything, and so that they don't mind it—*but then we have to mind it. So we have to continue struggling.*

Even as Daniel's identity politics are anchored in being "Filipino"—he is active with PCORE as well as a more radical, transnational Filipin@ youth organization—race and class were largely inseparable in his mind. He seamlessly interwove the race and class injustice that his Carson community and that other people of color suffered in the area, ultimately concluding that the government created a class who keep on getting richer at the expense of the poor who keep on getting poorer. Daniel also invoked morality when he said that the rich immorally pollute and accrete wealth to themselves for the signal purpose of *not suffering* transcorporeally; let the low-income minorities suffer so that we don't have to—the crux of Foucaultian biopolitics. As an example, LBACA health worker Tina and I had visited one low-income family in Long Beach to train them on asthma care for their cute, bright-eyed, brown-haired eight-month-old baby, who also had an extra appendage and other birth defects and a nasal tube, and was energetically crawling around in a diaper in the cramped apartment. On the way to the visit, Tina had informed me that the Latina mother, exasperated by her half Cambodian Samoan American partner's lack of help with their baby and his asthma, had told her that, for once, she would not be there—that Mike would be the one learning asthma care that day and teaching *her* what to do. Mindful of how racism feeds poverty, Daniel was speaking of his own working-class family and individuals like Mike, who were among the Asian ethnics who suffered some of the highest poverty rates in Long Beach and the country: Pacific Islander and Southeast Asian Americans (Pew Research Center 2018).

At the same time, when we take the narratives together, it becomes apparent that very few of the Asian and Latin@ immigrants invoked the precise language of "capitalism," excepting PCORE's radical Filipinx American leaders and Mexican American Jesse of CFASE, who vacillated between socialism and gentler capitalism. While in the interviews and during our campaigns the majority certainly talked around it by citing the injustice of "profit over people," "economics," and "class inequality," I never heard the word "capitalism/o," nor exegeses on owning the means of production versus being proletariat labor. To be sure, capitalism and class inequality are interconnected, and the whispers and shades of that interface seemed to enshrine the immigrants' politics, although that was rarely made explicit to me.

Just as class was always somewhere in the picture and remained significant for the Asian Americans, the same was true of race and ethnicity among the Latin@s. Like their Asian American counterparts, the Mexican immigrants did not restrict their identity politics to one axis of inequality and exploitation just because they decided to rally around a master injustice. When I queried the Mexican immigrants directly about race as a potential cause of disproportionate pollution, virtually no one denied its salience in determining life outcomes; almost everyone conceded that elite institutions' neglect had much to do with them being Mexican Latinos, as well. From the in-depth and ethnographic interview exchanges came a patterned series of one- to two-liners that identified racism as a (secondary) culprit. One example comes from soft-spoken Celia:

CELIA: It can be because they might think that immigrants only come to take from the country and not give to the country (*Puede ser que tienen en cuenta el inmigrante porque piensan que nomás viene a quitarles en lugar de aportar*).

NADIA: So sometimes do you think it has to do with being Latino, or—?

CELIA: Yes.

Concerning the same question, my exchange with thirty-year-old Maya, a mother and a newer activist on the scene, went as follows:

NADIA: What do you think about the fact that many are Latinos, and many aren't documented? Do you think that has any bearing on why they over-pollute your neighborhoods?

MAYA: Yes. Because they [Latinos] are afraid to speak up, to just say something, because they think they might be deported.

Some of the organizers more explicitly referred to racism, such as Erika, a high-energy mother who preferred a more rebellious look, complete with nose ring:

NADIA: Who is the majority that lives here [in her neighborhood]?

ERIKA: Here is the Hispanos.

NADIA: So are you saying it would be racism too, or—?

ERIKA: Yeah, racismo too!

Friendly, light-hearted, and passionate Yolanda, a middle-aged mother, echoed the same.

NADIA: So, you were mentioning racism. Do you think that you and the other activists moved into a community that was already polluted or do you

> think that they pollute more in your areas because of racism or because of your lower income? Which came first?
>
> YOLANDA: I think it's everything, like, low income and racism too.

It was not surprising, therefore, that the vast majority of Mexican ethnics were secondarily active in the movement for immigration reform, one which at its core foregrounded ethnoracial and citizenship hierarchies. Yet race could not overtake class oppression in terms of transnational history and livelihood. The fact that systemic racism was mostly a *nuevo* experience; that, relatedly, the activists demonstrated weaker recognition of it; and that they had been socialized by Latin American norms of hushed race talk (Roth and Kim 2013; Telles 2004) meant that the pauses and "I'm not sure's" became predictable whenever I asked some of them whether racism was the main source of the disproportionate contamination. Although the earlier narratives betray their clear identities as Mexicans, Latinos, and undocumented immigrants, and reveal their fingers on the pulse of racism, their treatments of environmental racism did not compare to their fluid ease and proficiency with class rhetoric, groomed as it was by years of internal community meetings; by practice for public testimonials, newspapers, and cameras; and by global human rights and labor migrant discourses. In this way, most of the Latin@s considered class to mediate race.

To be sure, one could argue that the loose coalition work of the leaders of the area's various organizations might have coalesced the differing viewpoints of the Asian American and Latin@ constituencies. The only groups that met regularly, however, were PCORE, CFASE, and EYCEJ, and all were led by those who had been community organizers for a longer period than most of the residents and who tended to hold more progressive, anti-capitalist, or anarchist viewpoints. In this vein, all three leaders saw racism and classism as equally yoked and pernicious, yet they focused on the community fighting the good environmental justice fight, not on forcing them to conform to their own political ideologies. What proved more significant was knocking on as many doors as possible to convince inactive or apathetic residents that the freeways, ports, railyards, and industry were causing their families' maladies, that they would not be deported if they got involved, and that the issues of environmental justice were connected to immigration and school reform; whether their constituencies tended to lean toward racism as the cause (Filipin@s) or classism as the cause (Latin@s) was secondary to the reality that they and their children were being killed quietly.

* * *

To come full circle to the opening vignette, recall that the Mexican ethnics like Laura made the political choice to broaden the community as much as possible, not only to make room for all marginalized racial and ethnic, legal-status, and contaminated groups, but to imagine a community that included privileged allies. That is to say, the embodied community would be too delimited and would even seem exclusionary if it were bound by race or ethnicity. Bound by poverty, any ethnoracial grouping who suffered neglect was part of the fray. Yet "the community" could also include those (upper-) middle-class members from environmentally privileged[3] spaces, so long as they empathized and organized with the immigrants; in this way, the embodied community was also imagined and symbolic. I would be reminded of this by moments in the field that would stay with me long after I left it.

For instance, recall from Chapter 3 the moment that the CPC staff leader, Marile, thought it "really big of me" to bring my five-month-old infant and her developing lungs to the contaminated air of West Long Beach. So arrested was I by her statement that I momentarily thought I might have misheard her: "Sorry, what was that?" I asked. Marile replied, "It's really big of you to bring your baby into this bad air." Soon after, I noticed that Marile was more open and talkative with me whenever I saw her. Although she had always been amiable and gave of her time whenever her stressful job would allow, somehow her perception that I was willing to endanger my baby's health to partake in the movement and to conduct my research project shored up her trust in me. In other words, I was willing to embody the community the way the immigrants did—to residents who prioritize body inequalities in the ways that we have seen, this was no small gesture. For me, the interaction with Marile immediately jolted me into a realization of my privilege, as living in a cleaner part of LA meant that I rarely thought about air quality to that extent. In that moment, Marile also had me questioning whether I was ruining my baby's fragile, growing lungs by bringing her to a three-hour meeting in air teeming with $PM_{2.5}$ and other toxins. My next thought was, but all these women's children, even crawling around at this meeting right now, live here all the time! Sometimes these reality checks over the course of the research could bring a sense of emotional overwhelming to me, as a mix of guilt, sadness, and demoralization would saddle my heart. At the same time, the activists would cite their hope in me to assist their movement by publicizing it to a world that kept them at arm's length or that knew nothing of them at all. Knowing that I would complete the study, I was heartened by their hope in me (when I was not pressured by the weight of that responsibility). Although they certainly differentiated between their embodied community and an imagined version of it, they made clear that the honorary members need *not reside* in the same polluted geographic space nor suffer the same physical and emotional adversity. In fact, a memorable fieldwork moment revealed that not all Latin@s were welcome within their embodied bounds.

That is, I had asked my Spanish-speaking Chicana undergraduate research assistant, Marisol, if she could, at times, attend meetings in West Long Beach whenever I could not make them because of teaching, meetings, children's after-school activities, or Los Angeles Sigalerts. Marisol was perfectly bilingual in Spanish and English, and I had asked her to tape record and take notes at one particular CPC meeting. Although she had performed this task at a meeting once before and although staff and regular attendees knew her as an assistant to me, that day when Marisol moved the tape recorder right under Carmen (the staff leader facilitating the meeting), Carmen suddenly stopped the meeting to suspiciously interrogate Marisol as to who she was, given her noncommunity status, why she was recording, and what her intentions for attending the meeting were. Two influential coalition leaders with whom I had more of a close relationship, Laura and Marta, quickly came to her defense by making clear that she was "Nadia's" assistant and therefore no suspicion of impropriety was warranted. I did not expect Carmen's treatment of Marisol, exposing my naivete that a young Spanish-fluent Chicana researcher among her ethnic and linguistic peers could make staff leaders uncomfortable when Carmen had been more accepting of me, a Korean American who spoke only very basic Spanish. Admittedly, my older age and professor and mother status likely helped.

More important, this moment demonstrated that even a fellow Spanish-speaking Mexican American could be deemed an outsider depending on potentially suspect political intentions, and perhaps on generation, social class, legal status, and zip code. To be clear, I was also not surprised by Carmen's behavior. As a staff CPC leader, she had actually always been *slightly* suspicious of me (despite my earnest efforts) owing to a longer history of "outsiders" such as corporate and public officials undermining the community's movement and of periodic internal conflicts that had made her generally wary. Regardless, as someone who was much more removed from the community in terms of race, ethnicity, and language relative to Marisol, I did not wholly expect for me to have so much more credibility than a fellow Spanish-fluent Chicana.

Beyond the imagined rendering of "our community," the activists bounded their collective by lines of embodied classism or embodied racism, left room for both, and used morality as an entry point: those whose bodies and feelings suffered, as their illnesses attested, and those who, by dint of their own immoral lack of empathy, did not. In this vein, the focus of this chapter was to examine and compare the influences behind why the two racial and ethnic groups drew their political boundaries in this manner. In the case of the mostly unauthorized, low-income Mexican immigrants, they pivoted their political identities and boundary-drawing on class inequality given transnational, contextual, and strategic influences. That is, transnationally and contextually, in Mexico's rural villages the activists suffered not the assaults of (nativistic) racism but the terror of poverty. And, in their minds, it was merciless class inequality and exploitation that ultimately explained why their US neighborhoods were contaminated and neglected, and why their bodies carried the community's illnesses.

While poverty, infirmity, and empathy were clear in the Mexican immigrants' conceptualization of who belonged in their embodied community, wealth, better health, and most important, the indifference that flowed from both, were the clear markers of nonbelonging. In drawing political and moral boundaries thus, the activists, even without an explicit linkage of capitalism to hyperpollution, revealed a view of poverty as a socially fabricated inequality imposed on them by the powerful, one that made them sick and perpetually low income. By extension, the US state's choice to *legalize* their populace would not just improve their health—imperiled by emergency-room-only options and exclusion from Obamacare—but also open the vaunted gates of socioeconomic opportunity. By design, however, the state and anti-immigrant civil society continued to "illegalize" them, explaining why their neighborhoods were hazardous and why class elites were slow (or loathe) to act on their behalf. At the same time, the lack of an explicit critique of (racial) capitalism and its anti-environmental machinations seemed to keep the Latin@s in a dance with the US state; as the US state obscures class inequality (Shipler 2018), the vast majority of the Asian ethnics did not explicitly connect capitalism to environmental injustice either.

To be sure, relative to the mostly Latin@ organizers of West Long Beach and Wilmington, most of the Filipinx and other Asian ethnics of Carson were not working class; they had the luxury of not centering class as the source of their disproportionate contamination nor as the main social axis that oppressed them. Beyond being citizens, living in the US longer, being intensively socialized by American race discourse, and living amongst and engaging daily White America, the transnational reminders of the blunt force of White US (masculine) power in their "homeland" also mattered. To be sure, all first-generation immigrants to the United States, irrespective of race or ethnicity, have to be baptized by American racial fire in order to fully grasp its legacy—and this holds no matter how much they might have previously engaged US influence in their origins (N. Kim 2006a, 2006b, 2008b). Yet I found that the Asian ethnics' strong racial consciousness owed in part to their pre-US activism and their ongoing transnational ties to progressive political movements there. In contrast, the vast majority of Mexican ethnics had not done formal political activism in Mexico and were not part of transnational collective mobilizations.

Departing from Foucaultian biopower, both sets of immigrants revealed that the process of bioneglect manifested in enlivened and agentic bodies; these bodies drew political boundaries that were based on the physical and affective inequalities spawned by racism and classism. As immigrants who have struggled with subjugation in the sending country and now nativist racism and environmental injustice in the United States, their transnational history and perspective also cast into relief embodied inequalities and political boundaries.

Finally, what we know across both the Asian American and Mexican ethnic activists is what Lamont (2000) found so crucial to her French and American working classes: that dignity and respect mattered. My findings reveal that dignity and respect are not the only reasons, however. When the groups I study are racialized as intrinsic "foreigners" and non-Americans, their resistance is animated by a worldview of the signal importance of having a community to which one belongs—a form of citizenship that they seek to, and indeed, construct on their own terms.

CHAPTER 5

CITIZENSHIP AS GENDERED CAREGIVING

NOW THAT WE have established the embodied politics of environmental racism, environmental classism, and capitalism, we have painted the systemic and institutional context of bioneglect against which the immigrant women resist. Each of the previous chapters has also offered the building blocks of their political raison d'etre—resistance by way of *embodied citizenship*—building blocks such as a multipronged negotiation of unequal feelings; political boundaries based on embodied privilege versus subordination; street science that is informed by this dividing boundary; and the confluence of all of these elements in blended movements that heretofore had been kept discrete, such as school reform and environmental justice. Recall that, broadly, embodied citizenship steps into society's empathy gap by ensuring that oppressed neighbors' bodies and emotions are cared for amidst environmental injustice, a form of embodied violence; indeed, in providing this form of citizenship for others, one ensures the *belonging and emotional support of oneself and one's family*. The Asian and Latina immigrant women's theory and praxis of citizenship therefore hew more closely to an emotional structure that imbues citizenship with resistance, collective belonging, and emotional support-giving (see M. Kim 2018) rather than a top-down paradigm. That is, beyond citizenship as a nation-state's legal apparatus to socially shore up blind patriotism (and military might) against the foil of the enemy outsider, and beyond the hegemonic use of emotions to do so (loyalty, desire, fear) (Fortier 2010), the affective citizenship of the margins as a form of resistance must be given equal due. Scaffolding from Chapters 3 and 4, this chapter's analysis of the bottom-up, horizontal, and subversive scale culminates in embodied citizenship; more specifically, in rounding out its remaining elements. For instance, the largely Filipina and Mexican immigrants tended to resist the state's (and the market's) environmental assaults and concomitant demands for "gratitude" by taking care of each other's embodied needs and refusing to apologize for their presence. From this standpoint, we grasp that the activist women do not see "America" as a "site of desire" from which to gain more rights and ideals (Fortier 2013) but as a site of physical and emotional assaults and legal oppression. As a result, they do not engage an "economy of gratitude," one that "operates in the politics of belonging for immigrants" whereby they feel pressure to be grateful for the state's conditional "love" and "hospitality" *if and only if* they prove themselves to be good "market citizens."[1] As those who rebuke the indexing of immigrant worthiness by dint of contributions to the economy, the Asian Americans and Latin@s do not in any way feel that they should be grateful to the country nor that they should genuflect in deference to the US state or corporate class.

THEORETICAL BACKGROUND

If citizenship is equally about processes crafted by everyday people at the local level, as Evelyn Nakano Glenn (2002:53) writes, citizenship is necessarily embodied. Kabeer (2005) enjoins for a view of citizenship as "embodied" rather than "abstract." To expand on its emotive dimensions,[2] Yuval-Davis (2011) distinguishes "citizenship" as the participatory dimension of membership while "belonging" is the emotive-cognitive facet tied to identity, social status, and ethical and political value systems. Such an emotive-cognitive politics of belonging, which can include the need to feel safe and secure, animates the boundary-drawing done by groups. Applied to the case of the Asian American and Latina women, however, no distinction between "citizenship" and "belonging" is made. In other words, they never separated citizenship—or participation—from belonging, for if they did not actively participate in making others feel that they emotionally belonged, then they did not feel that they themselves belonged either.

Finally, immigration relates to the emotionality of citizenship insofar as "care as action and emotion constitutes the critical politics of belonging for migrant women, as women's reproductive ability becomes a pretext to constrict their citizenship experiences" (M. Kim 2018:14–15). As we explored in-depth in Chapter 3, Latinas have been maligned as anchor baby makers, while Asian immigrant, refugee, and maternity tourist women have been censured as parasites, albeit to a less mainstream degree.[3] Against the racial and gendered politics of citizenship (Fujiwara 2008:47), immigrants make claims to social belonging, including civil and political claims, despite their status as cultural "outsiders" (Rosaldo 1994). These immigrant change-makers are somewhat different insofar as they root their cultural citizenship not just in ethnoracial "rights" but in mutual emotional and resource support; in this, they are keenly aware that community relations and health are directly linked. In this spirit, Campos and Kim (2017) found that immigrants surrounded by strong families and support networks—like the Latinx and Asian immigrants who often live in affirming sociocultural contexts—tend to have better health and longer lives than those who do not. By extension, epidemiological and laboratory studies have made clear that high-quality relationships are associated not just with better health but with longer life; poor relationships, or a lack of relationships, pose a mortality risk comparable to that of cigarette smoking (ibid.).

In Chapter 2 I specified the process in which the activists were ensnared in an emotionally laden dialectic of political contestation, one in which they sought to combat and subvert the emotive power plays of state and corporate institutions. Here, I chronicle the emotional burdens of suffering nativist racism and environmental injustice, of organizing against both, and how the women arrive at embodied citizenship as the crux of their resistance. As a methodological caveat, at the start of my fieldwork I did not necessarily expect their desire to focus our conversations on their emotional state; I fully expected to talk about structural racism, xenophobia, class inequality, organizing strategies, oil refineries, and freeways. To be sure, social psychological and public health studies have long documented the deleterious effects of racism on Asian, Black, and Latinx ethnics, from depression to suicidal ideation (for example, Williams 2018). Yet I was studying a resistance movement for which

I assumed the "vocabulary of sentiment" (Geertz 1973) would focus on the best ways to fight the power. While this was certainly a key element of my discussions in Los Angeles, they were also peppered with more refrains than I expected about other dimensions of affect: emotional suffering, needs, support, and power dynamics. To be sure, my status as a fellow woman, immigrant, non-White person, activist, and mother, along with the skillset I deployed as a trained interviewer (and my hope that I am easy to talk to) also explained why they wanted so much to articulate about their emotional lives and the politics of emotions. The participant ethnographic method of my research also showed me that the emotional processes that unfolded before me were, at times, telling much beyond our one-on-one interviews.

FEELING POLITICS: NATIVIST RACISM AND THE REFRAIN OF THE EMOTIONAL TOLL

Carmen, a lead organizer for CPC, echoed the sentiments of the vast majority of the immigrants who felt sorrowful or aggrieved by nativist racism: "I was thinking that one of the things that made you want to go to CPC [Community Partners Council] was *the sorrow that you were in a country that wasn't yours.*" Although one could contend that Carmen seems to have internalized her own racialized foreigner status, one could also argue that being circumscribed to a national outsider caused her sorrow, the sorrow she assuaged through politicized community networks. Similarly, Anais proclaimed her "depression" at the hands of unpaid bills and her mind on Mexico, her first country.

ANAIS: You know what, I feel I have the thing—depression.

NADIA: You're sad?

ANAIS: I'm sad. So Sunday I need to sleep and I don't have too much energy, you know, because I don't know, all my life is like, I don't have energy for nothing—just for sleep, sleep, sleep. I keep my mind asleep. I don't have nothing to do. . . . That's why [I'm involved in organizing]; I think it's the depression at home because you know how I live alone, so I need to do something else, not only make food, not only clean my apartment; you know, I need to busy my mind because I think about the [lack of] money, I think about Mexico, so, you know, that's why I want to look for some other things to do, for [my] depression. For example, the Community

> [Partners] Council and LBACA, that is my family because they keep me normal. . . . And in Mothers' Brigade, like, . . . you've . . . communicated with different people, [so] you feel good.

It was the mutual support and simpatico that Anais gained from the Mother's Brigade—the EJ-minded school reform movement—that gave her life meaning. In this way, Anais highlights the psychological and emotional nurturance that membership in a group of fellow mothers provides and that she strives, in turn, to reciprocate. Both for Carmen and Anais, not only were CPC and LBACA—and the community they represented—their emotional support but this "family" helped moderate and modulate loneliness, confusion, and depressive symptoms. In this way, they defined the "community" in opposition to the more atomized relationships within fortressed suburban America (Putnam 2000), where class privilege obviates the need for neighborly sharing and mutual assistance, especially in individualistic gringolandia.

Recall that we met Liliana in the opening of Chapter 3, a long-time LBACA leader who had suffered from intense depression owing to a life full of tragedy: her abusive family, the murder of family members, and her related insufferable bout with chronic illness. Compound upon that the gripping fear of surveillance by the authorities of a nation you have worked for and sought to make your own, and Liliana remarked that that sorrow, at times, was unbearable.

> And in 1999 I had insurance so I went to the hospital and they did a colonoscopy and they told me I had Crohn's. . . . When I told my story [to the doctor], that's when I started taking antidepressants. That helped me, even when I didn't believe the doctor that I was really depressed; I didn't believe him, [but] now I know. And so that's the thing that helped me. . . . That's why now I understand that I'm different, . . . that I went through really tough things, and um, that's maybe why I have depression, and have to take the medicine all my life.

So in touch were the women with their emotions and what impacted on them—sexual abuse, death, ICE raids—that their preorganizing days were filled with volunteering around issues of mental health and self-esteem. Liliana was no exception.

> LILIANA: Well, when I volunteered at the school, . . . we took training with the police department, and whenever something happens, we can go into

the school. And, then, there used to be a lot of fights between Blacks and Hispanics, Blacks and Tongans—and another race that I can't remember. . . . I think it was like four . . . or five years ago, the time of . . . the 187 reform, that they want to deport a lot of people and do a lot of bad things—

NADIA: What did you like about it [volunteering]? Why did you enjoy it?

LILIANA: Because I was able to see my kids, and also they have a role model in me, and I was so happy because when I went to the middle school, . . . then high school, I was following my son, . . . because I think boys can get more easily in trouble than girls: "Is he going to graduate? . . . How he's doing?" . . . I would volunteer when the kids had blackouts [from electricity shortages] at the school. . . . And later on I started a class in Jordan [High]—

NADIA: What are you giving classes on?

LILIANA: Self-esteem. . . . A lot of them have problems because they have emotional problems.

As previously noted, Rogers and Terriquez (2016) found that California public schools offered few counseling services. As California ranked last of all states in the number of students served by each counselor (Rogers, Bertrand, Freelon, and Fanelli 2011), the Latin@ and Asian immigrants, mostly women, often had to conduct emotional labor and organizing by stepping into this social-emotional development gap. Here again, the common affective politics required by the assault of environmental injustice and underresourced schools prompted the mothers to conjoin both social movements. After all, these Latina and Asian immigrant mothers must endure myriad lifecourse and psycho-emotional issues because contamination rained down on their schools as well as their streets. They endured a long list of hardships: having sick and disabled children laboring to study both at school and at home, neighbors with cancer (or, like Marta, their own), constant nosebleeds, fibromyalgia, occasional fainting spells, eyes forced shut, an inaccessible or ignorant health care system, along with sensory overload such as visibly obstructed vistas; undesirable concrete aesthetics; and constant noise, light, and shaking. Although the transcorporeal toll of hyperpollution and depression on the Latinas was caused by, and nested within, broader nativist racism, a significant part of it came from surveillance (and potential deportation) by the state and from anxiety about income. For the mostly legal and middle-class Asian Americans, their sadness, melancholy, and exhaustion, however, rarely had to do with ICE or finances. Rather, their difficult emotions stemmed from the exhaustion of enduring organizing itself, unbreathable air, and the sicknesses their entire family suffered. This marked a stark difference between the Asian ethnics and the Mexican Latinas, the latter of whom almost never talked about the organizing as causing sadness, dejection, or exhaustion.

Precisely because Mexican Latinas were made to feel that there was no place for them in the United States—both as racialized "illegals" and as "poor people"—organizing, no matter how draining and demoralizing, granted purpose and superarse (to the women especially); it made them feel part of their own "national home" with its own emotionally supportive civic life. Moreover, the Latinas were more skilled than the Asian Americans at consistently organizing social and self-care events, not just to gain new recruits, but to keep each other grounded and supported in a tightly knit community (that was, as we shall see, not without its conflicts). These events helped the women take their mind off of financial struggles and the alienation of living as aliens in a nation. For Yolanda, for instance, grassroots organizing provided emotional uplift after years of hiatus and of being "bored" at home taking care of the kids and household.

YOLANDA: I think my kids need time when they were little. And I stay in my house for six years but I was bored at home.

NADIA: You were bored?

YOLANDA: Yeah, because CPC made a difference in my life. . . . But I came back last year and I am very happy to come back. *And I need that. Because I'm happy to work for the community and happy to see other people; and [also] see Anglo people when they watch us* [and say], "Oh! The community of Latinos is over *here!*" (in joking, sarcastic tone).

Striking about Yolanda's words is that she conceded that stay-at-home motherhood, in her eyes, was boring. Rather than motherhood inspiring her politics, working with a community-based organization such as CPC did. Bucking trends in the maternal politics literature, Yolanda and others show that motherly concern for children and family was not always or necessarily what catalyzed their politicization and social justice work. As another point of evidence, Liliana worried about the fact that tireless community leaders like Marta were not able to perform their mothering duties because of the daunting life that was activism:

> I see that Marta is involved in a lot, *a lot*, of things, but I see she's so stressed right now, and I see that she do so much, and *she doesn't have time for her family*. And sometimes she tells me, "I don't know why, but I never sleep, I'm always working on the campaign!" And I said, "Oh my God!" *I* don't want to do that. I still have my kids!

Marta is a striking example of how the practice of embodied citizenship for superarse did not just depend on the organizers getting from the community but giving back to it. Premised on the notion that embodied citizenship was *both* practice and belonging, the fusion of the two, many activists expressed that no matter how slow or nonexistent the state (and corporate) response, grassroots efforts gave them purpose, communal membership, and support for a strong embodied life. Even Dr. Martin Luther King Jr., knew that the system would not "Let justice roll down like waters and righteousness like a mighty stream" without decades of blood, sweat, and tears first. On engaging a negligent state in particular, I queried Elena about a point she had previously made about inaction being the most prominent response from the top.

> NADIA: If you already know that the agencies are not going to pay attention to you, then why go and testify? What's your reason to still go?
>
> ELENA: Every time I have gone to testify it because it's for something that moves me. I do it because it *makes* me *feel good* knowing that I'm doing something good for my community. (*Cada cosa que yo he ido a testificar me mueve y la esta como por decir porque me siento bien porque yo se que estoy haciendo algo para mi comunidad.*)

Elena made clear that she did not organize simply because she was concerned with political efficacy, outcomes, and wins versus losses. Rather, she, like Yolanda, and other Latin@ immigrants, perceived her life to be less meaningful and less fulfilling when she took a hiatus from organizing, even if the efforts often seemed to be in vain. An undocumented youth leader from Communities for a Better Environment named Jonny, for instance, felt a similar void when he left to take a long break, albeit one he initially took to overcome perennial movement burnout.

> JONNY: I mean it's awesome to be working with students [who are] actually there to *solve our energy problem*. That's when I have the most fun. But it's also very draining.
>
> NADIA: So, could you see living a life with no organizing in it? . . . for a long time?
>
> JONNY: (pause) Um, I've done it. And it's, and it did feel, empty. . . . It made me see how just being a worker or just being a student doesn't allow me to really visualize something bigger, or be able to be part of something bigger. . . . I do feel like I do have the need to be part of something bigger than my own personal issues.

As with "bored" mother Yolanda, Jonny's articulation of being part of something bigger meant that a life without organizing yielded a "small" life, literally and figuratively. It was not just his or Yolanda's need to make a social justice intervention in the world, however. Another key reason why busy or burnt-out activists could not stay away from the community for long was the fictive kinship and the attendant emotional support that they lost as a result of that absence.

Since the Asian ethnics enjoyed the privilege of legal status (save for two Filipin@ Americans) and relatively stable jobs and incomes, they did not have to operate at a deficit of superarse. As organizing was not as strongly attached to their sense of self, the Asian Americans, as noted, tended to express more exasperation than the Mexican ethnics over having to do something they felt they should not have to do in the first place. To be sure, the drudgery of movement work, and its general lack of victories, had the tendency to demoralize the Mexican ethnic organizers as well; after all, no collective mobilization was without emotional highs and lows (Gould 2009). Consider the words of Mexican immigrant community leader Laura, who underscored that doing community politics was "always" in some way an emotional letdown.

> LAURA: We are fighting. . . . We are here (positions her hand low to the ground) and they are there (positions hand high above her head).
>
> NADIA: How do you feel about that; sometimes, do you get discouraged? Does it feel like (interrupted)—

LAURA: Yeah, oh, not sometimes, *every time.*

NADIA: *Every time,* wow. Why do you think you keep going, then?

LAURA: Because we have to. We cannot give up—*that's the worst.*

By not giving up, Laura seemed to be conceding to the knowledge that "despite the avowed goals and immediate demands of protest organizers, the effects of social movements are often indirect and become apparent only well after the thrill of massive collective action has diminished" (Tarrow 1998:164). Although a sense of hope, superarse, and perhaps delayed gratification propped up Laura's commitment to the slog of politics, such that inaction was the absolute "worst" route, her feelings of dejection were more commonly invoked by the Asian American women. Cindy shared how being sickened by the truck-washing company next to her school and the grimy air she breathed manifested an insufferable emotional toll; note that although exhaustion is not necessarily a conventional emotion, it is related to feelings of sadness, melancholy, disgust, and frustration.

CINDY: *I think [with] Shine [truck-washing company] and all the air problems we had, when Cara came to us, we said "Thank God! We are tired, we are* tired. *We are all* sick.*" And you just get to the point where you just want to give up.*

NADIA: You mean you were tired of the five of you teachers advocating for yourself without feeling like there was any kind of organization to support you?

CINDY: *[Not so much that], but physically tired, just the . . . , yeah, from our air conditions I have been diagnosed with fibromyalgia—and so have some of the others—and asthma, and a host of other symptoms.* So it has been really difficult trying to work on my doctorate, trying to raise a family, trying to be involved with my church, being involved with the community, being involved with the school. It has been *very difficult.*

Note that I incorrectly presumed, per my research interest, that Cindy's noted exhaustion might have owed to the lack of political resources or advocacy; she quickly clarifies that all she really wanted to convey was how tired she was of the felt and embodied effects of toxic hazard exposure, leaving the fulfillment of her most important obligations in life nearly impossible: raising her family, finishing her Ph.D., and giving back to her community. Cindy's remark reminded me of the frustration that even young high school students felt, like Lily, an undocumented Filipina American, who said that she could not walk around her community without feeling boxed in by the vast mini-cities of oil refineries with their nighttime blinding lights.

Nina, an Asian of Japanese and White American ancestry ("hapa" in Asian American parlance), similarly shared her embodiment of pollution and its enduring toll:

> The main evidence is our [teachers'] symptoms. So we've had to go to a lot of doctors to provide evidence and it's kind of a long process. The next step, you know, it's very cumbersome because you're working and [also] going to doctors. . . . I think, because of the health effects, *we're tired.* I know, definitely, I'm a lot more tired than I used to be . . . [laughs].

Here, Nina echoes Cindy's perpetual thematic: being sick and tired of being sick and tired. Nina was prematurely sick and tired at age thirty, therefore, she was even sicker and more tired at the time of this interview, at age fifty-two. She goes a step further by stipulating that part of that exhaustion came from having to prove in the first place that they were sick. Nina and her fellow teachers explained elsewhere in their interviews that, per worker's compensation law, they shouldered the burden of "verifying" that their environmentally polluted workplace had caused their chronic illnesses.

Of course, the emotional toll did not always originate in resentment and exhaustion concerning the ups and downs of political organizing. Taken together, the narratives reveal that no matter how anticipatory and analytical Lily, Laura, and teachers like Cindy and Nina had to be about political organizing, as we saw, they also proved that they just wanted me, PCORE leaders, and others to listen to their tales of maladies and fatigue as they battled unjust body politics; they wanted to be emotionally supported through dominant assaults on their built and natural communities and on their bodily, mental, and emotional health.

EMOTIONAL SUPPORT AND EMBODIED CITIZENSHIP

Nina, whom we just met, elaborated further on the primacy of emotional support when she recollected with breezy happiness the first time she met Cara, a PCORE leader, whose empathy the teachers found remarkable. Our exchange began with our discussion of what precisely compelled her to work with Carson-based People's CORE.

> NADIA: You said you guys were tired, you didn't have, I guess, any . . . formal organizational thing going on [for EJ], but was there anything else, was there anything about PCORE's message, like their ideas, or—?
>
> NINA: Well, I liked [that] when they, when Cara first came, she was sad for us too—*they really sympathized with us.* They just, they didn't even know us. But you could see that Cara was really moved by the stories we told, the things going on, *how we feel,* about the kids. That was quite impressive to me, *that they didn't know us or anything, and [that] they just found out and they really empathized with what we were going through.* And we felt, the group of us teachers felt, like, "Wow, we've finally got someone fighting for us"—

I began the exchange with Nina by asking what beside exhaustion and lack of infrastructure inspired her to become a community organizer with PCORE; I was trying to address my research question of whether PCORE's political messaging was impactful. Like her co-worker Cindy earlier, she corrected me that, rather, it was how much Cara, who had never met these teachers before, empathized with their plight—how she actually listened to their feelings and how moved Cara was by their students' suffering. It was Cara's emotional response, then, that shored up the teachers' willingness to jump into yet another social justice fight for which they had very little time, energy, or money. In posing the same question to Mexican immigrant leader Laura—"When you got involved with CPC, LBACA, what was it about what they were saying that made you want to get more involved?"—she would also correct me to say that it was not necessarily their political message: "Um, because they care about community. They are always there, so if you have questions . . . they just listen. I don't know how to say this in English, but in Spanish, "Nos dejan desahogarnos" ("They let us blow off steam"). Simply put, it was the fact that these community organizations let them vent their troubled emotions.

These narratives profoundly show emotional support to be a metric of good, real, or moral "citizenship." To the Asian Americans and Latin@s, this metric was one of the primary ways to countervail the two-headed bio-neglecting monster of environmental injustice against the poor and people of color. The women defined citizenship, then, not just as "rights," papers, and voting per se but as taking care of one's neighbor's feelings and resource needs, both of which were forms of emotional support (see Herd and Meyer 2002). That was Cindy's perspective when she chose to break the apathy barrier and convey her condolences to the Japanese American widow standing tentatively in front of BP and government officials at the public comment with which I opened the book; Cindy offered her the emotional support that the officials would not. Among the first-generation Mexican ethnic women, many shared that they could never have overcome the fear and isolation as unauthorized persons without the assistance and counsel they received from community organizations.

CPC, in particular, was well aware that social and emotional services were most in demand, and thus they offered myriad workshops and seminars, as Carmen, CPC's leader, explains:

> A lot of the women that I have known [have been getting jobs] because of their preparation in the programs . . . and they have been succeeding. One of the main reasons why you can't find a job is because you're undocumented. But a lot of the women are now documented and have jobs. Some of these people got their documents because of the help of CPC. We also have some people who lived with domestic violence, and the help of CPC, and having someone to talk to and people to support them, helped them get out of the situation. It also helped them find the resources to make decisions about their lives. And, at the same time, there was a lot of workshops about domestic violence and child abuse. . . . And there was big support for the community that made them feel *that they could do things even if they were undocumented*, or if they didn't have a career, they could still succeed.

And that is precisely how thirty-six-year-old Celia, mother of three, received the work of CPC. In the following narrative, she shares how she would not have survived the undocumented life had it not been for their knowledge, resource, and emotional support (as well as LBACA's). Upon my asking her what she would do if she became a citizen—maintain her devotion to grassroots community work or devote more time to voting, campaigning, or running for office—she replied,

> No, because, first of all, we need to look out for our community because my community starts with my family to everyone else. It has been a type of guide

> for me in this country." (*No, tenemos que ver primero pues en mi caso yo primero tengo que ver por mi comunidad porque mi comunidad incluye desde mi familia hasta todos los de mas . . .*). . . . I think because I don't have any family here, I have found people that support me, and I know that they are here for me unconditionally. *I stay there because that's where I started.* (*Yo creo que como no tengo familia he encontrado medios de apoyo y si el día de mañana necesito algo ellos van a estar allí incondicionalmente claro. Me he mantenido allí porque pues allí empecé*). . . . I've had the opportunity to go to conferences to advocate for my children and it has been a long process and *mostly it helped me lose the fear of living in a country that was unknown to me.* . . . They also help us know where there are resources and how to look for them, because a lot of people . . . are afraid because they don't have papers. *They [CPC] do not ask and, thanks to CPC, I haven't had those fears,* and it's an obstacle I have overcome.

In Celia's rendering, the linchpin that determined her political allegiance was emotional and resource support, which she dovetails insofar as providing resources necessary to survive and thrive is indeed the politics of caring (see Prindeville 2004) in the spirit of "nourishing bodies and social ties" (Pérez and Abarca 2007:141). Likening the CBOs to the family, a social unit rooted in emotional attachment and meant to be "there . . . unconditionally," she immediately invokes how they have helped her overcome emotions such as fear of being "illegal" and of being surveilled by the state. She affirms that these CBOs do not care whether or not one has papers and thus "do not ask." It was a citizenship coeval with emotional support. These narratives by Carmen and Celia also bespoke the primacy that the activists gave to socioeconomic mobility as part of the broader importance they placed on the general mobility of their bodies through the world.

Long-time LBACA leader Marta addressed another side of emotional support when she responded to the criticism from elites that community organizers like her were "involved in everything"—elites charged, so how could they be sure that they were expert on anything? With indignation and conviction, Marta replied,

> Oh, wow, why can't I just focus on one thing? I'm going to tell you what I think about that. I can't focus on just one, [like] just on education, *because Nadia has asthma problems and I need to support Nadia to support air quality and [oppose] contamination issues.* There are also people who are in

> [undocumented] immigration situations, so if I'm a citizen that can change the community but Alicia over here (gesturing towards our translator) doesn't have her documents and isn't a citizen yet, then I have to help.

Marta makes clear that she does not distinguish between working on school reform, offering health-related support to an asthmatic Nadia, and fighting against disproportionate air pollution and toxic contamination in her neighborhood. As we have seen, especially in Chapter 3, schools were sites of environmental injustice, and everyone's health was imperiled as a result, so the state and industry forced her to focus on more than "one thing." She did not get to *choose* her focus. All of the aforementioned profoundly made up Marta's life; how could she see them singularly, and focus on just one of these ones? She also implies that it is precisely by offering emotional support to the sick and the deportable that she is recruiting new members to the struggle, who together would battle polluters, INS in the early years, ICE in the later years, the regulatory state, and anyone else who embodied privilege. The other Asian and Latin@ organizers similarly demonstrated that their approach to politics was *not* to draw hard and fast lines between helping someone learn how to prevent asthma attacks, helping the young ones study and run around at school or in parks, and helping someone nab those pro-forma citizenship papers.

A Filipina Mexican ethnic, Vega, affirms this sentiment by conflating the politics of feelings and of structural change by way of her Christian faith. About PCORE, she remarks, "It has been a blessing, a huge blessing. Absolute God-send. . . . We don't have time to do any of that [fight Shine Truck Washing, refineries, and so on], so that has been such a blessing and a strength in our relationship, . . . that support of what we're doing that could help us to make a change in our air quality in our community, and also systemically throughout other communities also." In other words, supporting the feeling states of one's fellow citizens and improving the air through environmental justice were in no way discrete processes.

Tina, the Cambodia American "community health worker" from LBACA, identified not just resource support but emotional support as one of LBACA's greatest strengths.

> TINA: I think the community health worker really affects those families because we go in and provide them with information and with the [asthma]

supplies, and we . . . accommodate their schedule: weekend visits, after-hour visits. And, for me, I found out that . . . *sometimes they just need someone to talk to if there's another issue besides asthma*. . . . For example, this [one] family has so many health issues. Her husband is going through difficult times and she's just going nuts, and then when I went to go visit her last, her mom was there, she said, "*Mom, I couldn't have done it without Tina! She was just there to listen.*"

NADIA: Aw, that's so sweet.

TINA: So that makes you feel really good that she appreciates it, and that *I've affected her life. I couldn't do much for her personal issue, but I was there to listen to her,* at least, and she was so grateful. *So it's not just for asthma.* And then there are times where I walk into my first visit and, I don't even put my stuff down, and *she'll be crying. This is the first visit!* . . . And, I'm like, "What happened?!" *Then we talk first . . . sometimes you need to get it out. . . . And most of them, I would say, 90 percent of them will share their personal story with me. . . . And at the beginning I would cry because I was just so emotional.* It's, like, a lot and I feel like I have to be . . . focused and . . . strong, and to find ways to support them.

Tina repeats over the course of this narrative that her LBACA job as a health services provider was much more than about asthma supplies. It was to serve as the emotional support system that so many low-income, immigrant, undocumented, women and mothers of color needed, such that upon meeting Tina for the very first time, they would open the floodgates of their pent-up emotions and spill tears of gratitude. In turn, not only would Tina cry out of compassion but she makes mention of the difficulty of that emotional labor, which was "a lot" and forced her to "be focused and strong" and constantly thinking of "ways to support them."

In another instance, Tina addressed the affective politics of her City of Long Beach unceremoniously dropping the Cambodian New Year celebration given mounting costs to the city; central to this process was the emotional support her coethnics offered one another so as to channel their anger and frustration into action.

[S]o the people that did the New Year before, they owed the city money. And then the city kept pushing them and pushed them to do it in another city.

> And so we disagreed and said, *"Why? This is our home?"* You know, you have a birthday party and you can't go celebrate just anywhere. *I mean, we're tired from running. We fled from Cambodia and then you tell us to go somewhere else!?* [scoffs]. . . . And this is like the second largest Cambodian community besides Cambodia!

Rather than interpret Long Beach's decision as a matter of dollars and cents, Tina and her coethnics saw it as tantamount to the American War and the Khmer Rouge exiling Cambodians out of their own home country. That is, Long Beach had effectively turned Cambodian Americans into refugees pushed from "home" yet again. After a lifetime of weary feet and hearts, Tina, her husband, and other coethnics refused to run, however. They marshalled their negative responses into positivity (Eyerman 2005) and emotionally supported one another through the vagaries of bringing the parade back "home," which they did to much fanfare in 2014 after a long three-year hiatus. Thereafter, Tina vowed to "work more towards my Cambodian community," not just on issues like gang prevention, but, interestingly, on relationships based on emotional attachment, namely, preventing divorce and domestic violence.

The youth organizers also echoed the construction of "good" citizenship as emotional support. In the infectious spirit of her activist mother, Bella conveyed how familial love prompted her to fight for her sister, namely, to get her into a magnet school that was "blessed" with air purifiers. Her sister's current school, as with most in the community, lacked these and therefore high asthma rates among Latinx children prevailed.

> I would tell them [the officials] how my sister wants to attend a magnet school, and when she would go by it . . . [she noticed] like, trucks would pass behind that school . . . [but at least] the magnets would have filters, air filters for the classrooms. And . . . that made me, I guess that motivated me to go and testify, so that my sister could go and attend that school. So that's one of the reasons [I organize], is my sister.

Bella traces her start in activism to her need to look out for her sister, who was asthmatic in part because the polluting state and corporations would not even spare the expense of air filters. Yet these were schools where students spent at least six-and-a-half hours a day and were often immobilized and distracted by environmental hazards and emergencies. In effect, schools were also killing the youth quietly.

Socializing and "Girls' Time" as Emotional Movement Building

As noted, Latin@ immigrant women have come to dominate the leadership of the immigration reform movement since the late 1980s owing to a panoply of factors: the increased power and public engagement of the women given the migration process, the explosive growth of the movement that left gaps in leadership, and the women's feminist consciousness in a 1990s political culture more in tune with gender equality (Milkman and Terriquez 2012). The Latinas with whom I worked also bespoke what Zepeda-Millán (2017:198) discovered about the African, Asian, Caribbean, and Mid-Eastern American and Latinx organizers of the historic 2006 immigration protests in Los Angeles, New York, and Fort Myers:

> I heard again and again about how regular people utilized the various assets already present in their neighborhoods to facilitate major episodes of collective action—sometimes, even without professional social movement organizations or financial assistance from external actors, such as private foundations or national organizations.

As we saw in Chapter 2, not only did the immigrant women marshal everyday community resources to strategize emotions in their dealings with state and corporate officials—along the vertical axis—they also intensely did so to movement-build on the ground, along the horizontal axis. Respected community leader Marta lives out this political philosophy, for instance, when she builds emotionality into her organizing activities: "For me, personally, I like to do door knocking, to invite people to help with housing. I take some time to do that. *I like to give phone calls to people to tell them that I missed them because they didn't come.*" Much more than a phone tree reminder about this and that event, or about how industry will win if residents do not attend (which was how I used to organize), Marta makes it about how much *she misses the residents in their absence.* Similarly, Teresa never lived her day-to-day life without enacting the emotion work and emotional labor endemic to recruiting for the movement: "Yeah, and if I see someone coughing, I say, 'Hey, are you feeling this way? I heard this might be because of pollution. Come to our meeting to get more information.' For example, at the laundromat, the women who are there, the individuals who are there, they just start talking, and that's just a topic that I bring up in order to talk about it [joining the movement]."

In addition to the types of grants their organizations received that tended to fund more innocuous activities, the Mexicana immigrants—to a greater extent than the Asian Americans and more than any social movement I had ever engaged with—devoted a large chunk of time to social activities, albeit those that were never unrelated to the movement (for example, Figure 12). CPC, for instance, offered myriad classes such as line dancing, *danza Azteca*, aerobics, cake-baking, flower-arranging, and, of course, healthier cooking classes. The health-related classes were to achieve the physical health that they were denied and the other classes were to forge the community and support structures for mental health that they were also denied. Recall, as well, the emphasis that Latina activists put on workshops and weeks-long seminars on dressing, doing hair, and wearing make-up professionally. These social "sisterly" events that I

FIGURE 12. Celebrating Marta Cota's birthday after a Health and Housing meeting. Source: courtesy of the author.

thought might take too much time, resources, and energy away from the good fight instead taught me that these allowed the women to politicize neighbors; grow the movement; buck elites' race, gender, and class stereotypes; develop their own self-worth and sense of superarse; and ultimately compensate for a life deprived of country and good health. Once I began attending more of these events, I understood much more intimately and deeply why they were so central to their lives and their politics. Not only would we stand shoulder to shoulder in our aprons in a vast, brightly lit kitchen making fresh tortillas, trading space and knives to chop, smelling the aromatic fajitas as they cooked, and then sitting down to eat their deliciousness together, we would catch up about our struggles with our partners, children, their asthma, and our world. It was this type of sharing, venting, and emotional support through conversation that Coll (2010), in her study, found was vital to growing superarse among the Mexican and Central American women activists who sought the best ways to fight domestic violence and anti-immigrant injustice.

In addition to the LA-based women in my study gathering to cook, apply mascara, dance, and exercise, it was CPC members who had to spend many waking hours together performing the social services that the local governments (bio)neglected per the withered social contract, such as finding after-school programming for their children while clearing the parks of drug dealers, gang members, and sex workers that they did not want influencing their children (see Pardo 1998). As a result, social bonding and stepping into the social services deficit were the beating heart of embodied citizenship. In this way, it was a profound social justice achievement just to be able to form their own community in a land that barred, sterilized, detained, ousted, exploited, and segregated them. In their eyes, the resistance just by dint of "being a community" proved self-evident even if the Latin@s never eked one environmental concession from the state or industry.

Spending more time with the Filipin@ ethnic organizers also allowed me to understand that similar reasons were behind why PCORE activists centered cultural politics at most of their events. As noted in the previous chapter, the Filipin@s of Carson and elsewhere in LA's industrial belt primarily attributed the hazards and other forms of bioneglect to the nativistic racism that reduced them to racial placeholders: those who came from a poor, brown country who were neither politically visible nor truly "American." The ultimate irony was that the US colonizer had entrenched itself in their ancestral country and then forcibly Americanized and propelled Filipinx people to the colonial center. Therefore, an environmental justice rally that is also an event full of aromatic Filipinx food—adobo and pancit—and that prioritizes a program of honoring the straight-A students, civic leaders, and historic farmworker labor leaders of the community, was the norm. In a process parallel to their Mexican immigrant counterparts, the Filipin@ ethnics engaged in time-consuming circumventions of nativistic racism, such as taking English classes to rid themselves of Tagalog accents or working harder than White co-workers to avoid the bamboo or jade ceiling (often to no avail); hence, ethnic pride was never extricable from the environmental injustices that plagued their community. It was never to be taken for granted.

If I Move, the Movement Won't Move—Manifesting Embodied Citizenship

Another key source of the activists' anger was their indignation over the cavalier suggestion, "Why don't you move?" posed by elites and more privileged Americans. In pursuing what the activists thought about this question, I heard all but two people unequivocally declare that they would *never* move. Even the two individuals who considered it did so only out of fear for their children's (and their own) health, leading them to wonder, "Maybe I should move?" A third organizer, Filipina American Pia, vowed not to move, but her response was slightly unexpected; she was one of the longest-standing and fiercest community organizers, yet she was not as incensed as the vast majority of the activists, nor did she focus on the offensive nature of the directive. Rather, she specified the need to stay local to keep refineries accountable.

> PIA: Why would I do that? I bought the house. That is my house!
>
> NADIA: (playing devil's advocate, speaking as if a politician) "Well, you don't live in poverty, you could buy a house somewhere else."
>
> PIA: Well, but what you have to do is monitor them [refineries]. Because if they're responsible business people, they'd want accountability to the people to support their business. If BP refinery would be accountable to the residents around the area, they'd have the social responsibility to know that they cannot lose the residents around the area.

By implication, Pia revealed that she did not see the oil refineries as primarily concerned with accountability to the people; otherwise, she would be living in a clean(er) neighborhood. In her eyes, she would never move because only local residents like her could keep the oil refineries in check. She implies, by extension, that "regulatory" agencies were remiss. At the same time, Pia's remark that BP might even be concerned with actual social responsibility (as opposed to coopting care rhetoric) gave me pause, in the same way that most of the activists' hope, even if frail, in an intractable government did. On the other side of the token, they taught me that defeatism and unilateral demonization did not help their mental or emotional state, or their capacity to strategize at multiple scales.

In contrast to Pia, the overwhelming majority were enraged by the question, and categorically refused to move. As we shall see, they refused to do so out of a sense of loyalty to their neighbors and a sense of conviction that they needed to help them, in large part through organizing and by being part of a mutually supportive social network (with nary a thick line between them). Such a refusal is significant; it demonstrates a form of embodied citizenship that involves a willingness "to be killed quietly" in order to emotionally support and ensure the belonging of others and, by extension, one's own belonging.

Of course, as mostly low-income undocumented immigrants, the Mexican ethnics did not have the economic or even legal privilege to just get up and move, let alone to more environmentally privileged areas. Second-generation youth leader Bella incisively noted the classist presupposition of the "Why don't you move?" question:

> BELLA: Money! You know, you can't always have the access and mobility to move somewhere else. . . . Sometimes you can't because of your job or your kids.
>
> NADIA: So you'd say that you can't always pick up and move? . . . And how would you feel about moving to a new place?
>
> BELLA: For example, say that I'm going to school and I'm working towards my career, and I wanted to move: I wouldn't feel comfortable with my family living in an area where the air is so nasty; and me being good with my apartment and car (pause)—that would really bother me.

Furthermore, any move they would make would likely only be a moderate improvement in air quality, and their reliance on other people's cars (as well as public transportation) would mean that they would continually be exposed to the asthma triggers of car and bus exhaust and second-hand cigarette smoke anyhow. At the same time, living in an area with even slightly better air quality could make a major difference to children prone to asthma attacks, and the fact that the women rejected it spoke volumes on how politically committed they were to their fellow citizens of the embodied community. Recall that Tanya, a Mexican immigrant, opened this book with, "Well, if I want to leave, I'll leave! If I don't, I won't! I would be leaving them all alone!" (shaking her head).

Middle-aged Valeria's response to "What would you say to someone who tells you, 'Just move'?" reveals her desire to fight for and defend her communal family rather than escape as an easy way out:

> VALERIA: "Mmm, NO (laughs). I would say, "Let me chat with the right people who are working with [us] and learn what is going on and learn more from them what I can do, what I can do to help in order to live better."
>
> NADIA: Mhm, okay. So you feel like even if you could afford the move, maybe, that you would rather do something to make the community better?
>
> VALERIA: Right, . . . it's not always a solution [to move]. Because then they [the powerful] don't listen to you. You don't have a voice and they're not going to do [anything] for us as a benefit.

Similarly, part Japanese American teacher Lana echoed some of the Mexican women's sentiments in underscoring the deleterious effects of abdicating embodied citizenship for the movement: "I just tell them, well, first of all, if I move out of the position, I'm exposing another person to the damage. And the other thing I say is that all of us who are organizing are there, and it would fall apart if we weren't all there. It's too hard, it's really hard [to sustain, otherwise]." When I queried her teaching co-worker Cindy about why she refused to move, she replied as follows:

> CINDY: 'Cause my fight is here. God has placed me here. Do you know the story of Queen Esther from the Bible?
>
> NADIA: No, sorry!
>
> CINDY: Well, Esther . . . was a Hebrew, and she had to become a queen of Persia. But she was afraid. She didn't tell anyone including the king that she was Hebrew. And it wasn't until her [Jewish] people began to be per-

> secuted that her uncle Mordechai came to her and told her that, for such a time as this, God has placed you where you are. And this is your time to do what you've been called to do. *And for each of us we're all called to do something in our lives, in our families, in our communities.* And for me this is, I feel, part of what I've been called to do. . . . *Even if it costs my health, I need to fight for these children. . . . We have the people always tell us, "You can transfer, go to another school" but who is going to fight for these children? Who is going to fight for this community? Who is going to fight for my family, in the neighborhood?* So, leaving is *not* an option.

Fully cognizant that she is being killed slowly, not only does Cindy emphasize the political protection that she must provide her students, but the fact that moving would leave her without any protection for her and her family. The staunch opposition to moving flowed from a sense of duty to fight for each other, to hold each other up emotionally. The sense that doing otherwise equaled a dereliction of duty makes more sense when we consider the ways these teachers thought of their schools and students. As fellow teacher Lana noted,

> It seems to me that women teachers consider their classroom environment more as a home, in general, you know?—*a family*, and so maybe it has something to do with that. You should see us talking about the children [the students] . . . to our spouses at home. And I wonder if men take their work home in that way, and internalize them [students] like that.

Lana adds that she thinks this internalization of a teacher's love and sense of protection for their students owes to femininity, an emotional attachment that men might not approximate.

Yet the male organizers were on the same page as Lana on the conviction not to move. Ben of PCORE (hapa Filipino) and Jesse of CFASE (Mexican American) emphasized more an imperative to address the structural factors that led to environmental racism and classism, not the post-hoc symptoms. Ben remarked,

> I don't think that the industry has to be there in the first place. I would disagree with the basis of that argument; [I'd say] that we need to really start making a shift to what we should have made a shift towards already: green

> energy! By rolling over and not putting up a fight and just saying "OK, I'm going to move," is kind [of like], you know, when people say . . . I'm an American, I consider myself to be an American, and what an American would do is fight for what's right, and not just throw their hands up and leave the country.

Jesse invoked rights discourse to flout the premise behind "just move somewhere cleaner": "It is our *right* to live here. We *chose* to be in this community. It is our *right* to a clean environment. And it is our *right* to a quality life. *You* have no rights to pollute the air. You have no rights to deprive me of a good quality of life." In the same vein as Ben and Jesse, Celia resented the onus being placed on her and her disadvantaged community to clean up the environment. Why should she have to suffer the expensive and laborious process of moving neighborhoods, filling out the often confusing and convoluted English-language paperwork to do so, changing their children's schools, and the like?

> CELIA: That, I don't think it's right. *It's not right.*
> NADIA: And you feel that you, the community, have to fix the problem?
> CELIA: *They* have to fix the problem!

The statements of all of the activists here reveal that they never wanted to be bad, immoral embodied citizens, that is to say, give up on the community's health, and emotional needs so as to prioritize one's individual needs—leaving one's neighbors, and the social movement itself, alone to choke and die without their assistance. When the loss of community also means losing your own support network that you have built up, as teacher Cindy reminds us with her "Who's going to fight for us?", then the community takes precedence even over one's health, well-being, and life.

WHY MOSTLY WOMEN? EMBODIED CITIZENSHIP OWES TO ECONOMICS, PATRIARCHY, AND GENDER

One of the primary ways that the Mexican and Asian ethnics would conjure gender was to think of the dominant presence of women and mothers at protests, public comments, and media events. Some, like Cindy remarked, "Come to think of it, I don't think I ever saw one dad show up to our protests." Her view likely flowed from her own personal situation: an ex-husband who did not believe in getting too involved in politics, especially when it came to their daughter.

CINDY: The last campaign my daughter Holly and I were involved in was my former superintendent of Parks and Recreation. She ran for City Council, so Holly . . . , she was six years old, the youngest member on the committee.

NADIA: Wow, that is so cute.

CINDY: So she is accustomed her whole life to going to meetings with me, going to protests.

NADIA: Do you want to expose her to that?

CINDY: Yeah. But her dad says, "No, don't take her." But I want her to see. I want her to understand that there are things we have to fight for—not just for ourselves but for others. . . . When we had the LA Unified rallies downtown [against the pink-slip layoffs of teachers] he was really worried about me taking her.

As a community health worker and activist, Tina weighed in on the role of men in health justice work: "For the community health worker, I don't think it's a position for a male. Why? Because the family needs to be comfortable. Because when you go in it's mostly the mom; very little percentage where you find the male there." As previous research has shown, women have gotten more involved in the environmental justice fight owing to the greater number who rear children and interact with neighbors and who thereby notice the deteriorating health symptoms of all. Women tend to be on the front lines of all kinds of environmental suffering, whether it owes to their role as homemakers or those who work fewer hours than their partners or those who tend to have more time to organize (see, for example, Brown and Ferguson 1995; Louie 2001; Hay 2009; Krauss 1993; Pardo 1998). When I posed the question to the women as to their own interpretation of "Why all the women?" their answers constellated around patriarchy and economics.

Yolanda, for instance, immediately zeroed in on the machismo born of male dominance.

YOLANDA: Especially the Spanish men is, like, "Oh no, come on, you only go lose your time over there!" It's because some Hispanic people, especially men, is very, I don't know what to say in English (long pause)—

NADIA: Like, macho?

YOLANDA: Yeah! Yeah, machismo. My husband is one of these. When I start to go to CPC, he say, "Come on, you only lose your time over there." [So

> I said] "Okay, come with me and you will see." When he come the first time, he say, "I will stay here. I like it!"

In a similar vein, hapa Japanese American Lana quipped, "There's something about Oriental men. It's the way they're raised! You know, my husband, he's changed a lot." Although Lana identifies sexism and patriarchy within "Oriental" culture she, like Yolanda, has a sanguine ending insofar as her husband grew more gender egalitarian over time. Even Bella, a millennial, concurred with the first-generation women's sentiments when I asked her what she thought about Mexican ethnic men.

> NADIA: Do you ever think they say, "Oh, that's women's work" because it's about the kids?
>
> BELLA: Yeah, yeah, I'm sure they do!

CPC leader Carmen attributed the highly imbalanced gender ratio both to macho patriarchy and to the gendered nature of the capitalist labor market.

> The man thinks that you shouldn't go. Machismo still exists: "You can't go. You have to attend to me." Like, the meetings are at 4:30 p.m. so the women want to—they go to the morning classes [such as aerobics] but not to the meeting. They don't go to the meeting because they say "my husband is already at the house, he doesn't like me to leave the children, he wants me there." . . . But those women, one day, say that they want to advocate for their children or, one day, something happens that they have to come to CPC—and it's been happening. The group before was thirty or twenty people and now it's sixty or seventy. So that means that they're starting to think like us. I think the problems with the economy . . . is making people open their eyes. Before, a man never let his wife work, but now there are more jobs for women than for men. So now the women have to leave and have to work, and the man has to stay home.

Some, like Laura, stayed in the realm of gender statuses, noting both the attributes of women's femininity and the problematic nature of masculinity.

> LAURA: Um, I don't know if you know, but our Latino race: men do not get involved in things like children, education—
>
> NADIA: Aren't you doing politics too? . . . Because you guys are talking to government and you're trying to influence government.

LAURA: Yeah, but they think that it's a woman's job.

NADIA: Very interesting. So let me ask you something: if the men were not working, do you think they'd come and get involved?

LAURA: Um, maybe, but it's difficult because I ask and my husband laughs. Maybe he would go if I was spending days or months constantly encouraging him to go. Maybe he finally would.

NADIA: Fifty percent of the women are working, though, . . . and the men are working, but the women are showing up.

LAURA: I think, because we're smarter (both laugh). . . . No, it's because mothers, I think, mothers care, almost care more than fathers about our children.

NADIA: Do you ever hear the women say at CPC, LBACA, "They're not very supportive of me doing this?"

LAURA: Oh yeah, oh yeah . . . *a lot*. . . . They want them to stay at home.

NADIA: Do you think it causes fights?

LAURA: Oh yeah, yeah, it causes fights. . . . But there's a phrase in Spanish. . . . *El valiente vive hasta que el cobarde quiere*, the brave live as much as the weak will allow them. . . . So sometimes I have to help some of the women. . . . "Remember, while you do your job cleaning the house, cooking, you can still go where you want!"

NADIA: And what do they say?

LAURA: Well, sometimes they say, "No, I can't." I say, "Oh, yes, you can!" (both laugh). That's true, and maybe they [husbands] will get mad, but once they [the women] come back it will be OK; it's not a problem. Yeah, because we should educate them.

Laura's Spanish-language proverb is instructive insofar as she believes society deems women weak and men "brave," but that the brave's capacity to act depends on the weak enabling it; therefore, in her eyes, if the Mexican immigrant women pushed back against their male partners' patriarchy, the men would have to relent. If the women just ventured out of the house irrespective of what their male partners said, then what else could he do but let her go? Given all of the immigrants' emphasis on mobility, indeed, this was a form of gendered mobility. Interestingly enough, Laura did not believe that her job as an organizer was just to get the women to fight the power, but also to "educate" them to fight their husbands. Again, the latter enabled the former.

Her friend and co-organizer Marta was especially agitated by women deferring to their husbands, a view she delivered with her characteristic moxie and conviction.

> When it's people like my niece, sister-in-law, people who I trust, I tell them, "Permission from your husband? Your husband is working all day! Take advantage of the time! You could go learn at class about diabetes, about cholesterol, about the contamination and the environment, and your husband doesn't come home until the afternoon." They say, "Well, I don't know." So sometimes people, they don't have a sense of what [kind of struggle] happens to others.

While Laura interpreted patriarchy and machismo as a mentality that the women internalized (one that could be disabused by way of "education"), Marta interpreted it as some Latinas' inability to understand "struggle" as a collective phenomenon. Later in her interview, however, Marta remarked proudly that she used her power as a woman to draw a few men into Community Partners Council.

> MARTA: And now we have two or three men in CPC. . . . He said he saw me at City Council and he told all the parents at the class, "I know this woman, even though she doesn't speak English, I'm very proud of her because she spoke with all the men in suits. They [the translators] were interpreting for her and she was advocating for the community. Listen to her because *she is good*." He was the first one that came to CPC.
>
> NADIA: Good! So how do the men think about the women going to these meetings, becoming leaders, getting involved in the community?
>
> MARTA: That we have a lot of value, we're being brave—even though I'm a woman I can do a lot of things (*Que somos muy valientes, que tenemos mucho valor, valor de que aunque soy mujer yo puedo hacer muchas cosas.*)

Statements like these signaled one of the reasons that Marta was not just one of the strongest activists but one of the strongest people I knew. She seemed able to convince anyone to care about the cause and to care about someone else's suffering.

Affirming her coethnics' ethnics class-bound politics, Laura was quick to point out, however, that both women and men were fundamentally hurt by economics—that economic causes ultimately came before gender causes. In response to my question of what would get more men into the movement, Laura does not default to an individualized solution, but a systemic economic one.

> LAURA: First of all, um, fix the economy. . . . Put food and home first.
>
> NADIA: Put food on the table? Paying rent, yeah?
>
> LAURA: Yeah, . . . maybe they [residents] are interested in this, but they think, "I'd rather go to work."
>
> NADIA: What if the house and what if their family issues were OK?
>
> LAURA: Oh yeah, they would. . . . They would, because I find that some of them are very interested, and they want to go.

Laura's view aligns with Mary Pardo's findings on the 1980s activism of Mothers of East Los Angeles, many of whose male partners gradually grew supportive of the movement and partook in ways that made men feel like leaders but without the women losing control of the movement—the women's carefully crafted strategy (Pardo 1998). Here, Laura's counterpart, Teresa, similarly wished that more men would join the movement. Upon asking her what ideas she had to realize more gender balance, Teresa concurred with Laura that it all boiled down to economics: "Yes, well, it's because of work. . . . We need them to pay them more and then they'd have time off (mutual laughter)! That's really the only way."

Some women such as Valeria were more reticent to call out the men as macho patriarchs. Both she and Teresa attributed the lack of men to a nonvaluative statement about the nature of Mexican and Mexican immigrant culture. First, Valeria responded thus to my question of why so few men:

> VALERIA: Maybe this is part of our culture? They come from work, they don't want to, you know, go outside anymore and they want to have dinner and rest.
>
> NADIA: But some of these women are working, too, so why do you think there's this difference between men and women?
>
> VALERIA: I really don't know, this is something that we've been observing, not just in the United States, but in Mexico too. And it's something that I forgot to mention: when we have parties over there, all the ladies gather at

> one table and the guys are drinking at another place by themselves. So, it's not like you sit next to your husband and talk with everybody at the same time. No, they gather in one place and the ladies gather in another place.

Valeria traced Mexican immigrant norms to customs of gender segregation in Mexico, something that she found worth observing, but that she does not necessarily condemn. Teresa was much more willing to concede that the men's machismo fostered all kinds of opposition to women stepping out of the home to fight the power.

> Sometimes I've heard husbands say, "Oh, they're just going there to gossip, and 'You're just going to go and hang out with friends, just wasting your time.'" Another thing that the husbands may think is that it's not proper for a woman to be out of the home most of the day, out in public doing stuff for the community; the core is here, the home, that needs to be taken care of. But, for the most part, if the women are there [at the meetings, that means] they have husbands who are supportive of them.

Teresa implies that the men may be threatened or jealous of the women partaking in a domain that the men do not rule, hence the dismissive comments about going to political meetings as mere women's gossip sessions.[4] As Hirsch (2003) noted, in rural Mexican villages from whence most of the LA activists came, space is gendered such that women out on the street (*calle*) are deemed sexually transgressive; therefore, it is not surprising that most men want women to stay within the domestic realm—that is, stay "inside" (see Zentgraf 2002). Teresa ends her narrative, however, with the affirmation that most of the women who are grassroots organizers are those with supportive husbands and partners. And indeed, roughly half of the women gleamed with pride when they spoke of how supportive their husbands were. Tanya was a prime example:

> TANYA: The communication is there. It's important that I do have communication with my husband and I do inform him of what's going on [politically]. My husband even encourages me to go to the meetings, so he supports me in that sense—that the wife gets bored at home. And if I have time to go educate myself then, he says, go for it.
>
> NADIA: He also wants to know what goes on?

> TANYA: Yes, I go to the meeting or the workshop, and he asks me what it was about (smiling widely).

Youth leader Tomas, who was active in the immigrant labor movement, remarked on what he deemed the Latinas' subversive forms of strength: "These women think, 'We have our husbands in check.' . . . That would scare the hell out of me because these are tough ladies! . . . Kind of like, 'You know what? . . . The food is there and I have a meeting. I've got to run!'" Similarly, Tomas was keenly aware of women's socialized tendencies:

> Usually females are better listeners and more mature at the high school level, and I would see that when they would talk to the male or female truckers. And with the guys [males], I would talk about, like, you know some of them were dealing with drug problems or broken homes, and I could tell them, "Hey, yeah, I was homeless when I was fifteen. In the divorce we all got scattered." I had some stellar . . . students who were homeless. . . . And these were the key leaders who were leading other students.

As Tomas himself alludes to, gender affected the solidarity of the community. Lead organizers such as Cara of PCORE, a young woman in her twenties, also noticed that in the LA port-industrial basin most of the leaders of the environmental justice groups were men.[5] She traced this demographic pattern to patriarchy and the reproduction of its side effects: men valuing male definitions and styles of leadership and women not seeing themselves as leader types within that narrow rubric, therefore not assuming the role. Yet my observations of these clean air movements also found that these male-led organizations by and large did not reject the women's influence on their organizational strategies and tactics. For one, the men had to listen to their membership lest they fall prey to charges that they failed as a "community" and "grassroots" group, in turn losing a strong-willed constituency who could vote with their feet on a moment's notice. At the same time, I was witness not just to the men's keen eye on such pragmatism but also to their sensitivity to the women's own struggles and political goals, in large part because they often shared the same racial or ethnic background—sometimes the same immigration and class profile. Even if some of these male leaders talked too much and listened too little, as per conventional gendered norms of speech (Tannen 2007), the women would overtly or subtly reign the men in when, for instance, the women discussed how they wanted to testify to officials or what types of campaigns they wanted to trail-blaze next.

When relations between men and women were not smooth, however, the situations could verge on discord and conflict. For instance, Cara, the PCORE coordinator we just met, remarked bluntly and without self-consciousness, "I don't like men." Not expecting such a frank declaration, I paused momentarily before asking, "Do you mind organizing with them?" to which she replied, "I'd prefer not. Most of them haven't dealt with their male privilege yet." When Cara had to leave her post at PCORE to move back to the East Coast she was replaced by another Filipino American millennial, Paul, of whom some of the teachers were not fond. Addressing an inverse household gendered dynamic, PCORE's Lana opined, "He was always having to ask his girlfriend every time we were trying to schedule a meeting, and it's like, come on, if you're going to take this job, you have to have a partner who's going to accept that, sometimes, you can't always be home for her. My husband does that for me [when I organize]; why can't he ask her to do the same for him?" Although one could argue that Paul was being more feminist by putting his girlfriend's needs before his own, Lana's implication was that Paul and his partner were in an unhealthy codependent relationship.

Another problematic gendered dynamic was clearly evident at one LBACA-CPC meeting during the summer of 2009. Everything was proceeding as usual—perfunctory report-backs from the various committees and coalition partners—when something widened my eyes. One of the husbands of one of the well-known women organizers stood up and demanded to talk about the labor exploitation of Los Angeles-Long Beach port truck drivers by the trucking companies. This was the first I had seen of him. In a deeply resonant voice he made known his frustration with the meeting and the organizations for failing to devote enough of their general agenda to this labor struggle. Waxing in a tonal diatribe, he lashed out against the trucking companies for committing the perennial act of neoliberal exploitation: designating them not employees but "independent contractors," in effect, shirking all responsibility for their employees. Corporations thus enjoyed paying substandard wages and no benefits, farming out the cost of the trucks and their maintenance to the truckers themselves, and sidestepping unions altogether. Although the vast majority of the women at the meeting that night whole-heartedly agreed with everything he said, many became visibly upset by what they considered his displaced anger and frustration. One woman replied (and I'm paraphrasing): "Francisco, I get it, we all get it, but LBACA has chosen to focus right now on clean air. Look at our kids! They're practically choking! We can't do everything, as you know, so you're going to have to respect that that's what we decided. Once we feel like we've really gotten them to clean up the air, we can focus more on the truckers. But you can't just come in here and yell like this." Francisco would not stop, however. He kept criticizing the women for not focusing on both issues at once, they were related after all; if the companies would buy the truckers clean-energy trucks, he opined, then Latinx and other kids of color would have less asthma and the adults, less cancer. The women empathized, but they were not going to tolerate his refusal to sit down and yield the mic. The female meeting facilitators then grabbed their own mics and sonically overpowered him: "You can't come here and talk forever when each person only gets a few minutes! Have you seen anyone else here yell or talk as long as you?!" Women near the wildly gesticulating Francisco gently held his arm and steered him away from the mic, his words soon trailing off and his resistance soon breaking. Without once calling it "machismo" (even though later that is what most of the women privately considered it)—and without enraging Francisco to the point of his storming out—the women got him to calm down and sit down. Though in moments like these some women could get indignant and escalate conflict, most would simply shake their heads and handle such gendered tensions and machismo with enviable aplomb. It was not just the fact that they outnumbered the men, or that this activist space was, in essence, a female-dominated domain; years of life experience just seemed to teach the women how to handle hypermasculine men.

To be sure, there were also times when some of the women's gendered behaviors shocked me. At another meeting that same summer, an energetic thirty-one-year-old and conventionally handsome Robert Garcia, the first Latino and the youngest person ever elected to the Long Beach Council, interrupted the usual cast of meeting characters (police officers, nonprofit workers) by paying us a visit. I would discover later that he, flanked by some other prominent figures in Long Beach, was an ethnically Peruvian child immigrant and rising political star. After his stock speech in which he explained in fluent

Spanish that he wanted to introduce himself to the organization, learn of their concerns, and help out in whatever way he could, some residents told him a little about their struggles with air and health, as well as school, immigration, and crime. Upon wrapping up, saying good-bye, and motioning to leave, a woman who appeared to be in her forties loudly blurted out, "Hey, aren't you going to give us a hug and a kiss?" to which most in the room burst into raucous laughter or some, like me, breathed a collective gasp of shock. Robert, slightly unnerved, nonetheless flashed his handsome pearly white smile, chuckled sheepishly, and remarked that he loved meeting the women and that he looked forward to working with them. Stunned by the reverse sexual objectification that I had just witnessed, but equally unable to avoid a smile given the lesser consequence of low-income immigrant women without papers making romantic or sexual innuendo at a middle-class, US-raised male citizen in political office, the woman's moxie in speaking like that to a politician she did not know stayed with me. The fact that she said it, and that the rest of the room laughed boisterously, made clear that most of these women were not the least bit faint of heart on gender and sexual matters. I do not think these same women would have shied away from such innuendo even after he became city mayor in 2014 (although, in the interim Garcia would come out, making him the first openly gay person to lead Long Beach, as well as the youngest mayor of any big city in the country). Who knows? Maybe that would not have stopped some of the women.

TROUBLE IN COMMUNAL PARADISE

Among the Asian Americans and Latin@s, another layer of embodied citizenship was the need to convince cynical, despairing, unknowing, and ICE-fearing community members to join their organizations and the broader fight. Both often cited it as a moral imperative, while also lamenting its difficulties. Such despair as a result of unconvinced or inactive neighbors also reveal the underbelly of fictive kinship ties and the limits of embodied citizenship. Anais shared frustrations of working with community residents who knew "nothing" or with the undocumented who were paralyzed by fears of reprisal. She bemoaned,

> I know people [who] don't know what consequences the air has around us, you know, they know nothing. They just live and they go home and sleep and they watch TV, but they don't know nothing; because sometimes we need like

> letters . . . or . . . different things like [petition post-]cards. Like, for example, you want to close the factory in this area . . . and we want them signing it. [They're] like, "No, I'm not about it—I don't support [the fact] that we need [to] clean this area" . . . I'm like, "Please, can you help me to sign?
>
> Do you know about expand[ing] the [I-710] freeway?" . . . and she [a resident] told me, "I don't know about that so, no, I'm sorry, I can't help you," so that's sad because I say, "Hello! Nothing happens [to you] if you sign, only we need [it] for support to demonstrate [against] the government. We don't want more contamination going to us," you know, and people don't sign because they don't know what [is] happen[ing].

Without being explicit, Anais references the fear of her fellow undocumented neighbors. Although their fear of "outing" themselves in the form of a signature and zip code on a petition stood to reason, Anais attributed their refusals and inaction to more than just legal status. Remarking that they just "go home and sleep and they watch TV but they don't know nothing" she condemns their refusal to gain knowledge about the social ills around them, almost a willful ignorance, in favor of TV. In this part of the interview Anais's voice and scorn rose with each word, her gesticulating hands betraying the depths of her frustration with their apathy; after all, apathy killed. It was no wonder that even as her discouragement was redoubled, so was her determination to convince her fellow undocumented Mexican immigrants to see and smell the air the way she did. Cindy was equally exasperated as she shared the following in a tone of utter dejection:

> NADIA: Earlier you . . . mentioned . . . how some people of color come from a culture where obedience is prized and many people would just say, "Let's just obey." Does that matter here, or no?
>
> CINDY: Yes, and then they do [obey]. . . . Samoans will never get involved like this. . . . They're embarrassed to be out in front of other people, or think, "Oh, you know, I don't know English well enough to say anything," so I'm sure that's the reason for some people to not speak up. But I think another thing . . . is that many people, too, just think, "Ah, it doesn't matter. It doesn't affect me."
>
> NADIA: Even if you tell them that the reason your kids have asthma is—?
>
> CINDY: Yeah, people act like, "Oh, you know, it's not bad." They're in denial. . . . All the stuff that we've done, all the information we try to get

out to parents: we passed out fliers for people to look at, they just throw it away. I think many people are afraid to admit that there might be something wrong with the air because *then they have to acknowledge there might be something wrong with my child. . . . I know a lot of people who don't want the truth.* . . . They just want to go on living life . . . pretending that it's okay.

NADIA: Do you have an idea of what it would take to make them stop and see?

CINDY: Someone died.

So disappointed in the Samoan American community was Cindy that she was resigned to the fact that only the death of loved ones would spur action; otherwise, overextended lives, language insecurities, obsequiousness, unauthorized status, denial, or willful ignorance ruled the day. Fellow teacher Lana underscored the power of denial. Aptly summarizing the activists' sense of vexation over their neighbors resisting the idea that their smelly air may be causing their kids' health problems, she blames the individualistic mindset that teachers could never have:

> You know, they only see their one child but I see *all* the children and it seems to me that there's a denial for whatever reason. There's a denial to accept that it's due to the environment. And I don't know what it is. If it's economic—because then they'll have to face moving and they cannot? I don't know if it's because they'll have to face that they put the child here and they'd have to take major steps to remove them or to do something about it? And they're very busy. . . . It's just because they're both working.

Both Cindy and Lana surmised that inaction stemmed from denial, either parents not wanting to believe that their children were sick or not wanting to have to take responsibility for imperiling their child and then having to uproot their lives. Such denial was clear to Cindy in other ways:

NADIA: Have you done door-knocking with your child before?

CINDY: Yes, my daughter Holly and Cara [PCORE leader] and I went [door-knocking] before a protest at Shine [truck-washing company]. We went up and down the neighborhood right there where it's always affected them, and almost every single person said, "Oh yeah, oh they're terrible."

> They did! "All these bad smells, oh yeah, they need to get closed down." And one woman said, "Oh yeah, I'm so glad. I support you." People said they'd come out. *And no one came out* (sighs).

Yolanda felt the same way when members of her community would (literally and figuratively) stand on the sidelines of a march for housing rights and rent control in working-class West Long Beach, yet would not walk over two feet to be a part of it. Perplexed, Yolanda reasoned as follows:

> YOLANDA: Because I think that if the community is scared to come outside, . . . when they see a lot of community [protesting] maybe they think, "OK, maybe I can do that too." I remember when I [went] walking for housing . . . I remember a lot of people in their house saying, "All right, all right, I'll stay with you! I'll fight with you!" But they don't come outside! And I said, "OK, come on!"
>
> NADIA: So what did you do?
>
> YOLANDA: I thought, for sure, *next year* they'll listen, maybe they'll come because . . . if I'm coming to the walk and I don't have problems [with ICE] . . . [they] can do it too. . . . *Yeah, but then they don't join . . . the march, because they're scared.*
>
> NADIA: They're scared of being caught?
>
> YOLANDA: Yeah, they're scared.

Beyond incredulity, Yolanda invokes the theme of lost mobility owing to the threat of ICE detention and deportation, one of the reasons why physical mobility mattered so much to the Latin@ immigrants. Yolanda's thoughts are also redolent of Laura's point about people being in too weak a position to go out and protest and organize—being able to do that, to some extent, relied on certain privileges.

Rather than fear, however, Tanya attributed political inaction to laziness.

> TANYA: People are lazy and they don't want to help.
>
> NADIA: So it's not because they are working too many jobs or—?
>
> TANYA: No, because people are lazy. The people that want to help, help, and those who don't, don't help. (*No, porque es floja la gente que quiere ayudar va ayuda pero no quieren ayudar.*) I invite a lot of people and they don't want to.

NADIA: Do you think it might be because the husbands don't let the women go out and do that, or no?

TANYA: Yeah, that too.

Ben, the PCORE leader with whom I worked the longest, pointed to Catholicism among both the Filipinx and Mexican Latinx community as dampening political organizing.

> Because especially in Catholicism there is such an emphasis on suffering, it's like you have to suffer in order to cleanse yourself, so it really keeps people from taking action when they know things are wrong. They think, "Oh, that's the way things are, you're supposed to be put here so that you can go through them and have these trials and tribulations, and then you get your reward after you die." So . . . just looking back on that I think that might inform, you know, what [activism] I'm doing now, is that I'm really against that whole . . . mentality I was brought up in.

When it came to her own personal story, young Bella disagreed, however.

NADIA: Do you feel like your religious beliefs also shape your efforts to change society and to make it better?

BELLA: Yeah, because if you believe in a higher power then you're going to believe in something else—not just, "Okay, I'm agnostic and I don't believe in anything" and "I don't believe that [divine intervention] can happen." . . . If you believe in no God then you're going to believe that everything is cool.

Whatever the reasons for their afflicted neighbors choosing not to opt in—theological or otherwise—the impassioned leaders felt a keen violation of embodied citizenship when residents did nothing, and when they did do something, it was to complain. On many an occasion, for instance, I witnessed the diatribes of CFASE's leader against his fellow neighbors, aptly summed up by Tomas:

> I've heard him [Jesse] yell and he was like, "I called all you parents to get involved and *you guys didn't even answer any of the calls* and don't even respond. *But you guys complain, so stop complaining and get involved!*" And I understand Jesse's frustration—I share it.

Of all the reasons for inaction, there was one argument that Eva, a Mexican immigrant organizer, refused to internalize—that of defeatism. In what follows, Eva believed that continuing to be the proverbial monkey on the state's back until that back bent—no matter how long it took—was the only solution. Again, the immigrant change-makers refused to jettison the state altogether.

EVA: I've heard people say, "Why do those kinds of organizations exist and why are they always fighting to change something—don't they know that they'll *never* win, that they can't fight against big companies?

NADIA: What do you think about that?

EVA: Well, some people think that you're fighting in vain but I don't think that nothing will be achieved. I think we *will* achieve something. But people say, "You aren't going to make changes to have cleaner air." I know it's not going to happen tomorrow, but if the big companies know that there are people who are fighting, then at least they're going to worry and try to make policies in our favor.

Recall that one of the cornerstones of embodied citizenship was never to move—to stay and fight for one's neighbor—ensuring that one's neighbors would in turn defend them. The problem was, the neighbor did not always fight. From my own experience as a grassroots activist, I am certain I would have taken many more hiatuses or would have found a different (perhaps placeholder) social cause merely to ameliorate the disappointment and sense of despair generated by my main movement. Yet these admirable Asian and Mexican immigrants put their embodied citizenship where their mouth was. They said, and I witnessed the fact, that they would never move and would never give up attacking the corporatist state and, perhaps most important, would never stop trying to convince their neighbors to join them.

"FAMILY" FEUDS: IN-FIGHTING

As if it were not demoralizing enough to tolerate gender divisions and inequities, and apathetic, defeatist, and harried neighbors, embodied citizenship would also have to survive the emotional-political turmoil of the conflicts, in-fighting, distrust, broken bonds, and bruised egos and feelings common to social movements (Gould 2009) as well as the diverging goals and priorities of those within (Tilly 1999; Goodwin and Jasper 2004). In this vein, Johnson (2017) notes that, of all the challenges endemic to social justice work in local communities, getting along with other activists is among the hardest. She attributes this difficulty to the underbelly of oppressive systems themselves, which accounts for much of the internalized inferiority and insecurities among the marginalized on the ground, which, together, cause conflict. Operating within this context, Maria, for instance, had served as president of LBACA and CPC but had to quit because she began working in the labor force and the organization's own rules precluded her from doing both. Teeming with bitter frustration, she shared,

> They were asking me to always be at the meetings and be on time with things, but I couldn't. I told them that I could still help them by being secretary or another lower position, but then they said "no." So that's why I decided to leave the position [altogether]. So this hurt me a lot because you give your time and volunteer, but they don't value your work (*Entonces eso si me dolio mucho y son cosas que te quedan porque dices tu ok das tu tiempo voluntario y no lo valoran que es lo que pasa.*)

In fact, Maria's ire had been raised by Carmen, the facilitator who distrusted my Chicana research assistant whenever she appeared as my proxy. Maria alleged that Carmen had been "violating" the very meeting rules that she pressured CPC members like Maria to follow. For instance, Carmen brought her own child to meetings when the rest had to use the caregiving service or leave them at home. Another was Carmen's frequent breach of the expectation to be punctual to meetings, leaving a room full of time-strapped people restless as she would arrive anywhere from a full thirty to sixty minutes late.

Among the Asian Americans, recall the earlier discussion about Filipinx American PCORE's internal dissension when coordinator Cara moved away, and the teachers began interpreting Paul's leadership through the problematic of gender. Paul also began grating on the teachers, and admittedly on me, for less gendered reasons, especially when his unstable personal life and his high level of disorganization meant that we never knew when meetings were or whether or not events were actually being organized. As I am the perennial academic who values time over money and who lived 40 to 120 minutes away (Los Angeles Sigalerts willing), it was certainly frustrating when I would make the stop-start rush hour drive all the way to Carson only to find that the meeting or public event had been abruptly canceled, forcing me back into two-hour traffic. The members and I would also lament his nonresponse to our emails or voicemails, halting our organizing in its tracks. While I tried to cite Paul's erratic home situation as the culprit, Lana made clear that she believed that he alone was responsible: "He just didn't have the people skills that Cara did, and he just didn't relate to us in the same way." Needless to say, it was no surprise to the teachers or me when we eventually learned that Paul, under pressure from his underperformance and his annoyed girlfriend, had essentially "disappeared" from the organization; after PCORE could not locate him for many weeks, they replaced him with another Filipino American, Ben.

Part of the reason that the Asian and Mexican immigrants put such a premium on emotional support as their preferred form of citizenship owed precisely to how draining it was to deal with emotional power plays (top down) and internal emotional disappointments (horizontally). Interestingly, Johnson's (2017) research has found that when activists regularly practice meditative relaxation and are readily conscious of their privilege blind spots and oppression triggers and how they are felt in the body, they can obviate tensions as they become more aware of their thoughts through their bodies.

* * *

As with the previous chapter, the embodied citizenship that the women trailblazed saw emotionality as the through line for the pushback and belonging that they prioritized. Nearly all gave primacy to the power of emotions, both before they had entered the political arena (mostly volunteering as school mental health support) and more forcefully thereafter. As well, the Asian American and Latin@ organizers chose to articulate the emotional toll of being racialized as "foreigners," manifest in the disproportionate environmental hazards and underresourced schooling systems that both suffered, and the toll of draconian immigration and deportation policy against the unauthorized immigrants. The narratives also revealed that, notwithstanding the solace and beauty that was their community, the Asian American women (and men)—many privileged by US citizen and middle-class status, English proficiency, and previous decades of organizing experience (hence entrenched participation in US institutions from which the Mexican ethnics were often barred)—did not consistently associate personal fulfillment with political work; they, more than anything, were exhausted and exasperated by it. Although some of the Mexican ethnics lamented the same, they tended to be less frustrated on this point. As unauthorized, low-income, non-English-speaking immigrants who had not previously engaged in social justice work, they chose to focus on the superarse and emotional uplift they got from feeling like they had agency and were forging a real community within a national community that sought to oust them.

As both groups put a premium on emotional support, it was the reason they decided to join the movement, what kept them in it, and what kept them politicized. As the narratives showed, it was the empathy of a stranger ("We were so impressed that s/he cared"), the provision of resources (itself an act of care), and the lending of an ear and shoulder (the more traditional notion of emotional labor) that inspired them to start a life of activism. From their perspective, one of the hallmarks of this embodied citizenship was to vow to never move to cleaner air and "greener pastures," even as their neighborhood killed them; doing so was tantamount to community betrayal and even self-abandonment. It was a key benchmark of one's authentic membership in the embodied community and a signal way to denounce the power ploys of the (White) healthy wealthy.

Of course, this did not mean that in their devotion to embodied citizenship the community was free of fractures and internal dissension. Sometimes these faultlines fell along gender lines, sometimes along lines of status, pride, and ego. Yet just as the immigrants' conflation of community with fictive kinship reveals that caring for others under bioneglect is crucial to embodied citizenship, so was the understanding that "family" and "conflict" were redundant. And, impressively, the male leaders tended not to conflict with the mostly female organizers owing to a more progressive gender ideology and deference to the wishes of their female constituency.

At the same time, gender did not define the Angeleno women's political boundary lines. Although some of the women periodically mentioned male domination over them and the biased treatment from the suits that angered them, they ultimately did not trace environmental, education, or immigration injustices to patriarchy and sexism. Rather, gender was most central to the Mexican immigrant women in terms of using their feminine socialization to perform emotional labor, both of which serve to recruit others to the struggle; these events could also double for self- and community care given the violence of bioneglect. Hence, caring through cooking for a meeting and caring for others' children was just as political as protesting and testifying (via masculine-speak) (see Sevenhuijsen 1998). The Asian ethnics did not center social events as much, in large part because their version of embodied citizenship was less rooted in survival but hewed more closely to workplace, civic, and service models of giving to, and getting from, the community. And, as a largely middle-class demographic of activists, they did not have to socialize each other on middle-class styles of professional dress. For both groups, however, true citizenship did not have as much to do with the law, rights, voting, documents, and surveillance as with the politics of caregiving (Prindeville 2004; Herd and Meyer 2002). In this way, the study of raced, classed, and gendered emotional life cannot be separated from an analysis of the citizenship of participation and belonging. And, as the community organizers made loud and clear, they could never separate their own belonging from the inclusion of their neighbor.

CHAPTER 6

*p*OLITICS WITHOUT THE *P*OLITICS

THIS CHAPTER EXAMINES an interesting irony—that the Latin@ activists' resistance strategy of embodied citizenship meant a weak desire to partake in mainstream politics; such a belief held even if the unauthorized were hypothetically given the opportunity to do so. While this did not in any way mean that they would refuse to vote if granted the franchise, it did mean that they were not deeply invested in it. It was an arresting political projection on the part of the Latin@ activists, the focus of this chapter, as they indeed would not have refused full sociocultural belonging in the United States if utopia allowed it; what they did *not* desire was full political assimilation into mainstream electoral institutions as a way to approximate that very sociocultural belonging. Granted, this is one set of Latin@s in a region of Los Angeles, but such a choice countervails what much of the social science literature on immigration has been saying and predicting about the robust institutional, including political, assimilation of Latin@ people.[1] To be sure, the Latin@s' distance from formal, electoral institutions *excepted the local level*, and this chapter will explore why and at what potential costs. As a window into one explanation, newer activists like the Latin@ immigrants had little else but existing models of environmental justice organizing to guide them: to pressure the state not to site the freeway here or to cut toxic emissions there. Indeed, the state seemed to decide everything, since it decided if they could ultimately enter and stay in the country.

One could certainly chalk up their related aversion to "big-P Politics" (that is, the federal electoral level) to non-English fluency, or to their legal or historical exclusion from these political institutions; in turn, their lack of participation flowed from their lack of familiarity with—perhaps even resentment toward—inaccessible "big-P Politics." Yet I found that a transnational understanding of "community" and "health"[2] among the Latin@ activists was vital, as was their noted conviction that empowerment could only come from an ethics of care (Sevenhuijsen 1998), "nourishing bodies and social ties" (Pérez and Abarca 2007), and, I would add, their moral elements. After all, if the neoliberal state refused to give them care—a social good and a form of respect—then they were left with no choice but to give it to each other.

The second irony that this chapter explores is that a small but noteworthy number of the activists—in this case, *both* Latin@ and Asian American—were utter political contradictions, guided mainly by orthodox Catholic or Protestant doctrine and the irony of a body-focused politics. As we shall see, the most striking pattern among these political enigmas was the organizers' comfort with what seemed on the surface to be political contradictions—positions seemingly at complete odds with each other. I devote much of this chapter to these ironies and paradoxes, and why they might have existed in the first place. Needless to say, there was rarely a dull moment in the field with these immigrant clean air activists.

THERE'S "BIG-P POLITICS" AND "SMALL-P POLITICS"

Zepeda-Millán (2017:146) found that, in the wake of the historic 2006 immigrant protest wave in which most of the activists I studied participated, the state "devastated" the movement's attempt to expand and grow. He writes, "In 2006, anti-movement state-sponsored suppression was carried out through various federal, state, and local actions; specifically, immigration policing by proxy, deportation, and detention, and worksite immigration raids of potential protest participants." Although squashing the draconian and nativist Sensenbrenner Bill was not the number one campaign of the Asian American and Latin@ activists with whom I worked, any faith in the federal government was certainly tested (or lost) when the state drafted Sensenbrenner and decidedly portrayed and punished immigrants as the enemy.

In order to grasp why the Angeleno activists had no interest in partaking in formal politics beyond local and state realms, we must first explore how they defined "politics" in the first place. Most fundamentally, the Mexican immigrant women in particular distinguish between what I call "Politics" with a big "P" and "politics" with a small "p," the former being the electoral political system and the latter being the Latinas' activism. When I asked Celia, for example, about whether she ever talked to her friends about her beloved Obama and sought to sway them to vote for him, she replied, "No, not politics." While "Obama" and voting constituted big-P Politics, then, Celia distinguishes "Obama" from *political* issues, which she described as the following: "We focus more on our children and their schools and their futures, that's what we focus on. But that doesn't mean that we do not know what's going on because we *do* know what is going on in our city. We know when they are paving streets, when they are fixing them, which streets are safer. We're paying attention!" While she may not talk about Obama, the federal level, and other big-P Politics with her friends and peers, she talks about the "other politics," whether the government is taking care of the upkeep and safety of the streets—that is, the social resources that immigrants like Celia need to thrive and survive, but that the government often does not provide to low-income, unauthorized Latinx communities like hers.

Tanya also revealed a pattern of reserving the term "politics" for the formal, institutional realm, but of conceiving her own past volunteer work and current activism as "political." My exchange with Tanya went as follows:

NADIA: As women you are out in public and you're dealing with politicians: do you consider what you're doing political, or no?

TANYA: Well, I believe that it works in two ways: it's something that I like to do, to help. And, well, the other part is that it's necessary *politically* for the community.

In similar fashion, Maria explained her community organizing as a product of enjoying giving "help" to others (the micro-interactive level); also like Tanya, she foregrounded the "political" aspects of it (the societal level). Maria remarked, "I never really liked politics [government], but I like helping people and I don't like when there are injustices."[3]

One of the reasons that the Mexican immigrant women emphasized the joy they derive from "helping" their community owes to their self-selectivity—almost every one of these women had engaged in previous helping and volunteering behavior in their communities. To be sure, most of these women also originated from rural Mexican villages where collective identity and norms are more commonplace than in the United States (Hirsch 2003). The fact that the women linked their premigration helping practices with their grassroots organizing in the United States casts light on the transnational lens through which they understood themselves and their politics. Upon querying Theresa why giving back to her immigrant community was so important to her, for instance, she replied tersely, "Because I see the need and because I used to do the same thing in Mexico." Many others said they had engaged in serving on "committees at the schools" and coordinating relief-help or fundraising in Mexico for those who needed it. Counter to previous scholarship that has found Mexican immigrant women to conceive of their community organizing as an extension of their mothering (Pardo 1998; Hardy-Fanta 1993), the women in my study deemed their grassroots efforts to be political insofar as them enjoying "helping" the community was directly addressing political injustices. At the same time, they did politics for reasons redolent of superarse, such as feeling a sense of purpose—environmental justice organizing was not just a destination, it was a journey.

Why Formal Politics Has Little Appeal

Although one would not know it from most social science studies of immigrant political behavior and social movements, the non-US context is indispensable to understanding Latin@ and Asian ethnics' political sentiments and behaviors. One cannot talk about immigrants and their families without a historical and transnational lens, especially given the first generation's socialization in another country in which they spent a significant part of their life (for example, N. Kim 2006a, 2008b); transnationality is also manifest in the children's engagement of literal and imagined ties to the origin country, especially if they had partly grown up there (for example, N. Kim 2009; Levitt and Waters 2006). Consider, as well, the global nature of media and the explosion of border-crossing and time-space compressing communication since the 2000s: email, Skype, social media, popular culture, smartphones, and video chat apps. In the United States, such ongoing transnational tools, experiences, and frameworks profoundly shape the through lines they draw across contexts, which in turn influence their political perspectives. For instance, so jaded were the immigrant activists by Mexican electoral politics that they could not stop seeing the similarities between their sending country's system and that of the United States; importantly, this shaped, in turn, their attitudes toward big-P Politics. Carolina, for instance, remarked on the inaction of the government in the homeland by comparing it with US inaction.

CAROLINA: I don't like comparing the different countries, Mexico and the US, but [here] they allow you to speak sometimes and stuff like that, but there's not really any action.

NADIA: What do you think about focusing your time and energy on electing a Latino politician here in Long Beach who says she'll do what you want, rather than spending so much time working with your community?

CAROLINA: Well, on the basis of race, no. There have been Latinos who do not help the community. They look at their own interests and they promise . . . to help the Latinos, but in the end, they do nothing. . . . *It is the same in Mexico—*

NADIA: Have you kept up with Mexico's politics and been involved in any way?

CAROLINA: Not involved, but just watching it. The politics in Mexico aren't good. I wouldn't want to be involved.

Although Celia was not as explicitly critical of the Mexican political system that she engaged prior to migration, she still attributes her parents' lack of interest and involvement to the undemocratic and money-driven nature of local politics that did not always point to justice.

NADIA: Do you know why your parents haven't been interested in changing anything political in Mexico?

CELIA: Well, what happens is that where I'm from is a very small town and, there, whoever was the one with the most money would just go and make themselves the leader; and everyone knew each other.

NADIA: But did the person who made the rules, were they a good person who did things with justice or—?

CELIA: Sometimes—depending on the money.

Yolanda shared her disappointment in the more overt gender bias in Mexican institutions, especially in comparison to what she considered a more gender egalitarian United States.

YOLANDA: Over here in the United States it is different because in Mexico, for sure, they don't hear the women because there's machismo in Mexico and, over here in the United States, it's very different; because I see when I have protests or when I go to the City Council, there is more women to men, and they [officials] listen to everybody the same [equally]. So I think the woman is more listened [to] over here in the United States, but it is very important [that] the men become involved in the community too, because it's every community—not only the women for the kids.

NADIA: But do the men know that women are being listened to here? Because remember you said that they [men] just think that women are going to talk, gossip, and have fun [when they organize]. I mean, do they not know that women are listened to here?

YOLANDA: Yeah, they don't know—exactly!

Many of the activists' ongoing transnational ties to Mexico, largely by dint of keeping up with the political and cultural situation there, simply reaffirmed their disappointment in formal political institutions. When I asked Teresa and her husband Jose about how much they kept up with Mexican politics, Jose lamented the current violence and disarray in Mexico under a seemingly inept and corrupt government.

JOSE: These days, not much. Too much news about pure violence, so, no more.

TERESA: No, there are too many bad things.

NADIA: And Ciudad Juarez.

JOSE: Yeah, exactly. And it's not good mentally to be thinking of your country in that way because all they display is all the negativity and all the bad things that are going on: lots of drugs, and too many children being affected. Yeah, just mentally, it's not healthy because it's just saddening. I don't like to see it.

Bucking the trend of Latino men being more engaged with home country politics than local ones (Jones-Correa 1998), Jose almost seemed to have to protect himself from the onslaught of bad news about Mexico as a means to maintaining his mental and emotional health. For others, the monied, opportunist, and corrupt character of Mexican politicians helps inform activists' similar view of most high-level American politicians, even if they are coethnics, immigrants, and fellow people of color. In Valeria's case, to be sure, her clerical job with the city police department precluded her from commenting publicly on politics or on behalf of the department, but she did not equivocate in any way:

NADIA: So are you a member of a political party?

VALERIA: No.

NADIA: Why is that?

VALERIA: I don't like politicians.

NADIA: You don't like politicians.

VALERIA: No. I don't know, I don't like to be involved with politicians.

In the same vein, I asked Laura what her response would be to those who ask, "Why don't most Latinos try to vote for a politician who is Latino who says, 'Oh, I'll listen to your issues, your problems, and I'll solve them' and that's the way you get less contamination and better health?" Without missing a beat, and echoing what Martha said earlier, Laura replied, "Because the politicians, Latino or Black, have not demonstrated that they're interested in us. They have not done the work that we need." She echoes what Pardo (1998) found in her work on Mothers of East Los Angeles, wherein the mothers had to shout down and shame Latino leaders who betrayed their community's environmental justice cause.

Worth noting are the similar feelings of the first-generation Asian American activists. When I posed the same thematic question—"Why not focus on electing supportive officials, such as fellow Asian American ones?"—PCORE's Cindy replied,

> I take everything with a grain of salt. All humans are fallible. And even within my own political party, there are crooks everywhere. I believe in the honor of the office, but I also know that the holders of the offices are people just like us, who make mistakes, who will have their own issues and problems, and are imperfect. So people can say one thing . . . and then work with another group, and then say something else to gin up support and gain votes. But it's a game. Politics is a game and people who are wise at the game rise within their parties.

Cindy begins her explanation for why politicians can be problematic by invoking a "bad apples" rationale; in a striking pivot, however, she ends with a critique of the system of politics itself, a "game" in which actors are opportunistically maximizing and spinning just to get into office and stay there. A fellow Asian American teacher with whom she worked at the same school, Lana, was even more critical of the system: "Even elected people are influenced. Even if you think someone's in your court, there's lobbyists in their back pocket." Lana immediately conjures the corporate suits and other lobbyists that "influenced" politicians to work for them rather than for the people.

The irony was that despite the clear disdain for those politicians, especially at the higher levels of government, many of the activists made one exception: Barack Obama. My research spanned the last year of his historic campaign for the presidency through the first part of the second term of that presidency. In fact, as we shall see, it was the fact of Obama's immigrant family background, his non-Whiteness, his message of hope for a racially diverse immigrant America, and the intangible "X factor" that made the activists peer beyond their local political boundaries to see what politicians like Obama were up to at the federal level. For instance, Liliana had just finished discussing how she favored the Democratic Party for caring more about minorities, upon which I invoked Obama's historic candidacy:

NADIA: So do you feel like the fact that Obama was also a minority, like your family, do you think that maybe you look at him with more favor—or no?

LILIANA: Yes, and especially right now, especially the things they say. Because we do hear Romney saying a lot of bad things. I don't know if you heard about today, that he doesn't care about the— (pauses)

NADIA: The 47 percent . . . [who consider themselves "victims," "dependent on government," and so on].

LILIANA: Yeah, he cares only about the rich people.

Although Liliana starts out with Obama's fellow non-Whiteness, she tacks on at the end of her narrative that Obama's concern for the poor (contrasted from Romney's caring only about the rich) also sold her on the Democratic candidate. Like her fellow activists, she spoke the language of care and respect, not of rights. Yolanda, unable to vote but a local political guru, was not clear on what political party Obama belonged to and revealed cursory awareness of the Democratic Party. Her focus on the individual candidate himself became clear in this exchange:

NADIA: Yeah, so do you follow the political parties, like do you have an opinion on whether you like the Democrats better or the Republicans better, or some other [party]?

YOLANDA: I like Obama.

NADIA: You like Obama (both chuckling). Why do you like Obama?

YOLANDA: I like him because I think that he's for the people, he says "Yes." Everybody has the same right. Because he is a color person [*sic*]. And, finally, he is the Other. . . . When Obama's coming to the presidency, it's like he talks to the other people [non-Whites]. . . . Everybody has a dream and they can make a dream.

NADIA: So did you really feel that he can inspire people of color?

YOLANDA: Yeah, when he won, oh my gosh, I'm very happy! I was screaming (laughing)!

NADIA: You wish you could've voted for him?

YOLANDA: Yeah (laughing)!

Yolanda, who did invoke the language of rights, was not the only one who decided to like Obama's political affiliation because of Obama or who had a vague understanding of party platforms. I posed the same question to Tanya, who likewise was unable to vote but also entrenched in the local political scene because of grassroots organizing. In response to my inquiry into any interest or knowledge she might have of the national parties, she replied as follows:

TANYA: Well, the one that Obama won.

NADIA: Oh, Democrat.

TANYA: Uh huh, Democrático.

NADIA: Have you heard anything about the Democratic Party?

TANYA: Yes, justice for the people—for poor people, and that.

Responding to the same question about interest or knowledge in the national parties, another interviewee, Teresa, automatically replied with her take on Obama instead.

TERESA: Because President Obama got the presidency with the Latino vote, [hopefully] he'll understand a little more about Latino people.

NADIA: So, do you like Obama?

TERESA: Yeah, he seems good to me (both laugh).

To be sure, there were the activists who knew that they would be members of the Democratic Party if given the chance. Still, they made it a point to highlight that Obama prompted them to feel more energized about the national political scene, even if they could not quite put their finger on exactly why. It also evinces how unauthorized immigrants informally shape electoral politics (see Zepeda-Millan 2017). Like her fellow LBACA community leader Marta, Laura offered the following:

LAURA: Um, well, I'm a Democrat, although I cannot vote, but Democratic. . . . My parents can vote because they're citizens. So I tell them, "Go and vote for me" (both laugh).

NADIA: OK, when it was Clinton versus Obama, who did you like?

LAURA: Um, I liked Obama. I don't know why, yeah.

NADIA: You don't know why.

LAURA: I don't know why (both laugh).

Yet precisely because of Obama's promise to effect immigration reform within the first ninety days of his administration, the specter of disingenuous Mexican and US politicians that originally turned them off to high-level officials haunted their Obama love as well, effectively vexing the activists. Martha, for instance, bemoaned,

> They would say that they'd try to help the Latinos. They also said that they would not be able to make amnesty (*amnistia*). . . . [They said] give them time so that they can fix the papers, [but] then . . . they've not done anything. *Obama is the same thing because he said he would help the Latinos. He hasn't been able to do anything.*

At the same time, she had not given up on the POTUS of color: "The truth is that I did not believe in Obama. But, now that time has passed and I see what he's done, now he has convinced me that he is a good president and that he's trying to do something. . . . It will not be immediate that he can help with this recession, but he is trying." Despite Obama doing nothing on the issue of amnesty, Martha was willing to grant him some latitude given his earnest work on the recession. Liliana was similarly forgiving.

LILIANA: I think he promised a lot for Latinos but he didn't do immigration reform; but I think he's better than Romney. . . . Maybe because he's a minority. . . . And I don't think he had a lot of credentials to become the government [leader], he was always criticized, so I don't think he had a lot of time to do all the things he wanted to do.

Yet, Liliana was such an Obama loyalist that she, without the capacity to vote, still fervently sought to make an electoral imprint.

NADIA: Do you think it's possible if he gets reelected this November, that he'd do more for immigrants?

LILIANA: I hope so. I hope so. And also, I'm an influence for my family and my relatives—because when Obama was running for president, I was [studying] in college, and my cousins and my uncle [asked] me, "Who do I vote for? The propositions, which one do I vote for?" I remember that this guy didn't want to vote and I told him to register and vote, that it was important, for Obama. And he said he didn't like . . . Obama or McCain, [but] he went to vote.

NADIA: And he voted for who?

LILIANA: For Obama!

Although Liliana could not vote herself, she was very excited at the prospect of being a political influencer anyway, and at being quite successful to that end.

Some like Celia, however, were utterly disappointed in Obama's inaction on amnesty, as were the 2006 protest wave activists who campaigned vigorously to get his presidency and his immigration platform realized (Zepeda-Millán 2017). In her contaminated corner of Los Angeles, Celia registered his failure to embody the signal change upon which he banked his entire campaign and vision for a new America.

CELIA: Well, at first, I liked Obama because of all the things he wanted for students—he wanted to see them reach their goals. But now there is something I don't like—he's holding out on the immigration policy that a lot of us are waiting on and that he promised us.

NADIA: Why do you think he's not paying attention to immigration as much?

CELIA: *Well, because I think it isn't convenient for them.*

Celia betrays her awareness that Obama alone did not work on immigration but the issue was simply not convenient for "them" in the US government.

She therefore alludes to one of the reasons that most of the activists did not completely dismiss and condemn Obama as an individual leader—as much as they were disappointed in, and castigated him, they well understood that his hands were tied by the system that checked him.

My interview of married couple Teresa and Jose harkened back to the influence of transnational schemas for interpreting US leaders. Recall that when we met Jose earlier, he lamented Mexico's chaotic political state so much that he stopped reading any news about it. About Obama, he concluded, "He's a little bit of a liar." His wife, Teresa, then elaborated on why Jose thought so, juxtaposing his viewpoint with hers:

> TERESA: Even though, you know, he [Obama] is in OK standing with me, [my husband's] a little disappointed that he's been lying. I realize that with my experiences with [community] committees in the past, that it's not only a president who makes the decisions, but it's the Congress.
>
> NADIA (to Jose): So I'm curious, what do you think that the lies are about?
>
> JOSE: So the immigration reform within the first three months of his Administration—a lot more than ninety days has passed.
>
> TERESA: So, he's saying that in the presidency, he understands that things take a long time. He [Obama] needs to talk to other people and cabinets and make those decisions. But [Jose's] saying that during his candidacy, he shouldn't have said, "This is *exactly* what I'm going to do." [Obama] should've said . . . "I promise to try." [Instead] he said, "I will," so that's the problem [Jose] has with him. [Obama] didn't live up to the "I will" part. . . . So he's saying that it's not really a joking matter, you know, he promised something to the Latino people (*Es como algo de antiguo broma mio, pero este, en esos aspectos nos esta fallando a los Latinos*).

In a unique interview in which the wife spoke for the husband (the two were clearly still in sweet love with each other after many years), Teresa was disappointed in Obama's broken promise, but it was evident to me that Jose was more profoundly hurt by it. They implied that, as with the corrupt Mexican political system that they had condemned earlier, Jose and Teresa shook their heads at an Obama who had pressed pause on immigration reform and around whom swirled whispers that deportations were ramping up.[4]

It stands to reason that negative experiences in two of the only countries that the activists knew would spawn criticisms of, and distancing from, the official governments of both. It also makes sense that activists would seek alternatives for effecting changes in order to breathe easier, literally and figuratively. As we saw, the activist women had plenty to say about why they were disappointed in, opted for only nominal involvement in, and disliked formal institutional politics. They pinpointed federal governments' lack of knowledge, empathy, and solid action when communities came to them about any issues affecting the margins where they lived—whether farming crises in rural Mexico or health epidemics in LA's goods movement jungle and big oil belt. In El Norte, where they planned to live out the rest of their lives, ICE willing, why would the Mexican immigrant activists have faith in a system that primarily practices bioneglect and anti-immigrant exclusion, criminalization, surveillance, and deportation?

Deriving Power from Grassroots Politics

With conviction for community politics, Martha sharply censured racism as well as the indistinguishable "Republocrat" phenomenon when explaining why she stayed in the grassroots community and out of the political mainstream.

> I like to fight for our people and the Latinos because the White people stay away [from us]. They don't care about anybody. In reality, they say that they help but, in reality, no one does; because neither the Republicans nor the Democrats have done anything to help. Everybody promises, but *they don't do anything.*

As Martha made clear, she had long hoped that the powerful would care for and respect them, as that seemed the precondition for *doing something.* In a related interview, undocumented and well-respected community leader Laura had made plain her distinction between big-P Politics and small-p politics—that she considered herself to do "political work," but would not call herself "political" per se. Recall in Chapter 4 that, following the same logic, even if she were granted citizenship and the franchise, she would "never" decrease her grassroots community work. Not only was this a testament to her commitment to embodied citizenship for her neighbors, it was a biting commentary of her disdain for national-level politicians, those who "don't know anything" about living in pollution. While one might easily chalk this up to her exclusion from the US state, she underscored instead the feds' willful disconnection from her community and attendant inaction on the biopolitical injustices terrorizing their lungs. In her politics, her community would have to do everything themselves and thus would always come first, even if politicians promised that the solutions instead resided with them.

Celia was unequivocal about submerging national-level politics below local politics when I posed the question, "Do you think that if Obama made laws to help the environment, like clean air, would it reach us here or do you think it has to be our local government—or something else?" She replied, "I think that our politicians here [locally] are the ones that have priority because Obama is only going to see a study of what goes on here. He's going to send someone to be his eyes and he's not going to be here or living here, so it would be better for our politicians because they are the ones that are here and the ones that are breathing this air." Again, the very fact of national politicians not knowing their neighborhood, reading, rather, some study about it from DC, and therefore not having the capacity for an embodied understanding, disqualified the likes of Obama from being able to do anything to help the immigrants. From an ecological and transcorporeal lens, then, these activists prioritized the embodiment of their community—its air and blight, its sickness and beauty, its concrete and rivers—and placed a premium on outsiders embodying the residents' disadvantages as a disruption to their own embodied privilege. These were the officials who might be reachable ("might" being the operative word here). The federal politicians far, far away, sequestered in richer communities with breathable air and comfortably shielded from relentless contamination, were the ones who might write policies akin to sticking Band-aids on oil tanks, smokestacks, and diesel pipes. At the same time, the activists knew that local politicians sometimes did the exact same thing; as noted throughout this book, the immigrants' relationship to the state was fraught, to say the least.

CPC leader Carmen was more sanguine about the interface between social justice work and elected civil servants. Carmen was another activist who declared that she would never temper her community organizing to focus on getting "sympathetic" politicians elected, yet she underscored the need to "bring the community to them." Our exchange began with what I call my devil's advocate provocation:

NADIA: Why do community work? Why don't they just rely on these politicians to do what they [residents] need rather than go door-knocking and teach trainings? . . . Let the politicians work instead of them having to work.

CARMEN: Because the politicians are *over there*. They're *not here*; that was the importance for us. We can't know exactly what they're up to but *we can take community to the politicians*: "These are the problems that we live through here" (*pero si podemos traerle como comunidad a los políticos; estos son los problemas que vivimos*). . . . We don't get involved politically like promoting them . . . but we do want to make an impact on them in the time that they're governing in that district. Because, in reality, we want the politicians to get involved in the community so that they can help us when we have to advocate at a higher point [state, federal].

Carmen's mandate to bring the community to the politicians affirmed the importance of embodiment. If one could not achieve the ultimate form of embodiment by living in it, then one could embody it momentarily by visiting its airspace. Carmen's mandate also flowed from her confidence in her community's street science to use their expertise about pollution, asthma, and other illnesses to outsmart the bioneglecting officials who usually had little local literacy. This was the case, as well, when a multiracial group of CBE youth activists was incredulous that the staff representatives of a local politician (who consistently declined to meet with them directly), knew nothing about their community issues; the staff even conflated Wilmington's struggles with the Erin Brockovich story of Hollywood lore, never mind that the two were completely different issues and completely different communities. As this was precisely when average citizens could wield Foucaultian power-knowledge over the state, I asked if the community activists were often successful in leaving the officials stumped and tongue-tied. Carmen replied, "Of course you can. Of course, you can, because they [politicians] don't know local issues sometimes. You know more than they do. You live here and you work here, right? So, yes, you can win debates (laughter)!" In Carmen's eyes, local embodied knowledge was power.

Like Carmen, Liliana was salutary. When presenting Liliana with the same question on whether she was interested in focusing more on federal politics if she were to ever become naturalized, she quipped, "No." In response, I pressed, "So you mean that you think more change is going to come from people or—?" Liliana replied, "From organizations. . . . Yes, because the politicians are going to listen to the organizations when we have the control. When we organize the community, they're going to listen to us." Later, Liliana would conclude, "I think that only one person elected can't make that many changes." Lucid is her estimation, however, that the local community's moment to make the feds listen had yet to happen, that there was still much work to be done in order to organize the community first. Her response took me aback, as I believed that the communities were already organized; it was the state that was still trying to figure out its response. In Liliana's temporality it was "not yet." Like Liliana, the majority of the Asian American activists believed that progressive political change originated with the people, the roots from whence the "grass" grew. When I posed to Lana the same strategy of shifting energy and focus onto elected officials to achieve environmental justice, she, without flinching, disagreed. Upon asking her why, she replied, "Because I think great movements in history come from the grassroots. It creates a groundswell."

Jesse, the renowned second-generation Mexican American founder of CFASE, had devoted his entire life to the grassroots groundswell that Lana spoke of. Born and raised in the US, he was a 1960s radical leftist who admitted that he had to move more toward the center to get politicians in California's legislature to pay attention to his community. Here he narrates how he went from working outside the system to seeing the purchase of working selectively within it:

> JESSE: I still consider myself to be a socialist. When I came out of high school, the first political party I signed up with was La Raza Unida. I was active in La Raza Unida all the way up to [when] Tom Hayden announced he was going to run for US Senate, and so then I changed to the Democratic Party—
>
> NADIA: So are you still a member of the Democratic Party or what is your party affiliation?
>
> JESSE: No, I'm still a part of the Democratic Party.
>
> NADIA: If you don't mind, I'm wondering why don't you belong to one of the more progressive parties, if you're a socialist?

> JESSE: Well, if anything, I'd probably go join the Green Party. . . . But because of the work I do in Sacramento [CA State Legislature], that's the difference. . . . I do strategic lobbying in the Democratic Party.

Although Jesse would prefer to be an official member of the Green Party, CFASE's reliance on lobbying Democratic state representatives to pass environmental justice legislation necessitated mainstream strategy. Again, the activists had to be comfortable with political tension with the state, in part because of the occasional moderate victory they would win from engaging the state, such as Jesse's historic win in securing the unprecedented Port of LA's Clean Trucks Program.

To be clear, Mexican immigrants such as Eva did not minimize the daunting day-to-day grind of organizing a community—especially one with a largely overworked, underresourced population targeted with fear—nor the fact that such work often did not yield dividends. But, again, grim realities did not obviate her hope in harvesting local power. By way of her long-time residence in, and deep knowledge of, West Long Beach, leaders like Eva often took public matters into her own hands:

> I really enjoy going out to advocate. . . . You know how every person has their own goals and purposes, right? I really like seeing changes in my community and I want to see them, not just like some people who say that they're part of the community [but don't act]. For example, here on Pine [Street] there is a little bus that takes you to the beach for free. So what I did was, I wrote a letter and I asked my friend Victoria to do me the favor of translating it to English. I got signatures and then I took it to Long Beach Transit so that they could put the bike rack in the front, because those buses didn't have it [for low-income, cycling, and air-conscious people]. So now they have bike racks. These are things that I like because they make me feel good. I say that there are organizations that help, but the community also has to work and value their rights and go and advocate for what the community needs.

Here, Eva collapses her "A-Team" activism with her own personal transformation, which she illustrates with her ability to become the kind of person who pioneers her own political campaign to assist the impoverished and clean the air. As noted, a common theme among the activists was superarse, how self and community needed to work in concert for the two to exist and flourish as one. For CFASE's Jesse, superarse came in the form of burning the candle at both ends for the movement, to the point that I often worried about the bags under his eyes and whether he would get his justice in toto. Many of us worried that his personal life was consumed and eclipsed by organizing; regardless of whether that was an accurate assessment, his personhood was wrapped up in the movement.

Federal Politicians Do What for the Environment?

We have already seen how uninterested the Latin@ activists were in the major political parties in the United States and in what precise platforms they advocated. Conditions were ripe for disengagement given the callousness of a political system that was exclusionary on the basis of race and class; a lack of faith in politicians given a corrupt Mexican political system that, by all transnational news accounts, was not improving; and high-level American politicians' own resemblance to those Mexican officials. As a result, the activists would wax eloquent on any issue related to environmental and school justice at the local level, would name all the officials with whom they worked (Val Lerch, Tony Oranga, Laura Richardson, Bonnie Loewenthal, Allen Loewenthal, Jim Dear), and would get emotionally charged (positively and negatively) when talking about the local campaigns they were currently embroiled in. What follows, however, were characteristic responses on federal-level actions, such as Obama's, for the environment.

NADIA: Do you know the president's policy on the environment; if so, do you think it can help California communities, or no?

MARTA: What do the policies say?

Similarly, I inquired of Liliana, an Obama fan, "Do you . . . want to learn more about what Obama's doing about clean air?"

LILIANA: No. I'm interested in the clean air work that LBACA's doing.

NADIA: So you're not as interested in what the big-name politicians are going to do about it?

LILIANA: Not too much.

Striking is Liliana's passion for Obama as president but her noninterest in his executive or legislative ability to address clean air, in large part because she traces power and control to the grassroots. When I asked Sandra, a homemaker, the same question she replied, "*I don't know about that.* I know that the government brings projects and regulates. *But Obama, I don't think he knows what's happening here.*" I asked Tanya, a middle-aged mother and an Obama supporter as well, if she had heard anything about his views or policies on the environment or air. She replied, "*No, I heard nothing.*" She, like many others, went on to say that when it came to the federal level, their bigger concern was the issue of "immigration reform." Other activists, such as longtime community leader Marta, who had devoted the bulk of her organizing to environmental racism and classism at the local level, would not cite the environment, not even clean air, when I asked her about the national stage:

NADIA: What political issues are you most interested in, what do you follow most?

MARTA: *Education, for my kids. I work in the community because of my kids.*

Among many of these passionate, highly informed, intelligent, socially conscious activists, their demeanor and discourse changed dramatically when the topic turned to the federal level, so much so that, from my vantage, it was almost like speaking to a different person.

We're Not Going to Assimilate into Big-P Politics

Another major implication of committing oneself to embodied community politics was to consider mainstream (nonlocal) politics so immaterial that, when I asked the Latin@ activists if they would consider being a part of either of the national parties, they declared that they would *never* partake or would do the bare minimum required, even if they gained the franchise. Others, including citizens, expressed complete lack of interest in voting and other formal electoral activities for myriad reasons.

CPC leader Carmen was one of the undocumented activist mothers who in a mere eight words made clear her adamant opposition to involvement in nonlocal politics. The interview conversation began as follows:

NADIA: Would you want to be a member of the Democratic or Republican or other political party in the US if or when you gain legal status?

CARMEN: *No.*

NADIA: No, not at all?

CARMEN: *No. I maintain the margin. I'm not political.*

Importantly, the women's lack of investment in the federal level is set within a broader redefinition of "citizenship" and "politics." Given the women's intersectional location within the matrix of domination, it is from this standpoint that they see much of the complexity and contradictions of environmental classism and racism under neoliberal bioneglect. Another way to consider it is how these immigrant women, from the margins, could see the distinct self-formation processes of White America and of their own group, in the DuBoisian sense. Amidst this constant tension between the oppressive veil and bottom-up agency, poor health unified those on the bottom. Yet as we are about to explore, it was also this political marginality that fostered and afforded viewpoints that did not necessarily conform to standard ideological constellations in US politics. As a result of the matrix of domination (Collins 2000), the women (and the men) often had to choose the "lesser of evils" precisely because of their intersectional and marginalized positions.

POLITICAL CONTRADICTIONS ON LIBERALISM VERSUS CONSERVATISM

This vibrant and dynamic group of people would surprise me again when they began answering what I thought were perfunctory questions in ways that left me momentarily stunned and stumbling over my words. Committing subtle dereliction of qualitative research duty, I presumed that these anti-Establishment environmental justice activists would at least conform to the liberal social platform, such as on reproductive and LGBTQIA rights. Yet I stood corrected when some of the Latin@ activists made clear that their Catholic theology, relatively short activist tenures, lack of socialization by formal party politics and party ideology, keen perspective from their multiply marginalized social locations, and unconventional and redefining spirit promoted these environmentalists' paradoxical attraction to antichoice, traditional marriage, and even promarket stances. On the hot-button issue of marriage equality alone, the vast majority of my interviews and observations were prior to the 2015 US Supreme Court ruling that promulgated marriage equality as the historic law of the land. Regardless of the stock ideologies of most environmental justice organizers in the United States, the LA immigrants were staunch believers in, and felt no compunction about, the potential contradiction between fighting conservatives on the environment yet aligning with them on social issues such as abortion and gay marriage. Interestingly, two of the activist teachers—one ethnically AAPI and one ethnically Black American—not only were conservative on these counts, but were ardently procapitalist; most striking was that they saw no contradiction with holding conservative views whilst opposing corporate America's deadly pollution of their neighborhoods and their bodies.

Generally, the Asian ethnic activists who were legal, English-speaking, and long-time Americans had been intensely socialized by formal US politics and had long engaged the federal level as much as the local. For instance, Pia started out in more radical-progressive politics—anti-Marcos student movements in the Philippines, labor movements on the archipelago and on US soil—yet she has been a loyal and active member of the US Democratic Party for decades. Since my interviews and time in the field, I have been able to keep up with Pia by way of the Facebook social media platform. During the 2015 Democratic Primary between Hillary Clinton and Bernie Sanders, she posted frequently and with great fervor of her support for Clinton—the potential first US female head of state—and her posts intensified once Donald Trump became Clinton's opponent. So active is Pia in the Democratic Party that she is a delegate; many of her Facebook posts featured her travel from Los Angeles to Philadelphia to attend the Democratic National Convention where Clinton would make history as the party's first female nominee. In the 2020 Democratic presidential primaries, I witnessed her fervent backing of Elizabeth Warren, again over the more progressive Sanders (especially if one considers his entire political career).

In contrast, the shorter tenure of the Mexican Latinas' activist lives, exclusion from the formal political system both in Mexico and the United States (hence less mainstream electoral socialization), non-English-fluency, and the Catholicism of most translated into more political contradictions and redefinitions than reported by the Asian American activists. As with the latter, I would often find myself doing a double-take in interviews and casual conversations with the Latin@ activists who conformed to progressive political positions on corporate pollution yet who would support conservative social positions. Tanya would just finish telling me that she favored Obama and the Democratic Party owing to her concern for immigrants and the poor, and then pivot to, "But I don't support when the women have abortions. I do not agree that women should abort." Owing to Catholic theological doctrine, other unauthorized Mexican immigrants related their own internal conflicts over agreeing with liberal stances (or Obama) in part and then fervidly opposing them in part. Consider Teresa.

> TERESA: On abortion, I don't think women should abort.
>
> NADIA: But Obama supports the women's right to choose, are you okay with that or not?
>
> TERESA: No, I'm not.
>
> NADIA: But do you still think Obama's better than McCain, or—?
>
> TERESA: Si!

One could certainly problematize the contradiction between (unauthorized) Mexican immigrant women opposing women's ability to make their own reproductive decisions and yet opposing the state racializing, gendering, and sexualizing them as "(anchor) baby-making machines" and excluding them from the country, in part, for that reproductive excess (see Chavez 2017). The work of Elena Gutiérrez (2008) on the mid- to late-twentieth-century forced sterilization of Mexican American and other women of color could also point to a paradox: Latin@s' opposition to state control and abuse of the women's bodies—the circumscription of their choices about having children—and yet the Catholic penchant to support that control when abortion was the issue. To be sure, oppression breeds political contradiction, including the oppressed's reproduction of hegemonic power.

Another social issue that a few of the activists invoked was marijuana. Mexican immigrant Maria, for instance, was staunchly against legalization when the issue was still being hotly debated.

> *For example, if there are things that are bad for the community like the bad quality of air, it's because they [elites] have permitted the air to be contaminated. It's like, right now, they want to legalize marijuana.* . . . In the news they've shown how in many places they're letting people sell marijuana for medical purposes. . . . This is bad because it's like with alcohol and tobacco: they allow it, but now everyone doesn't want people smoking at bus stops and in restaurants, and then later when everyone is smoking marijuana, they're going to say that you can't smoke it here or there; so all this chaos that we're living is because the government has allowed it.

Of like mind but of different generation, Filipino American youth activist Daniel struggled to reconcile the cannabis stance of his Catholic Church and Catholic family, on the one hand, and that of his favored Democrats, on the other. Daniel's interview segment began with my inquiring about his views on the historic presidential election that had just passed.

NADIA: Were you disappointed that you couldn't vote last year?

DANIEL: No.

NADIA: What did you think of the two candidates?

DANIEL: McCain—yeah, I think he's a Christian, I think? I think that my church would be more happy with that decision [McCain]. . . . My family is Republican, my mother's Republican, my dad's Republican. I feel like I'm more Democrat . . . because, first of all, we're minorities, so I feel I should side with Democrats.

NADIA: So are you kind of in this position where on some things you feel like you're more with the Democrats, . . . but on other things you feel you're more with the Republicans? And if so, what are the things you feel more close to with the Republicans?

DANIEL: With the Republicans? Well, sometimes I'm scared of, what if the US turns way too liberal or lets things get out of hand? . . . Change is good but . . . I'm kind of scared of too much change in the US.

NADIA: What are you afraid that's changing?

DANIEL: Like, I felt like legalizing marijuana and then legalizing gay marriage: it makes the US look like a bad country, legalizing all the stuff that shouldn't be legalized. It just looks like a drug-dealing country.

Interesting about the last part of his commentary is that he embeds his critique of legalized gay marriage within his opposition to legalized pot, a change that was turning the US into a "bad" "drug dealing" country. His narrative demonstrates his internal conflict in which the conservative parts of his life—family, church—are at war with the Democratic Party's more liberal positions. Not surprising, however, is that the issues most irksome to him are the two onto which the Catholic Church has shifted its brightest floodlights.

Although I was not expecting the activists for environmental, education, and immigration justice to be conservative on reproductive choice, gay marriage, and/or the market, I was even more astonished to learn that their children—albeit males and *not* youth organizers—could, at times, be social conservatives. Even their more liberal activist parents and the undocumented or mixed status of their families could not pull them away from conservatism. For example, Yolanda, a woman who single-handedly got her friends to send letters to Governor Schwarzenegger to support the Dream Act, said the following:

YOLANDA: My son is Republican, I think.

NADIA: Why do you think he likes Republicans?

YOLANDA: I don't know!

Another example was the son of Teresa. In an interesting point of triangulation vis-à-vis the second generation, Teresa's own son invoked the very social issue that made him, a nineteen-year-old millennial US citizen, countervail his mother's Obama "fever."

DAVID: I actually voted for McCain.

NADIA: Why did you like McCain?

DAVID: Because I know that people want Obama because he's the first Black president, but . . . he votes no on [Prop] 8 and he thinks that abortion is okay. . . . Because also, because my mom says, not two men and two women [as couples], that's why. And there's also that: "Oh, the first Black president, let's vote for him!" but they didn't hear out another White president.

Here David implicates his mother in conditioning him to oppose queer relationships. Unbeknownst to David, however, and in large part because of Obama's convoluted position on the issue, the then-presidential candidate supported civil unions but opposed same-sex marriages, culminating in his guarded opposition to California's Prop 8.[5] It also surprised me somewhat to hear a young Latino man who grew up low income in a segregated part of Long Beach with undocumented parents lament the lack of opportunity for White men to be US presidents.

Samoan American Cindy, a staunch opponent of putting profit over people's health and the environment, nearly made me lose my entire train of thought when she stunned me with her party affiliation, her economic and social views, and her justification for their political concordance.

NADIA: Are you a member of a formal political party?

CINDY: Republican.

NADIA: Okay (shocked facial expression). And um, um, do you see, I mean, do you have a (pauses, regathers), do you see a difference between how you identify politically with Republicans and some of the campaigns you work in? Because I'm sort of confused . . . (Cindy laughs)–because, it's interesting, a lot of times the Republicans would side with these very companies like BP and—

CINDY: Well, I'm a strong supporter of the free market and the capitalist system, and people should strive to their potential to work and earn, but at the same time we need to be conscious of our duty to the public, our duty to preserve the safety of the public and the environment. As a Christian I believe that God gave us the earth in order to be good stewards of that earth and the environment and everything therein. So it's funny, I'm extremely conservative!

NADIA: Like in what way?

CINDY: Fiscally very, very; and socially, very conservative.

NADIA: You mean like issues like abortion?

CINDY: Yes, I'm prolife. I believe in strong national defense.

NADIA: What about gay marriage issues?

CINDY: I'm against gay marriage. I am very conservative. But when it comes to issues of the environment I'm a bit more liberal-progressive in that sense, because we just have, there are things we have to do. We cannot operate our businesses without considering the consequences, while I respect and believe everyone has the right to work and to own businesses. And, oh, I believe strongly in strong business period. They provide jobs and support the economy, but we have to be responsible. There has to be a balance there.

I gradually resolved my slack-jawed expression as I learned more and more of Cindy's conservative views on just about everything *except* environmental and immigration justice, a woman with whom I had been organizing for some months and who I assumed was progressive on every issue. When I listened to her colleague, Black American teacher Kelly, cite her political contradictions and revise mainstream political parlance to justify it, I could see how the two co-workers might reinforce each other's unconventional politics.

KELLY: My church and I actively worked to pass Prop 8. I want to make clear it's not because we want to interfere with LBGT lives, but, if you think about it, the Prop would intrude on heterosexuals' lives by making our church marry them, their lifestyles would be taught as acceptable, as if it's *the* lifestyle in schools. So we led the intercessory prayer for Prop 8, but we didn't make phone calls to people's homes. We [instead] donated money to the cause. Now, I do understand how the gay community was upset at the African American community for not supporting them, but we feel that we have to be led by Biblical values, first and foremost.

NADIA: Just to play devil's advocate, then what would you say to those who say that Southerners used the same exact Bible to justify slavery and Jim Crow?

KELLY: They took the Bible out of context; that was really the culture of the time, so the Word got twisted.

NADIA: Well, then, what would you say to the Bible's teaching that we should always obey authority?

KELLY: But God also said, "Only if it's in line with my values!"

NADIA: May I ask, are you a member of a formal political party in the US—and, if so, which?

KELLY: I don't want to say, but I will say that I vote for whomever represents our values.

NADIA: Can I ask, then, how do you identify yourself politically? Left, right, center—fiscally, socially?

KELLY: I believe in capitalism, because I believe in creativity. *But*, I don't believe in greed at the expense of people. On social issues, like LGBT issues, I guess I'm more conservative, I guess. *But since I'm for conserving the environment, why isn't that "conservative?*

NADIA: You'd be OK with that interpretation even if the mainstream parties don't define it that way?

KELLY: Yes!

Seeing as how I was used to organizing with people who subscribed to progressive stances on every issue—from social to fiscal—and how the activists of my current study were used to debate and rhetorical argumentation, I was clearly airing challenges to her political justifications, in part because I was surprised to hear them. I also pressed Kelly on her articulations because I truly wanted to understand how she, like Cindy, calibrated the political contradictions and redefinitions in her mind. Admittedly, she had thoughtful and creative ways of doing so. She argued that being against gay marriage was not so much telling the LGBTQIA community how to live, but being against changing the way straight people had to live (school curriculum, church praxis; to be sure, equality was not of concern here); being "conservative" could just as easily mean conserving the environment rather than destroying it. Capitalism was always creative, as opposed to socialists or communists being forced to do what the state told them, without any monetary incentive to create, no less; capitalism did not always have to approximate greed at the expense of the people. She punctuates our exchange by saying that she does not want to specify her party affiliation—likely Republican, as "our values" signaled the culture wars as well as the values of her church—and that she was perfectly fine with bucking the conventional Republican-Democratic party platform and ideological constellation. She, herself, was a political creative.

Cindy would extend from my discussion with her and with Kelly by invoking her position on public schools. Even as a K–5 teacher, she believed in localized school districts—meaning continued reliance on local property taxes which has been shown to produce more race and class inequality in education, such as racial segregation, public-private charters, and vouchers (Kirsch and Braun 2016). She, a primary school teacher in a racially diverse, middle-class (but also mixed-income) community, did not believe in centralized federal funding and oversight of K–12 education. Needless to say, I was floored.

NADIA: What about nationally? Do you feel like the national-level politicians get local issues or do they try to understand . . . , or not?

CINDY: I think it's difficult to understand each local community. I'm very against centralized everything, because you don't know—just like centralized school districts. You don't know what goes on here in Carson. They don't know what we need in my classroom and in our school, so I think states and local communities should have a bit more autonomy. I'm quite a federalist: state power and state authority. But our state isn't very authoritative and . . . hasn't been able to make decisions very well.

NADIA: So is that why you see grassroots stuff as important, then?

CINDY: Yeah, it's always important. Because we can't wait around for people at City Hall or Sacramento or Washington, DC, to come and take care of

> us. We've got to do that for ourselves. . . . And I think that helps people to empower themselves. . . . And that's another strong Republican conservative characteristic, strong belief in individualism.

Note Cindy's chosen parlance of taking care of themselves rather than waiting around for Washington, DC, to help. In her interview she would go on to say that she "couldn't stand" individuals who sat there and did not make things happen, who merely "complained" and failed to fight on their own. Essentially, by holding up Republicans' conservative individualist tenets, Cindy was making a bootstraps Protestant Ethic argument here—that if one failed to succeed it was figuratively one's own individual fault for letting those bootstraps drag along the ground as one lazily refused to work anything but one's complaining mouth. In this vein, Cindy was against what conservatives call "big government"—well-funded and well-resourced social welfare agencies and programs—which hewed to her precept that states (and local communities) should be self-contained and vested with more autonomy. Interestingly, she followed the Republican party line of equating individualism and localities when they are, in effect, different things. Although the more liberal-progressive Asian American and Latin@ activists also fought for resources and rights for their communities, they did not subscribe to this more extremist interpretation of "the local," such as gutting the very welfare state on which they relied to serve their low-income communities of color and which they sought to stretch and strengthen. As if she did not buck convention enough, she also collapsed grassroots activism, which has a progressive history and core, with localism and federalism—seemingly lost on her was the individualism of the latter. Cindy continued narrating another contradiction between her national and local political positions as if it was pedestrian. Consider the following exchange:

> NADIA: So when you look at your history of being politically active in the community, was some of it, like, to hold up conservative issues or elect conservatives?
>
> CINDY: [No], here at the local level, no. Here [Carson], all the candidates I have supported and campaigns I have worked on were all Democrats.

More than her Republican and conservative predilections, most striking was her absolute comfort with her contradictions. There was nothing dramatically discordant about being a pro-EJ and pro-immigrant progressive while a pro-market, profederalist social conservative—same for being a Democratic voter at the local level but a Republican voter at every other level. Although Cindy was an English-speaking US citizen and did not suffer as much marginality as the unauthorized Latin@ activists, her multiply marginal and intersectional social positioning made her completely comfortable with being a political contradiction. Second-generation Mexican American leader Jesse was also a US citizen but that did not spare him the political contradictions. He, a self-described socialist (noted previously), had no qualms about contradicting himself within one narrative.

JESSE: I support capitalism, but I just don't want it to be the hypocrisy that it is.

NADIA: Okay, so you do support our society being capitalist?

JESSE: I don't mind it being capitalist as long as there's a more equal distribution of wealth. It's just that we never achieve that.

NADIA: Do you think it's possible under capitalism?

JESSE: No.

NADIA: Okay.

JESSE: I'm learning that I don't believe it's possible. The few people that might achieve that, that are the good guys, you know, even with their great wealth and their great billions, they're not activists, . . . like Bill Gates.

In the course of a few minutes of his interview, Jesse established himself as a socialist who supported capitalism but who then unsupported capitalism. And, like Cindy, he showed little self-consciousness about it, in large part because they saw their role as activists as one of remaking, redefining, and reappropriating. Contradiction and complexity were the political order of the day, not the political aberration to avoid.

One of the most profound contradictions emerged when I was organizing, of all innocuous things, an Earth Day event with AAPI activists in Carson. We were confronted with a political calculation—nay, calculated contradiction—that, in my view, was not just ironic but utterly disturbing. It was early 2012. For all of us, Earth Day was a tough event to organize; it was the least progressive event that a very progressive PCORE usually put on each year, yet it was a lot of work. This annual event was mainly to raise consciousness among the wider community—to drown out bioneglect's anti- or faux-EJ discourse with the community's own version—and to recruit residents into the movement. For Carson families, they truly appreciated the giveaways, the food, and the highlighting of Mexican, Filipinx, Pacific Islander, and Black civic accomplishments; they often stopped by the tables for information in between.

As organizers, we often found ourselves in a conundrum about what community businesses and sponsors to tap for free giveaways to the many lower-income, immigrant, and of color residents. After missing one planning meeting, I asked at the next one what, if anything, people had been able to secure. Pia told me that she and the rest of PCORE had decided to give out free gas cards donated by Shell Oil, one of our Enemy Number Ones, as one of the bigger raffle prizes. Anticipating my opposition, she quickly explained that free gas would be even more coveted that year given the aftermath of the Great Recession and prohibitively high gas prices at the time. After softly gasping, I vividly recall that I momentarily scanned the dilapidated, fluorescent-lit white meeting room anchored by the groaning stained white fridge, a room that all of a sudden looked more sad and worn; I made sure to pause on the rickety table, then the mismatched folding chairs because I could not quite look her in the eye. Feeling like we were in the middle of big oil's cruel joke (all this work only to *endorse* and *enable* them?), I scanned everyone's faces without meeting their eyes and managed to blurt out, "You guys, are we serious?" Quickly rationalizing, Pia explained, "It's an *Earth Day*. I totally told them [the Shell representative], "You know, Don, I'm accepting it because it's Earth Day, but when you guys are—I told him flat out—when you guys have different issues you'll see me out there *against* you. This is *Earth Day*." Still slightly thrown, I replied, "But even for an Earth Day, isn't this too much of a contradiction? Aren't we indirectly saying that Shell is an acceptable community business, refinery, whatever, that the residents can put their faith in?" Pia: "I honestly think that the people just see it as free gas. And our main goal is to get people to come out, to get them to keep coming out."

As I sunk into my out-of-body experience with this political paradox, I was quickly reminded of how for the same Earth Day event we did not have much beyond the gas cards in terms of free donations. Mom-and-pops could barely give anything gratis. I had even failed to acquire free tote bags and gift cards from Carson's imposing IKEA that always looked to me like a giant blue whale in yellow ribbon imposing on the freeway. I was already uncomfortable with the political contradiction of dealing with this big box store. Just because IKEA sourced mainly from renewable forests did not mean that corporations were good for the earth or environmental justice or Carson; heck, that this billion-dollar company made it so hard to get a tote bag or a gift card (I felt like I had to talk to headquarters and sign my life away) only poured salt on the wound of political conflicts of interest. But gas cards from Shell Oil? I was well aware that these were the very "bribes" for which oil refineries spent chump change, yet which were highly successful in exploiting the community and appeasing it. In fact, the local newspaper *The Wilmington Wire* would later publish a story on such conflicts of interest from the perspective of an impassioned CBE youth environmental justice leader with whom I also worked:

> Twenty-four-year-old activist Ashley Hernández remembers getting free backpacks and pencils with oil company logos as a kid. "You get popcorn from them every Halloween," she said. For more than six decades, Phillips 66 has co-opted that holiday, painting one of its 3-million-gallon gas storage tanks orange to create an enormous grinning jack-o-lantern—"Smilin' Jack"—that towers over the community. Employees in bright yellow safety vests stand beneath chemical tanks and smokestacks, giving local families bags of caramel corn and plastic balls marked with the Phillips 66 logo. "They do community events, they'll fund carnivals, they'll do youth trips. They do it with an aim to silence them," said Hernández, noting the hold that local industries have over her working-class parents, originally from El Salvador.

In addition to free pencils and backpacks and cute gas storage tanks emblazoned with smiling pumpkins, Phillips 66 shared part of their largesse with local institutions, and yet could explode into three fires in 2019, two that were large scale and within weeks of each other in the spring. As Phillips 66 endangered the community and worsened lung capacities that would be needed to fight against the COVID-19 pandemic that would hit seven months later, some of the EJ activists helped launch a lawsuit against the refinery (Valdez and Rosenfeld 2019; *US News* 2019). No amount of caramel corn and plastic balls could change that.

Returning to my corporeal body, I finally made eye contact with the others, noting their expressions of discomfort mixed with resignation—resigned because these were the very organizers accustomed to contradictions and ironies under a bioneglecting system. Yet what kept racing through my mind was, "Why did the oil industry always win, even at Earth Day of all things?" Finally, I relented. Part of this owed to the fact that I did not feel completely comfortable pursuing an intense debate and attempting to overrule the remaining members since I was a newer member, and a quasi-member at that, given my visiting ethnographer status. As we witnessed, Pia had pristinely reconciled the paradox in her mind and seemed resolute in the way she delivered it. Perhaps it was her last point that quieted my mind and mouth—that of needing people to come out since this Earth Day was more of a recruitment than a social justice event. In that moment, and as I write about it in the summer of 2020, I am struck by the contradictory lengths to which activists have to resort—or are willing to resort—to swell the number of bodies in the movement. As someone who had followed a more traditional "party line" of organizing, these moments of cognitive dissonance kept me up many a night. My fellow activists in the struggle, both Asian American and Latin@, were much more comfortable with the ironies. After all, that is how they often started their political lives, and neoliberalism offered few other alternatives.

The activists' "choices" were often made to be so entangled and enmeshed with the corporate market that the market was always part of the equation. Ben, the anarchist EJ activist who spent much of his life fighting the polluters who sullied his hometown, was one of the people at the rickety table in the room that day; he, too, had acquiesced to the gas cards from the very oil and gas behemoth we were fighting and to helping Shell's "eco" image in the act of so doing. As if that was not enough of a contradiction, he also had a father who had worked his whole life as a contractor for the defense industry, a major environmental polluter. Nina, an Asian American activist teacher, also had a father who had spent his entire life keeping the well-oiled machine going, and yet here she was fighting to take it down:

NINA: My father was in the Navy and the Merchant Marines and ended up in the oil and petroleum business.

NADIA: Oh, so that's how you know so much about it!

NINA: Mhm. He was a refinery operator, . . . a unit operator. Yeah, he didn't have a high enough education degree.

Later, when she addressed her mother's respiratory problems, she admits that she never made the connection with their many years living amidst a bank of oil refineries.

> NADIA: So you didn't really know that her respiratory issues had to do with pollution until you were—
>
> NINA: No, I just thought it was her family history [of illness].
>
> NADIA: Had you grown up hearing anything?
>
> NINA: Never, never. . . . And, yeah, my father . . . told me how careful they had to be at his refinery: how many procedures and how they had to be careful, but I didn't think anything of it.

So normalized was the existence of oil refineries—part of nature like clouds—that no one in her family, including her father who had spent countless hours avoiding and carefully managing dangerously toxic chemicals, explicated the connection between her mother's respiratory illness and refinery-polluted air. The power of neoliberal capitalist discourse is that it obfuscates our own knowledge of our bodies, of our ecological and transcorporeal reality.

* * *

This chapter set out to explore two interesting ironies. First, the Latina activists' use of embodied citizenship to fight bioneglect channeled a weak desire to partake in mainstream electoral politics, even if finally given the opportunity to do so; second, a substantial number of the activists—in this case, both Latin@ and Asian American—were progressive and radical on environmental justice and immigration issues but, guided mainly by religion, were conservative on social issues (while some of PCORE's teachers were promarket and federalist). Needless to say, I was surprised; by the activist teachers, I was shocked.

When I gathered myself to think, I recognized, first, that transnational livelihoods and perspectives had to be centered in the analysis. The unauthorized Latin@ activists had no faith in federal politicians in the US because they had no faith in politicians in Mexico. Some of the activists could not even keep up with transnational news on Mexico because they could not bear to watch the violent and unstable political situation; it was too melancholy- and anxiety-inducing. Similarly, many activists prized working for and helping the community in the United States because that is what they had enjoyed doing in Mexico. Although in the US their community work was social justice organizing, one could consider their support of their communities in Mexico an indirect form of it since it was largely the product of a Mexican state that neglected its poor. And, as we saw, the Latin@s transposed that mutual and emotional support onto their performance of a more moral citizenship and political resistance in the United States.

On the Latina activists' lack of interest in federal policy and politicians (save Obama), their thinking was redolent of Foucault's thesis that thought was the product of seeing an object precisely because one steps away from it. Because the women stepped away from "big-P Politics," they saw its lesser worthiness to them—even the lesser worthiness of knowing what Obama was doing about environmental issues. To be sure, the federal level has largely not dealt with environmental justice, even when US presidents such as Bill Clinton have issued executive orders on it. Although the federal level tends to focus on environment as "nature," it stood to reason that Obama-loving Latina environmental justice activists would be interested in what the history-making president was doing about air quality. Yet they were not, and perhaps most noteworthy was their absolute comfort with this seeming irony. Their response was that their air quality problems were primarily local (and state-level), and, by the way, what had high-level politicians and branches done about that? When had they come into "our neighborhood," pierced our dirty air with their own bodies, and done the emotional labor (empathy, care, concern) and resource labor (forcing refineries and ports to stop polluting) to achieve social justice?

The confluence of these factors accounts for why the majority of the activists could not envision grassroots organizing without pressuring the state in the form of *local* elected officials and institutions; who else had the authority to improve their lungs and lives in their communities? Their key concern, to be clear, was not with acquiring rights from any arm of the state (see Boggs and Kurashige 2011; Paik 2016; Tang 2015). As we have seen thus far, the Angeleno organizers did not prioritize the nomenclature of "rights." Rather, their focus was on *respect*, on compelling the state to respect them regardless of the outcome or whether that respect was utterly contrived. In a manner akin to visibility politics, or the showcasing of a collective identity to change conceptualizations of the group and their issues (Whittier 2017), the Latin@ EJ activists sought to eke from the state the resources that their community lacked. They believed that the respect they demanded from the state, no matter how partial, was what ultimately got the state to offer some resources, decrease emissions, electrify transport, and stop siting hazardous entities in or near their homes. As resources did not come before respect, in their eyes, local, grassroots community work seemed the ideal vehicle. Not only did it allow the Latin@ immigrants to practice their embodied citizenship, but the only officials whom they held some (moral and political) sway over were those who served the municipalities of Carson, Long Beach, and Wilmington.

Although most of the Asian immigrant activists had been socialized by the formal, electoral realm, some similarly did not believe in the federal level and thus concurred with the Latin@ immigrants that the local political scene was where they could exercise, or derive, the most power. This was not at all to argue that both the Asian American and Latin@ activists did not believe that corruption, procorporate bias, and duplicity did not exist among local politicians; yet at least these familiar public figures embodied, to some extent, the community—they were part of it, even if only partially—and at least local officials understood what the activists meant when they referenced local schools, streets, hospitals, churches, and refineries. Local officials were most likely the ones who interacted face-to-face (or body-to-body) with the activists, which, to be sure, yielded complex and contradictory relationships fraught with friendly etiquette, begrudging respect, handshakes, and head shakes, as well as axed and mended fences. Indeed, there is no better example of local leaders' local embodiment, and no better reason to name freeways "racist monuments," than the state dumping in mostly Latinx Huntington Park[6] six hundred thousand tons of concrete rubble from the historic, earth-shattering 1994 Northridge earthquake. So gargantuan and hazardous was the rubble that the nearby residents dubbed it "La Montaña" (and "mountain of death") and demanded, with the help of CBE, that it be removed. Almost as soon as Huntington Park councilman Rick Loya visited the site, one of his lungs partially collapsed from the debris, after which he was raced to the hospital. Astounded by the absolute peril to residents' health, Loya lobbied for a cleanup, returned to La Montaña with a respirator, and waited in anguish for over ten years with the residents who could barely go outdoors for that entire time; it would not be cleaned up until 2006 (Schwartz 2007). Seeing the purchase in embodying the community—"to put a human face on this," as CBE's executive director Bill Gallegos described—CBE, LBACA, and others began offering "toxic tours" on vans and buses, which in about a decade also began attracting policymakers and elected officials (ibid.). Along the tour, they are forced to smell the diesel fuel, the chemicals, and even the stench of pig carcasses from the slaughterhouse ("smell pollution"); they cannot ignore the bellowing smokestacks from the oil refineries nor the heartbreaking stories of the schools they visit, the ones so contaminated that students either die or are rushed to the hospital *en masse*.[7] When local officials did act, sometimes because the bigger enemy was the mayor or richer communities in LA, it helped foster more productive or friendly relations with the activists, as we saw when the PCORE teachers joked with the AQMD's epidemiologist or CFASE leader Jesse was friendly with the same politicians he sometimes dressed down. Conflict-ridden examples were the local officials who refused to meet with the community organizers; at least the latter could, in turn, raise hell easily by getting down to their offices quickly to protest loudly, sometimes getting local TV crews to film. In this vein, the immigrants articulated that even if the state never conceded anything, losing focus on the fight for the community meant community death; it also meant the death of their sense of purpose and identity (superarse).

For some, their distaste for anything beyond local politics translated into the activists' focus on their preference for individual politicians on the national stage, rather than conceiving of the system as a whole. As noted previously, many of the Mexican organizers would remark, "I really like Obama, but now I'm not so sure because he has done nothing on immigration reform." From a transnational vantage, Obama began looking like all those politicians in Mexico who did not really care about—or truly respect—the downtrodden. At the same time, unauthorized immigrants like the Latin@s of my study are not electorally inconsequential—they anticipate when the franchise has teeth and partake in Get Out the Vote and other campaigns even if they cannot pull the lever themselves (Zepeda-Millán 2017).

The other major irony that I explored in this chapter were some of the atypical, diametrically opposed political stances among the Latin@ and Asian

American activists. On the hot-button issue of marriage equality alone, the vast majority of my interviews and observations were done prior to the 2015 US Supreme Court ruling that promulgated marriage equality as the law of the land. Perhaps interviews in the wake of that decision and in the wake of a more "gay-friendly" political culture would have produced altered responses to the gay rights question, but the ruling could have just as easily sparked outrage and deepened conviction. Furthermore, efforts for marriage equality had already germinated prior to my time in the field (vetoed by Schwarzenegger), as both the California Legislature and Assembly had passed a marriage equality bill in 2005, after Massachusetts became the first state to do so. I was bowled over both by the unconventional politics and by the sheer comfort with it.

But should I have been? I would come to realize that these activists had always lived lives of political irony and contradiction. Youth grew up learning that the oil companies were generous, kind, and fun (school-supply-giving, carnival-throwing, free-prize-donating), that they partially funded their schools (so why should we talk bad about them?), that they were "natural" (they made clouds!), and that they were so trusted by the youths' parents that they worked their whole lives there (hey, they put a roof over our heads and food on the table). As well, the activists were comfortable with paradoxes precisely because of their relational consciousness; the Latin@ and Asian American activists were able to see from, and cross-pollinate, multiple perspectives. Furthermore, the lack of political visibility of both the Asian and Latin@ ethnics, and the lack of formal party indoctrination of the latter, prompted a unique constellation of political views. For instance, not only was Catholicism undergirding some of the Latin@ activists' antichoice and antigay marriage stances, it stands to reason that a community that sees politics through bodily inequalities and bodily and emotional care would interpret abortion as the ending of a life and gay marriage as the union of two bodies that do not belong together. In other words, the women could be asking, Where was respect for the baby's life and for God's ordination for men and women to procreate and raise families?

Regardless of where the activists stood on the issues, they deemed what they were doing as unequivocally political, even if it was not "big-P Politics." As a praxis of embodied citizenship, one major dimension of "small-p politics" was their local knowledge, or "street science" expertise. Recall Carmen and others chuckling when they would outsmart elite officials who finally placed their bodies in her neighborhood and were quiet long enough to learn from the local experts: the residents. This was not mere one-up(wo)manship, this was, as Foucault would call it, an exercise of biopolitical power-knowledge from the bottom up. I would add that this exercise was part of a broader power play wherein Latin@ activists refused to compromise any aspect of their community work to gain power through institutional assimilation, *even if one day it guaranteed White America's systemic care and respect.* Institutional and voting power, in their eyes, was not the true meaning of citizenship anyway. These immigrants of Los Angeles spotlighted how much the state did not influence their newfound sense of politics, nor could it stamp out their reinventive, rogue, and rebellious spirit, especially at the national level. Sometimes US discourse and actions just had no hold over them because, to these immigrant activists, outcome was not always destiny.

CHAPTER 7

THE KIDS WILL SAVE US

IT WAS A GORGEOUS day in early August 2012. On this Saturday it would be the first time I was to be part of a training of the Youth for Environmental Justice (Youth EJ) activists of the well-respected Communities for a Better Environment. I would definitely be the "newbie," as this was the fifth in a seven-week summer series aimed at politicizing and recruiting local youth into the movement. The group had already bonded, even going on a Mono Lake trip together to learn of the politics of water, so I knew I would stick out like a sore thumb. My nerves were joined by excited energy when I walked into the drab grey building where Jonny, other CBE leaders, and some Latinx youth (in the sartorial moda of summery tanks and denim shorts) had already gathered and were chatting. I exchanged pleasantries, sensed the youths' positive energy, and settled into one of the student desk-chairs in the half circle, reminding myself that I was awkwardly appropriating my college students' perspective for once. I peered around a room that sharply contrasted from the drab building exterior: colorful walls covered in many floor-length pieces of butcher paper titled by phrases such as "race/ethnicity," "immigrant status," "class," and "ability." As Jonny opened the session, I was eager to soak in how an organization with one of the most renowned youth environmental justice programs in the country politicized teens and recruited their bodies, hearts, and minds into the struggle. What I noted right away is that CBE does not immediately launch into the ports or plastics manufacturers that bioneglected their community, but speaks of what they deem the *sources* of that bioneglect in the first place. Rather than stop at "race" or "class" in doing so, however—the two most commonly cited culprits of environmental injustice—CBE made sure to teach the youth about *all* systemic inequalities, especially given the interrelationship and interdependence of each, or what Collins (2000) calls "the matrix of domination." Therefore, CBE also taped up butcher paper helmed by the phrases "sexual orientation," "age," "gender," and "religion." Pointing at each sheet in turn and employing the Socratic method, Jonny asked each of us to proffer the characteristics of the oppression, which he wrote down in a panoply of color. The now full room of mostly Latinx teenagers from the area raised their hands and offered up, "police messing with us" or "stereotyping us as stupid" for "race/ethnicity," "ICE deporting us," for "immigrant status," and for class, notions such as "making sure we can't afford homes in rich areas." As an undocumented young adult originally from Guatemala, Jonny proffered powerful examples from his own life to round out "immigrant status." When it came to "gender" and "age," the students were a little less vocal, leaving more white space on the paper, and when it came to "sexual orientation" and "religion," Jonny had to fill in the sonic and written space even more, vocalizing examples from his own life as a queer man to fill the silence, having me riff with him a bit. As I obliged but did not want to transform the dynamic (lest I become "the old professor know-it-all" in the room), I noted to myself how easy "race/ethnicity," "immigrant status," and "class" had been to the group but how the other "isms" were not as prominent in the frontal lobe.

This framing was reinforced when the next segment of the day-long workshop involved CBE presenting an impressive diorama of toilet paper tubes, foil, and thread transformed into the ports, railyards, freeways, oil refineries, power plants, and toxic industries in close proximity to the students' domiciles, schools, homeless shelters, and other community institutions. In explaining the disproportionate hazards that imperiled their health, CBE noted that many studies confirmed that communities of color like theirs tended to be targeted the most, often more so than impoverished White communities;

they were careful to say, however, that both could, of course, be targets. Race also came to the fore at the very end of the day when Jonny asked if anyone had any other observations to add for the final debriefing segment. One member of a pair of conventionally attractive twin sisters, Grizel, boldly remarked that we did not talk that day about the fact that there are inequalities between minority groups too, where some minorities are given more educational opportunities while "us Mexicans" are denied them. She made sure to add, "And we even saw that today here." She did not look directly at me while she spoke, though I thought she briefly glanced my way from her peripheral vantage, but everyone who was listening knew she was referring to me; I was the only Asian American amidst a room of Mexican and Central American Latinxs and one (undocumented) Filipina American, the only one who had stayed the whole day (save one other Asian American staff facilitator of the diorama segment who had already left), and the only "professor" in the room (Jonny had introduced me as such at the top of the morning). Furthermore, save a few of the lighter-complexioned and White-passing Latinxs in the room, my skin tone was paler (although I had been tan most of my life from growing up on the beach, that ended in graduate school). Upon hearing the unexpected comment, admittedly my heart sank, my throat knotted up, and tingles invaded my spine. I had hoped, despite obvious differences between Mexican and Korean immigrants in the aggregate—how both were faring in the labor market and schools and how the latter were often exploitative employers of the former—that today we could get to know our individual biographies and do an analysis of how the White-led system of institutionalized racism, race-based economics, geography and geopolitics, and visa preferences were largely responsible for the disparity between the two (Park 2012). I wanted to discuss, then, how all non-Whites were hurt by racism in different ways and how the system wanted us, in millennial speak, to "hate on" each other so that we would stop fighting the White enemy above. I was excited to engage on the topics of how Koreatown Immigrant Workers' Advocates and Koreatown Youth and Community Center had long advocated for the rights of Korean *and* Latinx low-wage service workers over fellow Korean employers (Chung 2007); that even though neither Jonny nor I had mentioned it, today's lessons could potentially help youth grasp why Chinatown and its residents were subjugated by White developers' gentrification (Acolin and Vitiello 2018), another form of environmental racism, or why even its wealthier ethnoburb counterpart, Monterey Park, had faced a vicious onslaught of nativist backlash (no Asian signage or architecture!) (Saito 1998). Observant Grizel taught me an important lesson, however: that no matter how much I was in solidarity with the Mexican American teens on economic, class, and immigrants-rights issues, some were unwilling to erase my race, my race marked me as outside their embodied community, and race trumped all other social identities. To this day I am thankful to Grizel for being strident enough to teach me and her peers that lesson, and for helping me see how race was definitely on the frontal lobes of the second generation in a way that was different from many of their parents. Such was the beauty of ethnography.

At the same time, the youth were very much like their parents. As with most members of the Asian immigrant first generation, these youth activists adopted a race-then-class perspective, in part because of a shared transnational identification with US racism over their "homeland" as well as their own socialization growing up in a country that typically defined everything through race. And, in part owing to English fluency, the youth activists tended to wax poetic in even more embodied, transcorporeal terms than their parents about their community and about how racism and classism were impossible to understand without paying close attention to body inequalities (see Chapter 3). Perhaps more surprising is that they resembled their parents as those who had little faith in, and aspiration for, national politics, opting to focus instead on organizing the community to pressure local politicians who actually embodied the community and could be held to account for it, even if only in fragmented fashion.

BACKGROUND AND CONTEXT ON IMMIGRANT YOUTH ORGANIZING

The citizenship of children (and I would specify, adolescent youth) has also suffered from theoretical underdevelopment. In an effort to treat children as more than "citizens in the making" Lister (2007) cites the work of Cohen (2005:234) as clarifying the manner in which children "are citizens by certain standards and not by others," such as when children are "folded into the legal identity of their parents" (229).[1] I would argue that this is even more oppressive for the citizen children of unauthorized families when ICE banishes their parents to another country. In this vein, Daiva Stasiulis (2002:507) critiques "the relative failure of adult decision-makers to implement the participation rights of children" with the view advanced by "the contemporary children's movement . . . of children as empowered, knowledgeable, compassionate and global citizens, who are nonetheless, like other marginalized groups, in need of special, group-differentiated protections." Indeed, youth-organizing groups have vastly expanded in size and influence since the late 1980s (Warren, Mira, and Nikundiwe 2008), numbering in the hundreds by the early 2000s (Endo 2002, cited in Rogers and Terriquez 2016). These organizations that underpin American youth's orchestration of the Dreamer, DACA, gun control, climate justice, and Black Lives Matter movements in recent years were dismissed by President Trump as the knee-jerk immaturity and the unrefined, inconsequential musings of youth; his interjections ranged from ignoring March for Our Lives protestors, censuring some DACA activists as "hardened criminals," mocking teenaged Greta Thunberg, and tear-gassing BLM and its young supporters, whom he called "thugs" (see Arnold 2018; Smith 2019).

But what this proves is that those in power have noticed, and feel threatened by, these youth movements. And immigrant youth, especially the 1.5 generation, have played a profound role in the mushrooming of these and other movements (Abrego 2011; Bloemraad 2006; Terriquez and Kwon 2015), yet research has not caught up to the level of civic and political engagement among youth from immigrant families.[2] The Asian American and Latin@ youth whom I studied and their environmental justice efforts since high school—for some, middle school—certainly bucked the impolitic fear of threatened politicians and the trends in social science research. When they could have just been Snapchatting, playing video games, shopping, and attending parties, they chose a life of social justice work to contest their being killed quietly.

Bindi Shah's (2011) work on Asian American—specifically, Laotian American—teenage girl activists in Northern California provides a conceptualization of citizenship helpful for understanding the youth organizers in Los Angeles. Shah writes of a citizenship that the margins generate by way of critique and activism, and by dint of the relationship between such politics and other communal sites, such as the fraught family, school, and peer networks of which youth are part. The young activists of my study are quite similar to the Laotian teenage girls of the City of Richmond. Although I did not make youth the thrust of my study as Shah did, opting instead to supplement my analysis of the more established and larger first-generation movement, the Angeleno youth, like the Laotian teen girls, countervail simplistic "at risk" derogations of urban youth of color and simplistic caricatures of the "model minority." Further akin to the Laotian activists, the mostly Mexican and Filipin@ youth of LA critically incorporated themselves into the American political system but only by resisting, remapping, and redefining it, and by challenging the broader (nativist) racism and classism that upheld it. As some of these youth were secondarily active in immigration, Dreamer, and DACA movements, Nicholls's (2013) analysis of the Dreamers' political conundrum of fighting for legal belonging in the US nation while wanting to move beyond these exclusionary racist binaries was something that the youth here ruminated over as well. The difference was that, unlike the Dreamers of Nicholls's study, the youth here were not guided and constrained by the top-down strategizing of mainstream civil rights organizations (who, for instance, admonished Dreamers to be "perfect" to appeal to broader White America). Rather, the Mexican and Filipin@ ethnic youth often played a major role in deciding the agenda and political angle of their youth programs, one of the reasons why CBE's and PCORE's programs were so successful and had relatively long shelf lives. Therefore, the youth of my study were more able to negotiate seeming political conundrums, contradictions, and liminalities because, from the start, they were part of a generative process to do so. Although not to the extent of the young Latinx and Asian immigrant rights activists who have used the intersectionality of legal, queer, race, and gender identities as their main identity politics (Escudero 2020), the youth organizers here, as we shall see, meaningfully interrelated race, class, and citizenship in their fight for environmental justice.

To understand the perspectives of the youth activists of Los Angeles, it is imperative that we briefly familiarize ourselves with their day-to-day lives beyond what the previous chapters have shown. As those who struggle with life in working-class mixed-status families and who are afflicted with asthma, it is no surprise that the youth are most involved in environmental justice and in Dreamer mobilizations (DACA had not come into full force until the end of my fieldwork). In spending time with the youth and in explicitly asking them, I found racial conflict at school to be an issue for both the Latin@ and the Asian American ethnic groups (one over which their parents wrung hands as well). On their campuses, the Latin@ youth activists in particular cited their tensions and conflicts with Black Americans, while Asian American groups cited conflict between distinct Asian ethnics as well as with Latinx students. For the vast majority of Mexican and other Latin@ youth, anxiety and problems related to the immigration authorities were another major concern, while only two Asian Americans (that I knew of) had to struggle with being unauthorized. Then there were the youth activists such as Bella, a Chicana, who reminded us of the very simple practical reasons for why grassroots politics was not always an option for them: "Kids from middle school and from high school and kids from college, they can't sometimes go and testify because, first of all, they have school, and I think it's complicated."

It became more complicated for the youth if the CBOs did not have established and long-standing youth activist programs, which was certainly true of LBACA (as well as CPC), with which Bella and her mother worked. When I began my fieldwork and interviews with LBACA and CPC, they were in the infant stages of developing a youth program. CBE, however, had a long-standing youth environmental justice program of record dating back to 1997 (Figure 13). On its website, CBE notes this as a "unique" trait that distinguished it from most activist CBOs and nonprofits. Starting in Southeast Los Angeles, the program spread to Wilmington (and even Richmond in Northern California) and was premised on consciousness-raising, organizing, and leadership development (Figure 14). In addition, Filipinx American People's CORE has long incorporated youth into their EJ program.

Given the weaker youth environmental justice programs of CPC and LBACA, the older organizers felt that the youth were not doing enough. In this way, the movement in this port-refinery corner of LA was somewhat misaligned with the research trends on intergenerational political socialization writ large (Abrego 2011; Terriquez and Kwon 2015). For one, excepting Communities for a Better Environment, it was the first-generation (undocumented, low-income) parents who were politically socializing their children to get involved in environmental justice rather than the other way around, which research has identified as more common. Such influence is not wholly surprising since mothers and women have been on the front lines of EJ movements and since immigrant youth (versus youth who are not immigrants) seem to be less affected by lower socioeconomic status when it comes to intergenerational

FIGURE 13. Artwork from a youth program. Source: Communities for a Better Environment.

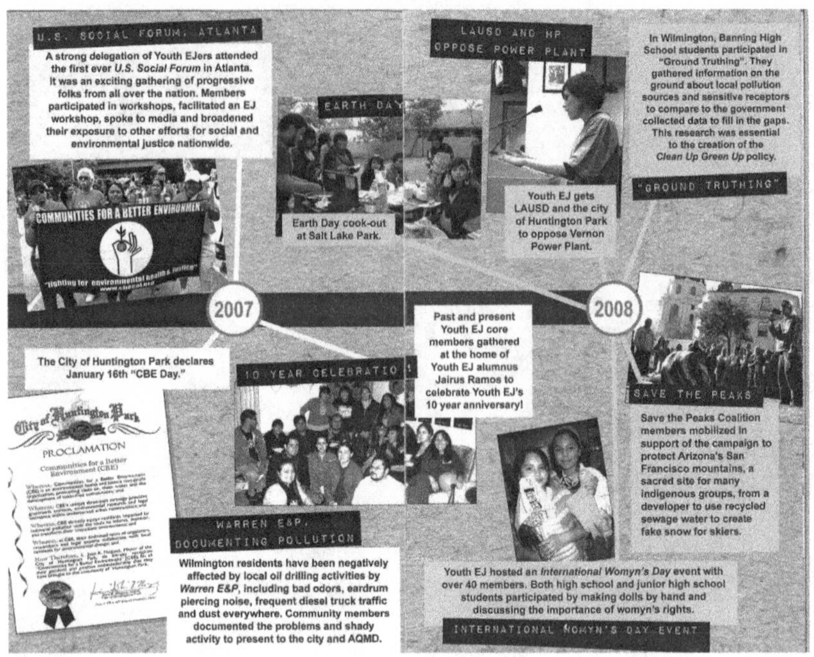

FIGURE 14. Ten-year anniversary of CBE's Youth for Environmental Justice (Youth EJ)—Achievements. Source: Communities for a Better Environment.

political socialization (Callahan and Muller 2013). The parents were also not more fearful or reluctant than the youth to get politically involved, which research has found (Abrego 2011). To be sure, and as we shall see, CBE's youth at times followed the more traditional trajectory by inspiring their parents to join the struggle (see Terriquez and Kwon 2015).

CPC leader Carmen implied that school and other centerpieces of youth life consumed and distracted the second generation from working on issues such as environmental justice, even though they were a critical (but missing) slice of the movement, in her eyes: "The young people are, they are the key to achieve a lot of things. The problem is that the young people have other things that they're worried about than air pollution . . . they don't know a lot so we have to find a way to educate them because their voice is key." Indeed, PCORE activist Vega bemoaned the fact that youth were not doing enough: "They should get more involved. Like the high school kids need to protest, testify more; and they could be educating themselves too!" Cindy of PCORE was more critical of youth's so-called distractions. In response to my question of what she thought of youth's role in the movement, Cindy replied with an air of frustrated lamentation:

> CINDY: People need to be more informed, and also to be more proactive and to just participate.
>
> NADIA: You think they're not participating?
>
> CINDY: Yeah, 'cause very typically, most young people get involved in other things: friends, you know, school, technology. . . . But I think young people in America, and probably Western society as a whole, tend to be more inwardly focused than outwardly focused. That's why with my church, with my family, Holly [her daughter] has done mission trips, we've gone to Mexico, we've gone to Skid Row. . . . My nephews *were four* when they first went digging dirt down in Mexico. . . . It's so important to expose children and to teach them and they need to have compassion for others . . . and not to be so . . . selfish, focused on themselves. *I can't stand it.*

From Cindy's vantage, the explanation for youth not committing to social justice was self-involvement and selfishness, reflective of the broader individualism of the US and Western world, which she countervailed by teaching compassion and volunteerism to her children and nephews; here, again, charitable service and grassroots organizing were not mutually exclusive but mutually reinforcing political domains.

Several parents also attributed the youth's wayward mindsets to the lack of a community space with youth-centered programming. Symptomatic of the neoliberal racism crucial to bioneglect, after-school programs in low-income communities of color were sparse or left much to be desired if they did exist. The dearth of youth-centered after-school, social service, and community programs was frequently cited by the first generation, in large part because parents worried that the youth would get caught up in gang-banging, drug dealing, and other criminalized underground economies or that their teen daughters would get pregnant. When I asked Valeria what she thought the government could be doing for youth (hence, what CBOs should be pressuring the system to do) she immediately invoked "drug rehab programs" for youth addicted to drugs. When I asked the same of another activist, Yolanda, she replied with an air of great concern:

> Yeah. Yeah, because I see a lot of young people in the streets and they don't have good times in the streets, so I think they need to come to CPC. I talked to CPC—Carmen—[that] they need to open one place for the teens. Because the teens need a special time, too, but I know that the teens don't like to stay with the adults. The teens like to stay with teens only. . . . My son is very, very happy when he starts to go to the California Endowment [a grant-making agency to improve health for Californians via progressive solutions] [because] they have some place [and programs] especially for teens. And he is very happy because he say, "Oh mom, for the first time, they heard me."

Again, not only do young people only want to be around young people, but Yolanda believed that the youth having a space to gather and do constructive things together—what the city and state should have been providing anyway—would allow young people to feel heard (and likely to preempt "destructive" activities like teen pregnancy). Indeed, one of the reasons that mother of tweens Diana appreciated CPC was that they offered nutrition classes "to show kids between ten and twelve to take control of their weight and their health." She, a devout Catholic, was not threatened by sex education and welcomed the fact that "last year they also had a health and safety fair for the teenagers [where] they talked to them about sex and how to protect themselves from STDs. So some of the doubts that the teenagers had that they couldn't ask someone else, they could ask, and they would listen." In other words, CPC was helping youth understand their bodies, not just in terms of how to feed and take care of them in the name of health but how to achieve sexual health—consider that these youth of color from immigrant families also had to learn very quickly that their asthma and other respiratory problems were fundamentally political and politically engineered. Repeated throughout these narratives, as well, was the importance of institutions doing the emotional labor of "listening" to the youth. As the bodies of working-class and (unauthorized) immigrant teenagers of color were under especial assault in the United States, listening to these youth was indeed a political act.

GENERATIONAL INTERFACE

The interjections thus far, and many of those that follow, imply that the older generation's role is to show the youth the way, whether it is to provide them youth centers; educate them on social justice issues; teach them to teach themselves; or impart to them compassion, a giving spirit of service, and a sense of the "we." I learned this when some of the older cohorts criticized the youth for lacking some of these characteristics and a vision. Among the first generation, there were exceptions, of course. Some, like Yolanda, took great pride in the possibility that her son would continue the legacy of her social justice work—owing to her tutelage—and would one day credit her with starting it, or being there in the beginning; in other words, he would see her superarse, and how it changed their city.

> YOLANDA: Like, for a project, maybe LBACA will get money to change Long Beach, and maybe I won't be here in ten years, but my kids will be here in ten years. I love it because as my kids live over here, maybe they'll see a lot of change, and they can say, "My mom was there for that change, so my mom worked to make this change in Long Beach."
>
> NADIA: So, then you feel like they will do it themselves?
>
> YOLANDA: Yeah! . . . I teach my son the same, because my son . . . asked me, "Why Bush doesn't like the gay community . . . being married?" And I said, "I don't know. You can write one letter to ask why he says no to marriage of gay people." And he did that.
>
> NADIA: Oh, he did?
>
> YOLANDA: Yeah, he did and he [Bush] answered, so my son learned to fight for their rights too. . . . Also he is the [CPC] representative of teens.
>
> NADIA: Oh, does he talk to other teens about the pollution?
>
> YOLANDA: Yes, other teens, . . . with other community members we talk about . . . pollution, about the bad condition of [the] air.

Yolanda made clear that she should show her kids the way (how to fight for the community, write to the president) and that she wanted her children to be proud of her for the social improvements she helped effect in Long Beach long after she hung up her activist gloves. Without discrediting the crucial role of stay-at-home mothering, she wanted them to see that she influenced society.

Cindy proudly touted how much she exposed her daughter to politics and even made clear that her ex-husband was opposed to such political socialization. Implying that as a woman and mother she was the more political one, she also demonstrated that her daughter's father did not control her parenting.

> So she [her daughter] is accustomed her whole life to going to meetings with me, going to protests and doing things. . . . I want to expose her. But her dad says, "No, don't take her." *I want her to see. I want her to understand that there are things we have to fight for . . . not just for ourselves, but for others. . . .* When [he opposed it], I took her.

Like most of the other first generation, Cambodian American activist Tina also felt compelled to teach her children a giving spirit and that the lines between service, volunteerism, and grassroots community mobilization were extremely fine.

> NADIA: For your daughter do you try to instill the same things [values]?
>
> TINA: Same thing! Oh, with her, . . . she'll go and clean her teacher and ex-teacher's classrooms. Very helpful.
>
> NADIA: Wow!
>
> TINA: My kids always have been like that. And my son, during the summer, he goes and helps his elementary school teacher; and my daughter . . . after she eats lunch, she's in third grade—she'll go help her Kindergarten or first-grade . . . teacher . . . grade and put things in order. *I love that.* I say, "Continue doing it, ask them how their days are, and share yours." She's very gentle.
>
> NADIA: Do you also want them to be community activists?
>
> TINA: I do! I always teach my son that if you don't say anything, you're not going to be effective, and so I say, "Don't be afraid, you have a voice!"
>
> NADIA: So you're encouraging both of them.
>
> TINA: Oh yes, I encourage *both* of them!

Tina's proud feelings derived not only from how much her children put compassion and other-focused service into action (I started feeling guilty that my own daughter does not clean up her teachers' classrooms or help them grade!) but derived from how successfully she had instilled such lessons into them, those that also boded well for their future in grassroots activism.

When I asked Jessica, a respected community leader, how she had successfully recruited both her college-age son and daughter into the movement, she immediately cited her long-time work in the Long Beach School District: "I'm a volunteer at the schools. . . . I was there close to the young people. I saw the needs they have, both the young people [adolescents] and the children [early grades]—like we would talk to the young people about drugs." Indeed, some youth organizers, like Tomas, were able to vouch for the influence of the older generations. First, he credited proudly but indirectly his life of social justice to the grandfather he never knew.

> My grandfather Roberto, he was probably the most active in the [labor] union. He was a ship scaler, but he died twenty years before I was even born, but we found his wallets and his IDs, and we heard old stories from our great uncles and aunts that all matched up. . . . He was involved with big strikes in 1946 to 1948. . . . And he immigrated from Mexico to the US during the Mexican Revolution and was working in the mines in Nevada and became a ship scaler in the '30s. . . . And died in 1964 of respiratory illnesses. But, yeah, he was involved in politics . . . and that did influence my dad to be liberal.

Although Tomas does not mention it, and I did not want to press him on his family's loss, my guess is that his grandfather died of respiratory illnesses, in part because of his job on ships powered by coal and diesel and his work in mines. When I also inquired into whether or not his parents had also politicized him, Tomas immediately invoked childhood memories of his mother transnationally following Mexico's political scene.

> She was always watching the Spanish channels on TV, and I remember she was devastated when they assassinated a Mexican presidential candidate in 1994, Colosio.[3] My mom was just like, "Man! That was our chance!" . . . She saw him as hope—a progressive Mexican candidate for president, and they just shot him! It was on TV, and if you YouTube it, it was quite sad. . . . But [I got it] from my mom. She's big now in politics, registering Latinos to vote, door-to-door knocking, working on campaigns, and really agitating a lot of females to wake up.

Although Tomas is Mexican American, he continued to explain that his mother's political fidelity to Mexico prompted his early transnational interest, and continued tracking, of Mexico's political system and developments. His mother's early influence and current grassroots work even extended to his present-day organizing. Tomas explained that in his very first days of mobilizing the community, he found most of the adults to be demoralized and defeatist (he quoted them as saying, "The pollution is here to stay; there's nothing to do, so get out of here!"). Undeterred, he recalibrated his generational focus: "So I said, we need to organize in the high schools . . . and our university students in San Pedro and up to Long Beach." I asked him, "So what gave you that idea, though? Where did you learn that concept?" Tomas replied, "I learned it from my mom."

Striking about Tomas and other young male activists was their openness about their emotional vulnerability despite socialization by a hegemonic tough-guy, "man up" masculinity.[4] For instance, Don of PCORE's youth EJ program, a twenty-three-year-old Black American nursing school student, big box store employee, and aspiring musician and writer, shared his emotional struggles over housing insecurity:

> DON: I would write about stuff, because I was homeless for a little while. So I would write about the street and the things about the street I'd hear, and I would see homeless people on the street, . . . [how] it just makes up the community and stuff like that. I kind of noticed *not* how bad it is, but like how *beautiful* it is, even when it's really grimy and dirty and people are picking up stuff out here; like, I still can be content. *I used to be really depressed, I was like on some stuff* [mentally struggling]. . . . I was in a different mindset—like a lightbulb went off and I started seeing things differently, and started writing about it, and I guess it came off kind of political, because when I'm about to spit it [rap or do spoken word], I think of all the issues.
>
> NADIA: Wow, how did you end up homeless?
>
> DON: My mom was working . . . [while my younger brother was sick], um, but I don't know, . . . she got kind of erratic . . . and I don't know . . . , I am not sure what happened with her. . . . My little brother . . . was fourteen at the time and she was talking about kicking him out of the house and stuff, and one night I got home and all the doors were locked, and basically my suitcase was outside: a suitcase full of clothes. And I didn't know what to do, so I just left, and I was staying at a homeless shelter in downtown Long Beach.

As this interview occurred early in my interactions with Don—all of which were on the level of "activist business"—it was telling that he had no problem divulging that he suffered from houselessness and related depressive symptoms, so much so that he journaled about it on paper and spit it into a mic on a regular basis. To be sure, analyses of the interview method reveal that it can take on a form of therapy (Chung 2016). Furthermore, my being a woman rather than a man likely put them at ease to share the vagaries of their emotional journeys (to be sure, in the context of the cruelty of family and of houselessness); yet even still, it was noteworthy that virtually every single young male in my study not only felt no qualms about doing so, but shared highly personal information about psycho-emotional illnesses and moments of debilitating fear, anxiety, and insecurity. When one thinks of the hypermasculinity (for example, Gould 2009) and toxic nationalist masculinity (for example, Collins 2000; Espiritu 1997; Moraga and Anzaldua 1981) common to social movements, their admissions are even more striking.

Another emotional dimension of which the youth were cognizant was how militant they appeared to be in these political settings. Referring to the importance of employing just the right emotional strategy, youth leader Ben of PCORE noted that the power of youth might be diluted by the following: "If it's more radical, like militant, they [officials] kind of just dismiss it. . . . Like, normally, the city council likes to see youth, they like to see them there, but then again, there's a line if it's too militant. Then, they don't hear us." Just as their parents had to calculate and deliberate over the emotional strategies of politics, the youth also had to walk the line between being heard as a novelty and being dismissed as angry militants. As a self-described anarchist who did not believe that power and injustice would ever cease under a state apparatus (hence, who wholly dismissed Big P Politics and decried voting), Ben was especially sensitive to the emotional politics tied to militancy and radicalism.

On balance, Ben and others whom we have met reveal that learning politics meant seeing it ecologically, as inseparable from their natural and built environments, and also transcorporeally, as inseparable from their bodies. They, like the first-generation parents, conveyed that politicization and politics were deeply emotional processes. Becoming politicized and combating the regime of bioneglect also involved a cascade of intergenerational, familial, and personal forms of discovery and development, as the activists' narratives about their parents' and grandparents' politics also made clear. The first generation also imparted the notion that the personal is political whenever they saw only a fine line between service or volunteerism and grassroots organizing.

FROM THE KIDS WILL BE ALRIGHT TO THE KIDS WILL SAVE US

Although it was over Miguel's life course that he learned of, and would be inspired by, his mother Eva's activism, at seventeen years he would finally overcome his fears of facing "the suits" and understand the power of youth. I asked Miguel if there were other reasons besides his mother's influence that he finally joined the movement. He explained, "Because I believe that if young people get involved, the people who own companies will actually realize and open their eyes that young people actually care about what they breathe and about their health. They're not just partying and all that stuff. They actually want to know what's going on with their health, they want to know what's around in their environment." Miguel realized the power of youth to make the officials change their perspective on them, from seeing them as teens who only care about the social scene to seeing them as social change agents who care about environmental justice.

Don, the PCORE activist we met earlier, believed that youth were more effective than adults in making the officials listen since young people were intervening in a mostly adult domain (politics). Extending this logic, PCORE's Mia believed that activist organizations were making a mistake not targeting a younger demographic than high school students.

> MIA: Like Earth Day, I don't agree [that we should be] presenting at the high school, to the audience of high school students. . . . I think we should just focus on the younger crowd.
>
> NADIA: Younger than high school?
>
> MIA: Yeah, like hold an actual Earth Day festival for the elementary where they're more likely to be open to the ideas, whereas when PCORE organized that concert, the concert is first, and the information is just secondary.

As Mia felt that the sharing of political information was secondary to head-nodding to loud beats with friends, she offered a more agentic take on our youngest students despite the common view that Kinder to fifth grade students would be too young to grasp the issues.

Young leaders like Tomas involved with youth programs of record had, in effect, been among the pioneers laying the groundwork for fledgling youth programs such as Miguel's (CPC, LBACA) and for programs that needed more members, like PCORE's. I asked Tomas what he thought of some activists who felt that state and corporate officials would not listen to youth precisely because of their youth. Per his experience of agitating and organizing high school and university students, Tomas declared,

> On the contrary! I think that the politicians were very much like, "Wait, these young folks are getting active and involved?!" . . . They [the students] were mailing off letters every other day and every time, I'm pretty sure, Congresswoman Jane Harman would be like, "Another one? Another one?"—a constant flow of letters, emails, Facebook comments for the Clean Ports Act of 2010, saying, "Please support clean air, . . . clean trucks now." And they're like, "Oh wow, the young brown people!" . . . And pipelining all the parents, teachers, the matriarchy—oh man, they can move a lot of people! . . . Students wrote 223 letters. They gathered 3,385 post cards. . . . And we developed leadership skills and it's scary to speak in public, but we had students write some speeches, and it was great! I miss those days!

Some of the older activists were also impressed by youth movement work. Nina of PCORE, for instance, commented as follows:

> NINA: Like even with the kids right now, I can see them coming back into environmental issues just like in the '60s, just like in the '70s.
>
> NADIA: Yes, uhuh!
>
> NINA: Where did that come from?
>
> NADIA: Maybe this whole talk of global warming? I don't know, Katrina?
>
> NINA: Or it might be that the world is becoming smaller and they have lots of loved ones who they care about getting sick and getting involved. . . . Yeah, you know, and I was thinking about this the other day, how the electronic age has changed everything and how it can be such a powerful tool, so that you don't have to be isolated from any movement, really. . . . Even my kids have had access to computers, and that makes all the difference. You can see students now, how they're organizing, they'll be there in a second. "And here's when we're going next or I'll meet you here." There's thousands of people showing up, right? But I think the

> older generations and different communities don't have that. It's hard to organize.

Interestingly, Nina attributed youth's mimicry of past environmental movements, in part, to the increasing sickness and EJ work of those around today's young people. Her view that the world was "becoming smaller" connotes the continued, if not amplified, importance of the local as the world becomes more global. Her perspective also aligns with the salience of the local in catalyzing and delimiting the EJ politics that she and most of the others practiced.

RACE IS OFTEN THE REASON FOR THE MISTREATIN'

Unlike the first generation who grew up in Mexico, much of the Latin@ second generation deemed racism the primary cause of oil refineries and diesel hubs concentrating in their areas. Recall from Chapter 4 that the Mexican first generation tended to see class as primary and as the mediator of race. For those who grew up, however, as "minorities" and "people of color" socialized by American racialization and racism, it stood to reason that race would have more currency than class, or at least mediate it. For instance, I asked CBE youth leader Jonny if race and class were part of his self-described embodiment of his community. He led with race and followed up with class, "Yeah, I think so, because it's heavily polluted. It's mostly people of color, immigrant, working class or low income." Jonny's own facilitation of the summer workshop that opened this chapter also revealed how much the younger people in his community saw the world, and the injustices they suffered at its hands, as traceable to race.

LBACA youth activist Bella also invoked a "race-then-class" perspective. She expressed in her interview how her neighborhood's disproportionate toxicity clearly had a *racial* breadcrumb trail, but that the breadcrumbs also led to poor people. Bella's sentiment in this regard came up when I questioned her about who was responsible for the disproportionate hazards in her community.

> BELLA: I think that the government is being racist.
>
> NADIA: So you think the government is responsible for the air condition?
>
> BELLA: Oh yeah, they are! They're very responsible for that.
>
> NADIA: How?
>
> BELLA: Because they can, like, they have the power to tell the companies,

> "Okay, you guys can't do this or can't do that, you know, you guys are close to a community." And I guess it's because of finance. . . . Because they [companies] go . . . where there is such [a] low income [demographic]. They know that the people here, they won't say anything because they're scared to leave or to be deported because they [companies] know we can't do anything about it. All we can do here is, is live with it.

After citing racism as the cause, Bella pivots to the impoverished status of the community, and then returns to the undocumented immigrants of color whom companies know are too fearful of deportation to fight back. Similarly, Tomas articulated the race-then-class account, prompted by my question, "Why do you think the youth were willing to get involved? What was it? Because lots of times when youth know they're being negatively affected . . . they don't necessarily get involved."

> [Because] I look like them. I'm from Banning High School. I'm from Wilmington by the Harbor and not too far away from Long Beach. My last name is Ramirez and my first name is Alberto—my personal story and my personal background, and the trust and the relationship. . . . But why is all the pollution here? [As if he were the youth:] "Uhhh, because we're Latinos or we're poor" and I go, "Is that right [acceptable]?" [Youth:] "Uh, no." "Is there anything we can do about it?" [Youth:] "I don't think so." I go, "We can!" I just stuck the mirror on them and framed it to put perspective [on it]: "If this was an all-White school, would we have these issues?"

First, Tomas focuses on organizing the Latinx (mostly Mexican) youth of West Long Beach. He invokes the economic vector of race by making plain that predominantly White and affluent cities rarely, if ever, struggled with disproportionate refineries, freeways, and railyards running through their well-manicured neighborhoods. It was precisely because West Long Beach was the opposite: Latinx and poor.

Similarly, as part of a longer tradition of youth environmental justice work for multilingual services and resources, such as Laotian teen girls fighting for Richmond's warning signs and emergency calls to be translated into Lao (Shah 2011), I spent time with youth at that particularly heated public comment meeting about how the I-710 freeway expansion committee had barely given the Spanish-speaking community time to read the translated Environmental Impact Report (see Chapter 2). It was late January in 2011, and in my post-work business casual threads I sat near many of CBE's youth activists in casual flannels, T-shirts, and jeans, who themselves sat opposite the well-coiffed officials in the stately emerald green room. When the youth approached the mic, they were armed with numbers, comebacks, and quips to counter the claims that residents had ample time to review a Spanish-language EIR on the expansion. My ears perked up when I heard one youth EJ activist—a tall, willowy, self-possessed Latina teenager with long brown hair—deliver particularly savvy, eloquent remarks on her calculations down to the minute of how long it would take her to read each page of the EIR and then tallied how many competing minutes were consumed by her school day, homework, and her part-time jobs. She made sure to add that her having to work was necessitated by "our struggles," by which she referred not just to those of Latinx immigrants but to those of *low-income* Latinx immigrants. Youth such as her needed to work, even during high school, in order to contribute to the family income. As the rest of us expected, she calculated that the time period given by the I-710 Community Advisory Committee would not have allowed her and her non-English-fluent parents to have gotten through even half of the Spanish translation—a woefully insufficient review period. Piercing whistles, hoots, and loud claps greeted her thoughtful and "scientific" numbers.

The Asian American youth activists' lenses were similarly fixed on a race-then-class rendering. As noted in Chapter 4, Filipino American youth activist Daniel shared,

> And, also, the ports: they're very close to Carson, Long Beach. There's a lot of people that are minorities: the Latino communities, the African American community. And if you go by San Pedro, that big bridge, there's also a port there and I've been by there, there is also . . . the low income and the Latinos and the African Americans.[5]

In Daniel's case, we the embodied community were "minorities"—"the Latino communities [including Filipinos], the African American community"—relegated to the undesirable zip codes, and then he moved seamlessly to "the low income" as well. Although Daniel is from a working-class Filipin@ family—his father is a special education assistant and truck driver while his mother is an immigrant personal attendant for the elderly—he has never joined an organization or conducted extensive grassroots work solely on the basis of class injustice. Certainly, he wove race, ethnicity, and class together, but his words and behaviors revealed that he sees class filtered through his identity first as Filipino. Ultimately, and in true embodied fashion, he drew symbolic boundaries between the White elites from the suburbs who made the decision to place polluting ports in and near communities of color, which tended to be poorer.

As I found in the case of the first-generation Asian American activists, the younger generations' belief that race and ethnicity were paramount was encouraged by transnational ties to their sending country. In this way, both of the generations prioritized ethnoraciality given the transnational social network of activists and the race-centered world of the United States and of US empire. For instance, in response to my question about whether or not Daniel thought that any of his activist organizations had been effective at galvanizing the community around environmental justice, he revealed his transnational orientation.

DANIEL: I think with KmB, [Kabataang maka-Bayan, or Pro-People Youth] a part of it is that we link struggles here at home to struggles back in the Philippines. . . . What I like about KmB is that they're exposing us to the history of it and it's up to you if you want to be opposed to, or want to go with, the government. I don't know, I feel like the Philippines could do so much better in terms of their presidency; there's so many things they need to fix, like the roads. There aren't enough. And a lot of the crime rates are kind of really high there 'cause of the poverty. The poverty there is really bad, and it's really hard to see [witness], but that's real life for them. And . . . *I want to keep the heritage going, so KmB is also trying to preserve the Filipino culture.* Even if you're still also an American . . . you can't be too Americanized. . . . *I wanted to learn more about . . . what things can be changed about ourselves that can help change [the US] and the Philippines also.*

NADIA: How often do you go?

DANIEL: Well, I was born there but came when I was five, so I don't have a real good memory of it, but I did visit [Manila and nearby provinces] last year summer and . . . I have to say, that must've been the most eye-opening two weeks I've ever had. 'Cause when you're a kid you only think about it as just play time, but now that you come back as someone who has learned more about social change and stuff and you look at another country as opposed to the US, you take things for granted that you didn't have. *And the air over there is very, very bad.*

NADIA: Like, you can tell that it's worse?

DANIEL: Their cars are always emitting gas, all the stuff in it.

NADIA: Like black smoke, you mean?

DANIEL: Mhm, and it smells like fire all the time. *The air always smells like fire.*

Striking about Daniel's comments is that he realized that the Philippines, as the arbiter of Filipino-ness, needed to be part of him since he could never really be "American" (read: White). As part of his politics he believed that making this change would translate into helping Filipin@ Americans and Filipin@s in the homeland, the latter of whom, in terms of environmental injustice, breathed even worse air than the former. At least in LA, the air did not always smell like fire. PCORE's Ben, a fellow KmB member but, unlike Daniel, a White-passing hapa Filipino, shared that he only became connected to his ancestral home country by way of politics.

NADIA: Before KmB, did you have a connection to the Philippines or did you feel a connection?

BEN: Not really, no, because my [Filipina] mom, too—she was born here.

NADIA: So was it really through KmB and People's CORE that you felt tied to the Philippines?

BEN: Yeah.

NADIA: And have you been there?

BEN: I haven't. Joe's [PCORE executive director's] talking about sending me now that we've had more of People's CORE set up over there, kind of like an exposure trip, so—

NADIA: So are you thrilled, or no?

BEN: Kind of, because he's talking about it like, I spend two months with the Moros and two months with Lumads—like the indigenous—which would be cool—

NADIA: Do you think being multiethnic Filipino also had something to do with whether you felt that connection or not to the Philippines?

> BEN: Yeah, I think so, and especially just like, you know, if I go to a Filipino event I don't look that much like a Filipino so, unless they know me, they're going to treat me like a non-Filipino. . . . If I go to the Philippines I am not going to be able to assimilate necessarily.

Despite often not being recognized as a coethnic by his Filipinx counterparts and never having traveled to the country of his ancestors, Ben engaged his mother's ancestral country by doing social justice work for it. Here, he conveys his pro-Philippines ideology through his political artistry:

> I made this shirt [for a political event] . . . and it was relating, actually environmentally, . . . to the recent floods that they had in the Philippines. . . . There's this mining act in the Philippines, the Mining Act of 1995, that basically allows foreign-based mining companies to come in and take 100 percent of the resources, and basically take everything. . . . So with large-scale mining there's also large-scale deforestation, so when the typhoons came, there wasn't anything to hold it back; so not only [did] the water and the mud and everything drown people, but also the logs from the logging industry hit people and basically wiped out the city. So my piece was kind of like this scene of tree stumps with Noah's Ark in the background, but instead of people in the ark, it was gold from the mining companies in the ark.

Ben's political battle against environmental racism stretched beyond the borders of Carson in Los Angeles and lapped the shores of the Philippines. Given his answer, I asked him about who he rooted for in World Cup and Olympic matchups between the ancestral "homeland" and the United States. He explained, "I'd probably root for the Philippines because, you know, the colonized versus the colonizer, mostly for that reason." So strong were Ben's social justice commitments to the Philippines that his more European than Filipino phenotype (prompting many to question his membership) and his lack of travel there did not stop him from forging a transnational political linkage. Like most of the second generation of all ethnic profiles, however, Ben's long-standing efforts to combat colonial environmental racism against the Philippines was never without a critique of neoliberal global capitalism, hence his analogy of transnational companies' Noah's Ark of gold at the expense of Filipinx lives. Striking, too, is that Ben's anticapitalist position affirms the connection that *Refusing Death* has discussed throughout: that those who supported or did not explicitly attack (racial) capitalism tended to engage the state more. In opposition, Ben identified capitalism as a key source of their hyperpollution and was a committed anarchist who was ideologically opposed to voting and other government practices. Yet he also understood the inexorable contradictions of living under a capitalist state, as he was one of the organizers who begrudgingly accepted Shell's free gas cards for our Earth Day and who lobbied local politicians and regulators when efficacy called for it.

Like Ben, Daniel was most devoted to two political organizations, PCORE and KmB: both were primarily Filipinx-identified, made explicit connections between Filipinx America and the Philippines, and understood economic injustice through a Filipinx lens. As Chapter 4 revealed, both the first and second generations of Asian American activists were of one mind that racism had a transnational basis—that race and nation cooperated in a form of imperialist racial formation (N. Kim 2008b). Transnational connections, therefore, were always a reminder of American racism (ibid.).

By virtue of the sending country being either a wisp away from San Diego or from Mexico's southern border, the Latin@ second generation was always in some way transnational—especially interpersonally and culturally. For the vast majority of the youth organizers, their trips back to visit relatives—grandparents, aunts, uncles, cousins—was the most common transnational social field in which they partook. In this way, the young generational cohorts lived with one foot, and one half of their heart and mind, in each country. I asked Tomas, for instance, the following:

NADIA: Do you follow what's going on in Mexico or do you feel any connection at all to other countries besides the United States politically?

TOMAS: Mexico, yes. Because those are my people even though my experience is different and I'm a different generation. I still have the same last name.

NADIA: Yeah, yeah.

TOMAS: You know, I mean, I learned about the Zapatistas. In 1998, Rage Against the Machine, who has a Chicano lead singer, sang about the dehumanization of women and the maquiladoras. Learning through that, I "go" to Latin America. I want to know what the hell is going on. Like, why are they killing everyone? Who is killing everyone? And, then, also like the issue on the border of the animalization of immigrants. . . . Like

> teachers asking for a pay raise and they're getting shot at, or their skulls caved in, you know, people being butchered at the border—families, even young children, are getting shot at!—fighting because the drug dealers are fighting for turf, and I'm just like, who is all behind this?

Tomas made clear that even though he was a third-generation Chicano, he never stopped, in his words, "watching CNN" or "reading *Huffington Post*" to find out not only about the bloody turmoil in Mexico but who or what might be behind it. He, like many other youth organizers, would also often state some variant of how the oppression they suffered in the United States stemmed from how Americans "look down on Mexico" as an inferior peoplehood that thus produced a "really poor country." Some would extend this race-then-class interpretation by commenting on how the maquiladoras emblazoned with American corporate logos showed that the US "exploits us there" just like they "exploit us here."

MAINSTREAM POLITICS? MEH

Although the Latinx youth diverged from the first generation on the race issue, both were of one accord when it came to electoral politics on the national stage. Like the first generation, Jonny was lucid on how the local level (including small business) was where they had to do battle, notwithstanding full acknowledgment of the neoliberal and corrupt dimensions of local politics and bought-off politicians. Given the injustices Jonny had suffered as described at the outset of this chapter, much of which he imparted onto the budding high school EJ activists—racism, classism, homophobia, undocumented status—he had learned firsthand from, and was inspired by, his devotion to people power. Community organizing taught him that everyday people's ingenuity, political malleability, and innovative strategy could force the mountain of mainstream politics to move—sometimes. First, one must start with the local, such as local mom-and-pop businesses, many of which were owned by fellow Latinx ethnics. To illustrate, he cites his involvement in CBE's groundbreaking campaign known as "Clean Up, Green Up" in Wilmington, one of three communities involved in combating environmental destruction. His grassroots campaign had brought a motion to the Los Angeles City Council in 2011, still awaiting passage, as a means not only to reduce and prevent pollution but to marshal support to help local businesses clean and green up as part of "green zone" creation. In the following exchange we begin with his response to my question of what he thought the best way to pressure reluctant politicians seemed to be:

> A very good example to use is *Wilmington,* because from there, you saw that the newly elected [LA city] council member . . . [finally acted]. . . . [Up to that point] petitions to him weren't working so we needed to move forward with organizations . . . , churches, and eventually moved into the business side of it—local businesses. . . . One thing that I feel like . . . , well, the Chamber of Commerce and even the major companies forget, is that small businesses still have quite a bit of control. . . . People [including small business] think, "Oh, environmental law or environment policies or justice things are very antibusiness." And so I think us . . . showing [local business] that there's a connection, like, we don't want to close down the mom-and-pop stores or the restaurants, . . . we just want to make sure they're following the law as much as everybody else, . . . but [also] that there's funding for them [to go green]. . . . They had the heart, I feel like, because they lived there, they know the issues, . . . so they saw how as a business they had more power than even as an individual who lived there. And so being able to gather about forty businesses to support Clean Up, Green Up was major. . . . So by then, like, the politician [LA City councilman] had no other choice but to see you have different supporters within the neighborhood, so he can't really say no. There's no justification [to say no] aside from, "I get funds from the refineries"—which he did—but the good thing [was] that he . . . [did] not let that stop him from seeing something better.

Jonny was clearly buoyed by his campaign's ability to convince small businesses that decreasing their pollution output was to their benefit as residents who lived and breathed—that is, embodied—the community, and thereby forced the hand of an unwitting politician to support "Clean Up, Green Up." A related exchange revealed how he parsed the national level.

> NADIA: Do you care about electoral politics in the United States? Any political parties?
>
> JONNY: Personally, I don't. But I do [think] there's a sense to how real they are. And, potentially, they do give a sense of power to people when people

> vote and it goes in their favor, but I do think there's also a reason why people don't vote; there's no faith in the system and, in some ways, I don't have a whole lot of faith . . . considering the fact that, whether we choose a Democrat or Republican, . . . there's still a lot of troubles in our communities and our lives are . . . impacted in similar ways [by both]. . . . And in terms of me doing that work, I do believe in city politics, maybe, I think I see it . . . working much more because it's more local, and so I think at some point I would want to be part of . . . the [city] councils, I think, . . . [rather] than something like country-wise. . . . *I feel like people care much more about their neighborhood than an entire country. And that's because we're not, I feel like, as a country, we're not unified. We're not the "United States of Americans," in that sense.*

In light of Jonny's special thoughtfulness as a youth activist leader, I further inquired, "What do you think about Obama and his historic election?"

> JONNY: I don't think one person can solve everybody's issues.
>
> NADIA: OK, what about . . . his administration, what about the Democratic party—*if* you think about them?
>
> JONNY: Well, for one, I must think about them because they're so everywhere. . . . I mean, obviously, there are small differences between the Republicans and Democrats, . . . I guess that's sort of the evils [of the] Democrats. . . . In terms of Obama, . . . it's cool that he's a person of color, but again, does that ensure anything? No. I do think he could be . . . a little more, maybe socially conscious? *Maybe*. Does that mean that I, I put all my faith in him for change? No—

In brief, Jonny cites multiple reasons for his lack of investment in mainstream political parties and national elections: the lack of impact they had on Wilmington and nearby localities; the Democratic Party's Machiavellian "evil" of pretending to be divergent from Republicans when in fact both propped up polluting capitalism, for instance; the many ineffective or unimplemented laws of national-level politicians; their inability or unwillingness to rectify environmental racism, immigration, and the like; and the dubious impact of a man of color occupying the most establishmentarian of offices. As Jonny explains, the Latin@ activists' rejection of mainstream political assimilation had more to do with the salience of *city politics* on their lives and on their day-to-day capacity to nudge local processes along, and, at times, to see results, in part because the politicians could see and breathe the diesel and benzene too. While the Latin@ activists like Jonny may not have closely followed the candidates, policies, or machinations of the federal level, they were also well aware that local officials were just as easily bought off by oil money, power, and opportunism. No matter how problematic, however, an official in the flesh was more useful than one projected on a screen from the DC Beltway.

In fact, as part of CBE's youth-organizing philosophy, they taught students not to be seduced by the status, power, or authority of politicians, whether in the local scene or on the (inter)national stage. Despite the racial watershed and the symbolic importance of the first Black president in US history, Barack Obama was also a paragon of the cult of personality in US politics. In fact, part of the mission of CBE's environmental justice youth activist program was to imbue self- and group confidence into students by unraveling romanticized, individualized hero worship in formal US politics. The first CBE youth EJ coordinator whom I had met a few years prior, an Asian American woman named Jane, remarked,

> I wanted to make sure they . . . didn't see there was a "star" behind the council member. . . . They're not a celebrity or, I mean, there's nothing special about them . . . ; they were voted in. . . . They're just another person. And so . . . we wanted to build that confidence . . . , also wanted to make sure they didn't fear this person or . . . were intimidated by this situation, because this was somebody who works for *them*. . . . We talk about how . . . we all have the ability, or the capacity [to fight the politicians], it's just whether or not we choose to take that role.

Such a political philosophy seemed to be working. Similar to her youth leader Jonny, a Filipina ethnic Lily, who like him was also unauthorized, articulates why she had no faith in the national political machine; she uses the grassroots work she was doing in Carson and Wilmington as a counterpoint.

> NADIA: When you think of politics, or when you hear the word "politics," what do you think about?
>
> LILY: A bunch of people sitting in a room deciding how to make the government better, but then failing at it.

NADIA: So are you talking about Congress, and things like that?

LILY: (Laughs) Yeah. . . . Like, do they ever come down to our meetings and *actually listen to our voices face-to-face, like sit down and have coffee with us and ask what our problems are,* and how they can help us solve them? Like, they don't do that!

NADIA: So would you give a different name to the stuff that CBE does, that people from the bottom up do, or—?

LILY: I think we're like more people's politics.

NADIA: People's politics—

LILY: Plus, they've only let us in this country until they don't need us anymore, then they're, like, ready to kick us out! *It's like someone you put all your effort into being friends with and then when they don't need you anymore, they just drop you!*

In line with sentiments expressed in Chapter 5, Lily condemns federal politicians for not doing embodied citizenship, that is, the emotional labor of sitting down and having coffee face-to-face with the people, listening to their voices, asking what their problems are, and how they can help solve them. To add insult to injury, it was precisely the highest-ranking officials who were simultaneously criminalizing and economically exploiting Filipin@ American "illegals" like Lily and her family. That she analogizes the deportation of immigrants to a friend discarding you after they have used you for your friendship affirms not just millennial flair but a likening of deportation to a calculating friend's emotional abandonment. While Lily perceives her work with CBE's environmental justice movement as "people's politics," she made clear that she perceived the federal level's dereliction of duty to the community that voted them in as quintessential "politics": failure and neglect. CBE's "people's politics" was therefore ideal.

In this same vein, I queried youth organizer Miguel about the historic 2008 McCain-Obama election, which fell just after his eighteenth birthday. Miguel's response resembled the disaffection of Jonny despite the fact that he, unlike Jonny, could in fact vote. Miguel, however, seemed more uncertain and contradictory as he spoke:

NADIA: So you can vote, so why have you not voted?

MIGUEL: Probably because when I was in high school one of our teachers, she gave us a voter registration, and I wasn't eighteen at the time so I couldn't fill it out. And when I was eighteen I just never registered to vote. But I have to register.

NADIA: When you turned eighteen, were you interested in the politicians who were running?

MIGUEL: Yes, I was. . . . Back then it was Barack Obama and— (pauses for a long while)

NADIA: McCain. So why didn't you vote if you were so interested?

MIGUEL: I guess because I wasn't registered—

NADIA: I guess my question is that why didn't you go find out how to register?

MIGUEL: Probably because it's like I was interested, but not to the extent . . . that . . . I want to go and make a difference and put my vote in—

As the exchange reveals, I did not readily or robotically move onto the next item on my interview schedule. I pressed him, as I wanted to grasp the seeming incommensurability between his nonvoting and his purported interest in the Obama-McCain election; why an intelligent, thoughtful Miguel would not vote, either for the US president or for propositions on the environment, housing, education, or taxes; why a youth activist who was excluded from the franchise until his eighteenth birthday would not be excited to cast a vote in any election, let alone one involving the first non-White general election presidential candidate (also from an immigrant family). I sensed strongly that there was something that he was not saying. At the close of our interview an hour later, I decided to ask point blank, "Do you trust politicians?" Finally, Miguel was unambiguous: "No. They just say what people want to hear." It seemed that in just one phrase, he filled the gaps in his arguments and clarified his terse, obscure explanations that I had struggled to make sense of.

Miguel's older sister Bella shared similar but more informed and nuanced sentiments about avoiding formal politics. This exchange began with her views on the major political parties.

> I've been aware of both the different parties, and I guess you could say that I do lean more towards the Democrat party. . . . But then again, I don't like to get caught up in that, all that is political. . . . I'm just like, "No, that's not for me." . . . *I'm active in politics in my community*. . . . Maybe because a reason why I don't want to be involved is, okay . . . you [politician] are saying some

> things, but you don't accomplish them. And that really ticks me off, *so I'd rather just not know.*

While we have already heard activists say that the neglect of politicians prompted their political disaffection, Bella connected her partial disengagement from national politics to a preemptive strike against the disappointment and frustration that do-nothing politicians incited. Ignorance, in this case, was bliss.

Although I was surprised by the first generation's almost complete lack of interest in environmental laws and policy at the national level, I presumed that the children of the parent activists—those more socialized by the two-party system, US elections, and climate justice—would be different. Yet most of them showed little to no interest in how the federal government was handling environmental issues. Bella, for instance, voted for Obama, and so I started the narrative with that:

> NADIA: And why did you decide to vote for him?
>
> BELLA: Hmm, because he was different, not just because of the color of his skin, but . . . he was promising that, "Oh, we would change this." But, to be honest, I really don't see anything that he's done. And now I'm thinking, "Why did I even vote for him?"
>
> NADIA: What kind of issues are you thinking about?
>
> BELLA: Health care, change for youth—
>
> NADIA: What do you want him to do about health care?
>
> BELLA: I would want him to give . . . people who were not born here [the undocumented] health care. . . . [T]hey come here for the reason to work. And I think that it's important that if you come here from somewhere else . . . you [need] to be healthy, so that you can still help the economy.
>
> NADIA: And, for you, what was he going to do . . . that didn't happen?
>
> BELLA: Well, I remember that Dreamer students were going to pay more for their fees for tuition. And I was like, wow, that's ridiculous.
>
> NADIA: Did you pay attention to his views on the environment?
>
> BELLA: No, I didn't.
>
> NADIA: Oh, okay. So is that just not an issue that is important to you then?
>
> BELLA: No, it is an important issue, I just didn't have time to actually see what he was thinking about.

Later in the interview, I asked Bella the following:

NADIA: You were telling me that you go to meetings and that you're interested in doing more youth programs in the future. You testify. What else, if anything, have you done to influence government?

BELLA: Something I also like to do is beach cleanup and just the environment.

NADIA: What makes you care about the environment?

BELLA: Animals. And, yeah, animals and people. It's really sad because when you go to the zoo or the aquarium, their cages will be empty and they no longer exist. It makes you think about them.

When Bella first told me that she did not have time to follow what Obama or other high-level politicians did on the environment, I presumed it could be for the same reason as much of the first generation—that high-level officials show greater concern for issues that wealthy White America wrings hands over, such as conservation, and much less for environmental justice, which largely affects people of color and the low income (Bullard, Johnson, and Torres 2011). But the reality was that Bella was actually interested in environmental conservation-type issues (animal cruelty via zoos, preserving beaches), not just local EJ concerns. Furthermore, this fell in line with the activists' overall ecological ethos within and without their urban community, that nature—rivers, trees, and parks—also defined "environmental justice." Yet what consumed her national-level political interests were not issues concerning the environment but (1) Obamacare or health care and (2) the Dream Act. As a twenty-one-year-old just beginning to learn about mainstream federal politics, she did not identify any contradiction here about which to be self-conscious. Like her first-generation parents who lived at the interstices of politics and could therefore define them unconventionally, Bella seemed to follow suit. Similarly, Tomas articulates the myopia of presidents and Congress on environmental issues in his broader narrative about the difference between the mainstream parties and his dejection by the Democrats' votes against the Dream Act:

> I mean, I know Republicans are going to be Republican and I know Libertarians are going to be Libertarian and fascists will be fascists and Democrats will be Democrats. You have a spectrum. . . . You know, Republican is anti-abortion and [for] God and liberty. Democrats are, like, save a dolphin, save

> the endangered whale, and I mean, that's fine, but it's just, like, I was just very disappointed that they voted against the Dream Act. . . . If the Green Party had power, I'd join the Green Party, but there's other forces at play.

Tomas points out the contradiction by slightly mocking the Democratic Party's concern for the natural environment and conservation, yet complete inability to care for the unauthorized child immigrants who faced deportation and could barely afford higher education.

Moreover, Lily, whom we just met, could speak endlessly about local politicians, laws, and issues just as the Latina mothers could, yet what top-of-the-ticket officials were doing with regard to clean air or environmental justice issues was nowhere in her political calculus:

> NADIA: What got you into politics? What are you the most interested in at the federal level?
>
> LILY: *The Dream Act, immigration.*
>
> NADIA: Do you ever follow what politicians, presidents are doing on the environment?
>
> LILY: (pause) *Not really!* (embarrassed laughter)

Lily, a youth EJ activist, was really the only one who expressed a modicum of embarrassment at the political contradiction, at least through her laughter and body language.

Taken together, it is no surprise that, just like their activist parents, the newly eligible second-generation voters were not excited about spending significant time and energy in formal political institutions despite what classic political assimilation might argue to the contrary (see Portes and Rumbaut 2001). When I queried youth activist Miguel about focusing more on getting sympathetic politicians elected rather than on convincing neighbors to join a movement, not only did he not trust opportunistic politicians who say whatever "we want to hear," but he just did not feel like getting involved. Surprisingly, this view held despite his knowledge that the Democrats advocated for (unauthorized) Latin@ immigrants like his family, while the Republicans largely did not.

> NADIA: Have you heard any stories, though, about what party is better for Latinos or better for low-income people, for immigrants?

MIGUEL: I've heard it was, I think, the Democratic Party—

NADIA: And what's your understanding of the Republican Party, who would they apply more to?

MIGUEL: They apply more to people who are rich—

NADIA: But, still, you don't lean more one way or the other?

MIGUEL: I don't lean.

From the overall interview and my time with him in the field, I concluded that Miguel's reluctance to invest in the national parties, or, say, to side with the party he knew supported his "people" (or to condemn the party that did not), seemed attributable to busy schedules (work and school); lack of exposure to national politics at home and in the community; the detachment on the part of the national parties themselves, especially in relation to mixed-status families like his; and his commitment to organize against the neoliberal state via grassroots environmental justice. He was neutral and uninterested, and many would allege that given bioneglect and other forms of inequality and injustice, he had every reason to be.

Even while an ascendant Obama was dramatically galvanizing youth, other members of the second generation were already jaded by the national political scene. In explaining her own reasons why, community college student Mia responded, as was common among the millennial set, by culling a personal example from high school:

> If you want someone's help, you can vote, but if you can do it yourself, do it! . . . Like, back in high school, I was part of [student] council; you know, we were a group of people that helped people. . . . They [council] weren't really good at making decisions and, you know, they would lag on videos, on presentations. And so it was just like, why would I have to wait on this [student] president to say something if I could just do it right now and get it done? Yeah, like, this doesn't need to go to Democrat or Republican!

Like Bella and Miguel—and before them, Lily and Jonny—Mia did not have faith in the parties, but she differs insofar as she believes that not only could she and the community do what they were trying to convince the parties to do, but that they could do it faster and, perhaps, better.

* * *

As Shah (2011) discovered, I found that sometimes it was very difficult and awkward to conduct ethnographic fieldwork with youth, such as Grizel from the opening fieldwork moment. Why? Because I was far from the archetype of a typical "Latina" (despite the fact that my mother is Asian Brazilian, as is her entire family) and because I was far from young and I was far from my student days. In fact, I was the authority figure over the student, and not even a primary, middle, or high school teacher, but a *professor at a four-year university*. And as the budding teen activist Grizel reminded us when she remarked that racial inequalities existed right there in the room that day, I was an (East) Asian American, someone from a group positioned above most Mexican ethnics under US racial hegemony and in the national imaginary. As a Korean American university professor living in a more well-to-do neighborhood than working-class Wilmington, I was a walking poster child for the model minority. Aside from the fact that we were both women and from immigrant families, the social distance with Grizel could not have been wider. But the moment was also instructive and revealing as to how race was a primary social axis through which youth received and grasped the world. An uncomfortable exchange that never once happened between me and the first-generation Mexican activists over a three-year period happened at one of the very first youth activist events that I attended. Grizel's comment about me, and the fact that no one else registered an opposing viewpoint, also cast into relief that we needed to find new ways to address White supremacy's reliance on racially subordinating all non-Whites whilst leaving room to simultaneously acknowledge that I was positioned above her in the mainstream race and class hierarchy. We would have to figure out how to address the fact that the large Filipinx community in Carson were, like the Latinx ethnics, victims of environmental racism. But myriad examples ranging from police profiling of Cambodian and other Asian youth in Long Beach, to AAPIs suffering some of the highest rates of hate crimes in many US cities since the 1990s (Fan 1992), to my family having been welfare recipients (Aid to Families with Dependent Children, as well as Canadian welfare) for years after my father had died in his forties just had no way of entering the conversation at hand. Yet the convergences could be powerful little antidotes to White supremacy.

While White supremacy was not gracious enough to allow that, it had certainly sharpened the budding youth activists' awareness of the complex and many layers of racism, including the transnational relationship between the United States on the one hand and Mexico and Central America on the other (whereas, among the parents, transnational lenses tended to reify only classism). The youth also keenly grasped race owing to their embodied struggle with bioneglect (neoliberal racism and classism tied to the environment and beyond) as well as to CBE's and PCORE's potent consciousness-raising about racism. Both of these experiences, enshrined by first-generation organizing, honed both the Latin@ and the Asian American youth's open critique of the notion of US assimilation and incorporation itself. The youth cast their disaffection into relief when they demonstrated weaker interest in political processes at any level beyond the local. This was one of the ways that the LA youth activists departed from the Laotian teen girls; while the teenage girls tended to see how their EJ activism, while a form of political assimilation, also redefined their notions of American citizenship and belonging (Shah 2011), the Angeleno youth of my study showed little interest in wanting to navigate the politics of Americanness. For one, they did not concern themselves with being seen as Americans or being centrally part of American institutions. Perhaps one would surmise that those who did would covet the privilege of voting or of being a national leader or of running for high office; that would not describe the mostly Mexican and Filipin@ ethnic youth here. Of course, even their investment and engagement in the local realm never nullified its fundamental market-driven and unethical nature. Youth such as Ashley Hernández, who discussed Phillips 66 pumpkins in Chapter 6, were well aware that local industry poured money and free pencils into their campaigns and into schools and hospitals to secure local silence and apathy. In this way, the youth of my study were also less concerned about challenging and redefining *American* belonging-citizenship through their environmental justice organizing as much as they cared about *community* citizenship. Further, like the activist first generation, the Angeleno youth were explicit about the embodied and emotional nature of political injustice, resistance processes, and their remapping of both. As we witnessed, the youth of my study were most lucid and waxed most poetic when it came to the ways that they embodied both the beauty of their community and the injustices that polluted it; they were the same when it came to the emotional layers of power, politicization, and social justice work.

In this context, the youth of my study did not engage or reify the "deserving versus undeserving immigrant" trope that ensnared the Dreamer movement and eventually compelled many Dreamers to emphasize their undocumented status over their overachiever one (Nicholls 2013). Although the EJ youth activists were secondarily involved in the Dreamer movement, they largely avoided that discursive trap because their political boundaries were drawn on the basis of who catalyzed (and benefited from) embodied racism and classism versus those who did not. Just as important, while Nicholls concludes that the Dreamer movement was ultimately unable to challenge the transgressive goal of postnational citizenship, the Carson and Wilmington youth seemed to move precisely in that direction. They did so by concerning themselves more with the grassroots community and with local political change than anything countrywide, as well as by maintaining literal, political, symbolic, or emotional ties with the ethnic "homeland."

Like the Laotian teenagers and the Dreamer activists, however, the Angeleno youth knew their own power and exercised it to the best of their ability. All of these youth movements also endured their fair share of conflict with older generations, but for different reasons. While the Laotian teens had parents who did not understand their feminism or American cultural mores and the Dreamers had older leaders telling them what to say, the Angeleno youth of CPC and LBACA (and to some extent, PCORE) often faced an older generation that did not think they were doing enough. Because CPC's and LBACA's critiques also stemmed from their lack of tried and tested youth programs in comparison to CBE, these first-generation organizers definitely felt that they were responsible for politicizing the youth. Perhaps precisely because of CBE's and PCORE's emphasis on allowing the youth to create or cocreate their theory and praxis, they were very well-received and growing (see Brodkin 2009).

One important concluding point: when state- and federal-level representatives and ballot measures of consequence for environmental justice, immigration, and education come up for a vote, these LA-based youth activists will certainly be there at the polling station. And those who cannot vote will likely help turn it out, as many unauthorized immigrants proved when they doorknocked for the post-2006 mega march midterm elections (Zepeda-Millán 2017). With Dreamer, DACA, and resources for K–12 often looming large on the national political scene, they would be voting against their interests if they did not. Latin@ youth knew their power in the grassroots world, and seemed to be aware of their increasing power at the ballot box. As Zepeda-Millán (2017:213) writes:

> [T]he fact that millennials made up almost half (44%) of the over 27 million Latinos eligible to vote in 2016 (Krogstad et al. 2016), and that the vast majority of Latino millennials overwhelmingly supported an openly socialist candidate—Bernie Sanders—during the Democratic primaries, suggests that we could expect the Latino electorate to become increasingly progressive and even more supportive of immigrant rights in the coming years.

Zepeda-Millán proved prophetic, as Sanders would mushroom his Latinx support in 2020 by capturing the hearts of the parents as well. What the activists of my study generally revealed, both younger and older, is that they would sit it out if these nonlocal elections did not bear on their community in some way, shape, or form. Why? Because they would much rather be spending their time talking to neighbors at school, at the laundromat, at church, and at the medical clinic about how industry was killing them, and asking them to join a movement whose power against bioneglect depended on the number of bodies it had.

AFTERWORD

TOWARD BIONEGLECT

NOW THAT WE have chronicled in seven chapters the neoliberal politics of the body and emotions tied to environmental racism and classism, and to resistance against both, it is possible to fully reckon with Foucault's biopolitics and biopower. While Foucault (and many of his interpreters) gave center stage to the "making live" process by presenting multiple case studies of states (and related entities) optimizing the health of a population in myriad ways, it left readers with a weak understanding of the varying processes, nuances, and vectors of "let die." Cultural critic Henry Giroux (2006) aptly writes that biopower does not attend to the "let die" function to the extent that it does "make live." Achille Mbembé (2013) similarly criticized Foucault for not theorizing about systems of violence and domination; in response, Mbembé originated the concept of necropolitics, or the politics of death, to mark sovereign decision-making on death, that is, "the power and the capacity to dictate who may live and who must die" (161). Indeed, this is one of the *privileges* born of subjugating others, a process that Giroux critiques Foucault for not theorizing enough. Discussed throughout this book are the privileges of corporate and political actors who perform the biopower of letting others die by circulating deadly air. Foucault (2007), in contrast, wrote at length about the circulation of beneficial forms (from money to fresh air) and the suppression of negative forms (circulated disease) as a cornerstone of "making live."

I contend that Foucault's underdevelopment both of "let die" and of the dialectic of privileged-subjugated is due *in part* to the distinct era in which we live, one in which modern neoliberalism has seemingly reached its apotheosis, and one that Foucault's premature death would deny him and his analytic eyes. To be sure, his sparse analyses of "let die" also have to do with subjectivity and materiality remaining in the shadows of Foucault's spotlight. Had he given both their due, he would have likely seen that the margins must continually find new ways to navigate the vagaries of neoliberal White nationalist wrath and, importantly, that the Establishment must perpetually find new ways to respond to the "positive power" of the bottom up (false choices, free backpacks and Halloween parades, buying school silence, redefining oil and gas as proenvironment, troubling the margins' emotions while normalizing their own). In broad terms, then, I also depart from Foucault insofar as I believe that the way power often works in the neoliberal era is in top-down and bottom-up form akin to a dialectic, and not always in a web-like mesh of localized circuits. The racial state and racial capitalism are slowly and quietly killing people (see Pulido 2017a)—including the Asian, Latin@, and other activists of color whom I came to know and care for—this is not the stuff of anonymous, "positive" power.

All told, Foucault's treatment of biopolitics could not fully account for the (White) "healthy wealthy" or the lives of today's Latin@ and Asian immigrant environmental justice activists and of many groups and immigrants of color; for one, the activists' resistance to biopower, and how biopower renegotiates itself in response to resistance—especially by way of an emotional economy—was nowhere to be found in his formulations. A theory of power over bodies that prioritized "let die" and its emotional or affective structures therefore grew out of necessity, and my case study was one of the first prompts. We saw that the activists, namely the women, resisted not just by deploying their own affective strategies in the face of emotional domination but by harnessing them to emotional support networks for their oppressed communities, redefining "good" and "moral" citizenship thus. In broad theoretical terms, then, emotions were what also did the explaining and were not merely something to be explained.

In addition to emotions, this concluding chapter rounds out the other key points of departure from Foucault's biopower, as fleshed out by the Asian and Latin@ immigrant clean air activists and in concert with the broader swath of existing theoretical critique.

RACE: SHOULD I STAY OR SHOULD I GO?

First, while race has been more of a flickering flashlight than a constant floodlight in Foucault's oeuvre, bioneglect gave primacy to racism and to the racial state (Goldberg 2002), using environmental justice to show that race could never be separated from the state (nor from capitalism or [neo]liberalism). However, race was not solely relegated to discursive systems or divorced from its relationality with gender and sexuality, class, citizenship, ability status, and the like. In a world formed by colonization, imperialism, and racial capitalism (Robinson 1983), bioneglect presupposes that every society has biologized its people in phenotypic or heritable terms (though it might be called something other than "race" [see N. Kim 2008b]). To extend Foucault's Europe-centric framework, I focused on the United States as case study. In this focus, the Asian American and Latin@ activists demonstrated how nativist racism (or what we now call "White nationalism") marks a rebuke to his view that racism is solely about society warring against itself and killing its own. For one, Foucault would have to posit that Europe's Jews—and in the US, immigrants and refugees of color—were national insiders at all, that they were deemed members of their nation-states. Seemingly biased by his nationalist French perspective—France hegemonically defines itself as the French (within society) against the foil of the not-French (without society)—Foucault would miss the fact that the US racializes Latinx, Asian, Mid-Eastern, Black immigrants and their children as un-American foreigners: illegals, the "dark terrorist threats," inscrutable exotica, and/or deportees. While no group that calls a nation home can be excluded from every institution and cultural formation in the country, akin to Yen Espiritu's (2003) notion of "differential inclusion," Foucault does not consider nativist racism and its "foreigner" bogeyman. Therefore, the society—the nation—is not at war with itself or with its internal population, but is at war with a population that the society-nation already sees as outside of itself, as belonging to another nation, and, often, as the enemy that never should have been within the boundary in the first place. Upon my working with the LA-based immigrants of color, the need to trouble Foucault's French and European biases and his inability to specify the different (but interrelated) racisms of biopower—such as between the nation, on the one hand, and imagined other-nations, on the other—became abundantly clear.

In fact, Ruth Gilmore's (2007:28) conceptualization of racism as "the state-sanctioned or extralegal production and exploitation of group-differentiated vulnerability to premature death" better captures the role of the state (or extralegal entities) to exact power, as her criterion for vulnerability is group differentiation rather than a presumption of national sameness in which one resides; it also better captures the capaciousness of such a system of injustice, as death is not always the inevitable outcome for racial Others, as it would likely be in Foucault's race war. Not everyone with whom I worked will contract asthma or die earlier than average, but the state inexorably positions them as *highly vulnerable to the possibility*. *Refusing Death* was thus anchored in the line between who is accorded life (longevity, health, cleaner air) for being the White insider and those who are vulnerable to premature death because they are the non-White immigrant. Indeed, the activists of my study and/or others from their group have been exposed to physical, emotional, and mental violence: sexual assault, sterilization, economic exploitation, deadly pollution, infirmity and immobility, non-empathy, surveillance, imprisonment, deportation, war-time internment, beatings and killings, and cross-border family separation, much of which grew more acceptable and deadly under the Trump administration (Merchant 2019). As we saw, environmental racism and nativist racism fomented among the Asian immigrant and undocumented Latin@ population palpable emotional distress—at times, and to my mild surprise, that was all they wanted to talk about.[1] As "there is no civil discourse that does not conceptualize the world into those who deserve inclusion and those who do not" (Alexander 1998:98), their distress stood to reason. Although I only worked with the immigrant activists of my study through 2013, it is no surprise that from the start of his 2015 presidential run, Donald Trump and advisor Steve Bannon maximally exploited this discursive trope, especially against Latinx and Muslim ethnics.[2] To the Filipin@ Americans, as well, the heavy (neo)imperial hand of the United States was a profound reminder of the Philippines's nonbelonging in the same echelon as "America" within the racialized (and gendered) global economic order (Espiritu 2003). The vestiges of US colonization in the form of US military bases leaking toxins and killing quietly their people was in part what spurred LA's Filipin@ activists to focus on environmental injustice.

THE STATE OF THE NEOLIBERAL, MATERIAL, TEXTUAL STATE

The second departure from Foucault's biopower-biopolitics is inspired by Stuart Hall's (2017) contention that the state must be understood to be as material as it is discursive (see also Giroux 2006; Sacchi 2011); most important, I connect the neoliberal state—something that Foucault would not live long enough to see—to the case of racism. On Foucault's rendering of the state, Stuart Hall (2017:104) contends that discourse theory is incapable of "theorising the necessary unevenness of a complex unity [that is, the state], or even the 'unity in difference' of a complex structure." While Hall agrees that the state is not a monolith that pivots on a singular flow of power, as Marxist theorists had generally conceptualized, he writes, "the state remains one of the crucial sites in a modern capitalist social formation where political practices of different kinds are *condensed*" (122). In this vein, Nicholas Fox (1998:421–422) mindfully writes that the body is also both material and discursive: "[C]apitalism, industrial development, the physicality of the body, particular historical events or whatever forms an unacknowledged backcloth . . . structure the analytical work of discerning the 'rules' of discursive formation." Like Fox, I contend that social processes, at times, involve the material informing the discursive. For instance, I would not be surprised if, at the birth of capitalism, industrialists did not know exactly how much profit they would earn before they started manufacturing products and banking for some time; some discourses of "profit"—such as "profit at all costs" or justifications for it—were likely constructed after the realization of how much profiteers could actually amass. Hence, to give primacy to discourse *at the expense of* materiality is to miss the nature of power, injustice, and inequality in toto, which I have argued is more negative and repressive than Foucault acknowledges.[3]

The intersection of materiality and discourse is seen in the state's prioritization of corporations and the economy over the people and children of color whom they imperil while they tell the story of how the "environmental justice community" is an equal, or bigger, priority (see Chapter 1) and that oil and gas juggernauts care as much about the earth's and people's health as they do the health of their stock value (in other words, "coopting care"). As another example, the oil refineries were willing to expend considerable effort donating to local schools, hospitals, and other cherished community institutions and throwing parties for the residents they polluted upon, since doing so allowed them to thwart resistance and discursively construct themselves as "caring." With respect to health care, Obama excluded undocumented immigrants from the Affordable Care Act, such as the chronically ill activists I studied. Although his was a dangerous and potentially deadly act, he banked both of his historic presidential campaigns on discursively celebrating immigrants, especially the Latinx.

Indeed, one of the reasons that both the Asian and Latin@ immigrants had such a controversial relationship to the state was the amount of power and jurisdiction that the state had over the built environment (which, in turn, bears on the natural environment). To be sure, and in the face of a failed neoliberal system, low-income communities of color should, to whatever extent possible, abdicate their reliance on the state to solve their problems (Pulido 2017b). To this end, visionaries and freedom fighters such as Grace Lee Boggs advise growing urban gardens to have access to (healthy) food and pretty neighborhoods, and to stop relying on polluting, corporate food production; to form freedom schools to learn a socially just, community-centered education; and to forge Peace Zones to keep each other safe from the abuses of the police, which was masterfully prescient for our post–George Floyd era (Boggs and Kurashige 2011). Such community citizenship is crucial, and through providing the resources, information, bodily care, and emotional support that bioneglect withheld, the LA activists were impressive on the point of self-determination. At the same time, theory and praxis do not always mesh perfectly, and low-income (unauthorized) immigrant communities of color cannot make (or unmake) streets and freeways, decide where they get placed, and do so unilaterally. They still have to get to work, to the market, to the school, and to the clinic or hospital, whether by bus or car. No one else builds those roads or freeways except the state. No one can build a school or community clinic without authorization from the state, let alone a cargo shipping port, a train yard, or an oil refinery. Again, in the words of Hall (2017), the state's power can be diffuse, multipronged, and multilateral, but it is often, as well, *condensed.* The activists of this study therefore perpetually navigated and vacillated between relying on a condensed state and relying on a condensed community.

THE STATE OF BIRTHING DEATH

Third, my examination of environmental justice in an uncelebrated hyper-hazardous corner of Los Angeles revealed that power is not exercised solely because often-unexpected *populationwide health* issues force the state's hand, another distinction from Foucaultian biopower. Take, for example, how Foucault writes about the role of leprosy (under the king), the plague (under discipline), or polio and grain scarcity (under security) in forcing the state to make calculated decisions about life and death. Studying the clean air activists through the prism of bioneglect demonstrates, rather, that the state (and industry) also *originate* major populationwide health crises, sometimes in questionably lawful or categorically unlawful ways, and not always under Agamben's "states of emergency" (1998; see also Han 2008). For instance, not only did the racial state germinate an environmental and climate crisis by being bought off by cozy industry (Pulido 2017b), but it engineers a health crisis by making immigrants of color, who keep the nation afloat and humming, collectively sick, tired and depressed, and prematurely in the morgue. Failing to treat asthma as the public health crisis that it is (Corburn 2005) means, in turn, a health crisis of too many sick people and not enough health care providers. Emergency departments and free and low-cost health clinics deluged with long lines of distressed, low-income, and undocumented patients is, indeed, a crisis.

By throwing into relief the role of the state (and industry) as originators of populationwide health crises, I contend that the modern state no longer needs a state of emergency nor to normalize it in the Foucaultian sense, in order to control populations or partake in bioneglect. It merely needs to normalize nonstatist and nonindustrial sources as responsible for public health crises ("It appeared out of nowhere") and to normalize actual neoliberal crises (soaring rates of asthma, now worsened by COVID-19) as *noncrises*. The most effective way for the state (and industry) to do so is to not act; that is, not talk, not legislate, and not enforce as if no crisis existed at all (akin to the way Trump discredited the "Kung-flu" global pandemic); as we saw in Chapter 1, let our government health website focus instead on changing how children and families manage asthma, inhalers, and dust mites (per Foucaultian discipline). In other words, disproportionate numbers of children of color suffering from asthma is not a crisis, it is a nondescript nonissue in the national background. How do we know? Because, in perfect teleological fashion, the state does not react to it as crisis. As *Refusing Death* has laid bare, the engineering of an asthma crisis shares some parallels with the engineering of an environmental one. To be certain, US state apparatuses have expended more effort to respond to the latter than the former. However, by dint of the federal government not declaring a national climate emergency decades ago (Kormann 2019) and not declaring Carson's and Wilmington's oil refineries or the Port of Long Beach's diesel plumes as partly responsible for that emergency, it conveys that the climate crisis, or local environmental justice crises, are, in fact, not of crisis proportions at all (with the Trump administration's climate change denial serving as apex). In other words, the widespread release of barely regulated chemicals into the air such that nearby children of low income and color *en masse* are made sick and live shorter is "normal"—a nondescript nonissue in the national background. That the state is, at once, the architect of racially oppressive health crises and of the nonresponse to them lays bare that the "biopolitics of racism," or what I conceptualize as the bioneglect of racism, operates within, rather than outside, the normal juridical order (Han 2008). It is precisely its juridical "normality" that enables the state (and industry) to be invisible throughout—invisible when creating public health crises and invisible as nonresponders (because there is no crisis to which to respond)—as invisible as the air we breathe.

The danger of this invisibility connected, importantly, to the Angeleno activists' contradictory relationship to the state: they knew that the state, alongside industry, was an architect of environmental racism and classism, so who else could they turn to but source? At the same time, the Asian Americans and Latin@s knew that the crisis itself, and the state's nonresponse, were invisible to the rest of the world; therefore the state had little incentive to un-engineer an invisible "problem." No one else was really watching anyway.

STAYIN' ALIVE: LET'S GET PHYSICAL AND IN OUR FEELINGS

In a fourth departure from standard biopolitics, the Asian and Latin@ immigrant activists made clear that we must understand bodies not just as discursive, but as corporeal material that is enlivened to think, feel, and act agentically in the world. Sociologists and other students of the body have tended to stay in the theoretical realm, devoting more attention to what is done to the body rather than to how social actors use the body to discern the workings of power and inequality, and construct political ideologies, identities, and emotional lives accordingly (see Davis 1995; Kang 2010).

My own thinking on this point has been inspired by the frequent application of Foucaultian biopower to the subjugation of Latin@ immigrants in the social sciences, Latinx studies, and related fields. For instance, Chavez (2007) likens the Minuteman Project's vigilante patrolling of the Arizona-Mexico border to Foucault's (1975/1979) concepts of "spectacle" (such as the king's public executions) and "surveillance" (for example, the discipline of prisoners by the Panopticon). Rather than opposing these two practices, Chavez views the Minuteman monitoring as both: performing surveillance to produce a spectacle on the Arizona-Mexico border. Finding clandestine border crossers became part of the "show," a "media circus." That is, in the final analysis and in a final twist, the Minutemen's success was not in numbers of border crossers found and detained, but on the attention that the project received and the disciplining it achieved, namely, the ability to discipline the state to align with a vigilante cause. Other examples of the biopolitics of racism against Latinx bodies, Chavez (2008) finds, are hospitals medically repatriating unauthorized immigrants for their inability to pay and White Americans lambasting the possibility of an unauthorized Latina receiving an "American" organ.

Similarly invoking Foucault, Cisneros (2016) has skillfully applied his concept of "massive elimination" under state racism to today's prison industrial complex and to the detention, deportation, and the state-fashioned "illegality" of migrants. Not only does Cisneros deem the prison a primary strategy of massive elimination,[4] she considers immigrant deportation to actually "rehears[e] and exten[d] what Foucault and his GIP [the activist *Prison Information Group*] called the 'intolerable' practices of the prison" (244; see also Dilts 2014). Cisneros specifies that the "confining society" defines and justifies prisons and similar institutions as tools of preservation (for example, reform) but, to Foucault, are "actually aimed at elimination" (246). Though Foucault's case studies do not spotlight the discourses and punishments of anti-immigrant and antirefugee regimes in a comprehensive or sustained way,

GIP documents do make mention of immigrant detainment under French jurisdiction; immigrants—namely, those from Algeria—are mentioned alongside workers and students as a group especially vulnerable to strategies of confinement.

As recent critical prison activism and theory have pointed us toward (James 2002), immigrant detainment in the United States has been subsumed under the prison industrial complex and its drastic expansion as "the privileged instrument" of racist "massive elimination" (Defert 1971, cited in Cisneros 2016:248). Foucault (1975/1979) also presciently observed that the self-justification of the criminal justice system has depended on its "perpetual reference to something other than itself" and its reinscription in nonlegal systems. While the detention center is certainly in the family of standard prisons, Foucault was also referring to nonjuridical forms such as morality discourse, itself inseparable from the state's power to punish. In accordance, regulators' and industry's normalization of their bioneglect could be read as instantiating moral authority. From the angle of resistance, the Angeleno activists of my study used their own morality tropes to resist the (White) healthy wealthy's immoral punishment regimes manifest in environmental injustice and resultant quiet death.

Brendese (2014) uses a Foucaultian framework to demonstrate how the Latinx population is read as both epidemic threat and vaccinating agent, as both cure and disease (by dint of discipline and biopolitics, respectively). In both cases, the immigrants in question are either tacitly or explicitly regarded as outside the human race. For instance, she writes, immigrants who perform jobs with a high probability of death or maiming—slaughterhouse labor, mining, logging, firefighting—or back-breaking farm and factory work, are living a life tantamount to "slow death." Yet until the Trump administration changed the policy, George W. Bush had solved military shortages by offering expedited citizenship to unauthorized immigrants. As "[m]ilitary service has long been used as an incentive to prove one deserves status, dignity, and even humanity," as was the case for African Americans in the Civil War (see Smith 2012) and for mass-incarcerated Japanese Americans in World War II, Brendese sees the Latinx, in the military, as a biopolitical cure (Brendese 2014:180). At the same time, Latinxs' large share of the armed forces is concomitant with their large share of the prison population; hence, they are at once a vaccinating agent and an epidemic threat (180).

Carney's (2014:3) research on Mexican and Central American migrant women who seek food under conditions of food insecurity finds, akin to my study, that ideologies of gender, race, class, and citizenship "obscure the very social processes in which these power relations are embedded and constituted." As she writes that these power relations "have allowed for an unevenness of ecological suffering, specifically at the locus of migrant women's bodies," she argues that the political ecologies of food reproduce the conditions of difference," even at the level of "affect and emotion" (13). Yet in the same vein as the LA environmental justice activists, the women contest state discipline of their bodies by way of "subjective transnationalism" (Segura and Zavella 2008), that is, resisting "the unevenness in food access and distribution that often exacerbates health and nutritional vulnerabilities"; the women also used the political strategy of "*cuidarse en la comidato*" (caring for each other through food) to achieve what neoliberalism failed to do: "nourish . . . bodies and social ties" (Pérez and Abarca 2007:141). In my study, as well, transnationalism undergirded the immigrant women's emphasis on bodily movement in the first place; they could never take such mobility for granted, as patriarchal sexual shame in Mexico and as ICE surveillance in El Norte limited their freedom in the streets.

In considering the confluence of these myriad studies, Foucaultian biopolitical processes of disciplining and letting die clearly have purchase for understanding the subjugation of Latin@ populations. At the same time, given the limitations of Foucaultian thought as I outline in this chapter (and have done throughout the book)—having a Eurocentric and nonnativist conceptualization of race, not attending sufficiently to racial capitalism and materiality, not centering the state's originating of public health crises, not foregrounding corporeality and emotion—I contend that we students of race, migration, gender, intersectionality, and citizenship need also to be stretching, problematizing, and enriching Foucaultian frameworks through these intellectual prisms that he himself underappreciated; those of us who occupy subjugated social locations can also craft critical reformulations per standpoint epistemology and strong objectivity (Harding 1993).

To be certain, Foucault's work on state power over bodies applies very well to the case of immigrants of color. Here, the Asian and Latin@ immigrant clean air activists see inequalities of the body as endemic to how society, injustices, and politics work. But, in a departure from Foucault, they also see body inequalities as endemic to their acts of resistance against being racialized as "foreign invaders," whether in cities or in suburbs (for example, Saito 1998). Foucault's framework also does not stipulate what intersectionality theorists have long told us, that systemic racism has hinged on defining people of color as (more) embodied, more emotional, and more sexual than White people (for example, Collins 2000). Feminist scholars also have excoriated Foucault for underappreciating gender more generally (see Naples 2003). It was therefore intersectionality and feminist scholars who underscored that, for instance, African American women have been subject to a form of domination that "reduces humans to animate nature in order to exploit them economically or to treat them condescendingly as pets" (Tuan 1984, cited in Collins 2000:144). In parallel fashion, heterosexual, able-bodied, upper-class, and ethnoreligiously dominant subjects have also defined themselves as more in their minds and less in their bodies (and less in their "negative" feelings) than LGBTQIA, disabled, poor, and so-called "terrorist" groupings (see Collins 2000, 2004; hooks 1984).

The underdevelopment of an enlivened, agentic, and resisting corporeal body cannot be laid at Foucault's feet alone. Although in the social scientific literature on nativist racism and White nationalism scholars have alluded to bodies and embodiment, they have not closely engaged the body research, not centered the body when theorizing or methodologically designing their work, and not sufficiently engaged (even if just to critique) biopower-biopolitical frameworks. For the social sciences to move toward more body-centered paradigms, we must first address the historical connection between nativist racism, on the one hand, and the body and citizenship, on the other. Doing so allows us to rewrite some of the history and politics of Asian and Latin@ America from the standpoint of the body and emotionality. For instance, the work of Gutiérrez (2008) and Stern (2016) reminds us that there is no nativist racism and sexism against Latina immigrants without the dominant group's efforts to scare or trick them (that is, emotionally manipulate them) into mutilating their bodies, so as to stop them from making more. Rachel Lee (2014) also shows us that the bodies of Asian Americans (and other people of color) often manifest as body parts, from exploded Chinese bodies along California's railroads to comedian Margaret Cho's exploding pussy. In the case of today's clean air activists in port-industrial Los Angeles, Asian and Latin@ immigrants did not just draw "us-them" boundaries along race and class lines; they drew political boundaries in terms of an *embodied* community suffering, in particular, an *embodied* racism and classism.

Admittedly, it might be impossible for people who embodied pollution-induced illness *not* to be fixated on the body and on how much healthier the bodies of richer White citizens were, the ones who got to live far away from the port, BP Arco, and Shine truck-washing company. At the same time, given how variegated and unrelenting the transcorporeal stimuli were for these immigrants, they also conceptualized and worked through the politics of embodiment in more textured, complex, and even paradoxical ways. Recall that the activists were inundated with visual, audial, and emotional stress from light and noise pollution and suffered very delimited physical mobility given ICE surveillance and imposing refineries (so omnipresent they made clouds!), as well as the lack of cars, sidewalks, air one could exercise in, and green spaces. Such a unique experience of day-to-day embodiment led, for instance, to the mothers' unique interweaving of physical and *socioeconomic* mobility. As this type of mobility was even more pressing for the low-income Mexican (and Filipin@) immigrant families, the activists inventively redefined environmental justice by fusing it with the school reform movement. The mothers focused not only on the hazards and pollutants at school that made studying difficult, but on the concept that studying itself involved physical education and taking breaks to run around at recess. Neoliberalism's false choices also meant that, at times, low-income Latina mothers had to prioritize the walkable distance of a school (mobility) over its low pollution exposure; that is, sometimes they just had to choose the school right next to the diesel-spewing, cancer-causing freeway.

In other forms of embodiment, the Latina organizers interestingly prioritized bodily adornment. Tutoring each other on clothes, hair, and make-up for testifying in front of officials and interviewing for jobs, the women would sometimes do this at the many social gatherings they organized to resist their exclusion from the national community and, importantly, to swell the resistance; more than just embodying environmentally induced illness, then, the body and community could also be dovetailed in positive ways that made them feel they could superarse. Both the Asian and Latin@ immigrants also invoked the body when they revealed weak interest in national politicians and policies; they were not interested in officials who were disembodied and distant from their community, one besieged by inequalities of the body and emotions (notwithstanding sharp criticisms, too, of local politicians). For the Latin@ immigrants who lacked papers, this sentiment translated into weak interest in formal citizenship and formal political assimilation: eventual voting, electoral campaigning, and office-seeking. All told, this book sought to show that these kinds of predilections were profoundly informed by the immigrants' ecological, transcorporeal, and intersectional perspectives on urban environmental justice movements.

Suffering bioneglect also prompted the activists to construct political injustice, boundaries, and strategies on the basis of another vector of embodiment: emotional life. In fact, the women often talked about their feelings—usually, demoralization and depression—more than I expected they would. When they chose to tell officials from state agencies about how they thought their four-year-old son was going to choke to death from a particularly violent asthma attack, I always felt unease. Not only did I feel empathy for such a speaker as she wept, but I felt supreme discomfort with the stone-faced state and corporate officials. I never felt that these elites appreciated the fact that to share one's personal story of chronic illness, poverty, or uncertain futures to seemingly uncaring (mostly White male) strangers—and in a non-English language such as Spanish or in Tagalog-accented English—required palpable strength, summoned strong emotions, and deserved at least a little more than stoicism.

Yet we often do not hear of institutions and policy as sites of emotion work. When emotionality is connected to the US nation-state, for instance, we typically hear of the state's hegemonic imposition of patriotic (blind) loyalty and desire and of populist fearmongering (Glassner 2018). Furthermore, intersectionality scholars have long shown us that racism and sexism have depended on seeing people of color and women as saturated with emotion, betraying their inferiority vis-à-vis the White and male superiority proven by *mental* fortitude. Although this false binary of mind-body has been challenged by emotions scholars who have discredited the Cartesian division of rationality and irrationality (Zembylas 2016), hegemony persists, such as when global northern scholars continue to see global southern nations, such as those in Africa, as proximal to nature and, thereby, weakness. "Feelings, emotions and sensations—not reason—are said to characterize The Sons of Ham,"

Hamilton (1993:71) writes, contradistinguishing advanced Western nations as mental, rational, and civil. Coining the phenomenon "Orientalism," Edward Said (1978) noted the same about the advanced West's hegemonic emotional rendering of the Middle East.

With regard to the US immigrants that hail from other countries of the Global South, such as Mexico and the Philippines (or Guatemala, Samoa, or Cambodia), we saw that bioneglect depended on state and corporate deployment of emotive structures to wield and maintain power institutionally, an underdeveloped area of study. The officials were particularly effective when they coupled their "nonemotionality" with knowledge—the "superior" mental state legitimized by scientific studies from in-house or contracted researchers and from other forms of technocracy (read: *not* "emotional stories"). This group of predominantly White men were thus unimpeachably "correct," calcifying policy and legal decisions with little to no input from "street science" or other lived, embodied knowledge about hyperpollution. Institutional emotive power also ultimately affirms (nativist) racism, sexism, and classism at a broader discursive level (those Asian Americans are "meek" or "dragon ladies;" those Latin@s are "fiery" or "unrefined").

At the same time, the margins resist with their own racial economy of emotions. Departing decidedly from a focus on electoral campaigns, for instance, these immigrants chose emotional support-giving as their key mode of citizenship and citizen resistance. Yet by addressing the activists' subversive, bottom-up, and horizontal processes, this book never lost sight of the assaults on their bodies and feeling states by bioneglectful racism and classism—nor the dialectic between the two. For instance, the immigrants' agitation was rooted in pressuring the neoliberal state *to exhibit some modicum of concern, even if contrived*—the kind that one might associate with a strong welfare state and social safety net. Expansive programs for job security, social security, health care, nutrition, the safety of women and children, education, and housing as compensatory measures mitigating against the injustices of racial capitalism bespeak the dictum that you will not be left *completely* alone, you will not fall into *the bottom* of the abyss (see Hall 2017). But as Giroux (2006) alludes to, the supplanting of the welfare state with unfettered neoliberalism, privatization, and militarism meant that the most marginalized *were* completely alone at the *bottom*. By dint of (low-income, unauthorized) people of color, especially women, having to step into the gap for each other, they were by definition engaging in political resistance. In the process of so doing, they were also ensuring each other's *belonging* in the face of nativist racist exclusion and delimited inclusion. This effort at communal self-determination was one of the reasons that, even if the activists never won a single environmental justice victory, "the trying" was the most important; trying together kept them networked in a communal web of mutuality, the social node within their milieu of control. The outcome of the fight against BP or Caltrans, the dimension out of their control, would fall where it fell. To be sure, it was also the clean air organizers' unceasing hope that the state would ultimately reward their trying that, in part, propelled them into a hot and cold relationship with it.

In this vein, *Refusing Death* sought to delve deeper into why the activists had hope in a state in which they often had little hope, to align ontologically with them to the extent that those of us who do not live their existence can. If day-to-day life is unbreathable air, looming oil refineries, football-field-size ships, trains, freeway overpasses, and constant reminders that our coughing children are moving toward premature deaths, it is hard not to empathize with the pressure-cooker call to tap every resource, call every official, and speak at every public comment, lest their silence be deemed indifference or concession. In some ways, *not* making demands on government agencies and officials could be read as remiss parenting, especially when losing precious time could mean the difference between a child living or dying.

In an effort to spotlight the privilege[5] and affective structures of dominant society, both of which elude the Foucaultian framework, bioneglect marks emotive power and its effects as, at times, repressive power and privilege. To be fair to Foucault, he theoretically name-dropped emotions, such as in his definitions of discourse: "Discourses are more than ways of thinking and producing meaning. They constitute the 'nature' of the body, unconscious and conscious mind and *emotional life* of the subjects they seek to govern" (Weedon 1987:108). Furthermore, in the *History of Sexuality* (2008), Foucault argues that once the "confession" was no longer the province of the Christian Church, it prompted the public to "tell the truth"—a form of knowledge production—about everything from their emotions to their sexual desires, crafting a new knowledge of the self as fundamentally defined by a sexual identity. Furthermore, with regard to the shift from the monarchy (sovereign) to the disciplinary regime, Foucault noted that "the locus of the new European mode of punishment shifted from the body to the soul . . ." (James and Davis 1996:99). On these punished and imprisoned bodies, Foucault (1975/1979:29–30) writes, "The man described for us, whom we are invited to free, is already in himself the effect of a subjection more profound than himself. A 'soul' inhabits him and brings him to existence, which is itself a factor in the mastery that power exercises over the body. The soul is the effect and instrument of a political anatomy; the soul is the prison of the body." Angela Davis brilliantly interrelates this rendition of the soul with race, arguing that "black slaves in the US were largely perceived as lacking the soul that might be shaped and transformed by punishment" (James and Davis 1996:99). While Foucault is keen to explain the soul (though not by way of race like Davis), it raises the question, What is a soul without feeling? In my view, the two are mutually constitutive: the soul, as with feeling, is not necessarily something we can fully grasp by way of mental processing or discourse; this explains, in large part, why the state can use it to such powerful effect, to the point of compelling people to objectify or subjectify themselves. Despite allusions like these to emotion, Foucault's was not a theory of emotions, as noted earlier, but a peripheral invocation of emotions as an end product to be explained. As this book sought to show, however, a bioneglect-centered body politics considers emotional life and emotive power to do the explaining as well.

As Foucault did not theorize resistance movements and their relationship to the state (or capital), feminist scholars in particular have minded the gap by interrelating bodies, emotions, and activism. In evaluating this intellectual trajectory, Fonow and Franzway (2016:2) noted that the recent turn to affect in feminist theorizing is beginning to make the connections between and among the body, emotion, and politics. Fonow and Franzway use the example of gender within patriarchy to flesh out (pun intended) this relationship:

> Since women undertake a significant proportion of the bodily care practices (Turner 1984) required by others' bodies, the question must be raised: What about the bodily practices required by the woman's body to undertake this work. Women and men do not labor equally over their own bodies; bodily practices are not gender-neutral. Women not only care for others' bodies but must also care for their own. (2016:4–5)[6]

Burrowing holes in previous thinking by way of these forceful questions, however, has not always prompted feminist studies to center the state and intersectionality. Gwendolyn Mink, for instance, critiqued feminists for not taking Congress and President Clinton to task for the welfare-to-work campaign, which effectively disappeared struggling Asian immigrant and refugee women as well (1999, cited in Fujiwara 2008:184). In turn, Clinton's shift to neoliberal welfare policy stifled these marginalized immigrant women's ability to convey that such "reform" was, in effect, state violence (and, taking a cue from the LA activists, we should specify physical and emotional violence).

CHICKENS COMING HOME TO ROOST

The fifth and final distinction from Foucault that bioneglect makes clear is that the larger arc of biopower ultimately hurts the privileged despite the interim benefits that accrete to the privileged and their institutions, a dynamic that is not clear within traditional biopower. As Hochschild (2016) and others show, the citizens who use government programs—from well-heeled elites to the less glittery working class in the US—can be the same ones who condemn and seek to destroy them. As Mills (1997) and McIntosh (1989) have shown, privilege often breeds a certain type of ignorance. And when bad schools and the bioneglect of children lead to the downfall of society, when nothing stands between the polluting company and the watershed, and when the toxic incinerators, guns, violence, and prisons seep their harm into the posh zip codes, everybody starts to be killed slowly and quietly, even if the margins are much more vulnerable to its premature realization (Gilmore 2007). This is not to argue that the Establishment and the White healthy wealthy lack social and environmental privilege (Park and Pellow 2011); they absolutely do. At the same time, they can do nothing about the fact that air (or water or soil) ultimately moves, that gas pipelines explode and poison rich communities like Porter Ranch, that the climate catastrophe's mudslides and fires do not care if the homes are in Malibu Canyon, and that none of these environmental crises will reliably stop at real or symbolic white picket fences. The government officials can do nothing about the fact that most of their workdays are filled with "even" non-English-speaking "illegal moms" from working-class communities of color ruthlessly shouting them down, protesting outside their office, embarrassing them in the news, and shaming them as cold-hearted snakes in public—not exactly gratifying. And witnessing the officials' patterned body and affective language (frowns, sighs, eye rolls, slumped shoulders, straightened backs) and verbal language ("no," "delay," "We'll get back to you," "That's not what our science says," "You're involved in too much," "Why don't you move?" "You procrastinate," "You're not the only ones who get cancer") seemed to betray a lack of occupational gratification. In other words, the privileged, in some way or form, are ultimately hurt by their own privileged power. Bioneglect casts into relief, as Malcolm X (or El Hajj Malik El-Shabazz) would quip, that "the chickens" eventually come "home to roost."

Taken together, bioneglect is a top-down, discursive-material process of "letting die" waged by neoliberal racial capitalism and the racial state, a process capacious enough for the nativist racism chronicled in this book. Although the subjugation and resistance of the Asian and Latin@ EJ activists flesh out the necessity of inserting bioneglect into a biopolitical-biopower framework, mine is not an eliminatory theoretical maneuver. Rather, bioneglect is meant to give equal due to the "let die" process and to be theorized in relation to Foucault's much more in-depth exegesis on "make live" (see Giroux 2006; Mbembé 2013), which itself could be more transformed by neoliberal, discursive-material, corporeal, and emotive power (and also beyond Europe's borders). In my treatment, bioneglect, on the one hand, and "make live," on the other (what I like to call biohealth), together constitute biopower. Analysts would, in turn, interrelate resistance movements with this more expansive paradigm whereby the two perpetually negotiate each other, such as when state regulators respond to EJ activists' emotive power by shaming them for it. Waging these kinds of analyses mirrors the pivotal role of bottom-up movements in state racial projects, as theorized by Omi and Winant (2014) in racial formation theory and by Bonilla-Silva (1997) in racialized social systems theory.

OTHER KEY FINDINGS OF *REFUSING DEATH* AND THEIR IMPLICATIONS

Although both the Filipin@ and Mexican immigrant organizers stressed the embodied and emotive politics of their environmental justice work, their distinct class, US-based, and transnational livelihoods also prompted divergent patterns. While these differentiated elements prompted the mostly Mexican women activists to cite class injustice as the source of the hyperpollution and the source of inspiration for their moral boundary drawing, the Filipin@ ethnic organizers cited racial injustice.

Future research might explore how Mexican society talks about its poor and about class inequality writ large. It would be interesting to see if Mexico's class discourse similarly dismisses the poor as "ignorant," as "uneducated," and as bringing down society.[7] It would be a worthy project to compare and contrast with the explicitly racialized class discourse in El Norte, one that punishes immigrants of color for not speaking English, doing all the "bad jobs," having "too many kids," birthing anchor babies (Chavez 2017), invading as rich maternity tourists, draining resources as refugees, and/or being too good at what they do ("foreign competitors").

Another motive behind the Mexican ethnics' fingering of class could have been their view that citing White racism and drawing boundaries between "you Anglos" and "us Latinos" might have seemed more incendiary and controversial in hegemonically "color-blind" and "post-racial" America (Bonilla-Silva 2006; Cunnigen and Bruce 2010, respectively). To be sure, Trumpism arrived after I left the field. Still, scholars might explore if discourses of race and racism seem less effective in their capacity to compel institutional officials into social justice solutions, perhaps even a liability and a countervailing force against it.

To be sure, although the Latin@ activists were always conscious of race—they merely preferred to have class mediate race—my key findings were that class inequality was the transnational, transcorporeal reality across both sets of borders; therefore, transnational lenses and livelihoods proved paramount in determining their politics. In this vein, I would caution against overdetermining the salience of race for working-class immigrants of color. I say this with trepidation, as I never want to imply that race has less power than class, especially in relation to race-centered social processes. When racism is the primary source or co-cause of disproportionate environmental hazards in non-White communities, however, we might consider all the reasons why a non-White group would *not* go to race first as the political beast to slay. Doing so would allow us to stop analyzing solely as academics but to see the world through the eyes of the activists who more directly suffer from it and who craft theory that aligns more with "street theory" about overpolluted neighborhoods. While the majority of the activists did not directly invoke "capitalism"—not surprising, seeing as how the US perpetually obscures social class and the full exploitative nature of capital—its specter seemed to loom over us whenever they shared "people over profit" and talked at length about how the US needed and exploited immigrants in the name of "economics." On the same token, we might explore whether a secondary racial analysis of environmental justice could unconsciously reinforce color-blind and postracial discourse (Pellow 2007; Pulido 2017b).[8]

In parallel fashion, the Filipin@ ethnic activists were largely middle-class English speakers with more intense engagement of White America, mainstream discourse, and transcorporeal, transnational politics—together, these elements shored up the primacy of racism to most of the Filipin@ activists across the generations. While in their eyes race mediated class, the Filipin@s' premigrant political and activist life on the archipelago and their ongoing work in movements against US toxic imperialism in the Philippines kept global and local racism front and center. While the Filipin@ American activists were not explicit about how blocking a plant or refinery in Carson would merely send it to another disadvantaged community or to a developing nation (see Pellow 2007), both generations were very aware of how race and (neo)colonialism fueled global environmental injustice.

Transnationalism also mattered to both the Latin@ and Asian immigrant organizers when they expressed their lack of interest in national-level electoral politics. While both racial groups lamented the corrupt political system and its officials back in Mexico, the Philippines, Samoa, and Cambodia, the Mexican immigrants in particular tied their weaker interest in voting and other forms of assimilation to their disengagement from federal US politics, including the Obama whom they adored but who "betrayed" them on immigration. Again, it stands to reason that neoliberal nativist racism would prompt disengagement from the US racial state, particularly if transnational connections reminded immigrants that the tentacles of corrupt political power wrapped around and choked the globe.

In partial defiance of political assimilation predictions about the Latin@ second generation, the youth activists were not as interested in national-level voting, especially in a system they deemed duplicitous and ineffectual. While, like their parents, they would certainly partake begrudgingly, they ultimately did not want their focus on grassroots "people's politics" to be truncated or impinged upon. In further defiance of neat and uniform assimilatory predictions, some of the youth's hardcore activist parents who were protesting oil refineries were so removed from formal political socialization that they constructed a unique politics of the body to oppose prochoice and pro-gay-marriage stances.

A focus on the body coupled with religious beliefs and political marginality, in effect, afforded (contradictory) political notions about the politics of the body. While the conservative body ideologies were only true of a small minority of the immigrants, I could not help but be completely taken aback by them, especially by the procapitalist and Republican identity of Cindy, one of the strongest AAPI environmental justice activists in the movement, or even of fellow teacher Kelly, a Black American woman. At the same time, no one ever said that subjugated people were without political contradiction; this was especially true of those whose tools to remap politics were myriad because of their exclusion from, and marginality in, formal political systems. At the same time, neoliberal power unfolded in the false choices they imposed on even the most progressive of the activists. Again, the activists had so little to work with, of which such "choices" made us painfully aware.

IMPLICATIONS FOR RELATED SCHOLARSHIP

As *Refusing Death* has underscored, work by sociologists and American and ethnic studies could more intensively focus on environmental and climate justice (Fisher-Fishkin 2005), and do so from underappreciated perspectives of the body (Alaimo 2010) and emotions (Norgaard and Reed 2017). Those who broadly study immigration, social movements, race and ethnicity, class, gender, and/or transnationality would be especially well-suited to do so. On transnationality, for instance, the activists of color show that local contexts matter and that local ecological dynamics fundamentally inform transnational ones, with the reverse flow applying as well (see Aparicio 2006). Furthermore, while race studies across disciplines still need to empirically and theoretically foreground environmental dimensions of racism (Pellow 2007), Asian American, ethnic, and American studies would be well served by expanding research on Filipin@ American social movements, such as their environmental justice legacy. Latinx studies could also widen the purview of social movements beyond the wide battery of studies on immigration and labor reform; more research should highlight Latin@s' indelible contributions to less studied efforts, such as environmental justice and interfaith alliances, particularly since these mobilizations often overlap with immigrant rights. In this vein, environmental justice scholarship would also benefit from examining how the margins are redefining EJ movements. In this LA-based clean air fight, for example, the Latin@ immigrant change-makers in particular wholly redefined environmental justice by making it inseparable from their organizing for school reform, while also accepting the contradictions that emerged from this political interface. Finally, drawing an arc across disciplines reveals that while sociology—and environmental justice sociology, in particular—could draw more on American studies approaches to empire, the body, affect, and citizenship, American studies paradigms could more seriously engage social science questions and methodologies as a matter of course (Lauter 2002).

As I introduced at the start of *Refusing Death*, women of color, many of whom are immigrants, have been changing the world, and not just on issues of environmental justice. They have led on immigration rights, welfare reform, school reform, domestic violence, Black Lives Matter (Chatelain and Asoka 2015), and #metoo (Pazzanese and Walsh 2018), among others. And as I write this final chapter, the country and the world have exploded in protest over the racist police terror waged on Black male bodies and over Trump Era racism more broadly. While George Floyd is now emblazoned across the world and has sparked a political revolution we have not seen since the 1960s era, we still struggle to prioritize the deaths of Breonna Taylor, Atatiana Jefferson, Sandra Bland, and the tragically long list of other names (Khaleeli 2016). We also do not hear enough about how Black American women's founding and leadership of the Black Lives Matter Movement account for its uniqueness and success. Our scholarly knowledge on grassroots leadership by Black American women and on Asian and Latin@ immigrant women, even in feminist and women's studies, is not commensurate with these women's felt impact on the streets. It is my hope that adding my study to the growing lexicon of (immigrant) women of color politics and movements will inspire and could inform more global, comparative, and intersectional orientations. Understanding the environmental justice movement in Los Angeles by way of an expanded Foucaultian paradigm—one enriched by the experience of (undocumented, impoverished) immigrant women of color—also bridges theory and empiricism, and opens up room for reformulating both.

Beyond my study of air pollution in the City of Angels, other cases of environmental racism and classism could certainly be studied by way of bioneglect, and, in turn, the relationship between bioneglect and resistance. As an example, Giroux (2006) used Hurricane Katrina to criticize Foucault's underappreciation of "letting die," an argument that inspired much of my analysis. Other myriad social phenomena to be studied could potentially be (but are not limited to) the health care system's treatment of undocumented immigrants, which this book only peripherally addressed; death and discrimination in medical research, such as clinical drug trials on Third World peoples or a look back at the Tuskegee experiment; the neglect of war veterans and of the rapidly growing houseless population; the police killings of unarmed Black populations but also the underappreciated high rates of police murders of unarmed Brown and indigenous peoples (Egelko 2019; Schroedel and Chin 2020); the hyperimprisonment of the same population since the "drug wars"; the US rejection of Syrian refugees fleeing a murderous authoritarian; the US rejection of Central American children fleeing crushing poverty, US-made gangs, and the climate catastrophe; and, equally important, the organized pushback against each of these.

To flesh out how a bioneglect-centered body politics would apply elsewhere, the state treatment of unauthorized immigrants living with HIV/AIDS is an apt case. As *Refusing Death* has noted, California's neoliberal nativist racist policies often intersected immigration and health policy. A prime example is Proposition 187, which California passed to criminalize undocumented immigrants, prevent their enrollment in public schools, and deny their use of health services, including HIV and STI screening services. New York state took it a step further and denied legal immigration status and citizenship to people with HIV except under extraordinary circumstances, fomenting an anti-immigrant culture in the health care industry (Aparicio 2006:353). New York law also required persons applying for a change in immigration status to be tested for HIV, and if positive, deprived them of basic health services such as emergency care and even mandated that professionals report them to Immigration and Customs Enforcement (ibid.:949). Although the policy has since changed, not only did New York exclude those deemed "undocumented" from state-run and -funded HIV and STI services, but it also denied prenatal care services to women (Gálvez 2011). In other areas expanding outward from New York, immigrant detainees have generally lost access to health services such as basic HIV medication and care owing to their inability to appeal to an independent judicial body or tribunal to challenge their detention. As immigrants have perceived these policies as sources of criminalization threatening to them and their families (Aparicio 2006:965), rates of mental health illness, including posttraumatic stress disorder, have dramatically increased, demonstrating that the ripple effects can sometimes be worse than the policy itself. A bioneglect-centered body politics exposes that the denial of subsidized health care, due process of law, and physical mobility (what was gold to the EJ activists) is the product of neoliberal state engineering. In this case, nativist racism, racial capitalism, class inequities, and homophobia undergird the system's physical and emotional assaults. The state (and private medical facilities) normalize the quiet killing of HIV/AIDS patients without need for states of emergency, as this populationwide health crisis besieging "illegal" immigrants is invisible to much of society, as is the system's nonresponse. In the final analysis, such quiet killing ultimately hurts the privileged. Since dominant elites prioritize an ample supply of cheap, exploitable immigrant labor and their own communities' inoculation from "the excess" of too many non-Whites (especially non-White crime) and too much sickness and death, they are ultimately inviting in all of the aforementioned, including protests and property destruction, the more they partake in bioneglect. The same applies for all of the unauthorized immigrants left out by the Affordable Care Act (Obamacare), who would not need to swell emergency departments and Medicaid offices if the government would just insure them.[9] As dominant groups and institutions do not seem to see, or care to see, how they ultimately hurt themselves and the collective, we are reminded that it is not just "disaffected White American voters" but *the rich, White, and powerful* who profoundly act against their own interests (see McIntosh 1989; Mills 1997).

One of the limitations of my research project is that the working-class Latin@ and middle-class Asian immigrants worked mostly in separation given the demographic make-up of their respective communities and constituencies. We require more research on how a movement of integrated ethnoracial, class, and legal status diversity, which is arguably rare, might have inflected or changed the story. To be sure, one commonality between the Filipin@ and Mexican immigrants was nativist racism: both, including the "model minority Asians" (N. Kim 2008a, 2008b; Okihiro 1994), were threats to "American" (White) jobs and to proper English; both came from poor brown countries; and both produced "exotic" baby-making women. Given the Mexican immigrant women's class and legal status, however, mainstream society racialized their Spanish language and reproduction as much more problematic. As Trump is the apotheosis of anti-Latin@ and anti-Muslim (as well as anti–Asian

American) nativist racism, Zepeda-Millán (2017:210–211) writes that we "cannot understand the politics of race in America without understanding the central role of Latinos and their relationship to the contentious issue of immigration" (see also Menjívar 2010; Romero 2008)). I would argue that this is also increasingly true not just of Muslim Americans but of the Asian American population as well; the latter is the fastest growing racial group as well as the fastest growing group of unauthorized immigrants (currently, at 13 percent of those without papers) in the United States. (https://aapidata.com/).

Bringing it back to the communities themselves, I never thought any of the organizations would *ever* dissolve. Yet tragically, the founder and executive director of People's CORE—Joe Navidad (an anti-Marcos guerilla who was tortured and, after release, came to the US)—passed away just before Trump's election. PCORE would disband soon after. While its millennial EJ leader, Ben, is now credentialed to teach high school art (recall his Noah's Ark in the Philippines painting), baby boomer Pia brimmed with movement news when I followed up with her; she shared that a newer Filipinx American group that she was part of had successfully gotten air monitors up in Carson to measure refinery and other toxic contamination, that Jane Fonda's climate justice group had joined CBE's protest against oil drilling in San Pedro neighborhoods (in front of a councilman's office who receives big oil money), and that she was awestruck by the glory of Manila's Sierra Madre mountains that had been shrouded in diesel plumes until COVID-19 isolation drastically cleared Manila's air. No matter how much I knew that the fight would endure here and abroad, I felt some relief that I had documented a snapshot of PCORE's environmental justice struggle and had given voice to its activists, such as Ben and Pia. Both of them reminded me that they, like the undocumented Latin@ immigrants, were doing everything they could to extend and enrich life, especially for the children, before a system of premature death got to them first. To do so, they marshalled their own street science, body and emotional support networks, the power of youth and schools, and their development of self and community. The immigrants used these tenets to enshrine what "good" and moral citizenship meant to them, marked by such commitments as "I'll never move!" In their final analysis, the only way to respond to neoliberalism's assault on their bodies and emotions was to be the angels who nourished life, and refused death, in The City of Dying Angels.

NOTES

INTRODUCTION: FIGHTING FOR BREATH IN THE OTHER LA

1. In this book, I mostly use the "-@" in Filipin@ and Latin@ to refer to the activists whom I studied, since gender was an axis on which the movements were organized (e.g., most activists were women) and gender dynamics shaped everything from the activists' identities to their political methods. Whenever it is not my aim to do this type of gendered analysis I use the "-x" in Latinx and Filipinx. When I refer only to women, I use "-a" or "-as" and when I refer to men only, I use "-o" or "-os." When I am quoting other authors, I use their designations. Please note that every person in this study identified as cisgender male/man or female/woman. One person identified as queer.

2. Although some scholars distinguish their operationalizations of "emotion" and "affect," I found that those distinctions did not make sense in my case and confused more than they helped. Therefore, I use these terms interchangeably unless specified otherwise. I provide more explanation in the subsequent chapters.

3. In addition to this chapter's discussion of neoliberalism, it is defined by the shift and diffusion of power from federal to state levels. Discursively, neoliberalism is also about the margins having to be "respectable," which itself rests on disavowing the racism, patriarchy, heterosexism, etc., of dominant society (hence, "You should be respectable") (see Hong 2015).

4. Working within the "black radical tradition," Cedric Robinson (1983) rewrote Marx to show that not only did capitalism emerge from feudalism (rather than as a break from it) but so did racism; both worked together to form a modern world system rooted in institutions of enslavement, imperialism, and genocide. As Western feudal society was already categorically racial—the first proletariat were *racialized* (Irish, Jews, Roma/Gypsies, Slavs) and European racialization was a *colonial* process involving "invasion, settlement, expropriation, and racial hierarchy" (Kelley 2017)—Robinson bucks Marxian precepts that race is a tool to divide the proletariat or to justify enslavement and privation.

5. Sometimes referred to as "EJ."

6. Although more men than women led the CBOs during my three-and-a-half-year period of fieldwork (including staff changes), this book conceives of the women as truly leading and shaping the movement since they ran the remaining organizations, were the

vast majority of the membership or unattached activists in each community, and were the ones who indelibly influenced the male leaders; that is, the male leaders often had to defer to the women activists' vision and wishes lest they lose the lion's share of their constituency.

7. Owing to the political histories and conditions of Central American nations, they tend to be more politically socialized than Mexican immigrants upon arrival.

8. See, for example, Abrego (2011); Escudero (2020); García Bedolla (2005); Gonzales (2015); Menjívar (2010); Milkman (2006); Nicholls (2013); Pallares and Flores-González (2010); Pérez et al. (2010); Terriquez (2011); Terriquez and Rogers (2011); Voss and Bloemraad (2011); Zepeda-Millán (2017).

9. At its simplest, biopower is power and control over bodies. On biopower, Foucault writes in his 1978 *Security, Territory, and Population* lectures,

> By this I mean a number of phenomena that seem to me to be quite significant, namely, the set of mechanisms through which the basic biological features of the human species became the object of a political strategy, of a general strategy of power, or, in other words, how, starting from the 18th century, modern Western societies took on board the fundamental biological fact that human beings are a species. This is what I have called biopower (2007:1).

Biopower makes "knowledge-power an agent of transformation of human life," one occurring at the level of disciplining the human body and the other at the level of regulating the broader population (Foucault 1980:142). This dimension of population regulation is "biopolitics," as in the "biopolitics of the population" or, as in when Foucault analyzed race, "biopolitical state racism."

10. See Bell and Braun (2010); Brown and Mikkelson (1997); Bullard (1993); Davis (1999); Di Chiro (1992; 1998); Epstein (1995); Gálvez (2011); Gibbs (2002); Gottlieb (1993); Hay (2009); Jenkins (1985); Kirk (1998); Krauss (1993); Pardo (1998); Park and Pellow (2011); Peeples and Deluca (2006); Pellow and Park (2002); Pulido (1996a); Smith (2005); Stein (2004); Szasz (1994); Taylor (1993); Verchick (2004). See also Montoya, Hardy-Fanta, and García (2000).

11. Although in my study the immigrants addressed health and health care issues, they primarily focused on environmental justice, hence, this book will mostly refer only to the latter.

12. Although American Studies has focused on social movements it has not sufficiently engaged those for environmental justice (Fisher-Fishkin 2005; Sze 2006) nor has it adequately used social science methods and models (Lauter 2002).

13. As the Asian American activists and leadership in this study were mostly Filipin@ ethnics, it must first be established that Filipinx Americans have occupied a precarious space within Asian American Studies and spaces; Ocampo (2016) found that, as "the Latinos of Asia," his younger-generation Filipinx Americans more closely identified with the Latinxs in their lives (save high school racial conflicts) than with the proverbial "Asians" that society primarily collapses with "yellow" Eastern ethnics. While all of the Filipin@ ethnics in my study saw themselves as Asian Americans and, therefore, I adopted their label, all disciplines would benefit from studying Filipin@ Americans' contributions to environmental justice, irrespective of identification.

14. Itliong and Vera Cruz are also credited with influencing Cesar Chavez to wage the massive farmworker strike that has been attached to Chavez (and Dolores Huerta) in the country's national imaginary. Asian Americans have much to learn from research on Pacific Islanders' environmental justice movements, such as Native Hawaiians' fight for the US military's restitution of Kaho'olawe island, degraded by target range for warplanes (Blackford 2004).

15. Asian Pacific Islander Desi American.

16. Others, like Marquez (2012) and Schwartz, von Glascoe, Torres, Ramos, and Soria -Delgado (2015), have taken up the mantle.

17. This is even more complicated by the fact that with migration and multiracial children, there are increasing numbers of, say, Asian Latin ethnics and Afro-Asian Americans (or "Blasians"). Furthermore, while American Indians, Pacific Islanders, and Eskimos/Aleutians are distinct groups, they share indigenous status to their lands or islands, hence drawing lines in between and around is not always clear cut.

18. For example, see Bloemraad 2006; Cheng 2013; Escudero 2020; C. Kim 1999; J. Lee 2002; Saito 1998; and Tang 2011. See also N. Kim 2008a and 2008b.

19. The deadly statistic stands despite the fact that in 2014 the South Coast Air Quality Management District had reported significant reductions in cancer risk over the previous decade.

20. See Centers for Disease Control, 2011.

21. While the National Institute of Environmental Health Sciences has funded work and helped build the capacity of EJ groups to work on asthma, and while the EPA has had environmental education and other grants for asthma, no federally directed program has ever existed (personal communication, Phil Brown). Moreover, as Corburn finds, the environmental justice movement was similarly delayed, only recently making asthma the focus of its organizing efforts. At a 2000 National [EJ] Advisory Committee meeting held to discuss environmental health, no sessions were dedicated solely to discussing the asthma epidemic in communities of color (NEJAC 2001). Other epidemic diseases get a lot more attention, like HIV/AIDS (which wealthy White Americans tend to fund) (Epstein 1996). No national asthma movement means that organizing around asthma remains focused at the neighborhood and grassroots level.

22. By 1991, over 71 percent of the African Americans and 50 percent of the Latinxs in the LA basin lived in areas with the most polluted air, while only 34 percent of the White population did (Ong and Blumenberg 1990; Mann 1991).

23. Lower socioeconomic status (SES) is also associated with increased asthma morbidity, and minority children are also disproportionately affected by lower SES; for example, in 2010, 20 percent of US children lived in poverty, with higher rates in Black (38.2 percent) and "Hispanic" (32.3 percent) children, compared with 17 percent of White children (US Census Bureau 2011).

24. Historically, asthma activism is gendered insofar as patterns in general and mothers in particular occupy a dominant discursive place in terms of beliefs in illness causation and management (Mailick, Holden, and Wather 1994; Prout, Hayes, and Gelder 1999; Marteau and Johnston 1986). In the past, mothers of asthmatics were thought to be ambivalent, overprotective and rejecting toward their children, thereby contributing to the develop-

ment of childhood asthma (Gabbay 1982; Guyer 2000). To be sure, this notion of maternal causation has been largely discarded.

25. Studies have found race to operate independently of class when predicting the distribution of (1) municipal landfills and incinerators (Bullard 1996); (2) the location of abandoned toxic waste dumps (United Church of Christ Commission for Racial Justice 1987); (3) air pollution in our society (Gianessi, Peskin, and Wolff 1979; Gelobter 1988; Wernette and Nieves 1992); (4) lead poisoning in children (Agency for Toxic Substances and Disease Registry 1988); and (5) contaminated fish consumption (West, Fly, and Marans 1990).

26. For the bamboo ceiling, see Tran, Lee, and Huang (2019). For anti-Asian hate crimes, see Lai and Arguelles (2003). For reports of discrimination, see Gee, Spencer, Chen, and Takeuchi 2007; N. Kim 2008a; and McMurtry, Findling, Casey, Blendon, Benson, Sayde, and Miller (2019).

27. Although I understand the intellectual fatigue that some scholars feel about the politics of "belonging" or of "belongingness," this alone does not mean that these issues are irrelevant to the human condition and social reality, especially to the immigrants who suffer when they are denied legal and sociocultural belonging. The fact that nation-states, social movements (especially those rooted in identity politics), and communities have all centered the discourse of belonging and membership makes it one of the most relevant political problematics. Most of us choose not to live as hermits for a reason, and the COVID-19 pandemic has driven the point home.

28. Unfortunately, both of these watershed eras arrived after I left the field in late 2013.

29. They cite Pellow and Brulle (2007) as one example of the focus on physical health and cite Bullard (1990) as a minor exception. On disasters, Bevc, Marshall, and Picou (2007) and Gill and Picou (1998). They elaborate on emotions and the environment: "Auyero and Swistun's (2009) work on environmental suffering builds on Bourdieu's (1999) concept of social suffering to articulate how long-term environmental decline interacts with cultural practices and state and corporate power in an Argentine shantytown. Similarly, Shriver and Webb (2009) use the ecological-symbolic perspective (Kroll-Smith et al. 1991) to describe how Ponca tribal members interpret and develop diagnostic frames concerning air contamination. These studies move closer to engaging the complexity of how the social meanings of emotional experiences can be part of the operation of power."

30. See, for example, Brendese (2014); Carney (2014); Chavez (2007); Cisneros (2016).

31. See Zembylas (2016).

32. Never mind the fact that focusing only on legal citizens excludes an analysis of noncitizens such as Latin@s and the growing number of unauthorized Asian and Black immigrants.

33. Other scholars have examined the necropolitics of Israel's targeted assassinations of Palestinians in Gaza as a form of control (Weizman 2017) and of the intensive surveillance of Turkish immigrants in Germany in the name of preempting threats to public order and law (what Topal [2011] terms immigrants' "death productivities").

34. For other excellent research studies done on CBE, and methodological reflections thereof, see Brodkin (2009); Brown, Brody, Morello-Frosch, Tovar, Zota, and Rudel (2012); and Carrera, Brown, Brody, and Morello-Frosch (2018).

35. One young woman was working class and unauthorized, while one young man was from a documented working-class family—both were of the second generation.

36. The groups with the most ethnically diverse staff and membership were PCORE, which included small numbers of Samoan, Cambodian, multiethnic, White, and Black American residents, and CBE, which boasted Latinx, Asian, Black, and other ethnics as their staff and membership.

CHAPTER 1: NEOLIBERAL EMBODIED ASSAULT

1. While the thrust of Giroux's passage is more than compelling and accurate, his point about the biopolitics of the racist murder of Emmett Till could be extended to include gender in addition to race and class; the premise for one of White America's most gruesome killings was the breach of the patriarchal code of White male sexual possession of "their" women by a Black *boy* who was seen and treated as if he was an *adult male* predator (the same tyranny of Black masculinity that sentences Black boys as if they are adults or has police shooting or choking them when they are unarmed, vending, and/or playing with toys). As White women still stand at the top of the feminine hierarchy, however, Emmett Till would not have been mutilated to death had he looked, ostensibly, at a Black woman; in addition, Black women were not gruesomely murdered as often for their (sometimes nonconsensual but always unequally yoked) relationships with White men.

2. In ways that converge and diverge from Giroux, Grace Hong (2015:19) defines neoliberalism as a direct epistemological response to the crises in racial capital that the Civil Rights and Third World decolonization movements presented, what she calls a changed distribution in the politics of respectability.

3. Throughout this book, I use "superarse" figuratively and literally, as noun and verb.

4. HIA: A combination of procedures, methods and tools that systematically judges the potential, and sometimes unintended, effects of a policy plan, program, or project on the health of a population and the distribution of those effects within a population. HIA identifies appropriate actions to manage those effects.

5. This is a pseudonym.

CHAPTER 2: EMOTIONS AS POWER

1. This is a pseudonym.

2. On apathy related to race and racism, see Forman and Lewis (2006).

CHAPTER 3: EVERY BODY MATTERS

1. As Fujiwara (2008:xvii) notes,

> However, contrary to popular narratives of Asian success and assimilation, the reality is that at the time of the welfare reform movement poverty among Asian Pacific American families rose from 11.9 to 13.5 percent from 1990 to 1994. The 1990 U.S. Census showed that, although 10 percent of all Americans were officially impoverished, 47 percent of Cambodians, 66 percent of Hmong, 67 percent of Laotians, and 34 percent of Vietnamese officially lived in poverty. Thus, public assistance was an integral form of income for keeping these families out of complete destitution. The increasing

use of public assistance by more recent Asian immigrant and refugee groups galvanized the anti-immigrant campaign, provoking accusations against Asian immigrants and refugees for welfare dependency and for failure to assimilate to the American way of life and work. It is necessary to reverse the systematic tendency to dismiss Asian American politics from larger discussions surrounding forms and patterns of social inequality in the United States.

2. Others subject to what would today be considered a crime worthy of jail time were also men and women who transgressed sexual norms, especially women who were deemed too sexually promiscuous for their own good.

3. "[I]n 1971, Donald Bogue, a prominent [University of Chicago demographer], delivered a paper at the annual meeting of the American College of Obstetrics and Gynecology in San Francisco in which he revealed that while 'Anglos and Jews' were reproducing at replacement level, most of the national population growth was a result of the behavior of 'high fertility remnants,' including 'the Spanish-speaking population'" (Bogue 1971, cited in Gutiérrez 2008:51–52).

4. Gutiérrez is careful to differentiate the sterilization campaign against ethnically Mexican women as compared to the more well-known assaults unleashed against Black American women. Citing the well-known case of the Los Angeles County Medical Center, national attention was paid to the sterilization of Black women in the cases of *Relf v. Weinberger* and *Walker v. Pierce*, particularly to the women's reliance on public assistance and their residence in the American South (Gutiérrez 2008:39). The sterilization case *Madrigal v. Quilligan* differed in that it took place on the West Coast in the land of White Hollywood and Latinx and Asian ethnics: Los Angeles. In this case, the mostly Mexican immigrant women were low income but not welfare recipients and, further, unlike the African American women defendants, had limited English proficiency.

5. The information in this paragraph comes from Gutiérrez (2008), Chapter 3.

6. Gutiérrez (2008) took these quotes from the *Madrigal* trial transcript, pp. 18–383.

7. For a full history of the model minority racial project, see Wu (2013).

8. With regard to body parts, anthropologists Nancy Scheper-Hughes (2001, 2007) and Lawrence Cohen (1999) have researched the industry of organ harvesting in Brazil and India, respectively, to reveal the vitality of the Third World donors' perspectives and to mute the elite viewpoints of the for-profit medical industries (biotech, pharma, practitioners). A similar inequality between a recognized political subject and an erased one can be found in the work of Rudrappa (2015) on transnational surrogacy by women in India. Here she does not aim to re-theorize bodies or emotions, but her findings have deep implications for body frameworks in particular. Not only does she conceptualize such "markets in life" and their "reproductive assembly lines" as a product of neoliberal global capitalism, she situates them in relation to the latter's other industry of garment work. Given the bodily harm of back-breaking, repetitive labor—not to mention, of verbal, sexual, and physical harassment—many of the women opt to let the markets use their bodies to gestate a child. Although this service required them to be separated from their families over the pregnancy, to deliver by C-section (much riskier than vaginal birth), and to subject themselves to a high rate of medical surveillance, the women are accustomed to this type of surveillance.

9. As oppression breeds contradictions, however, this Chinese YMCA also catered to the second-generation Chinese ethnics, who sought to be recognized as citizens by living a healthy, modern lifestyle (Shah 2001:33). In this way, good health was associated with US citizenship and, by extension, White Americanness.

10. As *Los Angeles Times* real estate editor Ray Herber wondered at the time, "Can suburban-loving, freeway-addicted Southern Californians be lured into a permanent downtown population?" (Napoli 2018). The answer that would emerge was no. As "Bunker Hill" and "Downtown" did not exactly conjure up visions of a desirable and desirous landscape, wealthier Angelenos saw instead a geography embodied by crime, disease, and neglect. Pushed-out community residents and fierce opponents of urban renewal engaged in a series of protests and lawsuits that dragged on for years.

11. This piece analyzes the perspectives of older Black women on health care providers.

12. As we have seen, although the fliers, presentations, and public comments are rife with systematic research studies that demonstrate the correlation or causation connecting environmental pollutants (diesel, PM, toxic chemicals like nitrogen oxide [NOX], Sulphur Oxide [SOX], etc.,) and disease, note that these are often not enough for the state and industry to change fundamentally.

13. Now called Warren Resources, Inc.

14. EYCEJ flier, "WHY A COMPREHENSIVE HEALTH ANALYSIS IN I710 EIR/EIS? (A BRIEF ON HEALTH IMPACT ASSESSMENTS)—Keeping them honest ('improvement' project)," October 29, 2009 and January 28, 2010.

15. EYCEJ 710 Draft EIR (Summer 2012) flier (their mottos are FIGHTING FOR LIFE; LET'S GROW POLLUTION-FREE!).

16. See, for example, Crosnoe (2006); Ream and Palardy (2008); Turney and Kao (2009); see also Lareau (2003).

17. To be sure, gangs have often provided brotherly and sisterly protection and bonds that underresourced inner cities of color, or their own families, could not provide (Bourgois 1995; Rios 2011).

18. This is a pseudonym.

CHAPTER 4: "OUR COMMUNITY HAS BOUNDARIES"

1. The original Spanish (for italicized): *Si ustedes se viven aqui en el barrio en donde nosotros estamos donde yo estoy no simple vayan alla para que sepan lo que es para esta en la contaminacion. Y si cuando ustedes tienen hijos enfermos me van a entender a mi.*

2. The original Spanish (for italicized): *Eso es la realidad tu sabes cuando la gente tiene dinero se va. Pero tienen una mansion hermoso o una vecina vive muy bien. No les interesa.*

3. The phrase comes from Park and Pellow (2011).

CHAPTER 5: CITIZENSHIP AS GENDERED CAREGIVING

1. For "economy of gratitude," see M Kim (2018); for "conditional love and hospitality," see Ahmed (2004:131).

2. For "emotive dimensions," see, for example, Werbner (1999); Fortier (2010); Ho (2009); Isin (2004); and M. Kim (2018).

3. When US racial projects fixate on the White-Black binary, Black American women's reproductive excess is most targeted.

4. On Latinx politics in New York, Jones-Correa (1998) found that the men tended to be more interested in transnational political engagement with the Latin American home country. In my study, not only did men not have time or energy to organize locally—and had, to some extent, gendered it as the province of women—they similarly could and did not organize transnationally or spend a great deal of time delving into home country politics.

5. At the time of my research, PCORE, CBE, CFASE, and East Yard Communities for Environmental Justice (a group with whom I only informally worked) all had male executive directors. CPC and LBACA were the only groups that were female-led, though PCORE had had Filipina leaders whom I had briefly known, as well.

CHAPTER 6: POLITICS WITHOUT THE POLITICS

1. For example, see Alba and Nee 2003; Bean and Stevens 2003; Gans 1999; Jimenez 2009; Lee and Bean 2004; and Portes and Rumbaut 2001.

2. Gálvez (2011) shows that Latinas, among many other migrants, become less healthy and more ill the longer they live in and assimilate to the United States.

3. It was not just the EJ activist women who claimed that their community work was indeed political. The male activists were explicit that the mothers were doing categorically political work. I asked long-time community leader Jesse, who has worked with many of these women, what seemed to be some of the factors that facilitated their politicization into activists despite being mostly low income, undocumented, unable to drive, and busy with children. He offered this explanation:

> JESSE: Men have been the bread winners going to work, where mothers have been the ones who care for the children. What's happening is that when a child gets sick with a serious illness, you know, yes they're concerned, concerned, concerned, but what happens when it's several children in their family? And then what happens when it's their neighbors too! So now, mothers have realized, "Wait a minute, there's more to this." Also, more mothers have graduated from a high school.
>
> NADIA: Than the fathers?
>
> JESSE: Than the fathers. So they have at least a high school education. Watching television and news. Most men will watch sports. Most women, most mothers, will listen to the news. So now there's been a more of a public education occurring where they're now more aware of the cause and effect, because of organizations like mine. Since our organization was founded in 2001, since 2002, we have been in one media [platform] every month, every year.

4. At this point, deportations under Obama were not clear, nor were they at the top of the news cycle, but evidence shows that Obama had started a conspicuous wave of deportations as soon as he entered office (Truax 2015).

5. In his memoir on running Obama's campaign, chief strategist David Axelrod would reveal that Obama had always supported same sex marriage but publicly did not out of political expediency. This explains why his administration made efforts for LGBTQIA rights

early on, culminating in Obama's about face on the issue and his administration's repeal of DOMA in 2011 (Axelrod 2016).

6. This is where CBE (Southern California) is headquartered. Although I mostly worked with their Wilmington office (in the port-oil region), which is further south, I kept up with the goings-on in Huntington Park and attended events and actions when I could.

7. Besides residents, I noticed that university students always seemed the most eager to learn. For instance, after LBACA had educated UC Irvine medical school students on the *environmental* causes of their community's illnesses (which many medical schools had not previously taught), the roughly twenty students clad head to toe in blue scrubs were eager to get into the "community classroom" through the toxic tour.

CHAPTER 7: THE KIDS WILL SAVE US

1. Children's citizenship practices in different spheres could be said to constitute them as *de facto* citizens even if they do not enjoy all the rights of full *de jure* citizens (Lister 2007).

2. See, for example, Bloemraad and Trost 2008; Callahan and Muller 2013; Escudero 2020; Gonzales 2016; Kasinitz et al. 2008; Nicholls 2013; Okamoto, Herda, and Hartzog 2013; Shah 2011; Terriquez 2015b; Wong and Tseng 2008.

3. Luis Donaldo Colosio Murrieta was a PRI party candidate in the 1994 Mexican election at a Tijuana rally; the official narrative is that he was shot in the head by an angry lone gunman, but many in Mexico believe that his murder was planned and enacted by his own party as well as the sitting President Carlos Salinas de Gortari (for veering too left of the party line).

4. For an enlightening ethnography on the masculinity of men of color, see Thangaraj (2015).

5. In the extended narrative, Daniel believes the "government" likely segregated people by race, pushing White Americans up the rich hills and pushing minorities down into overcrowded garage-homes and crowded streets bereft of restricted parking laws, areas that "the rich don't have to . . . mind." Simply put, he saw environmental racism as a top-down orchestration of residential race segregation via class oppression.

AFTERWORD: TOWARD BIONEGLECT

1. And in the latest installation of its emotional violence, the state rips babies and little children from their parents' desperate grasps; cages them in concentration camps; denies adequate medical care, soap, toothbrushes, blankets; loses thousands of children in the abysmal foster care system; and instills fear into antiracist protestors. The rounding up of migrants in these deadly conditions helps account for why at least twenty-five migrants, including several children, died in Trump's concentration camps (Merchant 2019), and that number will likely rise.

2. Although "illegals" are racialized as Mexican or Latin@ ethnics, Asian Americans constitute about 13 percent of the 11.2 undocumented immigrants in the country and growing (http://www.pewhispanic.org/files/reports/133.pdf) and were key organizers of the 2006 Mega Marches (Zepeda-Millán 2017). And, in unprecedented fashion, President Trump deported *en masse* Vietnamese and Cambodian Americans holding the most minor criminal

infractions after his administration redesignated the agreed-upon refugee status that was negotiated between the US and Asian governments after the US War in Southeast Asia.

3. For instance, I argue that scholars across disciplines did not predict the rise of a real estate tycoon, and certainly not based on a message of economic populism (tied to racist or xenophobic demagoguery), precisely owing to our underappreciation of the material effects of neoliberalism and, in particular, how these have been racialized.

4. Cisneros: "Understanding the way that the construction of citizenship is implicated in strategies of 'massive elimination' also demands a critique of particular goals of immigration reform. If the denial of residency or citizenship through detention or deportation is understood as a tool of 'massive elimination,' immigration reform that is not directed at resisting these practices will be ineffectual. Instead, refusing to tolerate racist normalization means resisting the criminalization of migration itself" (252–253).

5. Giroux (2006) contends that Foucault leaves us with little insight into the flows between privilege and subjugation.

6. In her book *Embodied Social Justice*, Rae Johnson (2017) argues that social systems are sustained and reinforced by the everyday nonverbal interactions with those whose social location differs, often unequally, from our own. These interactions manifest in interpersonal dynamics of body language, such as when someone of higher social status is availed of bodily gestures that the person of lower status is not, such as the right to walk a street without fear or through the front of an establishment and to sit in the front of a bus, the right not to bow and nod to an "inferior," and the right to spread one's legs in a subway or to grab or fondle the body parts of the stranger next to you. Another way to name these acts—and the unearned benefits that accrete to the person who performs them—are "body privilege." In this way, the subjugation and exploitation of bodies does not exist without their relationship to privileged bodies.

7. After much effort, and after asking many experts in the area, it was extremely difficult to find systematic English-language sociological research that delved into this topic.

8. For a related discussion of the dangers of such discourse for small business entrepreneurship, see Dhingra (2012).

9. Reactionary accusations of socialism and "death panels" were leveled at a plan (ACA) that was not single payer in nature and at a United States that passes much fewer socialistic policies than Canada and the UK, where single payer health care is in effect. Conservatives convey that, per bioneglect, forty-three million Americans without insurance will experience some "collateral" suffering, that some death was acceptable. Indeed, once the Trump administration could not sink Obamacare, it perpetually worked to depress enrollment and filed a lawsuit for its abolition. According to a health advocacy organization, Be a Hero (www.beaherofund.com), "Frankly, it's a miracle we can still sign up for health insurance at all, after the year we've had. Republicans cut our benefits, and they've allowed insurers to offer skimpy plans that don't cover hospitalization or preventative care. They've cut advertising funding, limited outreach, and axed enrollment assistance to obstruct the straightforward enrollment process *as much as possible*."

WORKS CITED

Abrego, L. J. 2011. "Legal Consciousness of Undocumented Latinos: Fear and Stigma as Barriers to Claims-Making for First- and 1.5-Generation Immigrants." *Law & Society Review* 45 (2): 337–369.

Acolin, A., and D. Vitiello. 2018. "Who Owns Chinatown: Neighbourhood Preservation and Change in Boston and Philadelphia." *Urban Studies* 55 (8): 1690–1710.

Agamben, G. 1998. *Homo Sacer: Sovereign Power and Bare Life*. Stanford, CA: Stanford University Press.

Agency for Toxic Substances and Disease Registry. 1988. *The Nature and Extent of Lead Poisoning in Children in the United States: A Reprint to Congress.* Atlanta: US Department of Health and Human Services.

Ahmed, S. 2004. *The Cultural Politics of Emotion*. New York: Routledge.

Alaimo, S. 2010. *Bodily Natures: Science, Environment, and the Material Self.* Bloomington: Indiana University Press.

Alba, R., and V. Nee. 2003. *Rethinking Assimilation. Remaking the American Mainstream: Assimilation and Contemporary Immigration.* Cambridge, MA: Harvard University Press.

Albas, C., and D. Albas. 1988. "Emotion Work and Emotion Rules: The Case of Exams." *Qualitative Sociology* 11 (4): 259–274.

Alexander, J. C. 1998. "Citizen and Enemy as Symbolic Classification: On the Polarizing Discourse of Civil Society." In *Real Civil Societies,* 96–114. Thousand Oaks, CA: Sage.

Alexander, M. (2016, July 9). "Following Horrific Violence, Something More Is Required of Us." Retrieved from https://billmoyers.com/story/following-horrific-violence-something-required-us/.

Alston, D., and N. Brown. 1993. "Global Threats to People of Color." In *Confronting Environmental Racism*, ed. R. D. Bullard, 179–194. Boston: South End Press.

Anderson, B. 1983. *Imagined Communities: Reflections on the Origin and Spread of Nationalism.* London and New York: Verso.

Andrade, S. J. 1982. "Social Science Stereotypes of Mexican American Women: Policy Implications for Research." *Hispanic Journal of Behavioral Sciences* 4 (2), 223–244.

Aparicio, A. 2006. *Dominican-Americans and the Politics of Empowerment*. Gainesville: University Press of Florida.

Arnold, A. 2018, March 24. "What Were Mike Pence and Donald Trump Doing During March for Our Lives?" *The CUT*. Retrieved from https://www.thecut.com/2018/03/what-donald-trump-and-mike-pence-did-for-march-for-our-lives.html.

Auyero, J., and D. A. Swistun. 2009. *Flammable: Environmental Suffering in an Argentine Shantytown*. New York: Oxford University Press.

Axelrod, D. 2016. *Believer: My Forty Years in Politics*. New York: Penguin Books.

Bagley, K. 2020, May 7. "Connecting the Dots Between Environmental Justice and the Coronavirus." *Yale Environment 360*. Retrieved from https://e360.yale.edu/features/connecting-the-dots-between-environmental-injustice-and-the-coronavirus.

Barth, F. 1998. *Ethnic Groups and Boundaries: The Social Organization of Culture Difference*. Long Grove, IL: Waveland Press.

Bean, F. D., and G. Stevens. 2003. *America's Newcomers and the Dynamics of Diversity*. New York: Russell Sage Foundation.

Bell, S. E., and Y. A. Braun. 2010. "Coal, Identity, and the Gendering of Environmental Justice Activism in Central Appalachia." *Gender and Society* 24 (6): 794–813.

Berezin, M. 2001. "Emotions and Political Identity: Mobilizing Affection for the Polity." In *Passionate Politics: Emotions and Social Movements*, ed. J. Goodwin, J. M. Jasper, and J. Poletta, 83-98. Chicago and London: The University of Chicago Press.

———. 2002. "Secure States: Towards a Political Sociology of Emotion." *The Sociological Review* 50 (2, suppl.): 33–52.

Berlant, L. 2007. "Slow Death (Sovereignty, Obesity, Lateral Agency)." *Critical Inquiry* 33 (4): 754–780.

Bevc, C. A., B. K. Marshall, and S. J. Picou. 2007. "Environmental Justice and Toxic Exposure: Toward a Spatial Model of Physical Health and Psychological Well-Being." *Social Science Research* 36 (1): 48–67.

Blackford, M. 2004. "Environmental Justice, Native Rights, Tourism, and Opposition to Military Control: The Case of Kaho'olawe." *Journal of American History* 91 (2): 544-571.

Bloemraad, I. 2006. "Becoming a Citizen in the United States and Canada: Structured Mobilization and Immigrant Political Incorporation. *Social Forces* 85 (2): 667–695.

Bloemraad, I., and C. Trost. 2008. "It's a Family Affair: Intergenerational Mobilization in the Spring 2006 Protests." *American Behavioral Scientist* 52 (4): 507–532.

Bloom, E. 2017, September 27. "See How Your Spending Compares with That of the Average American—and the US Government." CNBC. Retrieved from https://www.cnbc.com/2017/09/27/how-your-spending-compares-to-the-average-american-and-us-government.html.

Boggs, G. L. 1998. *Living for Change: An Autobiography*. Minneapolis: University of Minnesota Press.

Boggs, G. L., and S. Kurashige. 2011. *The Next American Revolution: Sustainable Activism for the Twenty-First Century*. Berkeley: University of California Press.

Bogue, D. J. 1971. *Demographic Aspects of Maternity and Infant Care in the Year 2001*. Paper delivered at the annual meeting of the American College of Obstetrics and Gynecology. San Francisco, CA.

Bonilla-Silva, E. 1997. "Rethinking Racism: Toward a Structural Interpretation." *American Sociological Review* 62 (3): 465–480.

———. 2006. *Racism Without Racists: Color-Blind Racism and the Persistence of Racial Inequality in the United States.* Lanham, MD: Rowman & Littlefield.

———. 2019. "Feeling Race: Theorizing the Racial Economy of Emotions." *American Sociological Review* 84 (1): 1–25.

"Born on Border, Twins Left Behind by Mexican Mother," *Los Angeles Times*, July 8, 1977.

Bourdieu, P. 1999. *The Weight of the World: Social Suffering in Contemporary Society.* Stanford, CA: Stanford University Press.

Bourgois, P. 1995. *In Search of Respect: Selling Crack in El Barrio.* Cambridge, UK: Cambridge University Press.

Brendese, P. J. 2014. "Borderline Epidemics: Latino Immigration and Racial Biopolitics." *Politics, Groups, and Identities* 2 (2): 168–187.

Brodkin, K. 2009. *Power Politics: Environmental Activism in South Los Angeles.* New Brunswick, NJ: Rutgers University Press.

Brown, P. 2007. *Toxic Exposures: Contested Illnesses and the Environmental Health Movement.* New York: Columbia University Press.

Brown, P., J. G. Brody, R. Morello-Frosch, J. Tovar, A. R. Zota, and A. R. Ruthel. 2012. "Measuring the Success of Community Science: The Northern California Household Exposure Study." *Environmental Health Perspective* 120:326–331.

Brown, P., and F. Ferguson. 1995. "Making a Big Stink: Women's Work, Women's Relationships, and Toxic Waste Activism." *Gender and Society* 9 (2): 145–172.

Brown, P., B. Mayer, S. Zavestoski, T. Luebke, J. Mandelbaum, and S. McCormick. 2003. "The Health Politics of Asthma: Environmental Justice and Collective Illness Experience in the United States." *Social Science and Medicine* 57 (3): 453–464.

Brown, P., B. Mayer, S. Zavestoski, T. Luebke, J. Mandelbaum, S. McCormick, and M. Lyson. 2012. "The Health Politics of Asthma: Environmental Justice and Collective Illness Experience." In *Contested Illnesses: Citizens, Science, and Health Social Movements*, ed. P. Brown, S. Zavestoski, and R. Morello-Frosch, 108–122. Berkeley: University of California Press.

Brown, P., E. Mikkelsen, and J. Harr. 1997. "No Safe Place: Toxic Waste, Leukemia, and Community Action." Berkeley: University of California Press.

Brown University News. 2017, November 7. "U.S. Spending on Post-9/11 Wars to Reach $5.6 Trillion by 2018." Retrieved from https://news.brown.edu/articles/2017/11/costssummary.

Bullard, R. D. 1990. *Dumping in Dixie: Race, Class and Environmental Quality.* Boulder, CO: Westview Press.

———, ed. 1993. *Confronting Environmental Racism: Voices from the Grassroots.* Boston: South End Press.

———. 1996. *Unequal Protection: Environmental Justice and Communities of Color.* 2nd ed. San Francisco: Sierra Club Books.

Bullard, R. D., G. S. Johnson, and A. O. Torres. 2011. *Environmental Health and Racial Equity in the United States: Building Environmentally Just, Sustainable, and Livable Communities.* Washington, DC: American Public Health Association Press.

Bullard, R., P. Mohai, R. Saha, and B. Wright. 2007. "Toxic Wastes and Race at Twenty: Why Race Still Matters After All of These Years." *Environmental Law* 38 (2): 371–411.

Bullard, R. D., and B. Wright. 2009. *Race, Place, and Environmental Justice After Hurricane Katrina: Struggles to Reclaim, Rebuild, and Revitalize New Orleans and the Gulf Coast.* Boulder, CO: Westview Press.

Bunders, J., and L. Leydesdorff. 1987. "The Causes and Consequences of Collaborations Between Scientists and Non-Scientific Groups. In *The Social Direction of the Public Sciences. Sociology of the Sciences (A Yearbook)*, ed. S. Blume, J. Bunders, L. Leydesdorff, and R. Whitley, 11. Dordrecht, Netherlands: Springer.

Calhoun, C. 2001. "Putting Emotions in their Place." In *Passionate Politics: Emotions and Social Movements*, ed. J. Goodwin, J. M. Jasper, and J. Poletta, 45–57. Chicago: University of Chicago Press.

Callahan, R., and Muller, C. 2013. *Coming of Political Age: American Schools and the Civic Development of Immigrant Youth*. New York: Russell Sage Foundation.

Campbell, R., and B. Hunter. 2000. *Moral Epistemology Naturalized.* Calgary: University of Calgary Press.

Campos, B., and H. S. Kim. 2017. "Incorporating the Cultural Diversity of Family and Close Relationships into the Study of Health." *American Psychologist* 72 (6): 543–554.

Carney, M. A. 2014. "The Biopolitics of 'Food Insecurity': Towards a Critical Political Ecology of the Body in Studies of Women's Transnational Migration." *Journal of Political Ecology* 21 (1): 1–18.

———. 2015. *The Unending Hunger: Tracing Women and Food Insecurity Across Borders.* Oakland, CA: University of California Press.

Carrera, J. S., P. Brown, J. G. Brody, and R. Morello-Frosch. 2018. "Research Altruism as Motivation for Participation in Community-Centered Environmental Health Research." *Social Science and Medicine* 196:175–181.

Carson, R. 2002 [1964]. *Silent Spring*. New York: Houghton Mifflin.

Centers for Disease Control and Prevention. 2011, May 3. "Asthma in the US." Retrieved from https://www.cdc.gov/vitalsigns/asthma/index.html.

Chatelain, M., and K. Asoka. 2015. "Women and Black Lives Matter: An Interview with Marcia Chatelain." *Dissent.* Retrieved from https://www.dissentmagazine.org/article/women-black-lives-matter-interview-marcia-chatelain.

Chavez, L. R. 2007. "Spectacle in the Desert: The Minuteman Project on the U.S.-Mexico Border. In *Global Vigilantes: Anthropological Perspectives on Justice and Violence*, ed. D. Patten and A. Sen, 25–46. New York: Columbia University Press.

———. 2008. *The Latino Threat: Constructing Immigrants, Citizens, and the Nation*. Stanford, CA: Stanford University Press.

———. 2017. *Anchor Babies and the Challenge of Birthright Citizenship*. Stanford. CA: Stanford University Press.

Cheng, W. 2013. "The Phenomenon of Hate Crimes in the United States." *Journal of Applied Social Psychology* 43 (4): 761–794.

Cherniack, M. 1986. *The Hawk's Nest Incident: America's Worst Industrial Disaster*. New Haven, CT: Yale University Press.

Christopherson, S. 1994. "The Fortress City: Privatized Spaces, Consumer Citizenship." *Post-Fordism: A Reader*, ed. Ash Amin, 409–427. Hoboken, NJ: Wiley-Blackwell.

Chung, A. Y. 2007. *Legacies of Struggle: Conflict and Cooperation in Korean American Politics*. Stanford, CA: Stanford University Press.

———. 2016. *Saving Face: The Emotional Costs of the Asian Immigrant Family Myth*. New Brunswick, NJ: Rutgers University Press.

Cisneros, N. 2016. "Resisting 'Massive Elimination': Foucault, Immigration and the GIP." In *Active Intolerance: Michel Foucault, the Prisons Information Group, and the Future of Abolition*, ed. P. Zurn and A. Dilts, 241–258. New York: Palgrave MacMillan.

Cohen, E. F. 2005. "Neither Seen Nor Heard: Childrens' Citizenship in Contemporary Democracies." *Citizenship Studies* 9 (2): 221–240.

Cohen, L. 1999. "Where It Hurts: Indian Material for an Ethics of Organ Transplantation." *Daedalus* 128 (4): 135–165.

Cole, L. W., and S. F. Foster. 2000. *From the Ground Up: Environmental Racism and the Rise of the Environmental Justice Movement*. New York, London: New York University Press.

Coll, K. M. 2010. *Remaking Citizenship Latina Immigrants and New American Politics*. Stanford, CA: Stanford University Press.

Collins, P. H. 2000. *Black Feminist Thought: Knowledge, Consciousness, and the Politics of Empowerment*. New York; London: Routledge.

———. 2004. *Black Sexual Politics: African Americans, Gender, and the New Racism*. New York; London: Routledge.

Corburn, J. 2005. *Street Science: Community Knowledge and Environmental Health Justice*. Cambridge, MA: MIT Press.

Crosnoe, R. 2006. *Mexican Schools, American Roots: Helping Mexican Immigrant Children Succeed*. Stanford, CA: Stanford University Press.

Cunnigen, D., and M. A. Bruce, eds. 2010. *Race in the Age of Obama: Research in Race and Ethnic Relations*. Bingley, UK: Emerald.

Das Gupta, M. 2006. *Unruly Immigrants: Rights, Activism, and Transnational South Asian Politics in the United States*. Durham, NC: Duke University Press.

Davis, A. Y. 1998. "Political Prisoners, Prisons, and Black Liberation." In *The Angela Y. Davis Reader*, ed. J. James, 41–44. Hoboken: Wiley-Blackwell.

Davis, K. 1995. *Reshaping the Female Body: The Dilemma of Cosmetic Surgery*. New York; London: Routledge.

Davis, M. 1990. *City of Quartz: Excavating the Future of Los Angeles*. New York; London: Verso.

———. 1999. "Philosophy Meets Practice: A Critique of Ecofeminism Through the Voices of Three Chicana Activists. In *Chicano Culture, Ecology, Politics: Subversive Kin*, ed. D. G. Peña. Tucson: University of Arizona Press.

Davis, N. Y. (2011). *The Politics of Belonging: Intersectional Contestations*. University of East London, UK: Sage.

Defert, D. 1971. "Quand L'information est une Lutte." *Archives d'une Lutte*, 69–73.

Dhingra, P. 2012. *Life Behind the Lobby: Indian American Motel Owners and the American Dream*. Stanford, CA: Stanford University Press.

Di Chiro, G. 1992. "Defining Environmental Justice: Women's Voices and Grassroots Politics." *Socialist Review* 22 (4): 93–130.

———. 1998. "Environmental Justice from the Grassroots." In *The Struggle for Ecological Democracy*, ed. D. Faber, 104–136. New York: Guilford Press.

DiFazio, W. 2006. *Ordinary Poverty: A Little Food and Cold Storage*. Philadelphia: Temple University Press.

Dilts, A. 2014. *Punishment and Inclusion: Race, Membership, and the Limits of American Liberalism*. New York: Fordham University Press.

Dixon, T. L., and D. Linz. 2000. "Overrepresentation and Underrepresentation of African Americans and Latinos as Lawbreakers on Television News." *Journal of Communication* 50 (2): 131–154.

Duggan, L. 2003. *The Twilight of Equality? Neoliberalism, Cultural Politics, and the Attack on Democracy*. Boston: Beacon Press.

Egelko, B. 2019, January 2. "Latinos Account for Nearly Half of 172 People Killed by Police in California in 2017." *San Francisco Chronicle*. Retrieved from https://www.sfchronicle.com/bayarea/article/Latinos-account-for-nearly-half-of-172-people-13504599.php.

Enck-Wanzer, D., ed. 2010. *The Young Lords: A Reader*. New York: New York University Press.

Endo, T. 2002. *Youth Engagement in Community Driven School Reform*. Oakland, CA: Social Policy Research Associates.

Epstein, S. 1995. "The Construction of Lay Expertise: AIDS Activism and the Forging of Credibility in the Reform of Clinical Trials." *Science, Technology, and Human Values* 20 (4): 408–437.

———. 1996. *Impure Science: AIDS, Activism, and the Politics of Knowledge*. Berkeley: University of California Press.

Escudero, K. 2020. *Organizing While Undocumented*. New York: New York University Press.

Espiritu, Y. L. 1997. *Asian American Women and Men: Labor, Laws and Love*. Walnut Creek, CA: Alta Mira Press.

———. 2003. *Home Bound: Filipino American Lives Across Cultures, Communities, and Countries*. Berkeley; Los Angeles; London: University of California Press.

Eyerman, R. 2005. "How Social Movements Move: Emotions and Social Movements." In *Emotions and Social Movements*, ed. H. Flam and D. King, 41–56. New York: Routledge.

Faber, M. 2008. How to Be an Ecological Economist. *Ecological Economics* 66 (1): 1–7.

"False Registration of Alien Babies Alleged," 1977, May 12. *El Paso Times*.

Fan, J. 1992. "Design-Adaptive Nonparametric Regression." *Journal of the American Statistical Association* 87 (420): 998-1004.

Feagin, J. R., and M. P. Sikes. 1994. *Living with Racism: The Black Middle-Class Experience*. Boston: Beacon Press.

Feliciano, C. 2005. "Educational Selectivity in U.S. Immigration: How Do Immigrants Compare to Those Left Behind?" *Demography* 42, 131–152.

Fisher-Fishkin, S. 2005. "Crossroads of Cultures: The Transnational Turn in American Studies: Presidential Address to the American Studies Association, November 12, 2004." *American Quarterly* 57 (1): 17–51.

Fleischer, M. 2020. "Want to Tear Down Insidious Monuments to Racism and Segregation? Bulldoze L.A. Freeways." *Los Angeles Times*. Retrieved from https://www.latimes.com/opinion/story/2020-06-24/bulldoze-la-freeways-racism-monument?_amp=true&__twitter_impression=true.

Fonow, M. M., and S. Franzway. 2016. "Embodied Activism, Transformational Leadership and Courage." American Sociological Association, Seattle, August 22.

Forman, T., and A. Lewis. 2006. "Racial Apathy and Hurricane Katrina: The Social Anatomy of Prejudice in the Post-Civil Rights Era." *Du Bois Review: Social Science Research on Race* 3 (1): 175–202.

Fortier, A. M. 2010. "Proximity by Design? Affective Citizenship and the Management of Unease." *Citizenship Studies* 14 (1): 17–30.

———. 2013. "What's the Big Deal? Naturalisation and the Politics of Desire." *Citizenship Studies* 17 (6–7): 697–711.

Forward, S., and C. Buck. 1989. *Toxic Parents: Overcoming Their Hurtful Legacy and Reclaiming Your Life*. New York: Bantam Books.

Foucault, M. 1975/1979. *Discipline and Punish: The Birth of a Prison*, trans. Alan Sheridan. New York: Pantheon/Random House.

———. 1980. *An Introduction: The History of Sexuality*, vol. 1., trans. R. Hurley. New York: Vintage.

———. 2007. *Security, Territory, Population: Lectures at the Collège de France, 1977–78*. New York: Springer.

———. 2008. *The History of Sexuality: The Will to Knowledge*. New York: Penguin Classics.

Foucault, M., and GIP. 1971. "Enqu ê te sur les prisons: brisons les barreaux du silence," FDE1, no. 88, 1047.

Fox, N. J. 1998. "Foucault, Foucauldians and Sociology." *The British Journal of Sociology* 49 (3): 415–433.

Frankenberg, R. 1993. *White Women, Race Matters: The Social Construction of Whiteness*. Minneapolis: University of Minnesota Press.

Franzway, S. 2001. *Sexual Politics and Greedy Institutions: Union Women, Commitments and Conflicts in Public and Private*. London: Pluto Press.

Fujino, D. C. 2008. "Who Studies the Asian American Movement? A Historiographical Analysis." *Journal of Asian American Studies* 11 (2): 127–169.

Fujiwara, L. 2008. *Mothers Without Citizenship: Asian Immigrant Families and the Consequences of Welfare Reform*. Minneapolis; London: University of Minnesota Press.

Gabbay, J. 1982. "Asthma Attacked? Tactics for the Reconstruction of a Disease Concept." In *The Problem of Medical Knowledge: Examining the Social Construction of Medicine*, ed. P. Wright and A. Treacher, 23–43. Edinburgh: Edinburgh University Press.

Gallegos, J. C. 1998. "Acequia Tales: Stories from a Chicano Centennial Farm." In *Chicano Culture, Ecology, Politics: Subversive Kin*, ed. Devin Peña. Tucson: University of Arizona Press.

Gálvez, A. 2011. *Patient Citizens, Immigrant Mothers: Mexican Women, Public Prenatal Care, and the Birth Weight Paradox*. New Brunswick, NJ: Rutgers University Press.

Gans, H. J. 1999. *Making Sense of America: Sociological Analyses and Essays*. Lanham, MD: Rowman & Littlefield.

García, Bedolla, L. 2005. *Fluid Borders: Latino Power, Identity, and Politics in Los Angeles.* Los Angeles: University of California Press.

———. 2014. *Latino Politics.* Cambridge, MA: John Wiley & Sons.

Garey, A. I., and K. V. Hansen. 2011. "Introduction." In *At the Heart of Work and Family,* ed. A. I. Garey and K. V. Hansen, 1–14. New Brunswick, NJ: Rutgers University Press.

Gaventa, J. 1993. "The Powerful, the Powerless, and the Experts: Knowledge Struggles in an Information Age." In *Voices of Change: Participatory Research in the U.S. and Canada,* ed. Peter Park, Mary Brydon-Miller, Budd Hall, and Ted Jackson. Westport, CT: Bergin and Garvey.

Gee, G. C., M. S. Spencer, J. Chen, and D. Takeuchi. 2007. "A Nationwide Study of Discrimination and Chronic Health Conditions Among Asian Americans." *American Journal of Public Health* 97: 1275–1282.

Geertz, C. 1973. *The Interpretation of Cultures: Selected Essays.* New York: Basic Books.

Gelobter, M. 1988, June. "The Distribution of Air Pollution by Income and Race." Paper presented at the Second Symposium on Social Science in Resource Management, Urbana, Illinois, 281–301.

Gianessi, L., H. Peskin, and E. Wolff. 1979. "The Distributional Effects of Uniform Air Pollution Policy in the United States." *The Quarterly Journal of Economics* 93 (2): 281–301.

Gibbs, L. 2002. "Citizen Activism for Environmental Health." *The Annals Of the American Academy of Political and Social Science* 584 (1): 97–109.

Gill, D., and J. S. Picou. 1998. "Technological Disaster and Chronic Community Stress." *Society & Natural Resources* 11 (8): 795–815.

Gilmore, R. W. 2007. *Golden Gulag: Prisons, Surplus, Crisis, and Opposition in Globalizing California.* Berkeley: University of California Press.

Giroux, H. A. 2006. "Reading Hurricane Katrina: Race, Class, and the Biopolitics of Disposability." *College Literature* 33 (3): 171–196.

Glassner, B. 2018. *The Culture of Fear: Why Americans Are Afraid of the Wrong Things.* New York: Basic Books.

Glenn, E. N. 2002. *Unequal Freedom: How Race and Gender Shaped American Citizenship and Labor.* Cambridge, MA: Harvard University Press.

Golash-Boza, T. 2018. "President Obama's Legacy as the Deporter in Chief." In *Immigration Policy in the Age of Punishment: Detention, Deportation and Border Control.* New York: Columbia University Press.

Goldberg, D. T. 2002. *The Racial State.* Hoboken, NJ: Wiley.

Gonzales, A. L. 2015. "Improving Health in Low-Income Communities with Group Texting." *Journal of Communication* 66 (1): 82–101.

Gonzales, R. G. 2016. *Lives in Limbo: Undocumented and Coming of Age in America.* Oakland, CA: University of California Press.

Goodwin, J., and J. M. Jasper. 2004. *Rethinking Social Movements: Structure, Meaning, and Emotion.* Lanham, MD: Rowman & Littlefield.

Gottlieb, R. 1993. *Forcing the Spring: The Transformation of the American Environmental Movement.* Washington, DC: Island Press.

Gould, D. B. 2009. *Moving Politics: Emotion and ACT UP's Fight Against Aids.* Chicago; London: University of Chicago Press.

Guillermo, E. (2015, September 8). "Eclipsed by Cesar Chavez, Larry Itliong's Story Now Emerges." *NBC News*. Retrieved from https://www.nbcnews.com/news/asian-america/eclipsed-cesar-chavez-larry-itliongs-story-now-emerges-n423336.

Gutiérrez, E. R. 2008. *Fertile Matters: The Politics of Mexican-Origin Women's Reproduction*. Austin: University of Texas Press.

Gutmann, M. C. 1996. *The Meanings of Macho: Being a Man in Mexico City*. Berkeley: University of California Press.

Guyer, R. 2000. "Breath of Life: Stories of Asthma from an Exhibition at the National Library of Medicine." *American Journal of Public Health* 90 (6): 874–879.

Hall, S. 1992. "The Question of Cultural Identity." In *Modernity and Its Futures*, S. Hall, D. Held, and A. McGrew, 274–316. Cambridge: Polity Press in association with the Open University.

———. 2017. *Selected Political Writings: The Great Moving Right Show and Other Essays*, ed. S. Davidson, D. Featherstone, M. Rustin, and B. Swartz. Durham, NC: Duke University Press.

Halse, C. 2009. "Bio-Citizenship: Virtue Discourses and the Birth of the Bio-Citizen." In *Biopolitics and the "Obesity Epidemic": Governing Bodies*, ed. J. Wright and V. Harwook, 45–59. New York: Routledge.

Hamilton, C. 1993. "Coping with Industrial Exploitation." In *Confronting Environmental Racism: Voices from the Grassroots*, ed. R. D. Bullard, 63–76. Boston: South End Press.

Han, S. Y. 2008, April. "The Conditional Logic of Strict Scrutiny: Race and Sexuality in Constitutional Law." In *Stanford Journal of Civil Rights and Civil Liberties* IV (1): 77–112.

Haraway, D. J. 1985. "Cyborg Manifesto: Science, Technology, and Social-Feminist in the Late 20th Century." *Social Review* 80:65–108.

Harding, S. 1993. "Rethinking Standpoint Epistemology: What Is 'Strong Objectivity'?" In *Feminist Epistemologies*, ed. L. Alcoff and E. Potter. London: Routledge.

Hardy-Fanta, C. 1993. *Latina Politics, Latino Politics: Gender, Culture, and Political Participation in Boston*. Philadelphia: Temple University Press.

Harrison, J. L. 2015. "Coopted Environmental Justice? Activists' Roles in Shaping EJ Policy Implementation." *Environmental Sociology* 1 (4): 241–255. doi:10.1080/23251042.2015.1084682.

Hay, A. M. 2009. "Recipe for Disaster: Motherhood and Citizenship at Love Canal." *Journal of Women's History* 21 (1): 111–134.

Hayot, E. 2007. "Chinese Bodies, Chinese Futures." *Representations* 99 (1): 99–129.

Herd, P., and M. H. Meyer. 2002. "Care Work: Invisible Civic Engagement." *Gender & Society* 16 (5): 665–688.

Heyman, J. M. C. 2004. "The Political Ecology of Consumption: Beyond Greed and Guilt." In *Political Ecology Across Spaces, Scales and Social Groups*, ed. S. Paulson and L. Gezon, 113–132. Newark, NJ: Rutgers University Press.

Heynen, N., J. McCarthy, S. Prudham, and P. Robbins. 2007. "Neoliberal Environments: False Promises and Unnatural Consequences." *Annals of the Association of American Geographers* 16 (1): 209–213.

Hirsch, J. 2003. *A Courtship After Marriage: Sexuality and Love in Mexican Transnational Families*. Berkeley: University of California Press.

Ho, E. L. E. 2009. "Constituting Citizenship Through the Emotions: Singaporean Transmigrants in London." *Annals of the Association of American Geographers* 99 (4): 788–804.

Hochschild, A. R. 1979. "Emotion Work, Feeling Rules, and Social Structure." *American Journal of Sociology* 85 (3): 551–575.

———. 1983. *The Managed Heart: Commercialization of Human Feeling*. Berkeley: University of California Press.

———. 2016. *Strangers in Their Own Land: Anger and Mourning on the American Right*. New York: New Press.

Hochschild, J. L. 1996. *Facing Up to the American Dream*. Princeton, NJ: Princeton University Press.

Holifield, R. 2007. "Neoliberalism and Environmental Justice in the United States Environmental Protection Agency: Translating Policy into Managerial Practice in Hazardous Waste Remediation." *Geoforum* 35 (3): 285–297.

Holmes, S. 2013. *Fresh Fruit, Broken Bodies: Migrant Farm Workers in the United States*. Berkeley: University of California Press.

Hong, G. K. 2015. *Death Beyond Disavowal: The Impossible Politics of Difference*. Minneapolis: University of Minnesota Press.

hooks, b. 1984. *Feminist Theory: From Margin to Center*. Boston: South End Press.

Ishizuka, K. L. 2016. *Serve the People: Making Asian America in the Long Sixties*. Brooklyn, NY: Verso.

Isin, E. F. 2004. "The Neurotic Citizen." *Citizenship Studies* 8 (3): 217–235.

James, J., ed. 2002. *States of Confinement: Policing, Detention and Prisons*. Basingstoke, UK: Palgrave.

James, J., and A. Davis. 1996. *Resisting State Violence: Radicalism, Gender, and Race in U.S. Culture*. Minneapolis: University of Minnesota Press.

Jasper, J. M. 2011. "Emotions and Social Movements: Twenty Years of Theory and Research." *Annual Review of Sociology* 37:285–303.

———. 1998. "The Emotions of Protest: Affective and Reactive Emotions in and around Social Movements." *Sociological Forum* 13 (3): 397–424.

Jenkins, J. 1985. *The Politics of Insurgency: The Farm Worker Movement in the 1960s*. New York: Columbia University Press.

Jimenez, T. R. 2009. *Replenished Ethnicity: Mexican Americans, Immigration, and Identity*. Berkeley: University of California Press.

Johnson, R. 2017. *Embodied Social Justice*. New York: Routledge.

Jones-Correa, M. 1998. *Between Two Nations: The Political Predicament of Latinos in New York City*. Ithaca, NY; London: Cornell University Press.

Jones-Correa, M. and M. Andalon. 2008, August. "The Prior Socialization of Immigrants and Their Political Participation in the United States." Paper presented at the annual meeting of the American Political Science Association, Boston, MA.

Kabeer, N. 2005 "Introduction: The Search for Inclusive Citizenship: Meanings and Expressions in an Interconnected World." In *Inclusive Citizenship*, ed. N. Kabeer, 1–30. New York: Zed.

Kang, M. 2010. *The Managed Hand: Race, Gender and the Body in Beauty Service Work*. Berkeley: University of California Press.

Kasinitz, P., J. Mollenkopf, M. Waters, and J. Holdaway. 2008. *Inheriting the City: The Children of Immigrants Come of Age*. New York: Russell Sage Foundation.

Kelley, R. D. G. 2017, December 13. "What Did Cedric Robinson Mean by Racial Capitalism?" *Boston Review*. Retrieved from http://bostonreview.net/race/robin-d-g-kelley-what-did-cedric-robinson-mean-racial-capitalism.

Khaleeli, H. 2016, May 30. "#SayHerName: Why Kimberlé Crenshaw Is Fighting for Forgotten Women." *The Guardian*. Retrieved from https://www.theguardian.com/lifeandstyle/2016/may/30/sayhername-why-kimberle-crenshaw-is-fighting-for-forgotten-women.

Kim, C. J. 1999. "The Racial Triangulation of Asian Americans." *Politics & Society* 27 (1): 105–138.

Kim, M. 2018. *Elusive Belonging: Marriage Immigrants and "Multiculturalism" in Rural South Korea*. Honolulu: University of Hawai'i Press.

Kim, N. Y. 2006a. "'Patriarchy Is So Third World': Korean Immigrant Women and 'Migrating' White Western Masculinity." *Social Problems* 53 (4): 519–536.

———. 2006b. "'Seoul-America' on America's 'Soul': South Koreans and Korean Immigrants Navigate Global White Racial Ideology." *Critical Sociology* 32 (2–3): 381–402.

———. 2008a. "Critical Thoughts on Asian American Assimilation in the Whitening Literature." In *Racism in Post-Racism America: New Theories, New Directions* (pp. 53–66). Chapel Hill, NC: University of North Carolina Press.

———. 2008b. *Imperial Citizens: Koreans and Race from Seoul to LA*. Stanford, CA: Stanford University Press.

———. 2009. "Finding Our Way Home: Korean Americans, Homelands Trips, and Cultural Foreignness." *Diasporic Homecomings: Ethnic Return Migrants in Comparative Perspective*, ed. Takeyuki Tsuda, 305–324. Stanford, CA: Stanford University Press.

———. 2013. "Citizenship on the Margins: A Critique of Scholarship on Marginalized Women and Community Activism." *Sociology Compass* 7 (6): 459–470.

Kirk, G. 1998. "Ecofeminism and Environmental Justice: Bridges Across Gender, Race, and Class." In *Chicano Culture, Ecology, Politics: Subversive Kin*, ed. D. G. Peña, 177–200. Tucson: University of Arizona Press.

Kirsch, I., and Braun, H. 2016. *The Dynamics of Opportunity in America Evidence and Perspectives*. Princeton, NJ: Educational Testing Service.

Kohl, T. 2014. "Do We Really Know That Trade Agreements Increase Trade?" *Review World Economics* 150: 443–469.

Koren, H. 1995. "Associations Between Criteria Air Pollutants and Asthma." *Environmental Health Perspectives* 103:235–242.

Kormann, C. 2019, July 7. "The Case for Declaring a National Climate Emergency." *The New Yorker*. Retrieved from https://www.newyorker.com/news/news-desk/the-case-for-declaring-a-national-climate-emergency.

Kosut, M., and L. Moore. 2010. *The Body Reader: Essential Social and Cultural Readings*. New York: New York University Press.

Krauss, C. 1993. "Women and Toxic Waste Protests: Race, Class and Gender as Resources of Resistance." *Qualitative Sociology* 16 (3): 247–262.

Krogstad, J. M., M. H. Lopez, G. López, J. S. Passel, and E. Patten. 2016, May 25. "Millennials Make Up Almost Half of Latino Eligible Voters in 2016." Retrieved from https://www.pewresearch.org/hispanic/2016/01/19/millennials-make-up-almost-half-of-latino-eligible-voters-in-2016/.

Kroll-Smith, J., J. Couch,, and S. Couch. 1991. "What Is a Disaster? An Ecological-Symbolic Approach to Resolving the Definitional Debate. *International Journal of Mass Emergencies and Disasters*, 9 (3): 355–366.

Krugman, P. 2005, September 19. "Tragedy in Black and White." *New York Times*. Retrieved from https://www.nytimes.com/2005/09/19/opinion/tragedy-in-black-and-white.html.

Lacroix, T. 2014. "Conceptualizing Transnational Engagements: A Structure and Agency Perspective on (Hometown) Transnationalism." *International Migration Review* 48 (3): 643–679.

LaDuke, W. 1993. "A Society Based on Conquest Cannot Be Sustained: Native Peoples and the Environmental Crisis." In *Toxic Struggles: The Theory and Practice of Environmental Justice*, ed. R. Hofrichter. Philadelphia: New Society.

———. 2005. *Recovering the Sacred: The Power of Naming and Claiming*. Boston: South End Press.

Lai, E. Y. P., and D. Arguelles. 2003. *The New Face of Asian Pacific America: Numbers, Diversity & Change in the 21st Century*. San Francisco: *AsianWeek*, with UCLA's Asian American Studies Center Press, in cooperation with the Organization of Chinese Americans and the National Coalition for Asian Pacific American Community Development.

Lamont, M. 2000. *The Dignity of Working Men: Morality and the Boundaries of Race, Class and Immigration*. Cambridge, MA: Harvard University Press.

Lareau, A. 2003. *Unequal Childhoods: Class, Race, and Family Life*. Berkeley: University of California Press.

Lauter, P. 2002. "American Studies, American Politics and the Reinvention of Class." In *The Futures of American Studies*, ed. D. Pease and R. Wiegman. 486–509. Durham, NC: Duke University Press.

Leal, D. L. 2002. "Political Participation by Latino Non-Citizens in the United States." *British Journal of Political Science* 32 (2): 353–370.

Lee, J. (2002). *Civility in the City: Blacks, Jews, and Koreans in Urban America*. Cambridge, MA: Harvard University Press.

Lee, J., and F. Bean. 2004. "America's Changing Color Lines: Immigration, Race/Ethnicity, and Multiracial Identification." *Annual Review of Sociology* 30:221–242.

Lee, R. C. 2014. *The Exquisite Corpse of Asian America: Biopolitics, Biosociality, and Posthuman Ecologies*. New York: New York University Press.

Lee, S., A. H. O'Neill, E. S. Ihara, and D. H. Chae. 2013. "Change in Self-Reported Health Status Among Immigrants in the United States: Associations with Measures of Acculturation." *Plos One* 8 (10): e76494.

Levine, A., and R. S. F. Heller. 2010. *Attached: The New Science of Adult Attachment and How It Can Help You Find—and Keep—Love*. New York: Penguin Random House.

Levitt, P. 2001. *The Transnational Villagers*. Berkeley: University of California Press.

Levitt, P., and M. C. Waters. 2006. *The Changing Face of Home: The Transnational Lives of the Second Generation*. New York: Russell Sage Foundation.

Lien, P. 2001. *Making of Asian America: Through Political Participation*. Philadelphia: Temple University Press.

———. 2017. "The Political Participation of Asian Americans." In *The Routledge Handbook of Asian American Studies*, ed. Cindy I-Fen Cheng, 355–366. New York: Routledge.

Liévanos, R. S. 2012. "Certainty, Fairness, and Balance: State Resonance and Environmental Justice Policy Implementation." *Sociological Forum* 27 (2): 481–503.

Lipsitz, G. 2001. *American Studies in a Moment of Danger*. Minneapolis: University of Minnesota Press.

Lister, R. 2007. "Inclusive Citizenship: Realizing the Potential." *Citizenship Studies* 11 (1): 49–61.

London, J., A. Karner, J. Sze, D. Rowan, G. Gambirazzio, and D. Niemeier. 2013. "Racing Climate Change: Collaboration and Conflict in California's Global Climate Change Policy Arena." *Global Climate Change* 23 (4): 791–799.

Lorber, J., and L. Moore. 2010. *Gendered Bodies: Feminist Perspectives*. Oxford, UK: Oxford University Press.

Louie, M. Y. 2001. *Sweatshop Warriors: Immigrant Women Workers Take on the Global Factory*. Cambridge, MA: South End Press.

Louie, V. 2004. *Compelled to Excel: Immigration, Education, and Opportunity Among Chinese Americans*. Stanford, CA: Stanford University Press.

Luft, R.E. 2009. "Beyond Disaster Exceptionalism: Social Movement Developments in New Orleans After Hurricane Katrina." *American Quarterly* 61 (3): 499–527.

Lutz, C. A. 1988. *Unnatural Emotions: Everyday Sentiments on a Micronesian Atoll and Their Challenge to Western Theory*. Chicago: University of Chicago Press.

Mailick, M. D., G. Holden, and V. N. Walther. 1994. "Coping with Childhood Asthma: Caretakers' Views." *Health and Social Work* 19 (2): 103–111.

Major, B., A. Blodorn, and G. M. Blascovich. 2016. "The Threat of Increasing Diversity: Why Many White Americans Support Trump in the 2016 Presidential Election." *Group Processes & Intergroup Relations* 21 (6): 931–940.

Mann, A. 2014, July 19. "What's Up with That: Building Bigger Roads Actually Makes Traffic Worse." *Wired*. Retrieved from https://www.wired.com/2014/06/wuwt-traffic-induced-demand/.

Mann, E. 1991. *LA's Lethal Air: New Perspectives for Policy, Organizing, and Action*. Los Angeles: Labor/Community Strategy Center.

Marquez, B. 2012. "Mexican Americans and Environmental Justice: Change and Continuity in Mexican American Politics." In *Latino Urbanism: The Politics of Planning, Policy and Redevelopment*, ed. D. Díaz and R. Torres, 163–180). New York; London: New York University Press.

Marteau, T., and M. Johnston. 1986. "Determinants of Beliefs About Illness: A Study of Parents of Children with Diabetes, Asthma, Epilepsy, and No Chronic Illness." *Journal of Psychosomatic Research* 20 (6): 673–683.

Martinez, A. D., L. Ruelas, and D. A. Granger. 2018. "Household Fear of Deportation in

Relation to Chronic Stressors and Salivary Proinflammatory Cytokines in Mexican-Origin Families Post-SB 1070." *SSM Population Health* 19 (5): 188–200.

Matias, C. 2016. *Feeling White: Whiteness, Emotionality, and Education*. Boston: Sense.

Mbembé, A. 2013. *Critique of Black Reason*. Durham, NC; London: Duke University Press.

Mbembé, J., and L. Meintjes. 2003. "Necropolitics." *Public Culture* 15 (1): 11–40.

McIntosh, P. 1989. "White Privilege: Unpacking the Invisible Knapsack." *Peace and Freedom* 10.

McMurtry, C. L., M. G. Findling, L. S. Casey, R. J. Blendon, J. M. Benson, J. M. Sayde, and C. Miller. 2019. "Discrimination in the United States: Experiences of Asian Americans." *Health Services Research* 54 (2): 1419–1430.

Menjívar, C. (2010). "Immigrants, Immigration, and Sociology: Reflecting on the State of the Discipline." *Sociological Inquiry* 80 (1): 3–27.

Merchant, N. 2019, December 26. "Congolese Migrant Woman, 41, Dies in US Border Custody on Christmas Day at Texas Hospital." *USA Today*. Retrieved from https://www.usatoday.com/story/news/nation/2019/12/26/congolese-migrant-dies-border-patrol-christmas/2754390001/.

Merton, R. 1972. "Insiders and Outsiders: A Chapter in the Sociology of Knowledge." *American Journal of Sociology* 78 (1): 9–47.

Milkman, R. 2006. *L.A. Story: Immigrant Workers and the Future of the U.S. Labor Movement*. New York: Russell Sage Foundation.

Milkman, R., and V. Terriquez. 2012. "'We Are the Ones Who Are Out in Front': Women's Leadership in the Immigrant Rights Movement." *Feminist Studies* 38 (3): 723–752.

Mills, C. 1997. *The Racial Contract*. Ithaca, NY: Cornell University Press.

———. 2017. *Black Rights/White Wrongs: The Critique of Racial Liberalism*. New York: Oxford University Press.

Mink, G. 1999. "Aren't Poor Single Mothers Women? Feminists, Welfare Reform, and Welfare Justice." In *Whose Welfare?* ed. G. Mink, Ithaca, NY: Cornell University Press.

Mirchandani, K. 2003. "Challenging Racial Silences in Studies of Emotion Work: Contributions from Anti-Racist Feminist Theory." *Organization Studies* 24 (5): 721–742.

Molina, N. 2013. *How Race Is Made in America: Immigration, Citizenship, and the Historical Power of Racial Scripts*. Berkeley: University of California Press.

Montoya, L., C. Hardy-Fanta, and S. García. 2000. "Latina Politics: Gender, Participation, and Leadership." *PS: Political Science and Politics* 33 (3): 555–561.

Moore, L., and M. Kosut. 2010. *The Body Reader: Essential Social and Cultural Readings*. New York: New York University Press.

Moraga, C., and G. Anzaldua. 1981. *This Bridge Called My Back: Writings by Radical Women of Color*. New York: Kitchen Table: Women of Color Press.

Moses, M. 1993. "Farmworkers and Pesticides." In *Confronting Environmental Racism: Voices from the Grassroots*, ed. Robert D. Bullard, 161–178). Boston: South End Press.

Naples, N. A. 1998. *Grassroots Warriors: Activist Mothering, Community Work, and the War on Poverty*. New York: Routledge.

———. 2003. *Feminism and Method: Ethnography, Discourse Analysis, and Activist Research*. New York: Routledge.

Napoli, L. 2018, November 28. "Bunker Hill's Redevelopment: Urban Travesty or Renaissance?" Curbed LA. Retrieved from https://la.curbed.com/2018/11/28/18115002/bunker-hill-towers-redevelopment-history.

National Environmental Justice Advisory Council (NEJAC). 2001. *Environmental Justice and Community-Based Health Model Discussion: A Report on the Public Meeting Convened by the National Environmental Justice Advisory Council, May 23–26, 2000.*

Nelson, A. 2011. *Body and Soul: The Black Panther Party and the Fight Against Medical Discrimination.* Minneapolis: University of Minnesota Press.

Nicholls, W. J. 2013. *The DREAMers: How the Undocumented Youth Movement Transformed the Immigrant Rights Debate.* Stanford, CA: Stanford University Press.

Norgaard, K. M., and R. Reed. 2017. "Emotional Impacts of Environmental Decline: What Can Native Cosmologies Teach Sociology About Emotions and Environmental Justice?" *Theory and Society* 46: 463–495.

Novotny, P. 2000. *Where We Live, Work, and Play: The Environmental Justice Movement and the Struggle for a New Environmentalism.* Westport, CT: Praeger.

Ocampo, A. C. 2016. *The Latinos of Asia: How Filipino Americans Break the Rules of Race.* Stanford, CA: Stanford University Press.

Okamoto, D.G., D. Herda, and C. Hartzog. 2013. "Beyond Good Grades: School Composition and Immigrant Youth Participation in Extracurricular Activities." *Social Science Research* 42 (1): 155–168.

Okihiro, G. Y. 1994. *Margins and Mainstreams: Asians in American History and Culture.* Seattle: University of Washington Press.

Oliver, M. L., and T. M. Shapiro. 1995. *Black Wealth/White Wealth: A New Perspective on Racial Inequality.* New York: Routledge.

Omi, M., and H. Winant. 2014. *Racial Formation in the United States* (3rd ed.). New York: Routledge.

Ong, A. 1996. "Cultural Citizenship as Subject-Making: Immigrants Negotiate Racial and Cultural Boundaries in the United States." *Current Anthropology* 37 (5): 737–751.

———. 1999. *Flexible Citizenship: The Cultural Logics of Transnationality.* Durham, NC: Duke University Press.

———. 2003. *Buddha Is Hiding: Refugees, Citizenship, the New America.* Berkeley: University of California Press.

Ong, P. M., and E. Blumenberg. 1990. *Race and Environmentalism.* Los Angeles: University of California Graduate School of Architecture and Urban Planning.

Padios, J. M. 2018. *A Nation on the Line: Call Centers as Postcolonial Predicaments in the Philippines.* Durham. NC, and London: Duke University Press.

Paik, A. N. 2016. *Rightlessness: Testimony and Redress in U.S. Prison Camps Since World War II.* Chapel Hill: University of North Carolina Press.

Pallares, A. 2014. *Family Activism: Immigrant Struggles and the Politics of Noncitizenhip.* New Brunswick, NJ: Rutgers University Press.

Pallares, A., and N. Flores-González, eds. 2010. *Marcha: Latino Chicago and the Immigrant Rights Movement (Latinos in Chicago and Midwest).* Urbana: University of Illinois Press.

Pardo, M. 1998. *Mexican American Women Activists: Identity and Resistance in Two Los Angeles Communities.* Philadelphia: Temple University Press.

Park, K. 2012. "Analysis of Latino-Korean Relations in the Workplace: Latino Perspectives in the Aftermath of the 1992 Los Angeles Civil Unrest." *Amerasia Journal* 38 (1): 143–169.

Park, L. S. 2011. *Entitled to Nothing: The Struggle for Immigrant Health Care in the Age of Welfare Reform.* New York: New York University Press.

Park, L., and D. Pellow. 2011. *The Slums of Aspen: Immigrants vs. the Environment in America's Eden.* New York: New York University Press.

Pazzanese, C., and C. Walsh. 2018, January 11. "The Women's Revolt: Why Now, and Where To." *The Harvard Gazette.* Retrieved from https://news.harvard.edu/gazette/story/2017/12/metoo-surge-could-change-society-in-pivotal-ways-harvard-analysts-say/.

Peeples, J. A., and K. M. Deluca. 2006. "The Truth of the Matter: Motherhood, Community and Environmental Justice." *Women's Studies in Communication* 29 (1): 59–87.

Pellow, D. 2007. *Resisting Global Toxics: Transnational Movements for Environmental Justice.* Cambridge, MA: MIT Press.

Pellow, D. N., and R. J. A. Brulle, eds. 2005. *Power, Justice, and the Environment.* Cambridge, MA: MIT Press.

———. 2007. "Poisoning the Planet: The Struggle for Environmental Justice." *Contexts* 6 (1): 37–41.

Pellow, D. N., and L. Park. 2002. *The Silicon Valley of Dreams: Environmental Injustice, Immigrant Workers, and the High-Tech Global Economy.* New York: New York University Press.

Peña, D. G. 1998. *Chicano Culture, Ecology, Politics: Subversive Kin.* Tucson: University of Arizona Press.

———. 2005. *Mexican Americans and the Environment: Tierra y Vida.* Tucson: University of Arizona Press.

Pérez, R. L., and M. E. Abarca. 2007. "Cocinas Públicas: Food and Border Consciousness in Greater Mexico." *Food and Foodways* 15 (3–4): 137–151.

Pérez, R. L., R. Espinoza, K. Ramos, H. Coronado, and R. Cortes. 2010. "Civic Engagement Patterns of Undocumented Mexican Students." *Journal of Hispanic Higher Education* 9 (3): 245–265.

Pew Research Center. 2018, July 11. "Income Inequality in the U.S. Is Highest Among Asian Americans. Retrieved from https://www.pewresearch.org/st_18-07-12_inequality_featrued-image_ft_blog/.

Portes, A., and R. G. Rumbaut. 2001. *Legacies: The Story of the Immigrant Second Generation.* Berkeley; New York: University of California Press and Russell Sage Foundation.

Prindeville, D. M. 2004. *On the Streets and In the Statehouse: American Indian and Hispanic Women and Environmental Policymaking in New Mexico.* New York: Routledge.

Prout, A., L. Hayes, and L. Gelder. 1999. "Medicines and the Maintenance of Ordinariness in the Household Management of Childhood Asthma." *Sociology of Health and Illness* 21 2, 137–162.

Pulido, L. 1996a. *Environmentalism and Economic Justice: Two Chicano Struggles in the Southwest.* Tucson: University of Arizona Press.

———. 1996b. "A Critical Review of the Methodology of Environmental Racism Research." *Antipode* 28 (2): 142–159.

———. 2017a. "Geographies of Race and Ethnicity II: Environmental Racism and Racial Capitalism." *Progress in Human Geography* 41 (4): 524–533.

———. 2017b. "The Personal and the Political: Evolving Racial Formations and the Environmental Justice Movement." In *The Routledge Handbook of Environmental Justice*, ed. R. Holifield, G. Walker, and J. Chakraborty, 15–24. London; New York: Routledge Handbooks Online.

———. 2018. "Geographies of Race and Ethnicity III: Settler Colonialism and Nonnative People of Color." *Progress in Human Geography* 42 (2): 309–318.

Pulido, L., and D. Peña. 1998. "Environmentalism and Positionality: The Early Pesticide Campaign of the United Farm Workers' Organizing Committee, 1965–71. *Race, Gender & Class* 6 (1): 33–50.

Putnam, R. D. 2000. *Bowling Alone: The Collapse and Revival of American Community*. New York: Simon & Schuster.

Pyke, K. D., and D. L. Johnson. 2003. "Asian American Women and Racialized Femininities: 'Doing' Gender Across Cultural Worlds." *Gender and Society* 17 (1): 33–53.

Ream, R. K., and G. J. Palardy. 2008. "Reexamining Social Class Differences in the Availability and the Educational Utility of Parental Social Capital." *American Educational Research Journal* 45 (2): 238–274.

Reay, D. 1998. *Class Work: Mothers' Involvement in their Children's Primary Schooling*. London: UCL Press.

Rios, V. M. 2011. *Punished: Policing the Lives of Black and Latino Boys*. New York: New York University Press.

Robinson, C. J. 1983. *Black Marxism: The Making of the Black Radical Tradition*. London: Zed.

Rogers, J., M. Bertrand, R. Freelon, and S. Fanelli. 2011. *Free Fall: Educational Opportunities in 2011*. Los Angeles: UCLA IDEA, UC/ACCORD.

Rogers, J., and V. Terriquez. 2016. "It Shaped Who I Am as a Person: Youth Organizing and the Educational and Civic Trajectories of Low-Income Youth." In *Contemporary Youth Activism Advancing Social Justice in the United States*, ed. J. Conner and S. M. Rosen, 141–161. Santa Barbara, CA: Praeger.

Romero, M. 2008. "Crossing the Immigration and Race Border: A Critical Race Theory Approach to Immigration Studies." *Contemporary Justice Review* 11(1): 23–37.

Rosaldo, R. 1994. "Cultural Citizenship in San Jose, California." *Political and Legal Anthropology Review* 17 (2): 57–63.

Rose, N. 2007. *The Politics of Life Itself: Biomedicine, Power, and Subjectivity in the Twenty-First Century*. Princeton, NJ: Princeton University Press.

Roth, W. D., and N. Y. Kim. 2013. "Relocating Prejudice: A Transnational Approach to Understanding Immigrants' Racial Attitudes." *International Migration Review* 42 (2): 330–373.

Rudrappa, S. 2015. *Discounted Life: The Price of Global Surrogacy in India*. New York: New York University Press.

Ruiz, V. L. 1998. "La Nueva Chicana: Women and the Movement." In *From Out of the Shadows: Mexican Women in Twentieth-Century America*, ed. V. L. Ruiz, 99–126. New York: Oxford University Press.

Rumbaut, R., R. Gonzales, G. Komaie, and C. Morgan. 2006. *Debunking the Myth of Immigrant Criminality: Imprisonment Among First- and Second-Generation Young Men.* Report for Migration Policy Institute. University of California, Irvine.

Sacchi, E. 2011. "The Biopolitical Paradox: Population and Security Mechanisms." *International Social Science Journal* 62 (205–206): 391–401.

Sadd, J., and B. Shamasunder. 2015. "Action in Los Angeles: Health, Land Use, and Environmental Justice Consequences." In *Drilling Down: The Community Consequences of Expanded Oil Development in Los Angeles*, 7–14. Los Angeles: Liberty Hill Foundation.

Safa, H. I. 1990. "Women's Social Movements in Latin America." Special issue: "Women and Development in the Third World." *Gender and Society* 4 (3):) 345–369.

Said, E. 1978. *Orientalism.* New York: Pantheon.

Saito, L. T. 1998. *Race and Politics: Asian Americans, Latinos, and Whites in a Los Angeles Suburb.* Urbana-Champaign, IL: University of Illinois Press.

Santa Ana, O. 2002. *Brown Tide Rising: Metaphors of Latinos in Contemporary American Public Discourse.* Austin: University of Texas Press.

Schaffner, B., M. MacWilliams, and T. Nteta. 2017. "Hostile Sexism, Racism Denial, and the Historic Education Gap in Support for Trump." In *The 2016 Presidential Election: The Causes and Consequences of a Political Earthquake.* Lanham, MD: Lexington.

Scheper-Hughes, N. 2001. "Commodity Fetishism in Organs Trafficking." *Body & Society* 7 (2–3): 31–62.

———. 2007. "The Last Commodity: Post-Human Ethics and the Global Traffic in 'Fresh' Organs." In *Global Assemblages: Technology, Politics, and Ethics as Anthropological Problems*, ed. A. Ong and S. J. Collier, 145–167. Malden, MA: Blackwell.

Schroedel, J. R., and R. Chin. 2020. "Whose Lives Matter: The Media's Failure to Cover Police Use of Lethal Force Against Native Americans." *Race and Justice* 10 (2):150–175.

Schwartz, N. 2007, February 20. "LA Tour Highlights Pollution Nightmares." NBC News. Retrieved from http://www.nbcnews.com/id/17156117/ns/us_news-environment/t/la-tour-highlights-pollution-nightmares/#.XwkEZ-d7lPZ.

Schwartz, N. A., C. A. V. Glascoe, V. Torres, L. Ramos, and C. Soria-Delgado. 2015. "'Where They (Live, Work and) Spray': Pesticide Exposure, Childhood Asthma and Environmental Justice Among Mexican-American Farmworkers." *Health & Place* 32:83–92.

Segura, D. A., and P. Zavella. 2008. "Introduction: Gendered Borderlands." *Gender and Society* 22 (5): 537–544.

Seitz, V. 1998. "Class, Gender, and Resistance in the Appalachian Coalfields." In *Community Activism and Feminist Politics: Organizing Across Race, Class, and Gender*, ed. N. Naples, 213–236. New York: Routledge.

Sevenhuijsen, S. 1998. *Citizenship and the Ethics of Care: Feminist Considerations on Justice, Morality, and Politics.* London: Routledge.

Shah, B. V. 2011. *Laotian Daughters: Working Toward Community, Belonging, and Environmental Justice.* Philadelphia: Temple University Press.

Shah, N. 2001. *Contagious Divides: Epidemics and Race in San Francisco's Chinatown.* Berkeley: University of California Press.

Shapiro, T. M. 2004. *The Hidden Cost of Being African American: How Wealth Perpetuates Inequality*. Oxford, UK: Oxford University Press.

Shipler, D. K. 2018. *Work Doesn't Work: From the Working Poor*. New York: Vintage.

Shiva, V. 1988. *Staying Alive: Women, Ecology, and Development*. New Delhi: Women Unlimited.

———. 1998. *Seeds of Suicide: The Ecological and Human Costs of Globalization of Agriculture*. New Delhi: Research Foundation for Science, Technology Ecology.

Shriver, T. E., and G. R. Webb. 2009. "Rethinking the Scope of Environmental Injustice: Perceptions of Health Hazards in a Rural Native American Community Exposed to Carbon Black." *Rural Sociology* 74 (2): 270–292.

Silbergeld, E., and D. Mandrioli. 2015. "Evidence from Toxicology: The Most Essential Science for Prevention." *Environmental Health Perspectives* 124 (1).

Simon, P. A., Z. Zeng, C. M. Wold, W. Haddock, and J. E. Fielding. 2003. "Prevalence of Childhood Asthma and Associated Morbidity in Los Angeles County: Impacts of Race/Ethnicity and Income." *The Journal of Asthma* 40 (5): 535–543.

Sims, C. M. 2010. "Ethnic Notions and Healthy Paranoias: Understanding of the Context of Experience and Interpretations of Healthcare Encounters Among Older Black Women." *Ethnicity and Health* 15 (5): 495–514.

Sinclair, A. 2005. "Body Possibilities in Leadership." *Leadership* 1 (4): 387–406.

Smith, A. 2005. *Conquest: Sexual Violence and Native American Genocide*. Boston: South End Press.

———. 2012. "Indigeneity, Settler Colonialism, White Supremacy." In *Racial Formation in the Twenty-First Century*, ed. D. HoSang, O. LaBennett, and L. Pulido, 66–90. Berkeley: University of California Press.

Smith, A. [Allan] 2019, November 12. "Trump Claims Some DACA Recipients 'Hardened Criminals' Ahead of Supreme Court Arguments." NBC News. https://www.nbcnews.com/politics/donald-trump/trump-claims-some-daca-recipients-hardened-criminals-ahead-supreme-court-n1080421.

Stasiulis, D. 2002. "The Active Child Citizen: Lessons from Canadian Policy and the Children's Movement." *Citizenship Studies* 6 (4): 507–538.

Stein, R. 2004. *New Perspectives on Environmental Justice: Gender, Sexuality, and Activism*. New Brunswick, NJ: Rutgers University Press.

Steinman, E. 2012. "Settler Colonial Power and the American Indian Sovereignty Movement: Forms of Domination, Strategies of Transformation." *American Journal of Sociology* 117 (4): 1073–1130.

Stern, A. M. 2015. *Eugenic Nation: Faults and Frontiers of Better Breeding in Modern America*. Oakland, CA: University of California Press.

———. 2016, January 8. "That Time the United States Sterilized 60,000 of Its Citizens." *Huffington Post*. Retrieved from https://www.huffpost.com/entry/sterilization-united-states_n_568f35f2e4b0c8beacf68713.

Suzara, A. 2003. "Reflections: A Filipina's Perspective." *Race, Poverty & the Environment* 10 (1): 18.

Szasz, A. 1994. *Ecopopulism: Toxic Waste and the Movement for Environmental Justice*. Minneapolis: University of Minnesota Press.

Sze, J. 1999. "Expanding Environmental Justice: Asian American Feminists' Contribution. In *Dragon Ladies: Asian American Feminists Breathe Fire*, 90–99. Boston: South End Press.

———. 2006. *Noxious New York: The Racial Politics of Urban Health and Environmental Justice*. Cambridge, MA: MIT Press.

Takagi, D. Y. 1993. *The Retreat from Race: Asian-American Admissions and Racial Politics*. New Brunswick, NJ: Rutgers University Press.

Talavera, E. 1977. "Sterilization Is Not an Alternative in Family Planning." *Agenda* 7 (8). (National Council of Raza).

Tang, E. 2011. "A Gulf Unites Us: The Vietnamese Americans of Black New Orleans East." *American Quarterly* 63 (1): 117–149.

———. 2015. *Unsettled: Cambodian Refugees in the New York City Hyperghetto*. Philadelphia: Temple University Press.

Tannen, R. 2007. *The Female Trickster: The Mask That Reveals: Post-Jungian and Postmodern Psychological Perspectives*. London; New York: Routledge.

Tarrow, S. 1998. *Power in Movement: Social Movements and Contentious Politics*. Cambridge, UK: Cambridge University Press.

Taylor, D. E. 1993. "Environmentalism and the Politics of Inclusion." In *Confronting Environmental Racism: Voices from the Grassroots*, ed. Robert D. Bullard, 53–62. Boston: South End Press.

Telles, E. 2004. *Race in Another America: The Significance of Skin Color in Brazil*. Princeton, NJ: Princeton University Press.

Telles, E., and V. Ortiz. 2008. *Generations of Exclusion: Mexican-Americans, Assimilation, and Race*. New York: Russell Sage Foundation.

Terriquez, V. 2011. "Schools for Democracy: Labor Union Participation and Latino Immigrant Parents' School-Based Civic Engagement." *American Sociological Review* 76 (4): 581–601.

———. 2012. "Civic Inequalities? Immigrant Incorporation and Latina Mothers' Participation in Their Children's Schools." *Sociological Perspectives* 55 (4): 663–682.

———. 2015a. "Labor Union Activity and the Civic Participation of Latino Immigrant Workers." In *Immigration and Work Research in the Sociology of Work*, ed. J. A. Vallejo, 55–73. Bingley, UK: Emerald.

———. 2015b. "Intersectional Mobilization, Social Movement Spillover, and Queer Youth Leadership in the Immigrant Rights Movement." *Social Problems* 62 (3): 343–362.

Terriquez, V., and H. Kwon. 2015. "Intergenerational Family Relations, Civic Organisations, and the Political Socialisation of Second-Generation Immigrant Youth." *Journal of Ethnic and Migration Studies* 41 (3): 425–447.

Terriquez, V., and J. Rogers. 2011. "Becoming Civic: The Active Engagement of Immigrant Parents in Public Schools." In *Bicultural Parent Engagement: Advocacy and Empowerment*, ed. E. M. Olivos and A. Ochoa, 186–205. New York: Teachers College Press.

Tesler, M. 2016, April 18. "Trump Is the First Modern Republican to Win the Nomination Based on Racial Prejudice." *Washington Post*. Retrieved from https://www.washingtonpost.com/news/monkey-cage/wp/2016/08/01/trump-is-the-first-republican-in-modern-times-to-win-the-partys-nomination-on-anti-minority-sentiments/.

Thangaraj, S. I. 2015. *Desi Hoop Dreams: Pickup Basketball and the Making of Asian American Masculinity*. New York: New York University Press.

Thoits, P. A. 1989. "The Sociology of Emotions." *Annual Review of Sociology* 15: 317–342.

Tilly, C. 1999. *Durable Inequality*. Berkeley: University of California Press.

Topal, C. 2011. "Surveillance of Immigrants from Turkey in Germany: From the Disciplinary Society to the Society of Control." *International Sociology* 26 (6): 789–814.

Tran, V. C., J. Lee, and T. J. Huang. 2019. "Revisiting the Asian Second-Generation Advantage." *Ethics and Racial Studies* 42 (13): 2248–2269.

Truax, E. 2015. *Dreamers: An Immigrant Generation's Fight for Their American Dream*. Boston: Beacon Press.

Tuan, Y. 1984. *Dominance and Affection: The Making of Pets*. New Haven; London: Yale University Press.

Turner, B. S. 1984. *The Body and Society*. Oxford, UK: Blackwell.

Turney, K., and G. Kao. 2009. "Barriers to School Involvement: Are Immigrant Parents Disadvantaged?" *Journal of Educational Research* 102 (4): 257–271.

United Church of Christ Commission for Racial Justice. 1987. *Toxic Wastes and Race in the United States, A National Report on the Racial and Socio-Economic Characteristics of Communities with Hazardous Waste Sites*. New York: United Church of Christ.

US Census Bureau. 2011. "Comparing 2011 American Community Survey Data." Retrieved from https://www.census.gov/programs-surveys/acs/guidance/comparing-acs-data/2011.html.

US News and World Report. 2017, September 18. "U.S. Spends Less as Other Nations Invest More in Education." Retrieved from https://www.usnews.com/news/national-news/articles/2017-09-18/while-rest-of-the-world-invests-more-in-education-the-us-spends-less.

———. 2019, December 25. "Phillips 66 Says Boiler Plant Fire Extinguished at Los Angeles, California Refinery." Retrieved from https://www.usnews.com/news/us/articles/2019-12-25/phillips-66-reports-fire-in-boiler-plant-area-at-wilmington-california-refinery.

Valdez, J., and D. Rosenfeld. 2019, May 2. "Crews Contain Fire at Phillips 66 Refinery in Carson; 2nd Fire at Site in Recent Weeks." *Daily Breeze*. Retrieved from https://www.dailybreeze.com/2019/05/02/fire-erupts-at-phillips-66-refinery-in-carson/.

Vera Cruz, P. 1992. *Philip Vera Cruz: A Personal History of Filipino Immigrants and the Farmworkers Movement*. Los Angeles: UCLA Labor Center and the UCLA Asian American Studies Center.

Verba, S., K. L. Schlozman, and H. E. Brady. 1995. *Voice and Equality: Civic Voluntarism in American Politics*. Cambridge, MA: Harvard University Press.

Verchick, R. M. 2004. "Feminist Theory and Envriomental Justice." In *New Perspectives on Environmental Justice: Gender, Sexuality, and Activism*, ed. R. Stein, 63–75. New Brunswick, NJ: Rutgers University Press.

Vickery, J., and L. M. Hunter. 2016. "Native Americans: Where in Environmental Justice Research?" *Society & Natural Resources* 29 (1): 36–42.

Võ, L. 2000. "Performing Ethnography in Asian American Communities: Beyond the

Insider-Versus-Outsider Perspective." In *Cultural Compass: Ethnographic Explorations of Asian America*, ed. M. F. Manalansan, 17–37. Philadelphia: Temple University Press.

———. 2004. *Mobilizing an Asian American Community*. Philadelphia: Temple University Press.

Voss, K., and I. Bloemraad, eds. 2011. *Rallying for Immigrant Rights: The Fight for Inclusion in 21st Century America*. Berkeley: University of California Press.

Voyles, T. B. 2015. *Wastelanding*. Minneapolis: University of Minnesota Press.

Warren, M., M. Mira, and T. Nikundiwe. 2008. "Youth Organizing: From Youth Development to School Reform." *New Directions for Youth Development* 117:27–42.

Waugh, C. 2010. "Only You Can Prevent a Forest: Agent Orange, Ecocide, and Environmental Justice." *Interdisciplinary Studies in Literature and Environment* 17 (1): 113–132.

Weedon, C. 1987. *Feminist Practice and Poststructuralist Theory*. Hoboken, NJ: Wiley-Blackwell.

Weizman, E. 2017. *The Least of All Possible Evils: A Short History of Humanitarian Violence*. New York: Verso.

Werbner, P. 1999. "Political Motherhood and the Feminization of Citizenship: Women's Activisms and the Transformation of the Public Sphere." In *Women, Citizenship and Difference*, ed. N. D. Yuval and P. Werbner. London: Zed.

Wernette, D. R., and L. A. Nieves. 1992. *Breathing Polluted Air; Minorities Are Disproportionately Exposed*. Washington, DC: Environmental Protection Agency.

West, P., F. Fly, and R. Marans. 1990. "Minority Anglers and Toxic Fish Consumption: Evidence from a State-Wide Survey of Michigan." In *The Proceedings of Michigan Conference on Race and the Incidence of Environmental Hazards*, ed. B. Bryant and P. Mohai, 108–122. Ann Arbor: University of Michigan School of Natural Resources.

Wharton, A. S. 2011. "The Sociology of Arlie Hochschild." *Work and Occupations* 38 (4): 459–464.

Whittier, N. 2017. "Identity Politics, Consciousness-Raising, and Visibility Politics." In *The Oxford Handbook of U.S. Women's Social Movement Activism*, ed. H. J. McCammon, V. Taylor, Jo Reger, and R. L. Einwohner. Oxford, UK: Oxford University Press.

Williams, D. R. 2008. "Racial/Ethnic Variations in Women's Health: The Social Embeddedness of Health." *American Journal of Public Health*:38–47.

———. 2018. "Stress and the Mental Health of Populations of Color: Advancing Our Understanding of Race-Related Stressors." *Journal of Health and Social Behavior* 59 (4): 466–485.

Wolkowitz, C. 2006. *Bodies at Work*. London: Sage.

Wong, J., K. S. Ramakrishnan, T. Lee, and J. Junn. 2011. *Asian American Political Participation: Emerging Constituents and Their Political Identities*. New York: Russell Sage Foundation.

Wong, J., and V. Tseng. 2008. "Political Socialisation in Immigrant Families: Challenging Top-Down Parental Socialisation Models." *Journal of Ethnic and Migration Studies* 34 (1): 151–168.

Woodruff, T. J., J. D. Parker, A. D. Kyle, and K. C. Schoendorf. 2003. "Disparities in Exposure to Air Pollution During Pregnancy." *Environmental Health Perspectives* 111 (7): 942–946.

Wu, E. D. 2013. *The Color of Success: Asian Americans and the Origins of the Model.* Princeton, NJ: Princeton University Press.

Young, A. A. 2006. *The Minds of Marginalized Black Men: Making Sense of Mobility, Opportunity, and Future Life Chances.* Princeton, NJ: Princeton University Press.

Yuval-Davis, N. 2011. *The Politics of Belonging: Intersectional Contestations.* London: University of East London; Sage.

Zamora, S. 2016. "Racial Remittances: The Effect of Migration on Racial Ideologies in Mexico and the United States." *Sociology of Race and Ethnicity* 2 (4): 466–481.

Zembylas, M. 2016. "Making Sense of the Complex Entanglement Between Emotion and Pedagogy: Contributions of the Affective Turn. " *Cultural Studies of Science Education* 11 (3): 539–550.

Zentgraf, K. M. 2002. "Immigration and Women's Employment: Salvadorans in Los Angeles." *Gender & Society* 16 (5): 625–646.

Zepeda-Millán, C. 2017. *Latino Mass Mobilization: Immigration, Racialization, and Activism.* Cambridge, UK: Cambridge University Press.

INDEX